RECORDS OF
THE CHURCHWARDENS OF
MILDENHALL

COLLECTIONS (1446–1454) AND
ACCOUNTS (1503–1553)

Mildenhall market place with the market cross and the parish pump. St Mary's church tower is in the background (see CWA, fol.23v). From the etching by M. Oliver Rae, c.1930.

RECORDS OF
THE CHURCHWARDENS OF
MILDENHALL

COLLECTIONS (1446–1454) AND
ACCOUNTS (1503–1553)

Edited by

† JUDITH MIDDLETON-STEWART

General Editor

DAVID DYMOND

The Boydell Press

Suffolk Records Society
VOLUME LIV

A Suffolk Records Society publication
First published 2011
The Boydell Press, Woodbridge

ISBN 978–0–85115–578–4

Issued to subscribing members for the year 2010–2011

The Boydell Press is an imprint of Boydell & Brewer Ltd
PO Box 9, Woodbridge, Suffolk IP12 3DF, UK
and of Boydell & Brewer Inc.
668 Mt Hope Avenue, Rochester, NY 14620, USA
website: www.boydellandbrewer.com

The publisher has no responsibility for the continued existence or
accuracy of URLs for external or third-party internet websites referred to
in this book, and does not guarantee that any content
on such websites is, or will remain, accurate or appropriate

A catalogue record for this book is available
from the British Library

Papers used by Boydell & Brewer Ltd are natural, recyclable products
made from wood grown in sustainable forests

Printed in Great Britain by
CPI Antony Rowe, Chippenham and Eastbourne

CONTENTS

List of Illustrations: plates, tables, maps and plans   ix

Preface   xiii

Abbreviations   xv

INTRODUCTION   xix

    The parish of Mildenhall   xix

    St Mary's church   xxii

    The liturgical necessities: books, vestments and plate   xxxi

    Priests and parochial personnel   xxxvii

    Remembering the dead   xliv

    The bells and the clock   liii

    Drinkings and drama   lv

Contents of the Collections and Churchwardens' Accounts   lix

Editorial Conventions   lxxii

THE COLLECTIONS 1446–1454   1

THE CHURCHWARDENS' ACCOUNTS 1503–1553   41

Appendices

1. Mildenhall under Queen Mary   133

2. Selected wills   137

3. Extracts from Lyndwood's *Provinciale* (1534)   181

Feasts and Festivals   183

Glossary   185

Notes on People   199

Bibliography   213

Indices *compiled by Heather Falvey*

    People and places   217

    Subjects   227

ILLUSTRATIONS

Frontispiece   Mildenhall market place with the market cross and the parish pump, St Mary's tower in the background. From the etching by M. Oliver Rae, *c*.1930

Plates

1. Mildenhall Warren Lodge, fifteenth/sixteenth century. The warrener's dwelling from the south-west   xx
2. The east window of the thirteenth-century vestry from within   xxiii
3. St Mary's church exterior: the east window, *c*.1300–10, with the east end of the thirteenth-century vestry on the right   xxiv
4. St Mary's church interior looking east to show the nave roof, chancel arch and east window, photographed by A.F. Kersting *c*.1950. © Conway Library, Courtauld Institute of Art   xxvi
5. St Mary's church interior: the north side of the fourteenth-century chancel arch showing the three blocked entrances leading to screen and rood. © Clifford Knowles 2007   xxvii
6. St Mary's church exterior: fourteenth- and fifteenth-century ashlar, carving and flushwork on the face of the north aisle and the north porch. © Clifford Knowles 2007   xxix
7. Exterior of St Mary's church, *c*.1930, from the south-east, with the ivy-covered ruins of the late fourteenth-century charnel chapel in the foreground. © National Monuments Record   li
8. A folio from the fifteenth-century Mildenhall collections, SROB, EL110/5/1, fol.8r, 1449   lxi
9. A folio from the sixteenth-century Mildenhall churchwardens' accounts, SROB, EL 110/5/3, fol.15r   lxvi

Tables

1. Vicars of Mildenhall, 1432–1559   xxxix
2. Priests and parochial personnel, 1469–1541   xli
3. Money raised by churchales in the collections, 1446–54   lvi
4. Money raised by May ales, May games, drinkings and churchales in the churchwardens' accounts, 1505–44   lvii

Maps

1. Mildenhall parish in the fifteenth–sixteenth centuries, drawn by Sue Holden   xvi
2. Mildenhall's proximity to the east coast via river and fen, drawn by Sue Holden   xvii

Plan

1. Plan of St Mary's church, adapted from Birkin Haward's *Suffolk*   xlv
   Medieval Church Arcades (1993)

The Suffolk Records Society and publishers are grateful to all the institutions and individuals listed for permission to reproduce the materials in which they hold copyright. Every effort has been made to trace the copyright holders; apologies are offered for any omission, and the publishers will be pleased to add any necessary acknowledgement in subsequent editions.

The Society is also grateful to Mildenhall and District Museum and the Scouloudi Foundation in association with the Institute of Historical Research for grants to cover the cost of the indices.

To my father,
Howell Gruffyd St Michael Rees,
who loved this church,
and to
Peter Northeast,
who explained to me that
Crockford's was not only a gaming house
in London.

PREFACE

In 1946, my parents decided to leave Liverpool. It had been a difficult war for my father, a general practitioner, and he thought it time to spread his wings. Why he decided that we should move to Suffolk I never knew, but we arrived in Mildenhall later that year.

Coming from a long line of Welsh clergymen, there was never any doubt but that he would take us to church – and it was to St Mary's that we went every Sunday. After extremely dull worship in a dreary late-Victorian church in a Liverpool suburb, church-going in Mildenhall was more of an occasion and, from the beginning, was almost the highlight of the week. It was not the services or the sermons that made an impression, but the size and beauty of the building. These were something which I had not experienced before, and so for many years it remained my church.

In 2001 Eamon Duffy telephoned. He was organising the Harlaxton conference for the following year and asked whether I could 'do something' on church officers. I knew that Mildenhall churchwardens' accounts existed and also those from Tilney All Saints in north Norfolk, another architecturally exceptional church like Mildenhall, but even older. I decided to compare and contrast the accounts of the two parishes and, since then, I have looked at Mildenhall in greater depth. It has taken a long time to get this far, but I have enjoyed the journey.

Along the way I have spoken to many people, one of the first being the late Peter Northeast who, always generous, shared his scholarship unselfishly over many years. As a post-graduate in the Centre of East Anglian Studies, I encountered A. Hassell Smith who made suggestions regarding my Harlaxton paper and commented on this present work. Meanwhile Robert Swanson explained pardons to me, Frank Woodman extolled the glories of Mildenhall's architecture, Magnus Williamson gave musical advice and Diarmaid MacCulloch brought the troubles of 1549 to life. Edward Martin and Sue Holden assisted with maps and a former Madingley student, Clifford Knowles, took photographs. At St Mary's, Marjorie Frape was welcoming. Nearer home Anne Holland and Jennifer Rogers have been skilful instructors in the computer field, and Alan, my husband, has undertaken many extra duties and has been a steadfast support.

I have the Mildenhall Parochial Church Council to thank for allowing me to publish the Mildenhall accounts. The staff of the Suffolk Record Office at Bury St Edmunds were patient and I thank them too for all their assistance so cheerfully given. Thanks are due to Michael Parker for giving permission to publish the illustration by M. Oliver Rae. I thank also the National Archives, the Norfolk Record Office, the Suffolk Institute of Archaeology and History, the National Monuments Record at English Heritage and the Courtauld Institute, all of whom have granted me permission to use manuscripts, publications and photographs in their care. I have also received encouragement and help from David Sherlock, the series editor.

My greatest debt is to David Dymond, the general editor, who has overseen this work through several years. He says in the preface to his Bassingbourn churchwardens' accounts, 'Many historians believe that the job of editing is merely to present an accurate transcription, prefaced by editorial notes and a brief history of the transcript. Belonging to a different school of thought, I have provided other supporting documents, copious footnotes, a glossary of English and Latin words, notes on people, a bibliography, and a sizeable introduction ... in the hope of making the documents accessible to the widest possible readership, both academic and general, national and local. For that I make no apologies.' He also added many will transcriptions to the Bassingbourn accounts, a volume of which has been my *vade-mecum* since 2004. It has been my intention that the Mildenhall collections and churchwardens' accounts should cover a similar range. I hope that they do.

Judith Middleton-Stewart,
Wenhaston,
St Agnes' Eve, 2010

The officers and council of the Suffolk Records Society regret to record here that Dr Judith Middleton-Stewart has not lived to see this volume in print. Soon after writing the Preface, and after a long and brave battle with cancer, she died on 12 May 2010 at her home in Wenhaston. Before this sad event, however, she did have the satisfaction of knowing that the book on which she had worked so hard for several years was finished, and would be sent to our co-publishers within a few months. We extend our deepest sympathy to her husband, Alan Middleton-Stewart, and hope that he will derive some consolation from this volume which meant so much to Judith in her later years. It expresses not only her passionate interest in late medieval social and religious life, in which she was so expert, but also her deep attachment to a corner of Suffolk which had been her home in childhood.

DPD

ABBREVIATIONS

BL	British Library
COED	*Compact Oxford English Dictionary*
Coll.	(Mildenhall) Collections
CPR	*Calendar of Patent Rolls*
CWA	(Mildenhall) Churchwardens' Accounts
LP	*Letters and Papers of Henry VIII*
NCC	Norwich Consistory Court
NRO	Norfolk Record Office
NRS	Norfolk Record Society
OE	Old English
PCC	Parochial Church Council
PSIA(H)	*Proceedings of the Suffolk Institute of Archaeology (and History)*
SIAH	Suffolk Institute of Archaeology and History
SROB	Suffolk Record Office, Bury St Edmunds branch
SRS	Suffolk Records Society
TNA	The National Archives (formerly the Public Record Office)

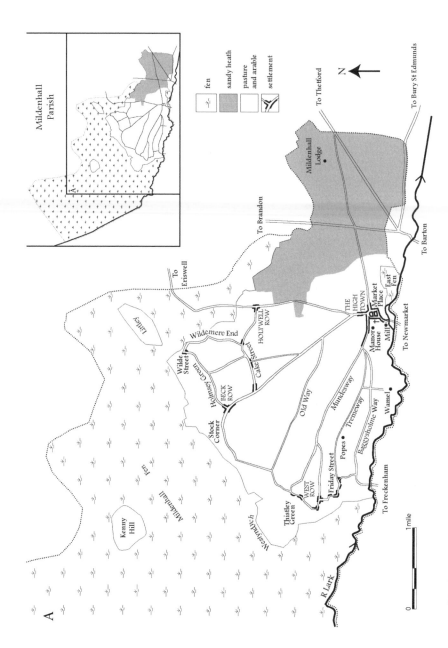

1. *Mildenhall parish in the fifteenth–sixteenth centuries, drawn by Sue Holden.*

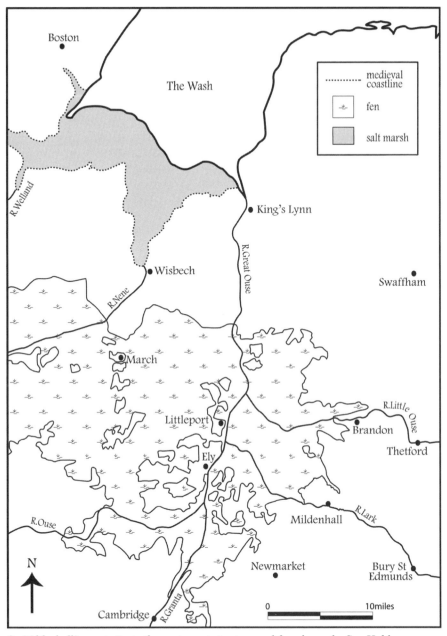

2. Mildenhall's proximity to the east coast via river and fen, drawn by Sue Holden.

INTRODUCTION

THE PARISH OF MILDENHALL

The history and prosperity of the market town of Mildenhall were largely dependent on the Fens which once covered parts of Cambridgeshire, Suffolk, Norfolk and Lincolnshire.[1] The area had been a chalky plain, but primeval flooding had swept across the lower areas of chalk, leaving the higher areas as islands, with peat deposits to the south of the Fens and silt to the north and east.[2] Mildenhall, then (and still) known locally as the High Town, was situated on a chalky promontory near the southern parish boundary. The name Mildenhall may come from the Old English *Middelen hale* meaning 'at the middle nook or place', but Margaret Gelling has proposed a different derivation, 'slightly raised ground isolated by marsh'.[3] This is an apt description of Mildenhall parish with the High Town and its various outlying settlements standing somewhat higher than the surrounding fen. All around is evidence of much earlier habitation, for example in the neolithic site at Hurst Fen and the Bronze Age sites in Mildenhall Fen and at Wilde Street.[4] The Mildenhall treasure, a priceless collection of Roman silver tableware, came to light at West Row.[5] This was during the 1940s when the plough dug into the chalk more deeply than usual and made the name of Mildenhall almost a household word.

Mildenhall parish is at its widest from north-west to south-east. The river Lark runs along its southern edge forming part of the county boundary between Suffolk and Cambridgeshire and it separates Mildenhall High Town from its two closest neighbours, Worlington and Barton Mills. To the north-east, the parish boundary is conterminous with Lakenheath, Undley common, which is not a parish, and Eriswell. Eastwards, the Breckland stretches away towards High Suffolk.[6] To the west lay the watery waste of the Fens, described by St Guthlac of Crowland as the 'hideous fen of a huge bigness' as he observed it from his tumulus on the banks of the river Welland.[7] Nevertheless, it was due to the later drainage schemes which started early in the medieval period that the rich alluvial fen-soil was recovered, with further improvements being made during the eighteenth and early nineteenth

---

[1]   J. Coles and D. Hall, *Changing Landscapes: The Ancient Fenland* (1998), p.3.
[2]   H.C. Darby, *The Medieval Fenland* (1974), p.16. In the southern peat areas settlements were founded on higher, drier islands.
[3]   M. Gelling, *Place-names in the Landscape* (1984), p.100. W.W. Skeat, *The Place-Names of Suffolk* (1913), p.45, suggested the name Mildenhall came from Milda's nook.
[4]   A.V. Steward, *A Suffolk Bibliography*, SRS, 20 (1974), pp.353–5; E. Martin, '13. The Neolithic: 14. The Bronze Age: 15. The Iron Age', in *An Historical Atlas of Suffolk*, ed. D. Dymond and E. Martin, 2nd edn (1999), pp.36–41.
[5]   T.W. Potter, *Roman Britain* (1997), pp.69, 81 and 86.
[6]   D.N.J. MacCulloch, *Suffolk and the Tudors* (1986), p.16. Mildenhall and Lakenheath have been called the monster parishes because of their size: W. White, *History, Gazetteer and Directory of Suffolk 1844* (1970), pp.592–593. Lakenheath contained 10,550 acres of land: N. Scarfe, *A Shell Guide to Suffolk*, 2nd edn (1965), p.71.
[7]   J. Campbell, *The Anglo-Saxons* (1991), p.82. Guthlac made his home in a barrow, like Beowulf's dragon, and lived, like Grendel, in a fen.

Plate 1. Mildenhall Warren Lodge, fifteenth/sixteenth century. The warrener's dwelling from the south-west.

centuries.[8] By 1844 the parish consisted of 15,990 acres, 8,540 acres of low, fertile and well-drained fen and 7,450 acres of skirt and high lands.[9]

In the fifteenth century the eastern half of the parish consisted of chalk and sand while the north-western half lay up against Ely in largely undrained fenland. On the edge of the fen minor settlements stood on small islands where the chalk had fragmented.[10] These islets were called Thistley Green, which lay to the west of West Row, Kenny Hill, Holmsey Green and Littley.[11] Larger settlements lying in an arc to the north of the High Town between the open fields and the fen were known as the Rows: West Row, Beck Row, Holywell Row and Cake Street.[12] These settlements were some distance from the High Town and were reached by ancient trackways, West Row for example lying a good two miles to the north-west of Mildenhall town.

---

[8] MacCulloch, *Suffolk and the Tudors*, pp.327–328. After the dissolution of the abbey at Bury St Edmunds, an elected body of leading Mildenhall yeomen called the Twenty-Four drained the parish fenland to reclaim more than 4,000 acres, as a result of which the population of the parish expanded to 2,000. J.S. Craig, 'Co-operation and initiatives: Mildenhall 1550–1603', *Social History* 18, no.3 (1993), and *Reformation, Politics and Polemics: the Growth of Protestantism in East Anglian Market Towns, 1500–1610* (2001), pp.35–63.

[9] White, *Suffolk*, p.593.

[10] Coles and Hall, *Changing Landscapes*, p.30.

[11] Thistley Green is probably derived from Ceciles or Cicily Green (SROB, E18/400/1:3); Kenny Hill is derived from Kine Isle; Holmsey Green is perhaps derived from the Old English meaning the island by the marsh in the hollow; Littley is derived from Little Isle. I have Edward Martin to thank for this information and for the following footnote.

[12] Beck Row may have derived from the Old Norse *bekkr*, meaning a stream (SROB, E18/455/102); Holywell Row is derived from OE *halig* (*helig*) holy-well; Cake Street in the fourteenth century was known as Cokes Green or Cokes Gate, probably derived from the surname Le Cok.

On the sand and heath to the east lay an extensive warren where Mildenhall Warren Lodge, a semi-fortified medieval lodge, still stands (Plate 1), built to house the warrener who had to protect his rabbits from poachers, and still occupied by a gamekeeper and his family in the 1930s. The warren at High Lodge ran to over a thousand acres. Rabbits were valuable for the food they provided and their fur was used for clothing and for household coverings such as rugs and bedding.[13]

On account of Mildenhall's position and the relative ease of access by water it had become a great emporium for fish brought up from the sea and fen, as well as for wildfowl, reeds, rushes and, of course, peat.[14] The waterways were vital to Mildenhall's economy as the river Ouse linked this part of Suffolk to the east Midlands. From further afield came coals from Newcastle, essential building stone from Northamptonshire and tar and timber from the Baltic.[15]

Originally a royal holding, Mildenhall manor, including its church, was granted to the abbey of Bury St Edmunds by Edward the Confessor in 1043.[16] The manor at that time was worth the considerable sum of £40 a year. In 1086, Domesday Book revealed that the manor contained twelve carucates of land (nominally 1,440 acres), 20 acres of meadow, a church with 40 acres, a mill and three fisheries. The manor changed hands again over the next hundred years, but was finally redeemed by Abbot Samson during the reign of Richard I.[17] From that time until the final dissolution of the monasteries in 1539–40, Mildenhall, the single most valuable manor in Suffolk, belonged to the abbey, and it was rich. In 1323, in addition to receiving arable produce from the manor, the cellarer of the abbey received cash worth £130.[18]

Mildenhall had long been a market town, its first market officially granted in 1220. Immediately after the Black Death, the town's cloth manufacture was buoyant. By 1377 Mildenhall was the fourth largest town in the county and seventy-sixth in the country, but gradually its fortunes waned.[19] To ameliorate the situation, the approach to the town from the river Lark was improved. The annual fair was moved from Lammas to Michaelmas, the weekly market-day changed and the present market cross and shambles erected, but the market continued to decline as permanent shops were set up.[20] It is against this unsettled economic background and the later divisive Reformation that the Mildenhall collections and churchwardens' accounts have to be considered.

---

13 R. Hoppitt, '29. Rabbit warrens', in *An Historical Atlas of Suffolk* (1999), pp.68–69, 200–201; M. Bailey, *Medieval Suffolk: an Economic and Social History 1200–1500* (2007), pp.227–30. See also Appendix 2:43, the will of Nicholas Meye, warrener, 1540.

14 Coles and Hall, *Changing Landscapes*, p.3.

15 Bailey, *Medieval Suffolk*, p.64. See Map 2.

16 H.G. St M. Rees, *An Illustrated History of Mildenhall, Suffolk and its Parish Church of the Blessed Virgin Mary* (1961), p.8; H.E. Butler, ed., *The Chronicle of Jocelin of Brakelond concerning the Acts of Samson, Abbot of the Monastery of St Edmund* (1949), p.51. In the margin is written 'and our charter speaks of the time of King Edward and that of his mother Queen Emma, who had eight and a half hundreds for her dowry before the time of St Edward, and had Mildenhall as well'. Aspal Hall was a small manor lying between Cake Street and Holywell Row which, by the fifteenth century, also belonged to the abbey at Bury. The ancient hall was demolished and its land sold for development in the 1960s.

17 Butler, *Jocelin of Brakelond*, pp.45–47.

18 Bailey, *Medieval Suffolk*, p.21; for further details of the relationship between Mildenhall and the abbey see C. Dyer, *Everyday Life in Medieval England* (2000), pp.80 n.14, 115, 225–228, 231, 233 and 235 (xii) on Margaret Wrighte of Lakenheath.

19 J. Sear, 'Trade and Commerce in Mildenhall, c.1350–c.1500', unpublished Master of Studies degree in Local and Regional History, Cambridge, 2007.

20 Bailey, *Medieval Suffolk*, pp.117, 231, 266–267 and 281.

ST MARY'S CHURCH

A church at Mildenhall is mentioned in Domesday Book (1086) but the earliest part of the present building is a short stretch of fabric in the south chancel wall. Here three distinct building campaigns can be detected below the fourteenth-century string course. The earliest of these are the banded flints lying west of the junction of chancel and nave, possibly of twelfth-century date, followed by a central section c.1220–40 with blocks of stone pitted to receive rendering, now lost, and finally the fabric to the east, lengthened during Richard de Wichforde's incumbency. This is the new building referred to on the funeral slab of de Wichforde, vicar of Mildenhall 1309–44, set into the chancel floor and inscribed *Hic jacet Ricardus de Wichforde quondam vicarius ecclesiae de Mildenhale qui fecit istud novum opus* 'Here lies Richard of Wichforde, formerly vicar of this church, who made this new work'.

On the north side, tucked between the chancel and north aisle, is the earliest complete structure, identified from the outside by its lancet windows overlooking the High Street. Stylistically this small chapel may be as early as c.1220 and was possibly the work of an Ely mason.[21] The date is deduced from its interior features which comprise the east window of three lights with detached columns, shaft-rings and stiff-leaf capitals (Plate 2), and single lancet windows in the north wall. The roof is stone-vaulted. References to this room being used as the vestry occur in the pre-Reformation accounts and it is used as the vestry today. Its original purpose is unknown.[22] In the sixteenth-century accounts the great hutch stood in the vestry. At the back of the church today stands an extremely large oak chest banded with iron, possibly the same vestry chest.[23]

The east façade of the church (Plate 3) contains the great chancel window with its seven lights, the narrow quatrefoil border of outer lights continuing around the window arch like a chain of medallions. It is dated to the first decade of the fourteenth century by Bony.[24] It is akin to contemporary court style 'micro-architecture' and is similar in some respects to Prior Crauden's chapel window at Ely, although that is later. The glazing may have had a Marian theme and the centre light, its shape resembling a mandorla, suggests that this may have been the Assumption of the Virgin.[25] The window is flanked by corner buttresses with niches set at an

---

[21] Nikolaus Pevsner and Enid Radcliffe, *The Buildings of England: Suffolk* (1974), p.364.

[22] H. Munro Cautley, *Suffolk Churches and their Treasures*, 4th edn (1975), pp.330–332.

[23] CWA, fols 5v, 25r. See also D. Sherlock, *Suffolk Church Chests* (2008), p.83.

[24] Jean Bony, *The English Decorated Style: Gothic Architecture Transformed 1250–1350* (1979), p.55 and ill. 377. Similar medallions decorate the tomb of Abbot Renaud de Montclar (d.1346) at La Chaise-Dieu in the Auvergne. Cautley suggests the chancel dates from the early thirteenth century and was finished at the end of that century, giving the window a date of c.1300. See *Suffolk Churches*, p.332.

[25] A contemporary English interpretation of the Assumption can be seen in L.R. Sandler, *Gothic Manuscripts 1285–1385: a Survey of Manuscripts Illuminated in the British Isles*, I (1986), pl.147; and E. Mâle, *The Gothic Image: Religious Art in France of the Thirteenth Century*, trans. D. Nussey (1972), pp.248–258. In 1829, this central light was filled with plaster. See D.E. Davy, 'Collections for the History of Suffolk by Hundreds and Parishes', BL, Add. MSS 19077–19113, in Add. MS 19095, fols 203–206. Davy also describes the carving on the beams of the chancel roof, the first beam from the east end bearing a Latin inscription translated as *Pray for the souls of Master William Cadge, William Buntyng and Agnes Rede of whose goods this chancel was made*. On the second, third and fourth beams the inscription, here translated, ran *Be it known repaired both in a new roof and in walls and other things AD 1507*.

Plate 2. The east window of the thirteenth-century vestry from within.

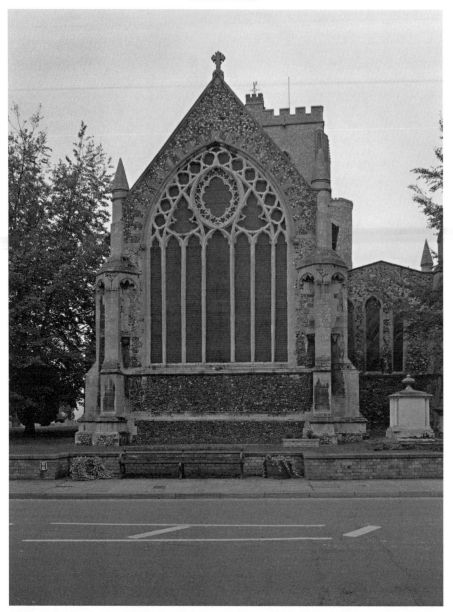

Plate 3. St Mary's church exterior: the east window, c.1300–10, with the east end of the thirteenth-century vestry on the right.

angle, their canopies joining together before continuing as octagonal pinnacles on the corners of the chancel. The early fourteenth-century tracery in the chancel side windows is unusual, perhaps unique, and the overall architectural design of the chancel is of the highest merit.

Within the chancel, the altar would have been set back against the east wall, raised either by a couple of steps or standing on a base. The double piscina for washing the eucharistic vessels, the *sedilia* for the priest, deacon and sub-deacon and an aumbrey remain in the south wall. To the north of the altar standing in a tabernacle was an image of 'the most glorious Virgin Mary', balanced on the south side of the altar by St John the Evangelist, to whom a tabernacle was bequeathed in 1515.[26] Also within the chancel was an Easter sepulchre, its presence entered annually in the churchwardens' accounts for Holy Week.[27]

The chancel arch is of a similar date and style as the vestry, the arch decorated with stiff-leafed capitals and dog-tooth carving on the east and west faces. Between the vestry and the north chancel aisle are steps in the depth of the vestry wall, which originally was the outer wall. The steps lead up to the roof where the sanctus bell would have hung. Off the steps are three doorways opening on to the west of the chancel arch. These would have given access to the rood and the rood-loft, the size and position of the openings indicating what an immense structure the rood-screen must have been. The north aisle chapel was originally dedicated to John the Baptist and St John's gild would have celebrated here. The chapel's piscina, with a blocked squint above, is still housed in the pier respond. The corresponding chapel of St Margaret in the south aisle has a pre-Reformation *mensa* of *c.*1420, incised with five consecration crosses representing the five wounds of Christ.[28]

The early sixteenth-century churchwardens' accounts suggest that either the rood-screen was a recent installation or that the existing screen had been altered, perhaps heightened.[29] At the beginning of the accounts, the vicar, Paul Geyton, donated 8s. towards the painting of the canopy above the rood.[30] Shortly afterwards, staging for the rood-loft was put into position and the 'alabaster man' was paid £1 6s. 2d. for painting the rood-loft, which probably means that painted alabaster panels were set into the framework.[31] Another entry shows that a further £1 9s. was spent on painting the rood-loft.[32]

Birkin Haward attributed a date of 1410–20 to the arcades, clerestory and roof of Mildenhall.[33] The arcades have five bays made of Barnack stone, the pier plan resembling that at St Nicholas in Bishop's (now King's) Lynn, which led Haward to suggest that a mason such as Robert Wodehirst from Norwich might have been the inspiration. The nave is lit by the wide aisle windows and the clerestory above. The north and south aisles, in typical fifteenth-century style, are both extremely wide. This is a feature to be found in many East Anglian churches, the result of the popu-

---

26 Alice Webbe, 1498 (NRO, NCC Typpes 146); Thomas Chylderston, butcher, 1477 (SROB, IC 500/2/11/235); and Margery Howton, 1515 (NRO, NCC Brigges 28). Margery also left 6s. 8d. to the gilding of St Christopher, but where this image appeared is not known.

27 Robert Pachett, 1488 (SROB, IC 500/2/11/410).

28 D.P. Mortlock, *The Popular Guide to Suffolk Churches*, I (1988), p.155.

29 CWA, fol.2v.

30 CWA, fol.1v.

31 See F. Cheetham, *Alabaster Images of Medieval England* (2003), p.4.

32 CWA, fol.3r.

33 Birkin Haward, *Suffolk Medieval Church Arcades* (1993), pp.308–310, 412–413. Haward suggested a possible link with Lowestoft St Margaret which he described as 'a grand re-build of the 15c', p.304.

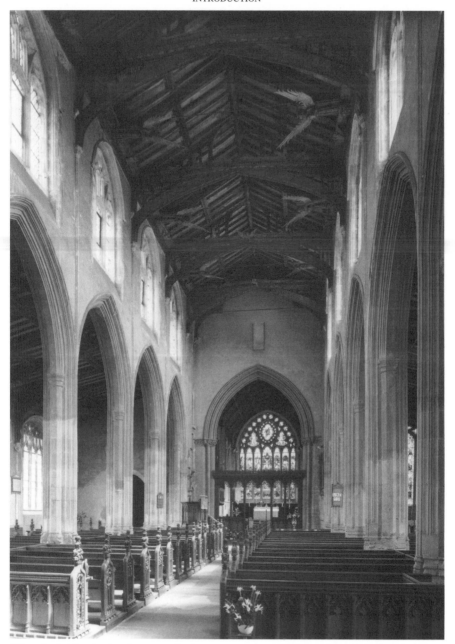

Plate 4. St Mary's church interior looking east to show the nave roof, chancel arch and east window, photographed by A.F. Kersting c.1950. © Courtauld Institute of Art.

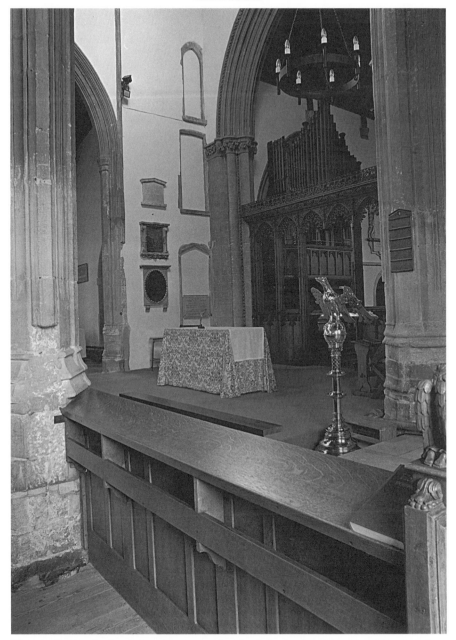

Plate 5. St Mary's church interior: the north side of the fourteenth-century chancel arch showing the three blocked entrances leading to screen and rood. © Clifford Knowles 2007.

larity of masses and commemorative prayers said for the laity by parish chaplains. Wider aisles made it easier to accommodate side-altars and, apart from the service chantries to be celebrated, there were religious gilds worshipping in St Mary's church, each one with its own space and a place for its patronal statue. Given that there were so many opportunities in this church for intercessory prayer, the absence of *piscinae*, blocked or open, is unusual. It may be, however, that the screens demarcating the area allotted to side altars were of stone with integral *piscinae*, all to be destroyed in the late 1540s.

Missing in this vast and colourless space are the wall paintings, from which the parishioners would have gained religious knowledge. Glazed imagery would have filled the huge fifteenth-century windows. The decoration of wall and window may have been complementary if the work had been undertaken as an integrated scheme, but the only definite fact is the churchwardens' accounts recording the whitewashing of the walls and the presence of the glazier replacing the shattered glass.[34] Little, too, is recorded of the painted and gilded statues to which prayers were offered and gifts bequeathed.[35]

Decoratively, the exterior of the south aisle is undistinguished. It is the exterior of the north aisle which is the more remarkable (Plate 6). Cautley believed that the north-aisle buttresses with their canopied niches, still retaining their socles, were fourteenth-century, perhaps carefully removed and then replaced after the fifteenth-century alterations to the aisle were complete.[36] The fifteenth-century work includes traceried stone parapets, the corbel table embellished by carved heads, both animal and human, and chequered flushwork which spreads over the face of the north aisle towards the north porch.

It is known from pre-Reformation wills that the Lady Chapel was situated in the upper chamber of the north porch.[37] This would have been the more important of the two porches because it faced the site of the manor house and led to the market place. The external walls of the north porch are decorated with flushwork, cresting, pinnacles, voided shields and two empty niches on each of the east, west and north sides. Within, the porch has a stone-vaulted roof with carved bosses, only one bearing the four evangelist symbols still identifiable. The original fourteenth-century doorways were re-set in the following century when the new aisles were built. The north doorway has carved emblems of St Edmund and St Edward the Confessor flanking a central niche within which would have stood the Virgin's image. The door itself shows clearly the woodcarver's skill although the fabric has been badly damaged. The Lady Chapel above is approached from inside the church through a doorway with spandrels bearing imagery of the Annunciation, and the chapel looks out over the nave through two arched openings. There was also a chapel dedicated to St Michael, its sole reference as *St Mykahall* appearing in Davy's notes which he made from the churchwardens' accounts of 1533, now lost.[38]

---

[34] CWA, fol.35r.

[35] In 1478 William Cootes asked to be buried before the image of St Leonard of Noblac (SROB, IC 500/2/11/238). St Leonard founded a monastery at Noblac near Limoges where he dedicated himself to the relief of prisoners. His emblem was a chain or fetters, depicted on the sixteenth-century screen at Westhall church.

[36] Cautley, *Suffolk Churches*, p.330.

[37] John Gardener, 1519 (SROB, IC 500/2/12/26); Alice Bateman, widow, 1527 (SROB, IC 500/2/17/250). In 1455, John Chylderston left four hives of bees 'to find a light of blessed Mary in Mildenhall parish church' (SROB, IC 500/2/9/179).

[38] Davy, BL, Add. MS. 19096, fol.203.

Plate 6. St Mary's church exterior: fourteenth- and fifteenth-century ashlar, carving and flushwork on the face of the north aisle and the north porch. © Clifford Knowles 2007.

The nave is topped by the famous angel roof of arched-braced tie beams supporting queen-posts and hammerbeams carved in the shape of human-sized angels holding stringed instruments or books. Angels bearing scrolls decorate the cornice. Traces of earlier decoration show that the roof was gilded. The south aisle roof is richly carved above with hammer beams below, and its cornice supports swans and antelopes, the heraldic emblems of Henry V (1413–22) which also embellish his chantry chapel at Westminster. The fifteenth-century font which stands below carries the arms of the City of London and of the donor, Sir Henry Barton. Sir Henry and, later, William Gregory, who were Mildenhall natives, both became Lord Mayor of London in the fifteenth century.[39] In the north aisle, the west face of the spandrels, being adjacent to the Lady Chapel, are carved with scenes from the life of Christ and Our Lady. The east face of the spandrels shows hunting scenes and St George killing the dragon. The defaced figures on the wall-posts shelter under an enfolding canopy of angels' wings.

Overall, St Mary's church must have been under reconstruction for two hundred years, beginning with the extension of the east end, followed by the new nave, aisles,

---

[39] William Gregory, 1465 (TNA, PCC Godyn 16); see Notes on People. Among the Mildenhall testators were three wood-workers but the church roofs predate all three. They were William Curteys, the elder, 1443 (SROB, IC 500/2/9/40): 'to Emma (my wife) all the utensils and bedding of my house, except what pertains to my body and my craft of carpentry, such as tools'; Henry Nowce, tourner, 1535 (see Appendix 2:39), his occupation was already appended to his name; and Richard Wengge, carpenter, 1434 (NRO, NCC Surflete 149): 'All my equipment belonging to the craft of carpenter to my son Thomas'. There was also a carver of Bury St Edmunds named John Myldenhale (d.1442), an example of a locative surname which may have later changed to Carpenter, see Haward, *Suffolk Medieval Church Arcades*, p.456.

roofs, two porches and finally a new tower. The fabric of the fifteenth-century tower received many bequests in late medieval wills, and the collections, of which perhaps only a fraction remain, were vital in recording the donations given towards the building programme.[40] It is not known how far the tower construction had reached when the collections began in 1446, but neither is it known if the collections started then or before 1446. The surviving manuscript is likely to be a fragment of a much larger body of accounts but, because the collections show income, not expenditure, there are few clues to follow. The only indication of any work going ahead at all was an entry in 1449 when the second bell had been made and the stock was set.[41] In 1450 the first donations were received for the bell-tower;[42] and it is from this evidence that it is supposed that the tower and its bells were the object of the collections.

The tower is a well-known landmark with a great western door and a huge window above, both renewed in the nineteenth century. Until 1831 a fifteenth-century spirelet and lantern stood on the top of the tower, the building of which was probably completed c.1460.[43] Its appearance and its date must have been very similar to that of the lantern at East Harling in south Norfolk. Now, Mildenhall tower appears as a very austere structure. It was refaced in the nineteenth century when quantities of thirteenth-century dog-tooth mouldings were revealed buried in the fabric. Within the tower is a stone gallery, set below the tower arch and decorated with shields. Overlooking the nave is a clock face, perhaps the remains of the clock which gave the churchwardens so much trouble in the sixteenth century.[44] The floor space below the gallery has been compared to a Galilee porch with a fan-vaulted roof which is likely to have been inserted between 1530 and 1555. The proximity of Mildenhall suggests that the creator of the vaulting was from Cambridge.[45]

St Mary's retains two of its ancient bells. Bell number 8, John, recast in 1913, is inscribed *In Multis Annis Resonet Campana Joahanis* and rings in G. Bell number 7, Magdalen, was recast in 1860 and in 1913. She previously bore the inscription *Nomen Magdalene Campana Gerit Melodie*, and she rings in A flat. The fifteenth-century wooden bell frame was removed in 1912.[46] It is worth noting that in 1447 Isabel Galyon donated one shilling for the repair of the bells and, two years later, a bill for sundry expenses included making the second bell and the setting of the stock. This was settled for seven nobles.[47]

Below and now at the back of the church is the parish chest with three locks, the equivalent of today's wall safe. Robert Gille, a chaplain in the late fourteenth century, bequeathed a chest with iron bands 'and to the common chest of the same

---

[40] In 1515 the churchwardens' accounts of St Mary's the Great in Cambridge recorded money collected each Sunday from 9 July to 24 December. This was to pay masons, carpenters and labourers for materials and work on the almshouse, and the porch and vestry of the church. See *The Churchwardens' Accounts of St Mary the Great, Cambridge, from 1504 to 1635*, ed. J.E. Foster (1905), pp.23–24. Mildenhall's collections do not describe such details, but the money gathered perhaps purchased the second bell and completed the bell tower.
[41] See CWA, fol.8r. This suggests the bell chamber had at least been completed.
[42] Coll. fol.10v.
[43] Mortlock, *Suffolk Churches*, I, p.151.
[44] See CWA, fol.27r and 'Mildenhall Church Clock', below, p.lv.
[45] Mortlock, *Suffolk Churches*, I, p.153.
[46] Rees, *Mildenhall*, p.24.
[47] Coll. fols 4r and 8r.

place 3s. 4d'.[48] The documents translated and transcribed in this present volume may have spent much of their lifetime locked away in such a chest.

THE LITURGICAL NECESSITIES

The parishioners, through their churchwardens, ultimately became responsible for the construction, maintenance and repair of the nave and tower. Outside they had to ensure that the churchyard was properly enclosed. The rector, whether a monastic or secular priest, was left with responsibility for the chancel. The archdeacon's annual task was to enquire of every parish in his charge whether divine office was properly conducted, to ensure that the sacrament was given to the faithful, to check the altar furnishings, linen and vestments and to make certain that the chrism and holy oil were under lock and key.[49] Inventories were to be drawn up for examination by the archdeacon on his annual parochial visitation.[50] The inventories included eight items of plate, eight liturgical books in manuscript form until the appearance of the printed page at the end of the fifteenth century, and a variety of vestments and cloths.[51] Other necessities included the principal image to the north of the high altar, the font, usually placed at the back of the church between the south and north doors, and the bells. These were the parishioners' responsibility.

Parishioners undertook these duties, but scant documentation from the parish has survived. In the reformed regime of the mid-sixteenth century, documents recording these now outmoded practices were of no use. Nevertheless, those churchwardens' accounts and church inventories which do exist, the latter mostly undated, testify to the generosity and pious provision of both clergy and laity, and lead to a more meaningful interpretation than would have been possible otherwise.

Books

The books to be supplied, at the least, were a lesson book, a troper containing short passages of music, an antiphoner providing music for divine service,[52] a psalter and a gradual or grail which provided music for the Mass. A missal (mass book), a manual containing occasional offices and an ordinal completed the requirements. The processional, which appears frequently in the Mildenhall accounts, contained

[48] Robert Gille de Schaftesbury, 1381 (NRO, NCC Heydon 194).
[49] For the full extent of the parishioners' responsibilities and a better understanding of the contents of churchwardens' accounts, see Appendix 3 taken from Lyndwood's *Provinciale*.
[50] C. Drew, *Early Parochial Organisation in England: The Origins of the Office of Churchwarden*, St Anthony's Hall Publications, 7, Borthwick Institute of Historical Research (1954), p.9.
[51] A. Watkin, ed., *Archdeaconry of Norwich: Inventory of Church Goods temp. Edward III*, part ii, pp.xvii–xviii. This is a valuable account of the provision of liturgical plate, books and linen used in the churches of the archdeaconry of Norwich in 1368. It identifies the profusion of church goods in even the smaller, poorer churches and contains detailed descriptions of various artefacts; see also E. Peacock, ed., *English Church Furniture* (1866), pp.175–179; P.S. Barnwell, C. Cross and A. Rycraft, eds, *Mass and Parish in Late Medieval England: The Use of York* (2005), pp.127–140, which includes illustrations from *Dat Boexken vander Missen*, ed. P. Dearmer; C. Oman, *English Church Plate 597–1830* (1957), p.10 n.3.
[52] Antiphoners were often in two parts, one for the immoveable feasts of the saints known as *antiphonale sanctorum*, the other *antiphonale temporalis* for the moveable feasts.

music to be sung in processions and was often included in the manual.[53] Milden-hall's collections bore no significant entry referring to books but, if an inventory had survived from that time, the books would have been in manuscript, not in print.[54]

Liturgical books were sometimes bequeathed by clerics to their clerical companions,[55] but those belonging to the church frequently appear in the accounts because repairs were regularly necessary. In 1510–11 St Mary's owned three anti-phoners at the least and their torn covers needed mending. The payment made to John Smith included the cost of a skin for the cover, shortly followed by repairs to an epistle book and a processional.[56] In 1514–15 the binding of a new mass book, given by Roger Barford, cost 2s. 6d. Board and lodging for the bookbinder was not entered in the accounts which suggest that the book was bound in Mildenhall by John Screvyner who, in 1516, was in charge of mending and covering books.[57]

Processionals suffered most from usage and appeared frequently in the accounts. A new processional made in 1512–13 cost 2s. 5d.[58] While antiphoners and graduals, of great size and weight, lay on a desk or a lectern around which several singers could gather at a time, a processional was 'carried on the move' and shared between two people.[59] In later inventories processionals are more numerous than other books, and the number of these in an inventory may be a guide to the size of the choir. Given that two undated pre-Reformation inventories from Mildenhall have survived, with five processionaries entered in one and six in the other, it may be that the choir consisted of ten to twelve singers. More information about Mildenhall's choir comes from a brief entry which reads 'Item for mend[ing] of the stole for the *rector chori*'.[60] This gives an indication of the sophistication of the psalmody in St Mary's, with a choirmaster leading the antiphonal singing. But it is not known where the choir would have been positioned. Would one of the three doorways on the north of the chancel arch have given access to a choir loft? From 1544 the processioner was printed in English, but Ronald Hutton has remarked that the pattern of parishes buying the new processioner indicates 'a limited interest in the positive aspects of Reformation'.[61]

No books are entered in the accounts between 1517–27 and 1528–36. It may be that there were no repairs, but missing folios make it impossible to say. In the spring of 1537, an anonymous bookbinder was employed for thirty-five days, costing the

---

[53] Watkin, *Inventory*, part ii, pp.xxv–xxxii; C. Wordsworth and H. Littlehales, *The Old Service Books of the English Church* (1904), plate opposite p.166.

[54] Printed books would not have been much in use before the turn of the century.

[55] See John Mason, Appendix 2:1; Thomas Sigo, Appendix 2:3; John Berton, Appendix 2:4; John Bryan, Appendix 2:9; Thomas Martyn, Appendix 2:16; George Gatynbe, Appendix 2:29; Roger Barforth, Appendix 2:30; William Reve, Appendix 2:44.

[56] CWA, fols 6v, 7v, 8r, 9r.

[57] CWA, fols 12v, 14r, 16v.

[58] CWA, fol.10v.

[59] M. Williamson, 'Liturgical music in the late medieval parish church: organs and voices, ways and means', in *The Parish in Late Medieval England*, ed. C. Burgess and E. Duffy, Harlaxton Medieval Studies, 14 (2006), pp.177–242, at pp.204–205; the Ranworth antiphoner, *c*.1470, measures 527 x 376mm, the Wollaton antiphoner, *c*.1430, measures 575 x 366mm, both in a good state of preservation precisely because they were not portable; K. Scott, *Later Gothic Manuscripts 1390–1490* (1996), pp.325, 204.

[60] CWA, fol.30v. M.E.C. Walcott, *Sacred Archaeology: a Popular Dictionary of Ecclesiastical Institutions* (1868), pp.492–493; A. Hughes, *Medieval Manuscripts for Mass and Office: a Guide to their Organization and Terminology* (1995), p.30, section 214.

[61] R. Hutton, *The Rise and Fall of Merry England: The Ritual Year 1400–1700* (1994), p.78.

wardens 14s.[62] The materials are detailed and cost a total of 11s. 1d., the bookbinder's board coming to an extra 10s., he being employed 'on holy dey and werking dey'.[63]

The injunctions of 1538 ordered priests in every parish to obtain registers for entering baptisms, marriages and burials.[64] In addition, a Bible in English was to be set up within the said church, 'the charge of which shall be ratably borne ... the one half by you [the clergy] and the other half by them [the parishioners]'.[65] Two keys bought for the hutch in which the injunctions were kept cost 6d. and the leather-covered lectern for the Bible was charged at 1s. 3d.[66] A bossed Bible was not bought until 1543, its purchase plus carriage coming to £1.[67] The expenses of the Reformation had begun.

Other words were dealt with in a different way. At some time previously, Mildenhall church and its congregation were granted a pardon by the Pope, or the Bishop of Rome as he is written in the accounts.[68] The fact that they were erased by a mason in the early days of the Reformation suggests that the pardon had been carved or painted on the wall. At the same time the name of Thomas Becket was removed from all liturgical books, but the accounts give no further details.[69] Later, Sir Richard, one of the priests, bound another new processionary and James Alexander, the painter, added the notation.[70]

The eight types of liturgical books were now described as the 'olde' books of the church, and would have numbered more than thirty volumes. These the churchwardens sold as scrap for 19s. between 1548 and 1549.[71] In their place the *Paraphrases of Erasmus* were purchased for the price of 5s. 4d.[72] A new regime meant new inventories and George Bassett was paid 6s. for 'a boke of the new order', later known as the *Book of Common Prayer*. A year later two further books 'of the new order' and four psalters were bought.[73] By 1552 the recently purchased Bible was in need of repair.[74]

The first indication of an organ in Mildenhall church referred to mending of the bellows in 1507, closely followed by the entry which suggests that the parish clerk was also the organist, he receiving 2s. 6d. for the 'organys kepyng'.[75] Never do the accounts reveal where the organ stood, or how many organs there were in that great

---

[62] CWA, fol.22v.

[63] Compare this with deleted payments in Coll. fol.22r.

[64] CWA, fol.24v, a locked hutch was provided 'for the cristyng and berrying' registers.

[65] C.H. Williams, *English Historical Documents, 1485–1558* (1967), p.811; E. Duffy, *The Stripping of the Altars: Traditional Religion in England, 1400–1580* (1992), pp.398 and 406.

[66] CWA, 24r and 30v.

[67] CWA, fol.29v.

[68] CWA, fol.24v. See also R.N. Swanson, *Indulgences in Late Medieval England: Passports to Paradise?* (2007), pp.97, 107, 366–367, 415 and 425.

[69] CWA, fol.24v and CWA, fol.29v. The commemoration of Becket's murder on 29 December 1170 had been entered in every calendar within every book required by the late medieval church, but Henry VIII ordered the complete removal of Becket's name. This often required the saint's name to be scraped off the vellum on which it had been written, the word 'rasse' used on CWA, fol.29v coming from the Latin to erase.

[70] CWA, 25v, 26v; James Alysander, 'paynter': Appendix 2:49.

[71] CWA, fol.37v.

[72] CWA, fol.38r.

[73] As the Reformation re-established the participation of the people in the services, the psalter was retained.

[74] CWA, fol.43r.

[75] CWA, fols 5r and 5v. 2s. 6d. was a quarterly payment.

church. It was not unusual for a small chamber or positive organ, at the least, to be placed in the building, perhaps in the Lady Chapel. The 'great' organ is identified in 1543–44, and this would certainly have had a permanent position.[76] It may have been lodged on the rood-screen or, as at Long Melford, in the rood-loft, 'a fair pair of organs standing thereby', or it may have had its own organ loft.[77] The clerk, who remains anonymous at this time, was paid steadily every quarter, receiving a pay rise of 10d. in 1528 which took his wage up to 3s. 4d. a quarter. The organist-cum-parish clerk in 1546–47 was Thomas Potter and, although he continued to be paid this enhanced salary, the last entry concerning the organs in use was in 1547.[78] In 1550–51, carpenters removed two organs, but on the following page of accounts one seems to have earned a reprieve, 3d. being paid for 'a keye of the orgones'.[79] This was not to last, however, for later the next year an entry in the accounts read 'sowlde to Thomas Colles, the sepulcker and the housse,[80] the sutte of the organs wythe other thinges belonging therto'.[81]

Vestments

Archbishop Winchelsey's constitution[82] of 1305 had contained a list of requisite garments for the clergy as well as coverings and hangings for use on and around the altar. Parishioners provided liturgical clothing and coverings of the finest materials and at the highest price that they could afford or that church funds would allow. Silk, say and velvet regularly featured in the inventories. Albs, rochets and surplices, altar cloths and individual cloths to be used during Mass were made from fine linen and appear in profusion in the accounts.

St Mary's church was well supplied. The accounts show new acquisitions as well as repairs, but the latter were not too frequent and were certainly not too expensive. In 1540 the vicar, John Wylkynson, gave 4s. 4d. for a surplice and two purses but, as the cost of linen for a surplice was 1s. and the making probably 2d., the purses were possibly made of an expensive woven silk, heavily encrusted with embroidery

---

76 CWA, fol.29r.
77 Williamson, 'Liturgical music', p.184; D. Dymond and C. Paine, *The Spoil of Melford Church: The Reformation in a Suffolk Parish* (1989), pp.2, 59; T. Easton and S. Bicknell, 'Two Pre-Reformation organ soundboards: towards an understanding of the form of early organs and their position in some Suffolk churches', *PSIAH*, 38, part 3 (1995), pp.268–295; J. Middleton-Stewart, *Inward Purity and Outward Splendour: Death and Remembrance in the Deanery of Dunwich, Suffolk, 1370–1547* (2001), pp.176–178.
78 CWA, fol.34r.
79 CWA, fols 41r, 41v.
80 The combination of sepulchre and house in the same phrase suggests an Easter sepulchre similar to that at Cowthorpe, Yorkshire, which in shape resembles a house made of oak and free standing, 216.5cm high to the top of the roof, 161cm wide and 65cm deep. See Charles Tracy, 'Easter sepulchre', in *Gothic: Art for England 1400–1547*, ed. R. Marks and P. Williamson (2003), pp.388–389. See also the Easter sepulchre in Gerald Randall's *Church Furnishings and Decoration in England and Wales* (1980), ill. 167; R. Bebb, *Welsh Furniture 1250–1950: a Cultural History of Craftmanship and Design* (2007), I, p.158, ill. 256.
81 CWA, fol.42v. Suit here means several things that are made to be used together, i.e. the organ bellows and the pipework, the one not being viable without the other, in the same way as a suit of vestments is made up of several distinct items of clothing. Organs were often referred to as 'a pair' of organs, again meaning two parts of a whole.
82 A. Watkin, ed., *Archdeaconry of Norwich: Inventory of Church Goods temp. Edward III*, NRS 19 (1948), vol. 2, p.xviii.

with an inner lining also of silk.[83] In 1543, four and a half yards of buckram, then a fine linen cloth, were purchased for making the best copes, although it is doubtful whether more than one cope could be made from this amount, the width of cloth being narrower than it would be today.[84] The buckram for the outer skin of the copes, canvas for the lining, silk and gold lace, crewel lace and threads 'of divers colours' came to £1 9s., excluding the embroiderer's work and his board. An entry in the accounts in 1505–06 shows £1 6s. 2d. paid out for making a pall cloth. This was not part of liturgical requirements but certainly necessary. A further 6s. was paid out for six ounces of ribbon silk, not a particularly expensive item, but the 'browder' who made the copes and the canopy was paid for eight days' board as well as for his work.[85]

Inventories give a complete picture of the stock of Mildenhall church. They appear towards the end of the churchwardens' accounts, but the folios at this stage are not always in numerical order and can be difficult to date.[86] The most impressive inventory is dated 1508 and lists a total of seventeen copes made from cloth of gold, cloth of tissue, white damask, blue velvet, red velvet and red damask among others. A suit of vestments did not necessarily include a cope, but the suit alone included a full complement of liturgical clothing for three clerics, the priest, deacon and subdeacon, with a chasuble for the first, a dalmatic for the second and a tunicle for the third as well as three albs, apparels, girdles, maniples and surplices. The entry describing the 'sute of vestiment for the Sonday with a cope of the same being of the colour popynggay grene damaskys' ran to over twenty articles of clothing and adornment and, like the suit of vestments bought for Bassingbourn church, may have cost as much as £24.[87] A bequest could be left towards the total price as Thomas Cake left 5 marks 'to the buying of a cope' in 1454.[88] When this cost is set against the average annual pay of a parish chaplain, which varied between 8 and 10 marks, the financial investment in cloths and clothing can be appreciated.

Mildenhall church contained at least five altars, the high altar, vestry altar, St Margaret's, St John's and Jesus altar, and another in the Lady chapel. The churchwardens would have been responsible for these, whereas side altars used by gilds and perpetual chantries would be decked out with their own linen and vestments provided by gild members or the chantry foundation. Pre-Reformation altars were made of stone and, by the late middle ages, the high altar stood against the east wall of the chancel gaining light from the east window. The framework on which the stone altar was placed was covered by the altar frontal decorated with orphreys, embroidered panels of cloth applied to hangings and clothing in the medieval church. Mildenhall had a variety of hangings of different colours,

---

[83] CWA, fol.30r. John Wylkynson died in the following year.

[84] CWA, fols 29r, 29v.

[85] CWA, fol.3r. From the frequent entries for boarding various craftsmen in the accounts it is clear that specialists of all types were brought into Mildenhall to undertake skilled work. The canopy, although referred to on several occasions, is never described and its position is never indicated.

[86] CWA, fols 49r, 49v, 50r and 51v, the last folio being very damaged. Though the labour was possibly quite reasonably priced, the cost of the materials was extraordinarily high. See F.E. Baldwin, *Sumptuary Legislation and Personal Regulation in England* (1926), p.142 n.58.

[87] CWA, fol.49r. See also Allan Barton, 'The ornaments of the altar and ministers in late medieval England', in Barnwell *et al.*, *Mass and Parish in Late Medieval England: The Use of York* (2005), pp.27–40; Dymond and Paine, *Spoil of Melford*, pp.15, 19, 22–23; D. Dymond, *The Churchwardens' Book of Bassingbourn, Cambridgeshire, 1496–c.1540* (2004), p.6 n.240.

[88] Thomas Cake, 1454 (SROB, IC 500/2/9/205). Five marks was the equivalent of £3 6s. 8d.

one described as stained, meaning that it was painted rather than embroidered.[89] The extraordinary number of towels listed in the inventory of 1508 would have been used to cover altars, not one at a time but in threes.[90] The first layer of textile to be laid on top of an altar was a thick hair cloth.[91] The towels came next, the roughest laid on the hair cloth, then one of an intermediate quality. Towels entered in the inventory 'of fifteen yards in length' would have been folded back upon themselves to acquire the correct covering.[92] Finally the altar cloth of finest weave was placed on top.

Testators were generous and occasionally very specific in their wishes but, with the paucity of written evidence remaining, it is difficult to match the bequest of an altar frontal in a parishioner's will to the presence of a similar frontal in a church inventory. It is possible, however, to trace the longevity of some of these hangings where several inventories have survived over a couple of hundred years. Wills include bequests of napery, the best or most prized article from the testator's household stock frequently being chosen. In her will of 1515, Margery Howton left her best diaper cloth to the high altar in St Mary's church, and within ten years her son-in law, Thomas Hall (Hull), had left instructions for his executors to buy a vestment for Mildenhall church 'for a priest to sing in it the time of my service and after to remain to the said church for ever'.[93] Humphrey Duffield's will of 1530 included instructions to his executors to deliver to the church 'my best coverlet and a black vestment for the priest to sing in and my best diaper cloth for an altar cloth'.[94]

Plate

In material terms and as moveable goods, plate was the great treasure of the medieval church and was almost indestructible until, of course, the Reformation. As the requirements of the Church had grown and become more stringent from the thirteenth century, what had been acceptable then was not so by the fifteenth century. Only in the poorest parishes would baser materials be substituted for precious metals and, in East Anglia, silver and parcel-gilt vessels were common. Mildenhall's inventory of 1508 gives an almost complete list of the plate required, but it should be read in conjunction with the undated inventory on the previous folio which includes items missing on the subsequent page.[95]

Mildenhall's parcel-gilt cross had a stave to which it could be fastened when carried in Sunday processions and on holy days. A copper-gilt foot into which the cross could be placed enabled it to be free-standing, although a cross was not placed on the high altar until the sixteenth century.[96] The writer of the inventory believed, as did the parishioners, that within Mildenhall's cross lay embedded a piece of Christ's cross. During Lent a wooden cross painted red was used and though not

---

[89] CWA, fol.31r. Richard Polyngton was paid 1s. 8d. for staining the altar cloths: see CWA, fol.49r. This inventory, which is undated and abbreviated, gives a good idea of what a smaller and less wealthy church might have provided before the Reformation. Compare it with Mildenhall's inventory on CWA, fols 49v, 50r and 50v.

[90] Barnwell, *Mass and Parish*, pp.31–32.

[91] See CWA, fol.15v.

[92] Dymond, *Bassingbourn*, p.9.

[93] Appendix 2:33 and 2:36.

[94] Appendix 2:38. This refers to Duffield's requiem mass at which a black vestment would be worn.

[95] CWA, fols 49v and 49r.

[96] J. Gilchrist, *Anglican Church Plate* (1967), pp.37–38.

mentioned in either inventory, the earlier inventory includes a hanging of white crossed with red silk 'for Lenton'. Four pairs of chalices were listed. A pair signified a chalice with its paten as two parts of a whole, the one being insufficient without the other. For that reason, chalices are frequently mentioned in late medieval inventories whereas patens are not.

Gifts of plate were infrequently bequeathed. A silver basin and a pair of cruets were left in the will of William Bakhote in 1461 'for the priest to wash his hands'.[97] In the inventory, a basin of silver and parcel-gilt is entered, perhaps Bakhote's gift.[98] Thomas Hopper bequeathed a pair of chalices in 1524, too late to be included in the 1508 inventory.[99] There is seldom any record of what was given during a parishioner's lifetime unless it was entered in the accounts. Nevertheless, the two inventories which have survived clearly show that St Mary's was well equipped.

Henry VIII died at the beginning of 1547 and the 'visitors scribes' arrived at Bury St Edmunds a few months later to assess the possessions of each church in the area. These they recorded in official inventories of church goods. Then the spoliation began. The hutch that had stood on the rood-loft was sold to John Peche for 6d. Nicholas Pollyngton bought another hutch from the churchwardens which cost him 1s.[100] Roger Langham and Robert Suckerman received £72 15s. for the church plate which they had sold, and Thomas Potter, Edmund Wryght and John Froste, churchwardens, collected 10¾ ounces of broken silver.[101] The stock of wax, valued at £2 4s. 8d. was gathered in, of which 2s. 7d. went to the poor, the wardens receiving a further 12s. 'less 2d.' which they paid out at a later date.[102] Silver plate under a separate entry realized £23 10s. and the wardens accepted a further £2 5s. 7d. for 'broke' silver; a pair of candlesticks was sold for 2s.[103] Neither latten nor copper was safe, four hundred pounds of a mixed load selling for £3 7s. 0d. The accounts at this time do not make comfortable reading, the entries are tragic, sometimes haphazard, and they are difficult to interpret. The impact of these measures upon parishes was profound but, for the historian, they are blurred by the fact that few of the accounts date individual items so that the precise chronology of change is usually irrecoverable.

PRIESTS AND PAROCHIAL PERSONNEL

In 2000 the third volume of the register of John Morton, the last archbishop of Canterbury of the fifteenth century, was published, edited by Christopher Harper-Bill.[104] It dealt specifically with the year 1499 and the Norwich *sede vacante*, meaning 'vacant seat'. The former bishop of Norwich, Bishop Goldwell, had died in February and, according to custom, the administration of a vacant diocese had to be undertaken by the archbishop of Canterbury until a new bishop was installed.

---

97   William Bakhote, 1461 (SROB, IC 500/2/9/303).
98   CWA, fol.49v.
99   Thomas Hopper. See Appendix 2:37.
100 CWA, fol.34v.
101 CWA, fol.35r.
102 CWA, fol.36r.
103 CWA, fols 36v and 37v.
104 C. Harper-Bill, ed., *The Register of John Morton, Archbishop of Canterbury 1486–1500*, III, *Norwich Sede Vacante*, Canterbury and York Society (2000).

This register covers but five months. The information it contains, however, is invaluable for, in the words of Harper-Bill, it 'provides, perhaps, the fullest account of the administration of any English diocese over a short space of time'.[105] In the visitation of the two Suffolk archdeaconries, names which have been noted from wills or from churchwardens' accounts, but have not been attributed to any particular clerical hierarchy, may now be apportioned to parish priests, parish chaplains or stipendiaries. The wills which have survived from this period are from across the diocese and, by taking a small sample of lay testators, it can be seen that one out of four testators, when making a will, empowered priests and chaplains to act as their executors. Testaments of the laity show how greatly the presence of the parochial clergy was valued and how it was incorporated into the life of the parish. Parish documentation, such as parishioners' wills and churchwardens' accounts – where they survive – give the impression of a buoyant Christian community rather than one clogged by redundant priests and a suspicious laity. With a good run of wills it is possible to trace a cleric through the testamentary minefield.

John Bryan of Mildenhall was a parish chaplain (for his will see Appendix 2:9). His father died in 1434 and left John, his only child, property in Mildenhall and the residue of his goods.[106] For Bryan this was a case of returning home – indeed, perhaps he had never really been away – and Bryan became, therefore, both chaplain and parishioner. This was not a unique occurrence for many requests were made by testators to clerical sons, godsons and nephews to return to their home parish to offer intercessions after the testators' death. Bryan first appears as executor in a will of 1438.[107] This was a common duty performed by clerics, either as witness, executor or supervisor. In 1439 Bryan was co-executor to Robert Sopere's will with Sopere's wife, Elizabeth, at Barton Mills;[108] in 1439 he was executor to Thomas Brynkele of Mildenhall,[109] and then supervisor rather than executor for William Curteys, the elder, of Mildenhall in 1443.[110] In 1448 he was supervisor to the estate of Isabel Fysch of Worlington.[111] Simon Bagot, the recently appointed rector of Worlington, was nominated as a witness. As a member of a well-to-do Mildenhall family Bagot had already appeared in a Mildenhall will of 1434 described as 'chaplain'.[112] Bagot, like Bryan, would have enjoyed his position both as priest and parishioner. Perhaps John Bryan never sought preferment. Recruitment to the clergy was high and the number of clergy always exceeded the number of posts to be filled. When Bryan died in 1454, leaving his portable breviary to his cousin, William Place, a chaplain, and his property to William's brother, Thomas, he was still described as chaplain.[113] At the time of his death, however, he was also churchwarden.

This position as one of the most trusted and respected members of the parish was not usually filled by clerics, and yet a priest as warden was not unique in Mildenhall. Sir Simon Etton, another parish chaplain, had been elected as churchwarden in 1505. When he wrote his will in 1516 he requested burial against the porch of the

105 Harper-Bill, *Register of John Morton*, p.1.
106 John Bryan, 1434 (NRO, NCC Surflete 172).
107 John Speed, 1438 (NRO, NCC Doke 67).
108 Robert Sopere, 1439 (SROB, IC 500/2/9/7).
109 Thomas Brynkele, 1439 (NRO, NCC Doke 87).
110 William Curteys, 1443 (SROB, IC 500/2/9/40).
111 Isabel Fysch, 1448 (SROB, IC 500/2/9/63).
112 Richard Bakhot, 1434 (NRO, NCC Surflete 181). Simon was Worlington's rector from 1447 to 1474.
113 John Bryan, 1454 (NRO, NCC Aleyn 215).

charnel chapel where one of Mildenhall's perpetual chantries was celebrated. This request suggests that he had been the chantry priest there. He leaves no other trace in the documentation.[114] His contemporary, Sir Thomas Wenge, was another local boy who had returned to his home town to celebrate a year's masses for his father's soul.[115]

The Vicars of Mildenhall

The benefice of Mildenhall had become a vicarage in the 1040s when Edward the Confessor granted it to the abbey at Bury St Edmunds. Vicars of Mildenhall were appointed by the abbey and, as long as their conduct was satisfactory, the appointment was for life. The careers of the first four vicars on Table 1 were only terminated by their deaths.

Table 1: Vicars of Mildenhall, 1432–1559[116]

Thomas Ryngstede	1432–1453
Thomas Oldbury	1453–1471
Paul Geyton (Gayton)	1471–1512
John Wylkynson	1512–1541
Thomas Scott	1541–1555
Roger Wright	1555–1556
Thomas Parker	1556–1559

The vicars from 1432 to 1541 seem to have spent far more time outside Mildenhall parish than in it, and their biographies, however short, show that they all held alternative occupations in plurality.[117] A vicar was expected to be resident and to minister the cure himself, but perhaps as many as a quarter of vicars did neither, although out of forty-eight parishes in the Norwich diocese which had non-resident vicars, there were only complaints about two of them for being absent in 1449.[118] For this very reason it was essential to engage a parish priest as *locum tenens* to undertake the vicar's duties. The duties to be undertaken were the administration of the rites of passage in baptism, marriage and burial, the provision of confession and communion and the other services which made up the religious life of the pre-Reformation church. Other more worldly but no less important duties included visiting the sick and sustaining those in need. The incumbent had to understand the Latin text and speak it clearly and to be able to administer sacraments other than the Mass: he had to be a perceptive confessor and a teacher of his flock.[119]

---

[114] Sir Simon Etton, 1516 (NRO, NCC Brigges 26).
[115] John Wenge, 1456 (NCC, NRO Neve 33).
[116] For more details of their careers, where these are known, see Notes on People.
[117] B. Kümin, *The Shaping of a Community: The Rise and Reformation of the English Parish c.1400–1560* (1996), p.130. Kümin suggests that absenteeism or pluralism had more to do with inadequate remuneration of the clergy than idle personnel.
[118] P. Marshall, *The Catholic Priesthood and the Reformation* (1994), pp.177–179.
[119] Duffy, *Stripping of the Altars*, p.57; G.F. Bryant and V.M. Hunter, eds, *How Thow Schalt Thy Paresche Preche: John Myrc's Instructions for Parish Priests*, part 1, *Introduction and Text* (1999). Myrc wrote his instructions in vernacular verse form, probably in the late fourteenth century, to inform the less well-educated clergy on how they should fulfil their duties.

Table 2 shows a continuous run of vicars from 1469 to 1541 because they were the only permanent members of the clerical staff in Mildenhall, even though they may have been pluralists or absentees. Because of their education, their details can be verified from university records and wills. Chaplains and curates were employed only in a temporary capacity, even though in some cases, such as Thomas Martyn's, they might be resident for many years. They are difficult to classify as will be seen below.

Chaplains and Curates

Mildenhall's vicars appear to have had reliable and responsible substitutes, but it is not always easy to place the various priests and chaplains who flit through the churchwardens' accounts into their correct position in the parish hierarchy. The first difficulty in deciding who belongs to which position in the clerical underclass of Mildenhall is the way in which the various titles were used. It could be assumed that the priest deputising for a non-resident vicar might be called parish priest or parish curate in the Mildenhall accounts, but often he is not. Mildenhall's parish priests were not as permanent a fixture as the chantry chaplains, but this may have been because they were more ambitious rather than more unsatisfactory. Evidence shows that priests, particularly those unbeneficed like the parish chaplains, were frequently on the move, seeking better positions, but they often stayed within the diocese which they knew and regularly returned to work within their home territory.[120] John Bryan was one of these in the fifteenth century and Robert Pachett another in the sixteenth.[121] The remuneration of unbeneficed chaplains was £5 6s. 8d., this being laid down as their annual stipend in the statutes of 1441.[122] What is certain is that Mildenhall had two perpetual chantries, both established in the fourteenth century, and each had its own chaplain. In Mildenhall's documentation, the incumbents of the two chantries are not identified until the *Valor Ecclesiasticus* of 1535 which heralded the dispersal of much ecclesiastical property. Then they were named as William Reve and Robert Pachett. A chantry chaplain was incumbent of what was regarded as a benefice, however small, and he would have been granted a dwelling as part of his remuneration. The profits from the land with which the chantry had been endowed would have provided his salary. Surprisingly, the chantry chaplains, William Reve and Robert Pachett, received less than £6 per annum each according to the *Valor.* On a chantry chaplain's death or resignation, the chantry's trustees would appoint a new chaplain. It was expected that he, in addition to his chantry obligations, would 'serve' the parish and, in the chantry certificates of 1548, drawn up under the boy king, Edward VI, this very point was made to the king's chantry commissioners.

There were nine religious gilds in the parish, perhaps not all active at the same time, but certainly the larger gilds of St Thomas, Corpus Christi, Holy Trinity and St Mary, could have engaged the services of two chaplains between them. It might be expected that the chaplains employed to undertake these services would be referred to as gild chaplains or gild priests, but this is not so. Table 2 consists of vicars, parish

---

120 Marshall, *Catholic Priesthood*, p.198.
121 J. Middleton-Stewart, 'Parochial activity in late medieval Fenland: accounts and wills from Tilney All Saints and St Mary's, Mildenhall, 1443–1520', in *The Parish in Late Medieval England*, ed. C. Burgess and E. Duffy, Harlaxton Medieval Studies, 14 (2006), pp.282–301 and at p.295 n.54.
122 Marshall, *Catholic Priesthood*, p.196.

priests and chaplains, all of whom may have served longer than they have been given credit for, and sometimes it shows too many chaplains in one year, sometimes too few.

Table 2: Priests and parochial personnel, 1469–1541

Year	Vicar	Parish priest	Chaplains
1469	Thomas Oldbury	Thomas Martyn	Thomas Barkere
1472	Paul Geyton		John Greene
1474			John Corbett
	Paul Geyton		John Austin
1477	Paul Geyton	John Coke	
1479	Paul Geyton		Thomas Barun Godynge
1480	Paul Geyton		Thomas Baron Godynge
1481	Paul Geyton		Thomas Barowne
1482	Paul Geyton		Thomas Baron Andrew Place
1483	Paul Geyton		Thomas Baron William Matthew
1484	Paul Geyton		Thomas Baron
1485	Paul Geyton		Thomas Baron
1486	Paul Geyton		Thomas Baron
1487	Paul Geyton		Thomas Baron
1488	Paul Geyton		Thomas Baron
1489	Paul Geyton		Thomas Baron
1490	Paul Geyton		Thomas Baron
1491	Paul Geyton		Thomas Baron
1492	Paul Geyton		Thomas Baron
1493	Paul Geyton		Thomas Baron
1500	Paul Geyton	William Bambour	
1501	Paul Geyton		Thomas Wynge[123]
1502	Paul Geyton	Robert Lane	Thomas Baron[124]
1503	Paul Geyton	George Geytonbye	Roger Barforth
1504	Paul Geyton	George Geytonbye	Roger Barforth Robert Algat
1505	Paul Geyton	Roger Oger	William Reve
1506	Paul Geyton	Roger Oger	Thomas Lawe
1509	Paul Geyton	John Grauntt	
1510	Paul Geyton	John Lee	
1512	Paul Geyton/ John Wylkynson		
1513	John Wylkynson	John Puwke	William Reve John Lee
1514	John Wylkynson	Thomas Tuppyng	

[123] Thomas Wynge, described as a priest in his will, was from a local family.

[124] Thomas Baron was described as 'priest of Mildenhall church' in Agnes Sygo's will in 1484 (SROB, IC 500/2/11/312). His will was proved 27 January 1503, which suggests that he served as a priest in Mildenhall for at least twenty-three years (TNA, PCC Blamyr 17), but no further details of him are known.

1516	John Wylkynson		Simon Etton
1519	John Wylkynson	John Ripley	John Lee
1520	John Wylkynson		William Reve
1521	John Wylkynson	Geoffrey Wilson	John Lee
1522	John Wylkynson	Geoffrey Wilson	
1524	John Wylkynson		John Lee
			Robert Pachett
1525	John Wylkynson	Edmund Warburton	William Reve
			Robert Pachett
1526	John Wylkynson	Robert Midelton	John Lee
1527	John Wylkynson	Thomas Anion	William Reve
			John Lee
			Robert Pachett
1528	John Wylkynson	James Mygely	William Reve
			Robert Pachett
1529	John Wylkynson	Thomas Anion	
1530	John Wylkynson	James Mygelay	
1532	John Wylkynson	John Wrighte	
1533	John Wylkynson	Richard Ferneley	
1536	John Wylkynson	Harry Olever	Robert Pachett
1537	John Wylkynson	Harry Olever	
1538	John Wylkynson		Robert Pachett
1541	JohnWylkynson/		William Reve
	Thomas Scott[125]		Robert Pachett

The Parish Clerk

The parish clerk was the only parish functionary apart from the sexton whose office partook 'of an ecclesiastical character'.[126] The origins of this clerk's position were religious rather than secular, the word *clericus* being used to describe this occupation in the early years of the church. The parish clerk assisted the priest during the liturgy, singing psalms, answering responses, reading the epistle at Mass and teaching children of the congregation.[127] Gradually the nature of the work changed from being one of deep involvement in liturgical offices to one more secretarial. Clerks could find work quite easily, being men of both education and erudition.[128] The early employment of musical clerks to assist in services had an honourable pedigree and in the late Middle Ages they were employed as organists and choirmasters. At Walberswick the clerk was paid 8s. for 'noting and wrytyng of the serwyes of owr lady' in 1483.[129] Elsewhere in England they certainly exercised a strong musical influence.[130]

The parish clerk, like the sexton, had his wages paid by the parish, either from

---

125 Thomas Scott's name does not appear in either J. and J.A.Venn, *Alumni Cantabrigiensis* (1922–7) or A.B. Emden, *A Biographical Register of the University of Oxford to AD 1500* (1957–1959).

126 J. Toulmin-Smith, *The Parish, its Obligations and Powers: Its Officers and their Duties* (1853), p.165.

127 E.G.C.F. Atchley, 'Medieval parish-clerks in Bristol', *Transactions of the St Paul's Ecclesiological Society*, 5 (1901–05), p.107.

128 F.L. Cross, *The Oxford Dictionary of the Christian Church* (1957), 1016; M. Williamson, 'Liturgical music', p.183.

129 R.W.M. Lewis, ed., *Walberswick Churchwardens' Accounts, AD 1450–1499* (1947), p.51.

130 P.A. Scholes, *The Oxford Companion to Music* (1988), p.759.

church funds or, as Kümin suggests, from an independent collection.[131] At Bassingbourn, a collection was taken for the clerk's wages.[132] At Mildenhall, however, it is difficult to decide how he earned sufficient money unless the incumbent also made a contribution towards his salary, as many parishes insisted.[133] The anonymous clerk at the beginning of the sixteenth century was paid 2s. 6d. a quarter: in other words his annual remuneration as far as the churchwardens were concerned cost 10s. a year. An extraordinary payment of 6d. 'for lokyn owte of bylls and wrytyn' would not have made much difference to his standard of living, even in 1507–08.[134] The stipend was not increased to 3s. 4d. a quarter until amendments were made in 1527–28, possibly due to a change of churchwardens.[135] This paucity of reward in Mildenhall may indicate that an independent collection was indeed the norm.

The mention of a school house in the accounts suggests that the parish clerk may also have been schoolmaster, the township paying his stipend, and Thomas Potter, both parish clerk and organist, may be one who had seen his way of life disrupted by the dissolution of the monasteries some six years before his name appeared in the Mildenhall accounts.[136] He was the first and only parish clerk to be named in the accounts and was also the last to keep the surviving accounts.[137] His wage remained at 3s. 4d. until the accounts ended in 1553. In 1548–49 a Thomas Potter was elected churchwarden and he appeared as witness to the will of James Alysander (see Appendix 2:49).

The Sexton

Like the parish clerk, Mildenhall's sexton was on the pay-roll of the church and similarly poorly paid.[138] His wage was entered in the churchwardens' accounts, starting at 10d. a quarter in 1505, when he was named as John Screvenere.[139] In Mildenhall's accounts the sexton can invariably be identified because he was paid for keeping the clock, which was frequently troublesome. In 1506 payments were entered, firstly to the clockmaker at 6s. 6d., then to John Gardener, a blacksmith, for mending the clock and finally an anonymous payment for 'kepyng of the clokke and mendyng'.[140] John Gardener replaced John Screvenere as sexton and his wage was enhanced by 5d.[141] By 1527–28 the sexton was Richard Pollington, who may have been a local blacksmith, and his wage remained at 1s. 3d. a quarter.[142] It actually stayed the same until 1550–51 when Richard's name was entered for the last time and, almost immediately afterwards, a clockmaker called Hynd charged 13s. 4d. for

---

[131] Kümin, *Shaping a Community*, p.100.

[132] N.J.G. Pounds, *A History of the English Parish: The Culture of Religion from Augustine to Victoria* (2000), pp.187–189, 232; Dymond, *Bassingbourn*, p.135.

[133] Marshall, *Catholic Priesthood*, p.202.

[134] CWA, fol.5r.

[135] CWA, fol.17r.

[136] CWA, fol.33v. Thomas Potter is first mentioned in 1546–47. His surname appears not to be local and his origins are unknown.

[137] A John Tyson is named as parish clerk in the Suffolk returns of 1524, receiving a wage of £1. See S.H.A. Hervey, ed., *Suffolk in 1524: being a return for a subsidy granted in 1523*, Suffolk Green Books, 10 (1910), pp.218–220.

[138] The word 'sexton' possibly comes from the Old French *sacristan*.

[139] CWA, fol.2v.

[140] CWA, fol.3r.

[141] CWA, fol.4v. On CWA, fol.13r, John Gardener is identified as a local smith.

[142] CWA, fol.18v.

wages and board.[143] Perhaps the clock had become too much for the elderly Richard and it was Nicholas Pollington, probably his son, who next assumed responsibility for this capricious piece of machinery, earning a pay rise of 5d. Nicholas remained in charge of the clock, receiving a steady 1s. 8d. a quarter until the churchwardens' accounts ran out at the beginning of Mary Tudor's reign.

REMEMBERING THE DEAD

Commemorative practices were diverse and catered for every section of society except the very poor, but even this impoverished class had a part to play, for the prayers of the deserving poor were considered to be of greater significance than the prayers of the well-heeled laity. The almost obligatory attendance of the poor at funerals was rewarded with a dole, often accompanied by cloaks, refreshment, torches and tapers.[144]

The most common bequest entered in churchwardens' accounts was the 'quetheword' or prayers for the soul.[145] R.W.M. Lewis, when transcribing the Walberswick accounts, explained quetheword as the announcement of the death of a parishioner.[146] As this announcement carried a bequest or legacy with it, quethewords were entered in the churchwardens' accounts under income. In the Mildenhall collections of the fifteenth century, bequests for commemorative prayers for twenty-five former parishioners use the phrase 'for the soul', rather than quetheword, and averaged three a year.[147] In the first folio of the sixteenth-century churchwardens' accounts, however, the terminology has changed and quetheword occurs at a rate of seven to eight bequests a year. These continue until the last quetheword or 'beqweth' is entered in the 1543–44 accounts (CWA, fol.27r). By 1546–47 the quetheword is no more and such a bequest is termed a legacy (CWA, fol.33r). Thereafter no further reference is made to the souls of the dead.

The variety of intercessory prayers chosen by testators can be seen in existing testaments where the last personal wishes for the care of the soul are written. The executors carry out the instructions *post mortem*, noting how the money should be spent, on what and for how long. Mildenhall's collections and churchwardens' accounts contain few references to the wide choice of commemoration available before the Reformation. However, the plan of St Mary's, Mildenhall (Plan 1), does strongly reflect the beliefs of priests and people in the late medieval period. The east ends of both aisles, and their great width, gave space for at least eight side altars for commemorative masses and prayers for both individuals and local religious gilds.

---

[143] CWA, fol.39r.

[144] S. Tymms, ed., 'John Baret of Bury, 1463', in *Wills and Inventories from the Registers of the Commissary of Bury St Edmunds and the Archdeacon of Sudbury*, Camden Society, Old Series, 49 (1850), p.17.

[145] *COED*, p.1490.

[146] Lewis, *Walberswick*, p.126. 'Quetheword' first appears in the Walberswick accounts in 1466, a few years after the accounts cease to be entered in Latin.

[147] Coll. fols 2r, 4r, 4v, 10v, 16r, 17v, 18r, 18v, 19r, 19v, 20v, 21r and 21v.

ST MARY'S CHURCH, MILDENHALL

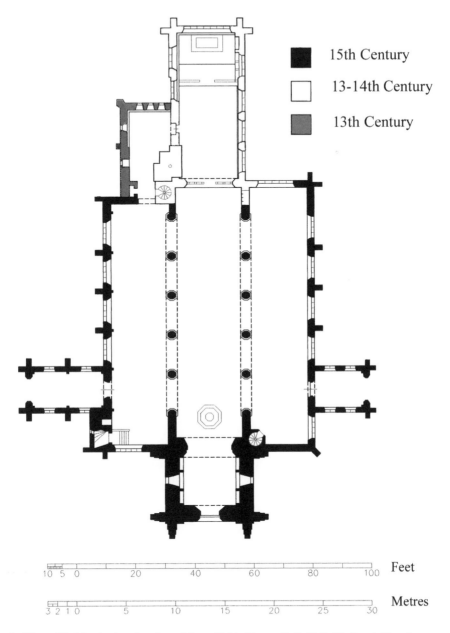

15th Century

13-14th Century

13th Century

Feet

Metres

1. Plan of St Mary's church, adapted from Birkin Haward's Suffolk Medieval Church
Arcades *(1993).*

Religious Gilds

Membership of the gilds was made up not only of parishioners but sometimes of outsiders also. Collectively they formed voluntary institutions similar to modern friendly societies, quite unlike the large trade and mercantile gilds in important towns and cities.[148] Parish gilds were created to pray for the souls of former members, to assist members who had fallen on hard times and to care for widows and orphans of past members. A fine or subscription was paid by each member, but the wealth of many gilds derived from bequests of land, some meagre, some generous, which could be rented out to other members of the gild or to parishioners. Gild accounts and minutes are exceedingly difficult to find, most documentation having been destroyed at the Reformation, but the gild returns of 1389 for parishes situated near navigable waterways make interesting reading, bearing in mind Mildenhall's situation.[149]

A total of nine gilds appear to have worshipped in St Mary's church although as one gild was founded, another gild may have foundered.[150] In the following list the earlier bequests, but not necessarily the earliest foundations, come first. Like any society or fellowship, a gild could be transitory, its strength determined by the cohesion of the aldermen and members, its income variable and sometimes uncertain. Within the church, a gild might have its own altar to which the members contributed vessels, or napery and imagery for the Mass. In Mildenhall church it is not possible to identify the site of the gild altars except that of St John at the east end of the north aisle.

Gild of St Thomas This gild was dedicated to Thomas Becket of Canterbury (d.1170), revered as a national martyr in England while also achieving great popularity in continental Europe.[151] Six testamentary bequests were made to St Thomas' gild between 1385 and 1506.[152] The gild is mentioned in 1546–47 in the churchwardens accounts (CWA, fol.33r) and there is also a list of the lands belonging to the gild (CWA, fol.46r). The latter is undated, but it mentions a messuage opposite the church with details of its abuttals and the names of occupants.

Gild of Corpus Christi Twelve testamentary bequests were made to this gild between 1439 and 1527.[153] Corpus Christi was a late entry into the liturgical life of the Church, but rapidly emerged as the most important feast in the late medieval

[148] J.J. Scarisbrick, *The Reformation and the English People* (1984), pp.19–39.

[149] H.F.Westlake, *The Parish Gilds of Medieval England* (1919), pp.217–18.

[150] Nine gilds are named in Mildenhall's churchwardens' accounts and local wills. A tenth gild, dedicated to the Blessed Cross, occurs in the Mildenhall rentals holding land in the open fields of the parish, but it is not mentioned in the accounts or wills. See A. Breen, *The Mildenhall Rentals 1501* (2008), pp.14–15.

[151] See CWA, fol.29v, n.293.

[152] William Wylde, senior, 1385 (NRO, NCC Harsyk 55); John Bakhot, 1464 (SROB, IC 500/2/10/379); Thomas Martin, chaplain, 1469 (NRO, NCC Jekkys 144); Richard Bakhott, 1474 (TNA, PCC Wattys 19); Thomas Playford, 1482 (SROB, IC 500/2/11/252); William Dey, 1506 (NRO, NCC Garnon 106).

[153] Edmund Childyrston, 1439 (NRO, NCC 119 Doke); John Bygge, 1450 (SROB, IC 500/2/9/122); John Staloun, 1452 (SROB, IC 500/2/9/148); Simon Chylderston, 1454 (SROB, IC 500/2/9/230); John Bakhot, 1464 (SROB, IC 500/2/10/397); William Chapman, 1464 (SROB, IC 500/2/10/379); Richard Bakhott, 1474 (TNA, PCC Wattys 19); John Playford, 1474 (SROB, IC 500/2/10/566); Thomas Playford, 1482 (SROB IC 500/2/11//252); William Bray, 1503 (SROB, IC 500/2/12/128);

period.[154] From its beginnings in a béguinage in Liège, the feast arrived in England at the beginning of the fourteenth century complete with indulgences attached to its celebration. It was a popular dedication for urban gilds, for example at Ipswich.[155] The gild hall, a barn and dovehouse called Corpus Christi yard, were destroyed in the Mildenhall fire of *c.*1568.[156]

Gild of St Mary Fourteen testamentary bequests were made to St Mary's gild between 1441 and 1510,[157] which seems to make this the most popular of the local gilds. It is not clear at which altar the gild celebrated its Mass, unless it was in the Lady chapel above the north porch, a fifteenth-century building of exceptional craftsmanship.

Gild of St Katherine Four testamentary bequests were made between 1448 and 1459.[158] The short period during which the bequests were made suggests that this may have been a gild which never achieved the popularity of larger gilds such at St Mary or Corpus Christi.

Gild of the Holy Trinity Five testamentary bequests were made between 1448 and 1523. The bequest of William Curteys included his messuage called Chelmys.[159] The ultimate release of the alderman and brethren to Robert Tyrrell and William Peche was dated 14 March 1535;[160] and a post-Reformation document dated 22 September 1573 gave a description of land previously belonging to the Trinity gild, then in the hands of an anonymous owner, with further lands at Cake Street Green which were in the tenure of William Cole.[161]

Roger Barforth, priest, 1504 (NRO, NCC Ryxe 27); and Alice Bateman, 1527 (SROB, IC 500/2/17/250).

[154] M. Rubin, *Corpus Christi: The Eucharist in Late Medieval Culture* (1991), pp.164–81.

[155] P. Northeast, 'Parish gilds', in *An Historical Atlas of Suffolk*, ed. D. Dymond and E. Martin, 3rd edn rev. (1999), pp.74–75.

[156] Richard Colman, 1461 (SROB, IC 500/2/9/286); SROB, E18/454/5, f.29r, Survey of Mildenhall 1574.

[157] Rose Place, 1441 (SROB, IC 500/2/9/22); Thomas Tydde, 1463 (SROB, IC 500/2/12/12); William Elys, 1493 (NRO, NCC Boner 16); Richard Morle, 1469 (SROB, IC 500/2/10/426); John Playford, 1474 (SROB, IC 500/2/9/66); Alice Morley, 1480 (SROB, IC 500/2/11/201); George Place, 1480 (SROB, IC 500/2/11/205); Simon Aleyn, 1481 (SROB, IC 500/2/11/255); William Charnoke, 1500 (NRO, NCC Popy 571); John Chistone, 1502 (NRO, NCC Popy 230); William Bray, 1503 (SROB, IC 500/2/12/128); John Wooderis, 1504 (SROB, IC 500/2/12/126); Thomas Cole, 1505 (NRO, NCC Garnon 34); Thomas Witwell, 1510 (NRO, NCC Robinson 143).

[158] John Frere, 1448 (SROB, IC 500/2/9/144); John Staloun, the younger, 1452 (SROB, IC 500/2/9/148); Simon Chylderston, 1454 (SROB, IC 500/2/9/230); John Stalham, the elder, 1459 (SROB, IC 500/2/10/341).

[159] John Frere, 1448 (SROB, IC 500/2/9/144); William Curteys, 1473 (SROB, IC 500/2/11/6); Richard Woodrise, 1474 (SROB, IC 500/2/11/111); Simon Etton, 1516 (NRO, NCC Brigges 26); John Deye, 1523 (SROB, IC 500/2/17/68).

[160] SROB, E18/400/1.

[161] 'County Suffolk: Lands which I have from Her Majesty in Mildenhall. Lands late belonging to the gild of the Trinity in Mildenhall. One messuage in Halywell street with courtyard, gardens, dovehouse, 16 acres of arable land, 1 close of meadow, containing by estimation 4 acres, late in the tenure of Christian Peache, widow, deceased, 1 close of meadow now or late in the tenure of Simon Sokerman; 1 other meadow and 2 acres of land at Swaye Cross and one piece of land at Cake Street Green now or late in the tenure of William Cole' (SROB, E18/400/1:2). See also CWA, fol.46r.

Gild of John the Baptist   There were eight testamentary bequests between 1452 and 1523.[162] This gild would have celebrated at the east end of the north aisle in the chapel of St John.

Gild of St George   Three testamentary bequests have survived between 1456 and 1504.[163]

Gild of St James   There was one testamentary bequest made in 1474.[164]

Gild of St Anne   There were three testamentary bequests between 1498 and 1506.[165]

No reference to a gild dedicated to St Margaret has been found in the parish documents, even though the south altar was dedicated to her. She was one of the most popular saints in the late medieval period, possibly because she was the patron saint of childbirth, always a dangerous undertaking.

Chantries

More individualistic commemorative foundations than the gilds were the chantries, either service chantries which ran for a specified term of years or perpetual chantries which were expected to run for eternity.

A service chantry depended on an endowment of property placed in the hands of feoffees or trustees by the chantry founder. The property was rented out, the rent providing sufficient income for the trustees to hire a stipendiary chaplain to perform a daily Mass for the founder's soul. The annual stipend in the late fifteenth and early sixteenth centuries was roughly 8 marks (£5 6s. 8d.).

Stipendiary chaplains played an important part in a parish forming a network of support often, as in the case of Mildenhall, travelling to visit outlying settlements. They also appeared in an executive capacity as executors and witnesses to wills. Service chantries were cheaper to found than perpetual chantries and rarely lasted longer than a year in Mildenhall, although elsewhere service chantries lasted for up to twenty years, or even in one case ninety-nine years. They were well established before the earliest surviving Mildenhall collections of 1446. Among the wills from the 1430s is a request for a one-year service at the standard cost of 8 marks.[166] In 1439 requests were made for a three-year service chantry and a service chantry for two priests praying for one year or, if more convenient, for one priest praying for

---

[162]   John Staloun, 1452 (SROB, IC 500/2/9/148) and his elder brother John Staloun/Stalonn/Stalham, 1459 (SROB, IC 500/2/10/341); John Bakhot, 1464 (SROB, IC 500/2/10/397); Thomas Martyn, 1469 (NRO, NCC Jekkys 144); Richard Bakhott, 1474 (TNA, PCC Wattys 19); Thomas Playford, 1482 (SROB, IC 500/2/11/252); William Dey, 1506 (NRO, NCC Garnon 106); John Daye, 1523 (SROB, IC 500/2/17/68).

[163]   Ralph Paynet, 1456 (NRO, NCC Neve 33) who also left 20d. apiece to three Lakenheath gilds dedicated to the Holy Trinity, St John and Blessed Mary; John Stalham, 1459 (SROB, IC 500/2/10/341) and Sir George Gatynbe, 1504 (NRO, NCC Ryxe 146).

[164]   Simon Goodrise, 1474 (SROB, IC 500/11/111). This is possibly another gild which, like the gild of St Katherine, failed for lack of support.

[165]   Alice Webbe, 1498 (NRO, NCC Typpes 146); William Charnoke, 1500 (NRO, NCC, Popy 571) and John Hart, 1506 (NRO, NCC Garnon 106). Hart also left 4d. to the reparation of the gild torches.

[166]   Robert Baron, 1438 (NRO, NCC Doke 84).

two years.[167] Requests for one-year chantries were plentiful from the 1450s to the 1480s and occasionally a quarter-year or half a year was requested. Seldom were chantries planned for a longer spell, although John Bakhot, one of the wealthier residents of the town, requested a four-year chantry in 1464.[168] Thomas Martyn, the chaplain, left money for a two-year chantry in 1469 and William Chylderston also planned for a two-year chantry in 1479.[169] Service chantries became less common and, in the sixteenth century, quarter-year and half-year services were more frequently requested in Mildenhall, with no substantial service chantries lasting for ten or twenty years.[170]

Perpetual chantries were ecclesiastical benefices requiring a licence from the Crown, the rents and profits from the endowment of land going straight to the chantry priest who was the freeholder. He, in his turn, would assist in parochial duties which often included teaching.[171] Both parishioners and priests might found perpetual chantries, of which Mildenhall had two. At the heart of these was a daily celebration of the Mass.

The sheer size of this parish and the need for adequate clerical personnel to service it was clearly stated in the chantry certificates of 1548, drawn up as the chantries were brought down.[172] The entry gives details of the two perpetual chantries in Mildenhall and adds, 'Mildenhall is a long and populous town with a great number of houseling people. It has sundry hamlets, having chapels distant from the parish church one mile or two, where the priest did sing Mass on sundry festival days and holy days. He also helped the curate to administer the Sacrament, who without help was not able to discharge his cure.'

Edmund de Mildenhall's Chantry   This was founded by licence during the reign of Edward III (1327–77) by Edmund of Mildenhall, a clerk.[173] It is unlikely that he was vicar of Mildenhall, no incumbent with that Christian name being listed during Edward III's reign. The whereabouts of his chantry chapel and the saint to which it was dedicated are unknown, but his endowment consisted of two messuages, forty acres of land, five acres of meadow and five acres of pasture. A chaplain was to celebrate daily in Mildenhall church for Edmund 'when he is departed this life' and for the souls of his parents, Adam and Emma, his sister Margaret, and his father's second wife, Joan de Chevington. Edmund paid forty shillings for the licence.

The chantry certificates of 1548 give the name of the chantry priest at that time as Robert Patchett, clerk, 'indifferently learned', a common way of describing a priest who was not a graduate but, at this time, perhaps a priest not of the current religious persuasion. Robert belonged to a local family who appear frequently in the church-

---

[167]   Thomas Sigo, 1439 (NRO, NCC Doke 113); Thomas Brynkele, 1439 (NRO, NCC Doke 87).
[168]   John Bakhot, 1464 (SROB, IC 500/2/10/397).
[169]   Thomas Martyn, 1469 (NCC, NRO Jekkys 144); William Chylderston, 1479 (SROB, IC 500/2/11/186).
[170]   Thomas Wynge, priest, 1500 (NRO, NCC Cage 135); see also Appendix 2.30: will of Roger Barforth (Barford), priest, 1504.
[171]   K.L. Wood-Legh, *Perpetual Chantries in Britain* (1965). For a unique record of the day-to-day expenses of a perpetual chantry, see K.L. Wood-Legh, *A Small Household of the XVth Century, being the account book of Munden's chantry, Bridport* (1956) where the introduction, pp.x–xxxiv, describes in detail the life of William Savernak, a chantry priest in Munden's chantry from 1453 until his death seven years later.
[172]   See V.B. Redstone, ed., 'II. Chantry Certificates, No. 45', *PSIA*, 12 (1906), p.32.
[173]   *CPR, Edward III (1354–1357)*, pp.47–348: *CPR, Edward VI (1548–1549)*, pp.294–95.

wardens' accounts and local wills (see Notes on People). He was forty years old in 1548 and had been in the post at least since 1535 when, in *Valor Ecclesiasticus*, he was named as chantry priest. The chantry foundation was worth £5 9s. 4d. a year and after certain deductions Patchett received £5 5s. 11d. By the time the chantry certificates were drawn up, Richard Sawer had already entered on one acre of land in Mildenhall field which had been given towards the priest's living by Katherine Playford.[174] This Sawer claimed as his inheritance.[175]

The Charnel Chapel The churchyard at Mildenhall was not extensive. It was bounded by the High Street to the east and by other buildings and occupied land on the other three sides. The extension of the east end of the church at the beginning of the fourteenth century had consumed precious space between the chancel and the road, and the subsequent rebuilding of the entire nave, aisles and tower at the beginning of the fifteenth century reduced the available ground even more. In cases such as this, where space was precious and burial plots were at a premium, a charnel house might be built to house bones disturbed either by new burials or new building, and this was sometimes referred to as the 'carnary' from the Latin meaning 'flesh'.[176]

The charnel chapel in Mildenhall churchyard was founded by Ralph de Walsham by licence in mortmain on 26 July 1386, during the incumbency of Simon Domynyk, vicar of Mildenhall from 1375 to 1408 (see Notes on Persons). The foundation consisted of four messuages, six cottages, 64 acres of land, 24 acres of meadow and 5s. rent in Mildenhall for a chaplain to celebrate daily within the parish of Mildenhall for the good estate of Ralph, for his soul after death and the souls of his ancestors and others.[177] The building in the churchyard was of two storeys, a vaulted chapel at ground level to house the bones and an upper chapel approached from either side by stone steps.[178] By 1516 a porch had been added against which Sir Simon Etton, the chantry chaplain, asked to be buried.[179] Little remains now, but it is possible to gauge the size of the chapel by the slight depression in the ground running east towards High Street.[180] The ruins of the fourteenth-century entrance were removed to make a bird bath in the vicarage garden in the nineteenth century and were replaced in the churchyard by a Victorian replica (Plate 7).

Little documentation has survived because parishioners made few testamentary gifts to the chapel in the churchyard. In 1503, however, it received a gift of land from William Bray in which five roods of land lying by Swath Cross were given on condition that Bray's soul was remembered in the bede-roll.[181] Katherine Playford left two acres in Mildenhall field near 'le Welmer', one acre to 'le Chernell' and another to the chantry of Edmund of Mildenhall.[182] Margery Howton bequeathed

---

174   Katherine Playford, 1522 (SROB, IC 500/2/15/45).
175   Redstone, 'Chantry Certificates', p.32.
176   The ruins of Bury St Edmunds' charnel house, built *c*.1300, stand between St Mary's church and the Norman gate. Bishop Salmon's two-storied carnary chapel, *c*.1316, in Norwich cathedral close is now the chapel of Norwich School.
177   *CPR, 10 Richard II (1385–1389)*, p.198.
178   By the late eighteenth century, only two ruined flights of stone steps remained. See the watercolour of Mildenhall Church in 1787 by Thomas Lyus in Ipswich Museum (IPSMG.R.1922–33. B0063) and H.C. Engelfield, *Archaeologia* 10 (1792), p.477 and fig.2.
179   Sir Simon Etton, see Appendix 2:34.
180   Mortlock, *Suffolk Churches*, p.153.
181   William Bray, 1503 (SROB, IC 500/2/12/128).
182   Katherine Playford, 1522 (SROB, IC 500/2/15/45).

Plate 7. Exterior of St Mary's church, c.1930, from the south-east, with the ivy-covered ruins of the late fourteenth-century charnel chapel in the foreground. © National Monuments Record.

6s. 8d. to 'both the chaunters in Mildenhall' and William Alen left a modest 4d. 'to the reparations of the chantry' but did not specify which.[183] John Haynes bequeathed half an acre of free land lying at 'Cestin's Wong' for prayers to be said for his soul.[184] Undoubtedly both the charnel chantry and the chantry within the church received gifts of cash and goods in return for individual prayers said by the chantry priests. In 1501 John Austyn was the chaplain of the charnel chantry.[185] In the *Valor Ecclesiasticus* of 1535, William Reve was named as the chaplain of Ralph de Walsham's chantry, which at that time was valued at £6 12s. 7½d. per annum. Reve died in 1545.[186]

At the dissolution of the chantries in 1548, Henry Wayneman was the chaplain of the charnel;[187] and, as so often happened when property was involved, a complaint was lodged because Richard Coole, whose name frequently appears in later churchwardens' accounts, had entered onto two roods of land, part of the five roods bequeathed by William Bray.[188] Nevertheless, the charnel and its endowments were let to Thomas Tirrell, gentleman, at a yearly rate of £6 6s. 9d. under seal of the Court of Augmentations. A bell weighing 23 pounds was recorded, but no other goods.

---

[183] Margery Howton: see Appendix 2:33; William Alen, 1536 (SROB, IC 500/2/20/170).
[184] John Haynes: see Appendix 2:35.
[185] Breen, *Mildenhall Rentals*, p.75.
[186] William Reve: see Appendix 2:44. Reve appears in a will of 1520 simply as 'priest'.
[187] TNA, E 322/154, 30 October 1547.
[188] Redstone, 'Chantry Certificates', p.32.

Anniversaries and Trentals

Anniversaries or obits were the re-enactment of the Office of the Dead with a requiem Mass on the eve and anniversary of the testator's death, the supposed corpse lying in the church beneath a pall.[189] Anniversaries are rarely mentioned in Mildenhall wills, being outnumbered by both service chantries and trentals, but an early example was that of Denise Constabill in 1473, who left her daughter Joan to make the arrangements.[190] The anniversary was to last for twelve years, 'disposing each year in bread, ale and cheese the value of 6s. 8d. for my soul and for the souls of Richard Cunstable, Robert Hynge, my husbands, and all my benefactors'.

Anniversaries or obits could range from the twenty years that Thomas Chyston requested to that of Thomas Geson, the tanner, who bequeathed to his own son seven acres, the profits from which were to finance a perpetual obit for the souls of Thomas and Margery Howton. Margery had already set up an obit on her own account in addition to a trental and a service-chantry lasting two years.[191] Geson, who had been Margery's executor, asked for a priest to sing for a quarter of a year for his own soul.

Intoning the names of the deceased from the bede-roll also ensured that their souls would not be forgotten. Robert Austen, a native of Mildenhall who had made his fortune as a member of the Salters Company in London, asked for prayers to be said in Mildenhall church 'there in the bederoll'.[192] No will has survived for Thomas Sherd (Scherd), and he is known only through the churchwardens' accounts: a *sangrede* for Sherd and his friends was charged at 4s. on the feast of the Purification in 1528.[193] In a later document, land called Shardes, containing thirteen acres of meadow and ten of arable in Mildenhall field, had been left to say Mass for dead souls.[194] This must be the foundation of Sherd's anniversary.

Other requests for prayers did not fit any particular category, such as that of Thomas Hopper who asked for a priest to pray for his own and his parents' souls 'for as long as £4 will extend and amount to'.[195] Both Sherd's and Hopper's provision for commemoration are a reminder that this was still a close society where much was arranged by word of mouth and carried out by mutual trust.

Trentals were a popular choice in Mildenhall. In the fifteenth century ten shillings would purchase thirty requiem masses which could be celebrated in the local church or in a religious house. Trentals could also be truncated and a half-trental would cost 5s. The masses could be said at one time or they might be spread over several days. Mildenhall parishioners chose both the parish church and local religious houses for these celebrations. Although St Gregory's trental had been popular, enthusiasm for it waned towards the end of the fifteenth century. There was only one instance of the St Gregory trental in fifteenth-century wills from Mildenhall, requested by Robert

---

[189] C. Burgess, 'A service for the dead: the form and function of the anniversary in late medieval Bristol', *Transactions of the Bristol and Gloucester Archaeological Society*, 105 (1987), pp.183–211.
[190] Dionesia Constabill: see Appendix 2:18.
[191] Thomas Chyston, senior, 1528 (SROB, IC 500/2/15/209); Thomas Geson, tanner, 1528 (SROB, IC 500/2/15/217); Margery Howton: see Appendix 2:33.
[192] Robert Austen, 1514 (TNA, PCC Holder 29). Austen's mother was buried in Mildenhall church in 1505–1506 at a cost of 6s. 8d. See CWA, fol.3v.
[193] CWA, fols 17v, 18r, 19r and 20r.
[194] SROB, E18/400/1:2.
[195] Thomas Hopper, see Appendix 2:37.

Chadenhalk some ten years before the surviving Mildenhall collections begin.[196] Dom John Lynne, a Benedictine monk of Bury, was nominated as the priest to celebrate half a trental for Thomas Puttock, a barker of Mildenhall, at a cost of 5s.[197] The bulk of requests, however, were for trentals to be said at the friaries of Babwell and of the Old and the New houses at Thetford.[198] Only one trental was requested in Mildenhall church, 'the priest of Mildenhall to celebrate a trental for my soul, parents, friends and benefactors' souls'.[199]

THE BELLS AND THE CLOCK

The first part of the accounts for St Mary's, Mildenhall, record weekly collections of money, but it is difficult to be certain for what purpose. The documents begin in 1446, perhaps twenty years after the completion of the nave and aisles. The 120-foot tower must have taken at least twenty years to construct for building in flint was limited to a height of roughly six feet of new work a year in order for the mortar to set within boarding shutters, and the working year was short because only the summer months were favoured for building. The contract for the construction of Walberswick's flint tower, for example, states that work was to be done between Lady Day (25 March) and Michaelmas (29 September).[200] It was probably the same for Mildenhall.

The collections received in the mid-fifteenth century were perhaps intended for the completion of the bell chamber or the bell frames, perhaps even for the bells themselves. The bell mechanism was contained within a wooden bell-frame or cage which rested on the floor of the bell chamber. Raven, writing in the late nineteenth century, argued that the bell-frame then in place in Mildenhall tower was earlier than the existing tower.[201] He had come to this conclusion because the frames were bolted together by wooden pins 'so long that they could not have been driven in after the walls were built'.

Bells were suspended from a wooden stock, and if the bells became loose on the stock, they were trussed or tightened (see Coll. fols 3r and 10r). The stock was attached to the bell-wheel. At this period bell-wheels were semi-circular which meant that the swing of the bell was restricted. Around the grooved wheel ran the rope which was pulled by the bell-ringer. Inside the bell, the clapper was suspended by a leather baldrick or strap from the eye of the bell. A common accident at this time was caused by the clappers falling out and injuring the ringers.[202]

---

[196] Robert Chadenhalk, 1434 (NRO, NCC Surflete 180): R. Pfaff, 'The English devotion of St Gregory's trental', *Speculum,* xlix (1974), pp.75–90.

[197] Thomas Puttock, barker, 1464 (SROB, IC 500/2/10/353).

[198] William Deynis, 1465 (SROB, IC 500/2/10/389); Thomas Symund, the elder, 1477 (SROB, IC 500/2/11/87); Roger Barford, priest, Appendix 2:30; John Deye, 1523 (SROB, IC 500/2/17/68); John Halsted, Appendix 2:40. The Thetford houses were, respectively, those of the Dominicans and the Augustinians. See D. Dymond, *The Register of Thetford Priory* I, p.64 (map) and II, p.486n.

[199] Katherine Bowne, 1471 (SROB, IC 500/2/10/571).

[200] BL, Add. Charter 17,634, the covenant for building Walberswick tower, 1426. See *PSIA* 25 (1952), pp.169–70.

[201] J.J. Raven, *The Church Bells of Suffolk* (1890), p.47. The fifteenth-century bell frame was finally removed in 1912 and a part of its timber was used to make the present high altar. The bells were re-hung on a steel frame. See Rees, *Mildenhall,* p.24.

[202] L.F. Salzman, *Building in England down to 1540: a Documentary History* (1952), p.242.

William Chapman, a parishioner from Beck Row, had already given to the collections a total of 3 marks in weekly instalments of 3s. 4d. between March and June 1446. Dame Isabel Galyon had also made several similar donations. Three years later, the making of the second bell cost £2 6s. 8d., the wheel, rope and stock costing extra. In 1450 bequests were made to the 'bell tower' and then the collections ceased for roughly six months. They petered out in 1454, but whether due to loss of records or completion of the work is hard to say.

The tower must have been completed by 1464. It was in that year that William Chapman, the earlier donor, wrote his will. It is not known what else had been salvaged from the previous tower, but it is clear that an old bell, known as the 'great' bell, was to be repaired. Chapman bequeathed 10 marks to the reparation of the 'great' bell hanging in the tower.[203] This must be the same bell described by Cautley as a fifteenth-century bell bearing the royal arms as altered after 1413 and inscribed *In multis annis resonet campana Johannis.*[204] It was due to be recast by Richard Brasyer, the Norwich bell-founder but, two years later when the work had not been started, the inhabitants of Mildenhall brought an action for breach of contract against Brasyer.[205]

The agreement was that the great bell be recast as a tenor to accord in tone and sound with the other Mildenhall bells. The contract stated that at Mildenhall's expense the great bell should be carried to the house of the defendant, Richard Brasyer, in Norwich, and that there it should be weighed and put in the furnace in the presence of a representative of Mildenhall.[206] The disagreement between the parties involved the weighing of the bell. Brasyer argued that it should have been weighed by the men of Mildenhall, but he lost the case. It seems that it was not until the 1530s that the bell was finally attended to. Henry Pope in his will of 1535 left £3 10s. to the making of the great bell, 'whensoever the town go about the making therof'.[207]

The churchwardens' accounts begin in 1503 and the running costs for bells and their appurtenances appear frequently. There was a constant demand for new ropes, clappers, wheels and baldricks. The latter were often made of white hide and the purchase of this commodity frequently occurs in the accounts. John Sadyler was paid 3d. for making the 'bawdrykks' in 1505–06.[208] The little bell or 'second' bell was hung and supplied with rests in 1505–06, and by 1510–11 a 'third' bell had been supplied with a new wheel made by Mandall of Thurston.[209] This may be the bell that is hallowed and appears as Bagot's bell on the next folio.[210] Although no evidence has survived to prove that any member of the Bagot family gave a bell to

---

203 William Chapman, 1464 (SROB, IC 500/2/10/379).

204 Cautley, *Suffolk Churches*, p.57; Raven, *Suffolk Bells*, p.219.

205 L.F. Salzman, *English Medieval Industries of the Middle Ages* (1923), pp.154–155; a bell was made up of four parts copper to one part tin. These proportions had been advised by Theophilus in his treatise *De Diversis Artibus* of *c.*1122, and were never questioned. Bells could be recast and often were, but if scrap metal was used more tin had to be added to obtain a purer sound. See C. Blair and J. Blair, 'Bell founding', in *English Medieval Industries: Craftsmen, Techniques, Products*, ed. J. Blair and N. Ramsay (1991), pp.89–93. When bells needed tuning, portions of the inner surface were pared away (see CWA, fol.12v).

206 Raven, *Suffolk Bells*, pp.49–51.

207 Henry Pope, 1537 (SROB, IC 500/2/20/51).

208 CWA, fol.2v. 'Sadyler', in this instance, must be an occupational surname.

209 CWA, fols 2v and 8r.

210 CWA, fols 9r and 9v.

the church, Bagot's bell appears frequently thereafter. In fact, it seems it was the only bell in Mildenhall church that ever received a personal name.[211] A fourth bell arrived some time later for, in 1547, the certificate of church goods indicates four bells then hanging in the tower.[212] The sanctus bell which was rung at the elevation of the host during Mass also had a wheel.

Mildenhall Church Clock

The clock may have been a fifteenth-century mechanical model but, despite its frequent occurrence in the churchwardens' accounts, little is known about it. Yet from the evidence of numerous churchwardens', sacrists' and bursars' accounts many clocks were acquired by towns and villages from 1400.[213]

Clocks at this time were constructed with a four-posted frame, the iron uprights standing on small feet. The posts were attached to horizontal members within which the clockwork was housed. These early clocks kept a steady pace by virtue of two constants, the first being a weight cast in lead or iron or hewn in stone; and the second was an escapement or a toothed wheel, the earliest of which had square, rather than pointed, teeth.[214] There are references within the county to fifteenth-century clocks such as John Baret's clock at St Mary's, Bury St Edmunds, complete with chimes, in 1464; or the church clock at St Andrew's, Walberswick, which cost the churchwardens 11s. 4d. in 1450 and a further 13s. 4d. in 1452.[215]

The expenses of the clock seem very meagre compared with those at Walberswick, although Mildenhall's wardens did make one payment to the clockmaker of 6s. 6d. This is comparable to the amount paid to John Payn, the smith of Southwold, who provided Walberswick church with a new clock in 1495.[216] Ordinary running repairs at Mildenhall were mostly carried out by the blacksmith of the time, and the payment for 'keeping the clock', which meant winding it daily, was paid at a quarterly rate of 10d. to 1s. 3d.[217]

The position of the clock may not have been in the tower at all at this period, for early clocks were placed inside the church so that the dial would have been visible at ground-level. Later, clocks were placed within the tower and clock dials were made visible on the exterior wall of the tower. The clock face which hangs today above the ground-floor entrance to the tower may well be an early one, but there is nothing to suggest its date or provenance.

DRINKINGS AND DRAMA

Mildenhall's collections reveal no sure evidence of theatrical productions, although it is possible that any churchale might have included a dramatic episode of some

---

211 Salzman, *English Industries*, p.150; Middleton-Stewart, *Inward Purity*, p.109.
212 The addition of a fourth bell may have been the reason that the bell-frame was rebuilt *c*.1541.
213 C.F.C. Beeson, *English Church Clocks 1280–1850: History and Classification* (1971), pp.22–24.
214 Beeson, *Church Clocks*, pp.11–12 and fig.1. The *horologium* at Dunstable priory had the earliest recorded escapement in England and, Beeson argues, the earliest in European records.
215 Tymms, 'John Baret of Bury, 1463', in *Wills and Inventories*, p.19: Lewis, *Walberswick*, pp.1–3: Middleton- Stewart, *Inward Purity*, pp. 108–110.
216 Lewis, *Walberswick*, p.73.
217 CWA, fols 3r, 3v, 4v and 7v.

sort. The various 'drinkings' of the parish, four in the summer of 1452 alone, would have given ample opportunity for lively presentations.[218] The money entered in the collections under the heading 'churchales', however, shows a fairly regular return with no suggestion that these were accompanied by entertainment requiring more expenses.

In the collections, the word used to describe a churchale is 'a drinking' (*potacio*). Table 3 shows the frequency with which this occurred, the profit made, the organizers of the events and the folio number in the original manuscript.

Table 3: Money raised by churchales in the collections, 1446–54

1446	May 15	£1 11s. 4d.	Holywell Row	fol.1v
1446	May 29	£1 15s. 0d	The Young Men and Women	fol.2r
1447	June 4	£1 4s. 0d.	The Town	fol.4r
1447	June 11	£1 0s. 0d.	West Row	fol.4r
1447	July 9	£1 0s. 4d.	Beck Row	fol.4r
1449	June 11	£1 3s. 0d.	Beck Row, Cake and Wilde Street	fol.5v
1450	June 28	£1 2s. 0d.	The Town	fol.10v
1452	May 21	£1 13s. 4d.	The Town	fol.16v
1452	June 25	£1 13s. 4d.	The Town	fol.17r
1452	July 2	£1 5s. 4d.	West Row	fol.17r
1452	July 16	18s.2½d.	Beck Row	fol.17v
1453	January 28	£1 4s. 0d.	Holywell Row	fol.19r
1453	March 25	£1 19s. 0d.	The Town	fol.19v
1453	May 6	18s. 7d.	West Row	fol.20r
1453	August 12	17s. 8d.	Beck Row, Cake and Wilde Street	fol.21r
1454	April 7	£1 3s. 4d.	Holywell Row	fol.23r

In the table of money raised by May ales, May games, drinkings and churchales (Table 4) the one outstanding entry is for the play of St Thomas, performed in 1505–06, which made a profit of £7. The overall profits entered in the sixteenth-century churchwardens' accounts are slightly higher than those of the churchales entered in the fifteenth-century collections.

A comparison, however, is hardly just as the collections appear to be almost complete while the churchwardens' accounts certainly are not. In similar accounts surviving from late medieval England, gaps occur in even the most complete series and, where one performance is noted, it may not be the entire entertainment staged that year.[219]

---

[218]   Coll. fols 16v (21 May), 17r (25 June and 2 July) and 17v (16 July).
[219]   D. Galloway and J. Wasson, 'Records of plays and players in Norfolk and Suffolk, 1330–1642', *Malone Society*, 11 (1980–1981), p.xi.

Table 4: Money raised by May ales, May games,
drinkings and churchales in the churchwardens' accounts, 1505–44

1505–6	£7 0s. 0d.	The Town: Play of St Thomas	fol.1v
1507–8	13s. 4d.	Holywell Row: May ale	fol.6r
1507–8	£2 0s. 0d.	The Town: May ale	fol.6r
1507–8	£2 4s. 0d.	Beck Row: May ale	fol.6r
1507–8 [damaged]		West Row: May [damaged]	fol.6r
1509–10 paid	1s. 1d.	to players at May ale	fol.7v
1509–10 paid 4d.		to the tabourer	fol. 7v
1510–11	£1 3s. 4½d.	The Town: May ale	fol.8v
1510–11	£1 17s. 0d.	West Row: May ale	fol.8v
1513–14	£1 16s. 8d.	The Town: churchale	fol.11r
1514–15	£2 13s. 8d.	The Town: churchale	fol.13v
1516–17	13s. 4d.	Holywell Row: drinking	fol.14v
1528–29	7s. 4d.	West Row: Lord of Misrule	fol.20r
1529–30	£2 4s. 0d.	The Town: Maygame	fol.20v
1540–41	£1 1s. 0d.	The Town: play	fol.30r
1543–44	£1 1s. 8d.	The Town: churchale	fol.27r
1543–44	£1 17s. 4d.	The Town: churchale	fol.27r

In the churchwardens' accounts of the sixteenth century a greater mix of terminology is to be found, but it is difficult to decide whether a churchale was only for eating and drinking as suggested by the figures given above. Players of some sort were certainly present at the May ale in 1509–10 at a cost of 1s. 1d. which was entered separately in the accounts. No indication, however, was given as to the type of act performed except that it included a taborer or drummer.[220] A dramatic presentation of some sort may have been included, but perhaps plays were performed only where the word 'game' occurs.

Non-professional drama fell into two categories: traditional village plays and May games performed annually and requiring only costumes and an audience; or the specially staged parish and community ventures which were performed only once or at most a few times. The aim was to make money, usually for a specific purpose, and production costs were deliberately held down.[221] This illustrates precisely the difference between the churchales or May games and the specific drama of St Thomas which was so profitable. Large towns such as Bungay, Bury St Edmunds, Bishop's Lynn and Ipswich had both pageants and plays, the former usually mounted on pageant wagons, but nothing suggests that these performances were in any way related to each other. In the smaller locations such as Mildenhall processions might take place, but plays were the exception.[222]

Churchwardens' accounts and other related manuscripts supply much relevant information on plays and players elsewhere in East Anglia. There were various presentations in the area on the theme of Thomas Becket, such as an 'interlude of St

---

220 CWA, fol.7v.
221 Galloway and Wasson, 'Records of plays and players', p.xv.
222 Galloway and Wasson, 'Records of plays and players', p.xi.

Thomas the martyr' at Bishop's Lynn in 1384–85 and a service of Thomas Becket with a procession at Bungay.[223] A second 'servyce' of Becket had been corrected by Sir Richard Charnell and it was to be performed at the chapel of St Thomas in the churchyard of St Mary's, Bungay, in 1539.[224] At the beginning of the fifteenth century in the Corpus Christi procession at Ipswich, the barbers and wax chandlers mounted a pageant for St Thomas, and this continued throughout the fifteenth century.[225]

Mildenhall lay only a few miles from Thetford, an important market town with its ancient castle and several religious foundations, including the thriving Cluniac house. It was also well placed on the intersection of roads from London to Norwich and from Bury St Edmunds to Bishop's Lynn. The Cluniac brethren happened to be at the heart of both visiting and local dramatic productions and they were entertained by travelling players at an average rate of two visits a year.[226] The monks contributed towards dramatic productions in various parishes in the area, two of these being Shelfanger, just to the north of Diss, and Mildenhall lying to the southwest. In the Cluniacs' financial year from June 1505 to June 1506 is the entry, 'to the play of Mildenhall 1s.'.[227] This was most likely to have been the play of St Thomas Becket, medieval England's most important saint.

---

[223] Galloway and Wasson, 'Records of plays and players', pp.235 and 230.

[224] Galloway and Wasson, 'Records of plays and players', p.142: St Mary's church had been the convent church of the Benedictine nuns. The nunnery, founded in 1183, was suppressed in 1536 under Henry VIII's Act for the suppression of smaller houses.

[225] Galloway and Wasson, 'Records of plays and players', pp.170, 171, 173 and 175.

[226] Dymond, *Thetford Priory*, I, p.49.

[227] Dymond, *Thetford Priory*, I, pp.51 and 204.

CONTENTS OF THE COLLECTIONS AND CHURCHWARDENS' ACCOUNTS

Much has been written about the men who served as bishops, but the most important of the ecclesiastical officers from the standpoint of the parish, and arguably for the entire structure, were the churchwardens.

John Craig, *Reformation, Politics and Polemics:*
The Growth of Protestantism in East Anglian
Market Towns, 1500–1610 (2001), p.34.

Mildenhall's collections (1446–1454) and churchwardens' accounts (1503–1553) are held in the Suffolk Record Office at Bury St Edmunds (SROB, EL 110/5/1–3). These late medieval manuscripts bring us as close to this particular church and its parish in the fifteenth and sixteenth centuries as is possible. They reveal a building which is representative of the pre-Reformation church, a concept no longer common to most people either in construction, plan or practice. The collections disclose a community which planned and worked together to create and maintain the church which we see today, while the accounts highlight the artefacts and decorative art based on the beliefs of the time and record the worship and performance which expressed those beliefs.

Churchwardens, sometimes also referred to as churchreeves, are first heard of nationally in the mid-fourteenth century, being the people through whom certain responsibilities were realized.[1] They raised and held funds and kept accounts of income and expenditure on behalf of the parishioners to whom the accounts were presented at an annual meeting. Wardens administered property belonging to the parish, cared for the books, vestments and plate, and ultimately were the parishioners' representatives, thus linking their church, their parish and its people to the wider world of their patron, in this instance the abbot and convent of Bury St Edmunds. It was incumbent on the wardens to attend the visitation of the archdeacon so that the accounts could be presented.

Churchwardens were chosen by the parishioners and their term of office was usually for three years, but in Mildenhall this is difficult to substantiate because the accounts are incomplete and erratic. From the earliest entry in the collections, it appears that the parish had more churchwardens than was normal custom, two coming from the High Town and another two from the outlying areas of West Row and Beck Row. Nevertheless, the size of the parish and the isolated positions of its various hamlets appear to have produced well-balanced wardenship and supportive parishioners, despite problems of communications within the scattered community.

The churchwardens named in the collections, which run from 1446 to 1454, appear to be men of middling status and, during this period, no women were appointed. Of the seven identifiable wardens, five left wills, suggesting that they were men of

---

[1]   C. Drew, *Early Parochial Organisation in England: The Origins of the Office of Churchwarden*, St Anthony's Hall Publications, 7 (Borthwick Institute of Historical Research, 1954).

some substance. Generally they were required to possess wealth beyond a level of subsistence.[2] Several of them were related, some by marriage, and they came mainly from well-established and locally respected families of yeomen and husbandmen. At least one of them, John Bryan, was not only a member of the local families of Bryan and Patchett, but also a parish chaplain.

Between 1503 and 1553, some churchwardens are unnamed or their names are illegible in the accounts, but over sixty wardens can be identified. Gardener, Patchett, Peachey, Duffield and Childerston are all local names that occur as wardens and they appear to be from the same background as their predecessors in the previous century. Many were local tradesmen and craftsmen and, yet again, one was a parish chaplain.

Four wardens served between August 1503 and November 1505, but only John Heynes and Thomas Mey can be identified by name. The other two were both called Thomas but their surnames are illegible. These accounts record receipts but no disbursements, and the length of time that they served as wardens is difficult to assess. They were followed by Simon Eton (Etton), the chaplain, Thomas Gesye, William Ballis and John Dey, but only 'for one year'. These accounts appear complete and they were well kept in a businesslike manner, and yet the same cannot be said for many of the accounts that follow for much has been destroyed or just mislaid.

The Collections (1446–54)

Late medieval churchwardens' accounts may be rare, most being destroyed as having no further use, but it is more unusual to find collections or gatherings.[3] These differ from general churchwardens' accounts in that they record the collecting of extra funding for specific projects.[4] The collections of Mildenhall are uneven in what they record and irregular in their layout, and yet they are a remarkable survival. They are written on soft sheets of a roughish hand-made paper with a watermark of a set of hand-held weighing scales.[5] The sheets measure 295mm x 440mm and are folded longitudinally. They have been professionally repaired where necessary and are currently lying loose in a cardboard folder. The collections are written in Latin, an exception being eight entries at the top of fol.8r. which are written in English and are shown on p.13 with the original spelling. The collections cover nine years during which they are written in ink in four or five different hands, but overall the lay-out is neat. The pages that remain may be the best copy and possibly the remnants of a larger gathering. As they do not record expenditure they give little indication as to where the money was to be spent, but they illustrate the vital

---

[2] Craig, *Reformation, Politics*, p.43.
[3] The early records of St Mary the Great in Cambridge refer to gatherings and gatherers rather than collections and collectors. See Foster, *Churchwardens' Accounts of St Mary the Great*, p.34; also Lewis, *Walberswick*, pp.198, 216.
[4] The accounts of St Mary the Great show weekly sums ranging from 5s. to 8s. 3d. gathered by the 'rolles' between July and December 1515 to pay masons, carpenters and labourers for materials, stone and iron work for the almshouse, and for the porch and vestry of the church, Foster, *St Mary the Great*, pp.23–24. In 1518 a parchment skin was purchased for 1d. to make the 'gathering roll' on which names of donors and donations were recorded, *ibid.* p.37; see also Lewis, *Walberswick*, p.256. In 1495, 10s. were received from the wives of Walberswick town from a gathering for a glass window.
[5] Thanks are due to Dominic Wall of the Suffolk Record Office for this information.

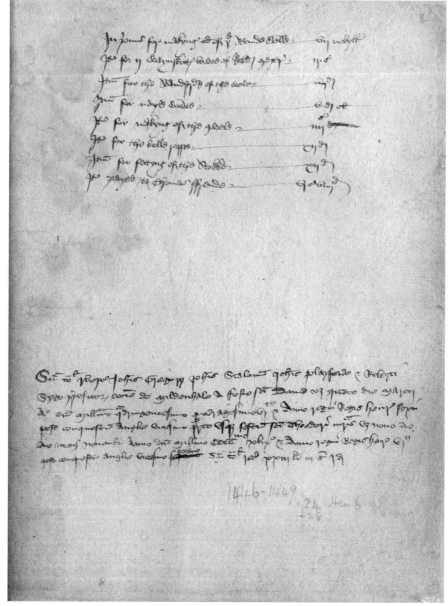

Plate 8. A folio from the fifteenth-century Mildenhall collections, SROB, EL 110/5/1, fol.8r, 1449.

drip-feed of church economy undertaken while building works were carried out.[6] There are, therefore, no disbursements such as appear in typical churchwardens' accounts which consist of income and expenditure. These are to be found in the sixteenth-century churchwardens' accounts which make up the second part and bulk of this volume.

Mildenhall's collections may not be complete, and it is not possible to assess how much money was raised or for how long the collections continued, but they give a good idea of the slow and painstaking accrual of small sums gathered for a communal end, although what this was is not directly revealed. The weekly tally raised was from 1s. to 4s. 6d. The collections are literally a record of variable sums given by inhabitants of the High Town as well as West Row, Holywell Row and Beck Row, the latter sometimes being paired with Cake Street and Wild Street.

The collections record special events such as churchales, sometimes called potations. These were both profitable and enjoyable, and sums raised from such convivial gatherings were substantial and might show a profit of £1 to just under £2. In the summer of 1446 two churchales are recorded, one at Holywell Row raising £1 11s. 4d., the second in Mildenhall raising £1 15s.[7] These revenues need to be compared with the money gathered from the normal weekly church collections, the average weekly takings during the six weeks from 26 June to 31 July in the same year being under 4s.[8] Frequently the collections reveal that holding a churchale meant that no other monies were gathered that week. Holywell Row, for instance, held a churchale in January 1453.[9] £1 4s. 0d. was raised, yet the following week Holywell contributed nothing to the weekly collection. January may seem an unusual choice for an event which was usually held during the summer, but two months later the next churchale was held on Palm Sunday, well in advance of the better weather, suggesting that more funding was urgently needed.[10]

Individual bequests or 'quethewords' left to provide prayers for the health of testators' souls were sometimes included in the collections. Although these are unusual, they can be identified by the phrase 'for the soul of ...'. A few wills have survived in which specific amounts are left for the good of the testators' souls, and the amount specified in the will corresponds with the entry in the collections.[11] Of the eight bequests received for the souls of dead parishioners on another page, none has testamentary support;[12] yet, from those eight bequests, the churchwardens received £1 3s.

In the 1450s John Fuller's name appeared three times as a debtor of Dame Isabel Gallyon.[13] In 1450 he paid 6s. 8d. towards the bells and in 1453 he paid a further two installments of 6s. 8d., a project close to Dame Isabel's heart for she had already

---

6   K.L. French, *The People of the Parish: Community Life in a Late Medieval English Diocese* (2001), pp.114–15. See also K.L. French 'Parochial fund-raising in late medieval Somerset', in *The Parish in English Life 1400–1600*, ed. K.L. French, G.G. Gibbs and B.A. Kümin (1997), pp.115–32.

7   Coll. fols 1v, 2r.

8   Coll. fol.2v.

9   Coll. fol.19r.

10 Coll. fol.19v.

11 See John Staloun's (Stalham's) will of 1452 in Northeast, ed., *Wills of the Archdeaconry of Sudbury*, no.708 and the entry on Coll. fol.19v below; Robert Tyd's will of 1452 in Northeast, ed., *Wills of the Archdeaconry of Sudbury*, no.598, and the entry on Coll. fol.21v below.

12 Coll. fol.17v.

13 Coll. fols 10v, 19v, 20r.

made a couple of small donations on her own account in 1447.[14] Individual items, too, might be recorded, such as 8d. raised from the sale of straw to Thomas Play-forde, the gift of a cloth of 'twilly' given by Margaret Helgey or the stone for a cistern given by the chaplain, John Bryan.[15] It is almost as though these are embry-onic churchwardens' accounts, but they actually represent individual contributions towards a specific purpose.

If the rebuilding of the church was completed c.1420–30, the building of the tower could have followed on immediately, yet the collections give no indication as to how the money gathered weekly was to be spent. Ancillary documentation such as wills might provide the answer, but here the wills are silent. Peter North-east compared the difference between the funding and re-building of the churches of Lavenham and Long Melford, both of which are reflected in many testamentary bequests, to the rebuilding of Beccles, which went largely unnoticed by testators.[16] He continued, 'similarly, on the other side of the county, the extensive fifteenth-century work in the impressive church of Mildenhall received no mention'. Sir Henry Barton, Lord Mayor of London in 1416 and 1426, 'notable in his native village as the traditional enlarger and re-builder of the church', may have under-written further building after the completion of the nave, aisles and clerestory.[17] Nevertheless, this is supposition, and works of major construction are more likely to have been built under contract, the great sums of money involved never passing through the churchwardens' hands.[18]

The collections fall into three sections:

a. 1446–49 (fols 1r–8r)
The earliest folios, 1r–8r, represent an accounting period running from the feast of St David on 4 March 1446,[19] to that of St Theodore, the martyr, celebrated on 9 November 1449. The collections began within two weeks of the wardens taking up their duties and continued intermittently until their term of office expired three and a half years later. When the churchwardens of these earliest accounts retired in 1449 they were named as John Gregory, John Staloun, John Playforde and Robert Sygo.[20] Collections had been made on the following Sundays:

1446   20, 27 March; 3, 10, 24 April; 1, 8, 15, 22, 29 May; 12, 19, 26 June; 3, 10, 17, 24, 31 July; 2, 16, 23 October; 20, 27 November; 4, 11 December.
1447   8, 15, 22, 29 January; 30 July.
1448   No collections were recorded but two donations were received during the year and three churchales were held on 4 and 11 June and 9 July.
1449   4, 11, 18, 25 May; 1, 8, 15, 22, 29 June; 6, 13, 20, 27 July; 3, 10, 17, 24, 31 August; 7, 14, 21, 28 September; 5, 12, 19, 26 October; 2, 9 November.

---

14   Coll. fol.4r.
15   Coll. fols 1v, 10v and 12v.
16   P. Northeast, 'Suffolk churches in the later middle ages', in *East Anglia's History: Studies in honour of Norman Scarfe*, ed. C. Harper-Bill, C. Rawcliffe and R.G. Wilson (2002), p.96.
17   Rees, *Mildenhall*, p.21.
18   Middleton-Stewart, 'Parochial activity', pp.291–292.
19   Within the octave of St David, whose saint's day was celebrated on 1 March.
20   Coll. fol.8r.

b. 1449–52 (fols 9r–16v)

The variations in the accounts in this period are similar to those above. The election took place on 7 December, 1449. The incoming wardens received 2s. 4d. from their predecessors. The new churchwardens were William Sutton, a glover, John Paynet, a smith, and John Bryan, a chaplain (d.1454).

Collections were made on the following Sundays:

1449   7, 21, 28 December.

1450   4, 18, 25 January; 1, 8, 15, 22 February; 1, 8, 15, 22 March.

On Palm Sunday it was announced that there would be no more collections until further notice, and they were not resumed for another nine months.

1451   31 January; 7, 21, 28 February; 7, 14, 21, 28 March; 4, 11, 18 April; 2, 9, 16, 23, 30 May; 6, 20, 27 June; 4, 11, 18, 25 July; 1, 8, 15, 22, 29 August; 5, 12, 19, 26 September; 3, 10, 17, 24, 31 October; 7, 14, 21, 28 November; 5, 12, 19, 26 December.

1452   2, 9, 16, 23 January; 6, 13, 20, 27 February; 5, 12, 19, 26 March; 2, 16, 30 April; 7, 14, 21, 28 May.

Having received £12 10s. 9½d. during their term of office, John Bryan, chaplain, and John Paynet presented their accounts on 29 May 1452, two and a half years after their election, and resigned.

c. 1452–54 (fols 17r–23v)

A week later, new churchwardens assumed office, but they cannot be identified because the introductory page to their wardenship has not survived and much information from this period has perished. The collections are comparatively full, however, and run from Trinity Sunday in 1452 to the middle of September in 1454. They are not brought to an end with a grand flourish, but peter out in the early autumn of 1454, the last pages presumably destroyed or lost, the wardens still anonymous.

Collections were made on the following Sundays:

1452   Trinity Sunday 4, 11, 18, 25 June; 2, 16, 23, 30 July; 24 September; 1, 8, 15, 22, 29 October; 5, 12, 19, 26 November; 3, 10, 17, 24 December.

1453   7, 14, 28 January; 4, 11, 25 February; 4, 11, 18, 25 March; 8, 15 April; 6, 13, 27 May; 3, 10, 17, 24 June; 1, 8, 15, 22, 29 July; 5, 12 August; 16, 23, 30 September; 7, 14, 21 October; 2, 9, 16 December.

1454   6, 13, 20, 27 January; 3, 17, 24 February; 3, 10, 17, 24 March; 7, 14 April; 26 May; 14, 28 July; 15, 22 September.

There had been only one collection entered in July 1447, but this was followed by entries of bequests in October and November made on the deaths of several parishioners, the donations ranging from 2d. to 6s. 8d.[21] This suggests that, despite the drip-feed economy of the collections, the money required to rebuild, renovate and maintain a parish church the size and stature of Mildenhall was enhanced and achieved by outright gifts, such as money left in a quetheword or earned from a churchale.

The most important work being undertaken at Mildenhall in the mid-fifteenth century may well have been the building of the tower, but the monies raised by the collections were probably used to finance the bells. When the first section of

21 Coll. fol.4r.

the collections came to an end in 1449 the four churchwardens had received the sum of £23 3s. 1d. They entered the expenditure, the only time it is recorded in the fifteenth-century documentation. It reveals that the making of the second bell cost seven nobles (£2 6s. 8d.), the bell wheel, the standard, the bell rope, the setting of the stock and the labour costing a further 15s. 8½d.

Churchales

(See 'Drinkings and Drama', above, p.lv) Churchales or 'drinkings' as they were called, were the pre-Reformation's answer to today's coffee mornings, but were probably more fun. They were held to raise additional funds for the local church. As many as four churchales might be held in one year, taking place at Mildenhall and the Rows. The total revenue raised from the churchales entered in the collections amounted to £20 6s. 9½d.

Churchales are entered in the collections on the following dates:

1446   15 May at Holywell; 29 May 'of the young men and women'.
1447   4 June in the town; 11 June at West Row; 9 July at Beck Row with Cake Street.
1449   8 June in the town; 15 June at Beck Row with Cake Street and Wild Street.
1450   28 June in the town.
1452   21 May in the town; 2 July at West Row; 16 July in Beck Row.
1453   28 January at Holywell; 25 March in the Town; 6 May at West Row; 12 August at Beck Row, Cake Street and Wild Street.
1454   7 April at Holywell; 10 June at West Row.

The Churchwardens' Accounts (1503–53)

Mildenhall churchwardens' accounts are written in Latin and English. Entries translated from Latin are headed *Latin* in italics within square brackets. Entries written in English keep their original spelling. The accounts are written in ink on sheets of finer paper than that used for the collections, but there is no watermark. Each sheet is folded and measures 355mm x 180mm. They have not been bound, but at some time, probably in the late nineteenth century, were sewn together along the spine and, at several points, collated in the wrong order. Nevertheless, this haphazard arrangement saved the remaining folios from destruction. Those that have survived are incomplete, ten years missing between 1516 and 1528, for instance, and other years lack either complete receipts or payments. There are at least twelve different hands and the appearance of many folios becomes untidy as the Reformation takes hold.

These accounts differ from the collections since they record expenditure as well as income. By the early 1500s, the church re-building, begun in the early fourteenth century, had been finished, yet there was still much to be done within the walls. Day-to-day expenses are noted and these make possible a better understanding about the running and administration of a church of this size. Although many artisans were resident in the parish, help was frequently summoned from outside for specialist trades. This applied both to the making of new vestments and the binding of church books; the organ, too, required frequent attention, and the entry referring to *rector chores* indicates a sophisticated musical tradition at St Mary's.[22] There was

---

[22] CWA, fol.30v. See also the Introduction, 'Liturgical Necessities', p.xxxi.

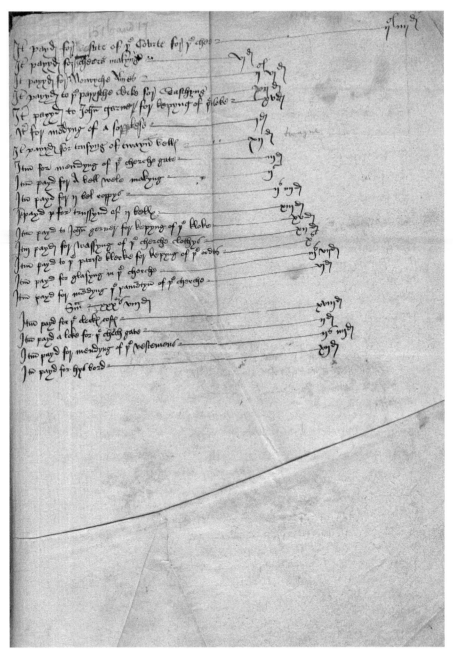

Plate 9. A folio from the sixteenth-century Mildenhall churchwardens' accounts, SROB, EL 110/5/3, fol.15r.

also a school at Mildenhall, expenditure on the school house being entered in the accounts.[23]

Payments balanced against profits can be seen, the play of St Thomas (Becket) performed in the Hall Yard making a profit of £7, more than the annual income of a chantry priest of Mildenhall.[24] The money left in parishioners' wills to cover the cost of their interment was also entered in the accounts. Interment within the church cost extra and, when this is noted, it reveals who had sufficient class or money to earn a place inside.

There are many references to pardons in the earlier accounts.[25] There were five pardon days at Mildenhall held on the feasts of Candlemas, Corpus Christi, St Philip and St James, Michaelmas and Dedication Day, the latter celebrated either on the anniversary of the presentation in the temple or the Immaculate Conception. The pardon days are entered on the first folio of receipts in 1504 and thereafter appear regularly, later intermittently until they are abolished in 1539.[26] The Bishop of Rome's pardon, either carved or painted on a wall, was destroyed in 1539.[27] The money raised had averaged £1 over a year, takings from the pardons varying from 2s. to 5s. a time. In the 1528 accounts, the word pardon was changed to indulgence and, from 1529, indulgence became collection or gathering. These were still collected for a while, but only Michaelmas survived as a gathering day up to 1546. Pardons had been important in establishing communal obligation, and for them to continue as collections after 1536 illustrates that although the pardon might have declined, the obligation remained.[28]

Much may be learnt about the parish itself from the accounts. There are references to the condition of the land in the sixteenth-century accounts, the flooded area between Ely common and Mildenhall common being referred to as a lake.[29] Sedge Fen is mentioned and the waterside cottage rented by Thomas Hopper is referred to as Hopper's Cot, the Fysche Cote lately Hoppers and the Old Coote in the Fen.[30] Lampland, the land given by parishioners for the upkeep of the candles in the church, is also noted, giving the names of James Salter, Henry Pope and John Dobson as tenants.[31]

In the years 1516–28, 1530–36, 1539–42 and from 1546 onwards many folios are missing. Despite this, the later folios reveal the impact of the Reformation on this church including the erasure of the pardon received from the Bishop of Rome, the removal of Thomas Becket's name from liturgical books, the payment to the carpenter for pulling down the rood loft, the destruction of the stone altar and the

---

[23] CWA, fol.22r.

[24] CWA, fol.1v.

[25] Money collected on the various pardon days ensured commemorative prayers for the parishioners; and it was believed that it also guaranteed a shorter stay in Purgatory. A pardon was synonymous with an indulgence, the remission of a penance imposed for sin committed. Mildenhall church had received a pardon from the Pope, who was also known as the Bishop of Rome.

[26] Swanson, *Indulgences*, p.97. Where the pardon benefited the parish as a whole, income should probably appear in the churchwardens' accounts as it does at St Edmund at Salisbury, Swaffham and Mildenhall. Swanson describes these three survivals as 'a poor harvest' and states that almost every church in England may have had a pardon annually on at least one day, pp.365–67. No parochial accounts have survived which show a pardon's full financial history.

[27] CWA, fol.24v.

[28] Swanson, *Indulgences*, p.415.

[29] CWA, fol.16r.

[30] CWA, fols 20r, 30r.

[31] CWA, fol.17r.

purchase of a communion table in its place. The sale of church plate is entered and the inventories reveal the extent of the wealth of this important church, not only in plate, but also in sumptuous hangings, vestments and books.

Parishioners feature throughout the collections and the churchwardens' accounts, and families can be traced from this archive to the recent past, the surname Childerston appearing in the 1440s and disappearing only in the 1920s. Names such as Mortlock, Rolf and Peachey are still frequently found in this part of the county, and a fuller account of Mildenhall's former inhabitants has been gained from the use of testamentary evidence in local wills.

The Churchwardens' Accounts fall into the following sections (original spellings of names have been retained):

CWA, fols 1r–1v, 1504 – 15 November 1505
Churchreeves: John Heynes, Thomas M[*damaged*], Thomas Mey and Thomas B[*damaged*]. The churchwardens' names appear at the top of the first folio, followed by the accounts which record income from 1504 to 15 November 1505.
Receipts only.

CWA, fol. 2r
Undated, deleted and probably misplaced.

CWA, fols 2v–4r, 15 November 1505 – 1506
Wardens elected: Symonde Eton, Thomas Gesye, William Ballis and John Dey.
Receipts, payments and debtors.

CWA, fols 4v–6v, 1507–1509
Wardens: John Gardener, Wylliam Gesyn, Robert Page and John Place.
Receipts and payments.

CWA, fols 7r–9r, 8 October 1509 – 1510
Wardens: Thomas Hopper, Edward Webbe, Thomas Gardnyr, Rychard Holme.
Receipts and payments.

CWA, fols 9v–12r, 1513–1514
Wardens: John Clement, Wylliam Costyng, Roberd Petche and John Alen.
Receipts and payments.

CWA, fols 12v–13v, 1515–1516
Wardens: William Pachet, Nicholas Willes, Thomas Rolff and John Bradley.
Receipts and payments.

CWA, fols 14r–16v, 1516–1517
Wardens elected: Humfrey Duffyld, William Langham, George Place and John Dockyng.
Receipts and payments.

CWA, fols 17r–20v, Easter quarter 1528 – 1530
Wardens elected: Nicholas Palton, Thomas Cotes, Thomas Wederes and John Peche.
Receipts and payments.

CWA, fols 21r–23v, 31 May 1536 – May Day 1538
No wardens named.
Payments.

CWA, fols 24r–24v, May 1538 – 1539
Wardens elected: Pawle Duffeld, John Lane, Thomas Skott and Robert Peche, the yonger.
Payments.

CWA, fols 30r–32v, 1540–1541
No wardens named.
Receipts and payments.

CWA, fols 25r–26r, 1542
No wardens named.
Payments.

CWA, fol.26v, 2 November 1542
Wardens elected: Thomas Venall, John Gerold, Richard Clyff for West Row and Thomas Dockyng for Beck.
Receipts and payments.

CWA, fols 27r–29v, 1 November 1543
Wardens in post: John Jerold, Thomas Fenall, Thomas Dockyng and Rychard Clyfte.
Receipts and payments.

CWA, fols 33r–34r, 6 December 1546 – 1547
Wardens elected: Thomas Quasshe, Wylliam Clerke, Henry Morby and Thomas Jacobs.
Receipts and payments.

CWA, fol.34v, 1547
Receipts.

CWA, fols 35r–35v, 12 August 1548
Receipts and payments.

CWA, fols 36r–36v, 6 August 1548
Payments.

CWA, fol.37r, 1547
Linen inventory.

CWA, fol.37v, 1548
Receipts.

CWA, fols 38r–39r, 6 August 1548 – 15 August 1549
Wardens elected: Thomas Potter, Edmund Wryght, John Froste and William Pechey.
Payments.

CWA, fol.39v, 1 October 1551
Wardens resign: names unknown.
Payments.

CWA, fol.40r, 12 October 1550
Inventory.

CWA, fols 40v–41v, 13 October 1550 – 15 November 1551
Wardens elected: Robert Thurston, George Bassett, Humfrey Currey and William
Chylderston.
Receipts and payments.

CWA, fol.42r, 1 November 1551
Wardens resign: George Bassett, Robert Thurston, Humfrey Currey and William
Chylderston.
Receipts and payments.

CWA, fols 42v – 45r, 1552 – 1 November 1553
Wardens resign: Thomas Cottes, John Layne, John Shene and Symon Clarke.
Receipts and payments.

CWA, fol.45v, 6 November 1553
Wardens elected: Stephen Cook, Mylles Hull, John Sparhawke, Peter Petchey.
No accounts.

CWA, fol.46r, undated
Survey of lands held by the alderman and brothers of the gild of St Thomas.

CWA, fol.46v, c.1516–1519[32]
Land bequeathed to the lamp hanging at the high altar.[33]

CWA, fol.47r
Two sums of money: £ 6 19s. 9d.
                    £17 10s. 9d.

CWA, fol.47v, c.1506–1507
Receipts.

CWA, fol.48r, 1550
Obligations delivered in the fourth year of King Edward VI, 1550.

---

[32] This document, written in Latin, contains a reference to the Lord of York, a title borne by Henry
Tudor, later Henry VIII, from the death of his brother, Arthur, in 1502 until Henry succeeded to the
throne on the death of his father, Henry VII, in 1509. The land mentioned in the document must have
been held by Henry before he became king.

[33] This document, written in Latin, records various pieces of land given towards lighting the lamp
which hung above the high altar. Land such as this was usually called Lampland. Two copies of this
document, written in English but in two different hands, can be found in a leather-bound book from
the Bunbury papers (SRO, E18/400/1:3 at p.79 (first version of a rental of 1500–01), or p.69 (second
version of the same)). In comparing the three copies there is little difference between them except
that those in the Bunbury papers refer to 'my lady of York' rather than 'my lord of York'.

CWA, fol.48v
Payments, a partial copy of CWA, fol. 43r.

CWA, fol.49r
Inventory of pre-Reformation church goods.

CWA, fols 49v–50v
Inventory *c.*1508.

CWA, fol.51r, *c.*1549–1550
Undated fragment of receipts for sale of church plate.

CWA, fol.51v
A damaged pre-Reformation inventory similar to CWA, fol.49v.

EDITORIAL CONVENTIONS
AND
WEIGHTS, MEASURES AND MONEY

The Collections

With the exception of eight insertions in English at the top of fol.8r, the collections are written in Latin but, in the present edition, the entire corpus has been translated into English. The collections record the money gathered weekly on a Sunday from the High Town and from the outlying settlements. They run intermittently from 20 March 1446 to 22 September 1454, but can be divided into three sections which date from 1446–1449, 1449–1452 and 1452–1454.

The Churchwardens' Accounts

These are written in English and the original spelling has been preserved. Where Latin occurs it has been translated into English. The accounts run intermittently. They begin during the nineteenth year of Henry VII's reign which ran from 22 August 1503 to 21 August 1504, and the first entry is made at Candlemas, 2 February 1504. The names of the churchwardens appear at the top of that document. It appears that many folios were never dated, or numbered; nor were they sewn together. Consequently, several folios were lost and of those that survive some have been renumbered later and others replaced in the wrong position. In this edition some folios without original numbering have been re-sited in what seems to have been their most likely place.

The following symbols have been used during editing:

\ / for insertions
< > for deletions
[*blank*] for words that have been omitted
[*illeg.*] for illegible letters, words or phrases
[?] before a word in the text to show that its meaning is doubtful
[ ] editorial insertions are in italics in square brackets.

fol. *folio*
r recto – of a folio
v verso – of a folio

Weights, Measures and Money

Weight
> 1 pound (lb) was equal to 16 ounces (oz) or 0.45kg.
> 14 pounds was equal to 1 stone.
> 1 hundredweight (cwt) was equal to 112 pounds or approximately 50.8kg.

Liquid measure
> 1 gallon (gal) contained 8 pints (pt), approximately 4.55 litres.
> 1 quart (qt) contained 2 pints, or approximately 1.14 litres.

Corn measure
> 1 quarter (qtr) contained 8 bushels (bush.), approximately 217kg.
> 1 bushel contained 4 pecks, approximately 27kg.
> 1 coomb contained 4 bushels.

Length
> 1 foot (ft) measured 12 inches (in.), equal to 30cm.
> 1 yard (yd) measured 3 feet, or 0.9m.
> 1 perch was equal to 5½ yards.

Land area
> 1 acre contained 4 roods, approximately 0.4 hectares.

Money
> 1 pound (£) was equal to 20 shillings (s.) or 240 pennies (d.).
> 1 shilling was equal to 12 pennies (d.) or 5p today.
> 1 mark was equal to 13s. 4d., but it was used for accounting purposes and was not a coin. It would be worth approximately 67p today. Half a mark was therefore 6s. 8d.

The inconsistent survival of many of the Mildenhall churchwardens' accounts makes it difficult and unsatisfactory to attempt to give a final sum at the pages' end. Often more money is spent than has been collected and vice-versa.

THE COLLECTIONS
1446–1454

Suffolk Record Office, Bury St Edmunds
EL 110/5/1

[SROB, EL 110/5/1, *fol.1r*]   *[1446]*

		£	s.	d.
[*20 March*]				
Third [*damaged*] of Lent [*Quadragesima*][1] next after				
the reckoning,[2] from the town[3]			2	9
[*damaged*] from Westrowe[4]			1	0
[*damaged*] from Halywelle[5]			1	2
Item from Bek[6]	<5d.>			9
Item from William Chapman[7]			3	4
	Sum		9	0
[*27 March*]				
Fourth Sunday of Lent, from the town			2	1
[*damaged*] Westrowe				9
[*damaged*] from Halywell				6
[*damaged*] from Bek				4
[*damaged*] from William Chapman			3	4
	Sum		7	0
[*3 April*]				
Sunday in the Passion of the Lord, from the town			2	6
Item from Westrowe			1	1
Item from Bek				8
Item from Halywelle				10
Item from William Chapman			3	4
	Sum		8	5
[*10 April*]				
Palm Sunday, from the town			1	10
Item from Westrowe			1	0
Item from Bek				4
Item from Halywelle				8
Item from William Chapman			3	4
Item from Thomas Ryngstede,[8] clerk, by the hand of				
Richard Machoun, chaplain		1	0	0
	Sum	1	7	2
	Sum of [*this*] side	2	11	7

---

[1]   The top left-hand corner of the first folio is torn, but the absent words, being part of the regular formula used throughout these accounts, are predictable.

[2]   The reckoning was the presentation of the accounts to the parish by the retiring churchwardens, followed by the acceptance of the accounts by the parishioners, who then elected new churchwardens for the next term of office.

[3]   In these accounts, Mildenhall is referred to as the 'town', sometimes even as the High Town, as today on the modern sign on the northern entrance to the town.

[4]   This hamlet is now called West Row.

[5]   This is Holywell Row which lies north of the High Town. The spelling of this hamlet varies throughout the manuscript.

[6]   This is now known as Beck Row.

[7]   See Notes on People, p.200.

[8]   Thomas Ryngstede, perpetual vicar of Mildenhall from 1423 to 1453; see A.B. Emden, *Biographical Register of the University of Cambridge to 1500* (1963), pp.499–500.

[fol.1v]   **[1446]**

		£	s.	d.
[24 April]				
Low Sunday [Dominica in albis], from the town	<3s.>		2	6
Item from Westrowe			1	0
Item from Bek <with Cakestrete>[9]				8
Item from Halywelle			1	2
Item from William Chapman			3	4
Item in the sale of straw [stramine vendicione]				
to Thomas Playforde[10]				8
	Sum		9	4
[1 May]				
Second Sunday [after Easter], from the town			1	8
Item from Westrowe			1	0
Item from Bek with Cakestrete				5
Item from Halywelle nothing <illeg.>		–	–	–
Item from William Chapman			3	4
	Sum		6	5
[8 May]				
Third Sunday, from the town			2	10
Item from Westrowe			1	0
Item from Bek with Cakestrete				5
Item from Halywell				9
Item from William Chapman			3	4
	Sum		8	4
[15 May]				
Fourth Sunday, from the town			2	1
Item from Westrowe				11
Item from Bek with Cakestrete				7
Item from Halywell				10
Item from William Chapman			3	4
Item from Ryngestede, clerk		1	0	0
Item from a churchale [potacione] at Halywell		1	11	4
	Sum	2	19	1
	<Sum	2	19	1>
	Sum of [this] side	4	3	2

[fol.2r]   **[1446]**

		£	s.	d.
[22 May]				
Fifth Sunday, from the town			1	5
Item from Westrowe			1	0
Item from Bek with Cakestrete			1	0
<Item from Westrowe>		–	–	–
Item from William Chapman			3	4
Item from Halywelle				10
	Sum		7	5

---

[9]   Cake Street is still known by this name and is an extension of Beck Row.
[10] Member of an important fifteenth-century local family. See Notes on People, p.207.

		£	s.	d.
[29 May]				
Sunday within the octave of the Ascension of the Lord, from the town[11]			1	11
Item from Westrowe				11
Item from Bek with Cakestrete				5
Item from Halywelle			1	0
Item from William Chapman			3	4
Item from a churchale of the young men and women[12]		1	15	0
Item from timber sold to the vicar			1	8
Item from William Thomson, tailor, for the soul of John Speed[13]			13	4
	Sum	2	17	7
[12 June]				
Sunday in the feast of the Holy Trinity, in the 24th year of the reign of King Henry VI [1446], from the town			2	4
Item from Westrowe			1	1
Item from Bek with Cakestrete <8d.>				7
Item from Halywelle			1	0
Item from William Chapman			3	4
	Sum		8	4
[19 June]				
First Sunday after the feast of the Holy Trinity, from the town <1s. 9d.>			2	1
Item from Westrowe				11
Item from Bek with Cakestrete Nothing here because nothing collected				
Item from Halywelle				8
Item from William Chapman			3	4
	Sum		7	0
	Sum of [this] side	4	0	4

[fol.2v]   **[1446]**

		£	s.	d.
[26 June]				
Second Sunday, from the town			1	10
Item from Westrowe			1	0
Item from Bek				6
Item from Halywelle				9
	Sum		4	1
[3 July]				
Third Sunday, after Trinity			1	11
Item from Westrowe				10

---

11 Originally the octave was the eighth day after a feast, and so it always fell on the same day of the week as the feast itself. Later the term was applied to the eight days following a feast.

12 In several churchwardens' accounts references occur to the fundraising of the young men and women, or wives, gathering money for specific church funds; see Lewis, *Walberswick*, pp.249, 256.

13 John Speed's will (see Appendix 2:2) of 1438 did not specify a sum of money for his quetheword, and the payment shown above may have been an extra-testamentary arrangement made between Speed and William Thomson. Three further payments of 6s. 8d. were received for his soul on Coll. fols 4r, 18r and 20v, paid by Thomson and John Dobyn.

	£	s.	d.
Item from Bek with Cakestrete			8
Item from Halywelle			9
Sum		4	2
[*10 July*]			
Fourth Sunday, after Trinity, from the town		1	9
Item from Westrowe			11
Item from Halywell			9
Item from Bek			8
Sum		4	1
[*17 July*]			
Fifth Sunday, from the town		2	1
Item from Cakestrete			5
Item from Halywell			9
Sum		3	3
[*24 July*]			
Sixth Sunday, from the town		2	1
Item from Westrowe			11
Item from Halywell			8
Item from Bek			9
Sum		4	5
[*31 July*]			
Seventh Sunday, from the town		1	1
Item from Westrowe			11
Item from Bek with Cakestrete			6
Item from Halywell			10
Sum		3	4
Sum of [*this*] side	1	3	5

[*There are ten Sundays missing between fols 2v and 3r.*]

[*fol.3r*]   **[*1446*]**

[*2 October*][14]			
Sixteenth Sunday [*after Trinity*], from the town		1	0
Item from Westrowe			4
Item from Bek			3
Item from [*Ha*]lywell			6
Sum		2	1
[*16 October*]			
Eighteenth Sunday, from the town			5
Item from Westrowe			6
Item from Bek			2
Item from Halywell			3
Sum		1	4

---

[14] The collection raised this Sunday was more than usual, but there is no entry for the following Sunday.

5

		£	s.	d.
[*23 October*]				
Nineteenth Sunday, from the town				5
Item from Westrowe				1
Item from Bek				2
Item from Halywell				4
	Sum		1	0
[*20 November*][15]				
Twenty-third Sunday, from the town				4
Item from Westrowe				2
Item from Bek				3
Item from Halywell				3
	Sum		1	0
[*27 November*]				
First Sunday in the Advent of the Lord, from the town <*illeg.*> nothing collected				
	Sum			6
[*4 December*]				
Second Sunday in the Advent of the Lord, from the town			1	1
Item from Westrowe				6
Item from Bek				2
Item from Halywell				8

[*fol.3v*]   **[1446]**

		£	s.	d.
[*11 December*][16]				
Third Sunday in the Advent of the Lord, from the town				11
Item from Westrowe				3
Item from Bek				4
Item from Halywell				5
	Sum		1	11
[*8 January*][17]				**[1447]**
First Sunday after the octave of the Epiphany, from the town				8
Item from Westrowe				2
Item from Bek				2
Item from Halywell				4
	Sum		1	4
[*15 January*]				
Second Sunday, from the town				7
Item from Westrowe				2
Item from Bek				2
Item from Halywell				4
	Sum		1	3
[*22 January*]				
Third Sunday, from the town				8
Item from Westrowe				2

---

15   This is the first collection entered for four weeks.
16   This was the final collection for 1446.
17   The following entries are the first four for 1447 after which none are recorded until 30 July 1447.

	£	s.	d.
Item from Bek			2
Item from Halywell			4
Sum		1	4
[29 January]			
Fourth Sunday, from the town			10
Item from Westrowe			4
Item from Bek			4
Item from Halywell			5½
Sum		1	10½

[fol.4r]   **[1447]**

	£	s.	d.
[30 July][18]			
Eighth Sunday, from the town		1	3
Item from Westrowe			8
Item from Bek and Cakestrete			6
Item from Halywell			11
Item from the lady Isabell Galyon for the repairs of the bells[19]		1	0
Sum		4	4
[22 October]			
Twentieth Sunday, for the soul of the Reverend John Massage of Thakstede		5	0
Item for the soul of Henry Morle[20]			5
Item from a donation from the lady Isabell Galyon			6
Item from a donation from Robert Hall			2
Sum		6	1
[12 November]			
Twenty-third Sunday, from William Thomson, tailor, for the soul of John Speed		6	8
Sum		6	8
[4 June]			
Sunday in the feast of the Holy Trinity in the 25th year of the reign of King Henry VI, from a churchale in the town	1	4	0
Sum	1	4	0
[11 June]			
First Sunday after the feast of the Holy Trinity, from a churchale from the Westrowe	1	0	0
Sum	1	0	0

---

[18] This folio is unusual in that only the first four lines record collections and the following entries are for donations or churchales. In other words, the folio is a precursor to later churchwardens' accounts. No further collections are entered until 4 May 1449.

[19] Dame Isabel was the widow of William Gallion, esquire, of Mildenhall. She made several generous donations to the new bells in Mildenhall's tower. She died in 1472 and was buried in St Mary's chapel in Bailey End, Thetford, of which she had been a patron: P. Northeast, ed., *Wills of the Archdeaconry of Sudbury, 1439–1461*, SRS 44, p.188 n.13; *CPR 1441–46*, pp.135, 178; Dymond, *Thetford Priory*, I, p.28.

[20] Only the probate remains of Morle's [Morley's] will, 24 October 1443 (SROB, IC 500/2/9/40).

		£	s.	d.
[*9 July*]				
Fifth Sunday after the feast of the Holy Trinity, from a				
churchale from the Bek with Cakestrete		1	0	4
	Sum	1	0	4
[*12 November*]				
Twenty-third Sunday [*illeg.*], received from Thomas				
Ryngstede, clerk				8
	Sum			8
	Sum of [*this*] side	4	2	1

[*fol.4v*]²¹   **[*1447*]**

			s.	d.
[*10 December*]				
Second Sunday in the Advent of the Lord, for the soul of				
Nicholas Mareyner			2	0
	Sum		2	0

[*3 March*]   **[*1448*]**

			s.	d.
Fourth Sunday in Lent in the 26th year of the reign of King				
Henry VI in one old [?] processional sold to				
Richard Constable.²²			3	4
Item in [?]grass that is thatch sold to the wife of John				
Barker²³			1	2
	Sum		4	6
14 April]				
<Third Sunday after Easter period paid Wrytle, the				
carpenter, for great works> [*illeg.*]				
[*21 April*]				
Sunday fourth after Easter for the soul of John Woderys			4	0
Sum			4	0
Item from <Thomas Tyd> William Thomson by the hands				
of Thomas Tyd paid to John Bryan, chaplain			6	8
	Sum of [*this*] side		17	2

[*fol.5r*]   **[*1449*]**

Memorandum because [*deleted*] the churchwardens
    began the collection in the church on the third
    Sunday after the festival of Easter in the 27th year of

---

²¹ Entries on this folio refer to income from items sold or from commemorative payments. The lay-out of the folio is quite different from those previously recording collections, the entries here spreading the width of the page rather than being limited to neat blocks on the left-hand side.

²² This entry in the manuscript is abbreviated and the most likely translation is 'processional'.

²³ Although this word reads as 'glass', the correct word must be 'grass', referring to thatch which was probably of inferior quality.

the reign of King Henry VI after the conquest of England.

[4 May][24]		£	s.	d.
From the town			1	8
From Westrowe				8
Item from Bek with Cakestrete				5
Item from Halywelle				7
	Sum		3	4
[11 May]				
Fourth Sunday, from the town			1	8
Item from Westrowe				10
Item from Halywell				4
Item from Bek				7
	Sum		3	5
[18 May]				
Fifth Sunday, from the town			1	8
<Sunday> from Halywell				10
Item from Bek and Cakestrete				7
Item from Westrowe			1	0
	Sum		4	1
[25 May]				
Sixth Sunday, from the town			2	4
Item from Westrowe	[illeg.]			11
Item from Beke				7
Item from Halywell				8
	Sum		4	6
	Sum of [this] side		15	4

[fol.5v]   **[1449]**

[1 June]		£	s.	d.
Sunday in the feast of the Pentecost, from the town			1	10
Item from Bek				4
Item from Westrowe			1	0
Item from Halywelle				5
	Sum		3	7
[8 June]				
Sunday in the feast of the Holy Trinity, by a book sold to Richard Constabele[25]			3	4
Item in a gift from <illeg.> the same day				2
	Sum		3	6

---

[24] The collections continue after a hiatus, either because sufficient money had been gathered already or, more probably, because several folios are missing.

[25] Constabele (Constable) had already been sold the old processionary on Coll. fol.4v.

9

		£	s.	d.
[*15 June*]				
Sunday after the feast of the Holy Trinity, from the churchale made in the Bek with Cakestrete and Wildestrete[26]		1	3	0
	Sum	1	3	0
[*22 June*]				
Second Sunday, from the town			2	2
Item from Bek				6
Item from Halywell				9
Item from Westrowe	<2s. 10d.>			10
	Sum		4	3
[*29 June*]				
Third Sunday, from the town	<1s. 10d.>		2	0
Item from Westrowe				8
Item from Bek with Cakestrete				7
Item from Halywell				7
	Sum		3	10
[*6 July*]				
Fourth Sunday, from the town			1	9
Item from Westrowe			1	2
Item from Bek				8
Item from Halywell				9
	Sum		4	4
	Sum of [*this*] side	2	2	6

[*fol.6r*]   **[*1449*]**

		£	s.	d.
[*13 July*]				
Fifth Sunday [*after Trinity*], from the town			2	6
Item from Westrowe			0	9
Item from Bek			0	7
Item from Halywell			0	7
	Sum		4	5
[*20 July*]				
Sixth Sunday, from the town			1	10
Item from Westrowe			0	11
Item from Bek				nil
Item from Halywell			0	6
	Sum		3	7
[*27 July*]				
Seventh Sunday, from the town			1	10
Item from Westrowe			1	3
Item from Bek			0	6
Item from Halywell			0	6
	Sum		3	11

---

26 Wilde Street was a hamlet adjacent to Beck Row.

		£	s.	d.
[*3 August*]				
Eighth Sunday, from the town			1	10
Item from Westrowe			0	5
Item from Bek			0	8
Item from Halywell			0	8
	Sum		3	5
	Sum of [*this*] side		15	4

[*fol.6v*]   **[*1449*]**

		£	s.	d.
[*10 August*]				
Ninth Sunday [*after Trinity*], from the town			2	1
Item from Westrowe				8
Item from Bek				4
Item from Halywell				5
	Sum		3	6
[*17 August*]				
Tenth Sunday, from the town			1	3
Item from the gift of Agnes Robb of Fordham			11	0
	Sum		12	3
[*24 August*]				
Eleventh Sunday, from the town			1	0
Item from Westrowe				5
Item from Bek				7
Item from Halywell				3
	Sum		2	3
[*31 August*]				
Twelfth Sunday, from the town			1	11
Item from Westrowe				7
Item from Bek				7
Item from Halywell				9
	Sum		3	10
[*7 September*]				
Thirteenth Sunday, from the town			1	4
Item from Westrowe				7
Item from Halywell	<2d.>			5
Item from Bek				7
	Sum		3	1
	Sum of [*this*] side	1	4	11

[*fol.7r*]   **[*1449*]**

		£	s.	d.
[*14 September*]				
Fourteenth Sunday [*after Trinity*], from the town			1	2
Item from Westrowe			0	7
Item from Bek			0	6
Item from Halywell			0	5
	Sum		2	8

	£	s.	d.
[*21 September*]			
Fifteenth Sunday, from the town		1	8
Item from Westrowe		0	7
Item from Bek		0	6
Item from Halywell		0	7
Sum		3	4
[*28 September*]			
Sixteenth Sunday, from the town		1	9
Item from Westrowe		0	7
Item from Bek		0	6
Item from Halywell		0	3
Sum		3	1
[*5 October*]			
Seventeenth Sunday, from the town		1	5
Item from Halywell		0	7
Item from Westrowe		0	8
Item from Bek		0	5
Sum		3	1
Sum of [*this*] side		12	2

[*fol. 7v*][27]   **[1449]**

	£	s.	d.
[*12 October*]			
Eighteenth Sunday [*after Trinity*]		1	9
Item from Westrowe			11
Item from Bek			8
Item from Halywell			7
Sum <4d.>		3	11
[*19 October*]			
Nineteenth Sunday, from the town		1	3
Item from Westrowe			6
Item from Bek			6
Item from Halywell			3
Sum		2	6
[*26 October*]			
Twentieth Sunday, from the town		1	5
Item from Westrowe <7s.>			7
Item from Bek			6
Item from Halywell			11
Sum		3	5
[*2 November*]			
Twenty-first Sunday, from the town		1	2
Item from Westrowe			7
Item from Bek			5
Item from Halywell			5
Sum		2	7

---

27 Folio 7v is divided longitudinally by a line separating the collections on the left of the page from five dissimilar entries on the right. The latter are comprised of money totalling £1 1s. 8d. collected as donations, as payments for debts or for the indulgences, otherwise known as pardons, on St Philip and St James's Day (1 May) and the feast of Corpus Christi (12 June).

		£	s.	d.
[*9 November*]				
Twenty-second Sunday, from the town			1	0
Item from Westrowe				4
Item from Bek				2
Item from Halywell		—	—	—
	Sum	6	0	0
Firstly for the indulgence on Philip's and James's day			3	4
Item for the same on Corpus Christi day			4	6
Item from Dom Robert Meyer			5	0
Item received from Dom John Dobyn			10	0
Item received from George Playforde[28]			6	8
	Total sum received	23	3	1

[*fol.8r*]
[*English*]   **[*1449*]**

Firstly for makyng [*ed*] of the secunde belle[29]   7 nobylls

	s.	d.
Item for 2 waynskotts bowte of Robert Meyer[30]	2	0
Item for the standerde of the wele		7
Item for nayle bowte		5½
Item for makyng of the qwele	4	0
Item for the belle roppe	1	0
Item for settyng of the stokke	1	0
Item payed to Thomas Frende	6	8

[*Latin*]
The total sum received from John Gregory, John Staloun,[31]
    John Playforde[32] and Robert Sygo,[33] churchwardens of
    Mildenhall church, from the feast of St David, viz the 4th of
    March in the year of Our Lord 1446 and the 24th year of the
    reign of King Henry VI after the conquest of England, up to
    the feast of St. Theodore, the martyr, viz the 9th day of the
    month of November in the year of Our Lord 1449 in the 28th
    year of the reign of the King Henry VI after the conquest of
    England.[34]

	£	s.	d.
Sum total received	23	3	1

---

28 See Notes on People for John Dobyn and George Playforde, pp.202, 207.
29 Seven nobles were equal to three and a half marks or £2 6s. 8d.
30 This entry and the seven subsequent entries are written in English and refer to the general expenditure when setting up the bell.
31 John Staloun the younger died in 1452. A translation of his will appears in Appendix 2:8. The will of his brother, John Stalham the elder, proved in 1461, refers to the younger brother as John Stalham. See Notes on People, p.210.
32 John Playford of Beck Row wrote his will in 1468 (SROB, IC 500/2/10/404); but it reveals that there were three other Playfords called John at the time, a son, a brother and the son of Thomas Playford.
33 The Sygo (Sygoo, Sigo) family were similar to the Playfords in that the will of an earlier Robert Sygoo refers to a second Robert Sygo, the son of William, perhaps the same man as the third Robert Sygo whom he makes co-executor with his wife, Matilda (SROB, IC 500/2/9/11).
34 Here the four retiring churchwardens present the collection accounts to the parish. There are no further disbursements. The three incoming churchwardens are named on the following folio.

[fol.9r]   **[1449]**

John Bakhot John Chylderston[35]   **£   s.   d.**

[Latin]
Memorandum that William Sutton, glover,[36] John Paynet,
  smith, and John Bryan, chaplain, were elected churchwardens
  by Mildenhall town the 7th day of December in the year of our
  Lord 1449 and in the 28th year of the reign of King Henry VI,
  after the conquest of England.[37]

[illeg.]
The same received from [deleted] 2s. 4d.[38] received from
  the predecessors

[7 December]
Second Sunday in the Advent of the Lord, from the town   1   11
Item from Westrowe   3
Item from Halywell   3
Item from Bek nil this [week] because nothing collected   –   –
                                                            Sum   2   5
[21 December]
Fourth Sunday in the Advent of the Lord, from the town   1   1
Item from Westrowe   5
                                                            Sum   1   6
[28 December]
First Sunday after the feast of the Nativity of the Lord,
  from the town   1   0
Item from Westrowe   6
Item from Halywell   3
Item from Bek   3
                                                            Sum   2   1

[4 January]   **[1450]**
Second Sunday, from the town   10
Item from Westrowe   4
Item from Bek   2
Item from Halywell   nil
                                                            Sum   1   4

                                    Sum of [this] side   19   8

---

35 John Bakhot was from a family of wealthy Mildenhall mercers and John Chylderston was from the
   very extensive Chylderston (sometimes Chiston) family. It is not clear why their names appear at the
   head of this folio.
36 William Sutton was a prosperous glover living in Mildenhall. His brother was Richard Sutton.
   William's will of 1474 reveals a web of prestigious social acquaintances and contacts (SROB, IC
   500/2/10/523).
37 For details of Bryan and Paynet see Notes on People, pp.200, 206.
38 This was the amount handed over to the incoming churchwardens.

[fol. 9v]   **[1450]**

[18 January]
Third Sunday, from the town   1   4
Item from Westrowe   6
Item from Bek   5
Item from Halywelle   5
                                                          Sum   2   8
[25 January]
Fourth Sunday, from the town[39]   1   2
Item from Westrowe   9
Item from Bek   6
Item from Haly]well   6
                                                          Sum   2   11
[1 February]
[Septuagesima] Sunday, from the town   10
Item from Bek   5
Item from Halywell   4
Item from Westrowe   5
                                                          Sum   2   0
[8 February]
[Sexagesima] Sunday, from the town   9
Item from Bek   5
Item from Westrowe   7
Item from Halywell   7
                                                          Sum   2   4
[15 February]
[Quinquagesima] Sunday, from the town   1   6
Item from Westrowe   5
Item from Halywell   7
Item from Bek   4
                                                          Sum   2   10

                                                          Sum   12   9

[fol. 10r]   **[1450]**

[22 February]
First Sunday 40 [in Lent], from the town   11
Item from Westrowe   5
Item from Bek   5
Item from Halywell   3
                                                          Sum   2   0

---

[39] The year 1450 had no fourth Sunday after Epiphany. Because there is no indication of whether the second, third and fourth Sundays entered here are those 'after the Nativity of the Lord' or those 'after Epiphany' it is difficult to attribute accurate dates. Only when Septuagesima is reached is it possible to give the correct date of 1 February. The collections ceased on Passion Sunday (see Memorandum on Coll. fol.10v), and it is impossible to say how the books were balanced.

		£	s.	d.
[1 March]				
Second Sunday 40, from the town			1	0
Item from Bek				4
Item from Westrowe				6
Item from Halywell				4
	Sum		2	2
[8 March]				
Third Sunday 40, from the town				6
Item from Westrowe				7
Item from Bek				5
Item from Halywell				6
	Sum		2	0
[15 March]				
Third [sic] Sunday 40, from the town				7
Item from Westrowe				8
Item from Bek				4
Item from Halywell				2
	Sum		1	9
[22 March]				
Sunday in the Passion of the Lord, from the town				7
Item from Westrowe				4
Item from Bek				4
Item from Halywell				4
	Sum		1	7
	Sum		9	6

[fol.10v]   **[1450]**

	£	s.	d.
[7 June]			
First Sunday after the feast of the Holy Trinity, for the soul of Henry Mors		6	8
[28 June]			
Fourth Sunday from a churchale, for the town	1	2	0
[5 July]			
Fifth Sunday for the soul of Isabell Skynner and her benefactors		6	8
[12 July]			
Sixth Sunday for one cloth of twylly given by Margaret Helgey and in money		1	0
Sum	1	16	4

16

		£	s.	d.
[*September 13*]				
Fifteenth Sunday, for the soul of John Frere by the hand of				
Alice, his widow [*relict*], granted to the bell tower[40]			6	8
Nothing by recompense in another place			–	–
And from John Fullere in the name of a debt to Isabel				
Galyon of pence granted to the bell tower			6	8
And [*sic*]	Sum		13	4

**Memorandum because on Passion Sunday the collection ceased
and was reinstated on the fourth Sunday after the feast of
Epiphany in the 29th year in the reign of King Henry VI
after the conquest.** [*1451*]

			s.	d.
[*31 January*]				
That day from the town			1	9
Item from Westrowe				8
Item from Bek with Cakestrete				6
Item from Halywelle				5
	Sum		3	4
[*7 February*]				
Fifth Sunday, from the town			2	1
Item from Westrowe				8
Item from Bek with Cakestrete				7
Item from Halywelle				6
	Sum		3	10
	Sum of [*this*] side		7	2

[fol.11r] [*1451*]

			s.	d.
[*21 February*]				
Sunday in 70 [*Septuagesima*], from the town			1	4
Item from Bek				5
Item from Halywelle				4
Item from Westrowe				11
	Sum		3	0
[*28 February*]				
Sunday in 60 [*Sexagesima*], from the town			1	3
Item from Westrowe				6
Item from Bek with Cakestrete				5
Item from Halywell				7
	Sum		2	9
[*7 March*]				
Sunday in 50 [*Quinquagesima*], from the town			1	10
Item from Westrowe				8

---

40 This donation is not mentioned in John Frere's will, but he left 40s. to the church fabric. Agnes, his
second wife, was to profit from the sale of property at Fornham St Martin, part of the proceeds of
which were to find a priest to sing for the souls of John and his first wife, Margaret.

17

	£	s.	d.
Item from Bek with Cakestrete			5
Item from Halywell			3
Sum		3	2
[14 March]			
First Sunday 40 [*in Lent*], from the town		1	2
Item from Westrowe			8
Item from Bek with Cakestrete			6
Item from Halywelle			4
Sum		2	8
Sum		11	8

[*fol.11v*]   **[*1451*]**

[21 March]	£	s.	d.
Second Sunday 40 [*in Lent*], from the town		1	2
Item from Westrowe			9
Item from Bek with Cakestrete			4
Item from Halywell			6
Sum <2s. 11d.>		2	9
[28 March]			
Third Sunday 40, from the town		1	7
Item from Westrowe			6
Item from Bek with Cakestrete			6
Sum		3	2
[4 April]			
Fourth Sunday 40, from the town		1	4
Item from Westrowe			7
Item from Bek with Cakestrete			6
Item from Halywell			4
Sum < 2s. 9d.>		2	8
[11 April]			
Sunday in the Passion of the Lord, from the town			11
Item from Westrowe			6
Item from Bek with Cakestrete			7
Item from Halywell			4
Sum		2	4
[18 April]			
Palm Sunday, from the town		1	7
Item from Westrowe			4
Item from Bek with Cakestrete			4
Item from Halywell			2
Sum		2	5
Sum		13	4

[fol.12r]   **[1451]**

	£	s.	d.
[2 May]			
Low Sunday [first Sunday after Easter], from the town		1	10
Item from Westrowe			6
Item from Bek with Cakestrete			6
Item from Halywell			3
Sum		3	1
[9 May]			
Second Sunday, from the town		1	2
Item from Westrowe			6
Item from Bek with Cakestrete			5
Item from Halywell			6
Sum		2	7
[16 May]			
Third Sunday, from the town		1	4
Item from Westrowe			10
Item from Bek with Cakestrete			6
Item from Halywell			5
Sum		3	1
[23 May]			
Fourth Sunday, from the town		1	3
Item from Westrowe			7
Item from Halywell			6
Item from Bek with Cakestrete			5
Sum		2	9
[30 May]			
Fifth Sunday Nil because nothing collected			
Sum		11	6

[fol.12v]   **[1451]**

	£	s.	d.
[6 June]			
Sixth Sunday [after Easter], from the town		1	2
Item from Westrowe			10
Item from Bek with Cakestrete			6
Item from Halywell			2
Sum		2	8
[20 June]			
Sunday on the feast of the Holy Trinity, from the town		1	6
Item from Westrowe			6
Item from Bek with Cakestrete			6
Item from Halywell			4
Sum <2s.11d.>		2	10
[27 June]			
First Sunday after the feast of the Holy Trinity, from the town		1	3
Item from Westrowe			8
Item from Bek with Cakestrete			5

		£	s.	d.
Item from Halywell				5
	Sum		2	9
[4 July]				
Second Sunday, from the town			1	6
Item from Westrowe				7
Item from Bek with Cakestrete				5
Item from Halywelle				6
	Sum		3	0
[11 July]				
Third Sunday on the feast of the Relics, from the town[41]			1	3
Item from Westrowe				9
Item from Bek with Cakestrete				6
Item from Halywell				5
Item from John Bryan, chaplain, for one stone				
called the Coyne for the cistern[42]				3
	Sum		3	2
[18 July]				
Fourth Sunday, from the town			1	1
Item from Westrowe				6
Item from Bek with Cakestrete				5
Item from Halywelle				3
	Sum		2	3
	Sum		16	8

[fol. 13r]   **[1451]**

		£	s.	d.
[25 July]				
Fifth Sunday, from the town			1	2
Item from Westrowe				7
Item from Bek with Cakestrete				7
Item from Halywell				5
	Sum		2	9
[1 August]				
Sixth Sunday, from the town				8
Item from Westrowe				7
Item from Bek with Cakestrete				8
Item from Halywelle				2
	Sum		2	0½
[8 August]				
Seventh Sunday, from the town			1	6
Item from Westrowe				6
Item from Bek with Cakestrete				5
<Item from Westrowe 6d>			—	—

---

[41] Relic Sunday was celebrated on the first Sunday after 7 July in dioceses where the Sarum rite was used, but other churches might celebrate on days of particular importance to them. At Mildenhall, Relic Sunday was celebrated in July: see Coll. fol.23v. Norwich, however, celebrated Relic Sunday on 16 September.

[42] Coyne should perhaps be translated as 'quoin' – but where was the cistern?

		£	s.	d.
Item from Halywelle				3
	Sum		2	8

[*15 August*]
Item from the town on the eighth Sunday, nothing from
   the others on account of the feast of St Mary,[43]
   nothing was collected therefore nothing   nil

[*22 August*]				
Ninth Sunday, from the town			1	1
Item from Westrowe				4
Item from Bek with Cakestrete				nil
Item from Halywell				3
	Sum		1	8
	Sum		9	1½

[*fol.13v*]   **[*1451*]**

[*29 August*]				
Tenth Sunday, from the town			1	0
Item from Westrowe				4
Item from Hallywelle				3
	Sum		1	8
[*5 September*]				
Eleventh Sunday, from the town			1	3
Item from Westrowe	<4d.>			5
Item from Bek with Cakestrete				3
Item from Halywell				1
	Sum		2	0
[*12 September*]				
Twelfth Sunday, from the town			1	1
Item from Westrowe				7
Item from Bek with Cakestrete				2
Item from Halywell				7
	Sum		2	5
[*19 September*]				
Thirteenth Sunday, from the town			1	4
Item from Westrowe				6
Item from Cakestrete				3
Item from Halywell				6
	Sum		2	7
[*26 September*]				
Fourteenth Sunday, from the town				10
Item from Westrow				9
Item from Bek				5
Item from Halywell				5
	Sum		2	5
	Sum		11	7

---

43 This refers to the Assumption of the Virgin Mary, celebrated on 15 August.

[fol.14r]   **[1451]**

	£	s.	d.
[3 October]			
Fifteenth Sunday, from the town		1	1
Item from Westrowe			7
Item from Bek with Cakestrete			3
Item from Halywell			3
Sum		2	2
[10 October]			
Sixteenth Sunday, from the town		1	1
Item from Westrowe			5
Item from Bek with Cakestrete			2
Item from Halywell			4
Sum <1s. 11d.>		2	0
[17 October]			
Seventeenth Sunday, from the town			11
Item from Westrowe			4
Item from Bek with Cakestrete			2
Item from Halywell			4
Sum		1	9
[24 October]			
Eighteenth Sunday, from the town			11
Item from Westrowe			9
Item from Halywell			4
Item from Bek with Cakestrete			2
Sum		2	2
[31 October]			
Nineteenth Sunday, from the town			11
Item from Westrowe			6
Item from Bek with Cakestrete			5
Item from Halywell			1
Sum		1	10
[7 November]			
Twentieth Sunday, from the town			10
Item from Westrowe			5
Item from Bek with Cakestrete			4
Item from Halywell			3
Sum		1	10
Sum	1	1	10

[fol.14v]   **[1451]**

	£	s.	d.
[14 November]			
Twenty-first Sunday, from the town		1	2
Item from Westrowe			4
Item from Bek with Cakestrete			3
Item from Halywell			2
Sum <1s. 9d.>		1	11

		£	s.	d.
[*21 November*]				
Twenty-second Sunday, from the town			1	0
Item from Westrowe				4
Item from Bek and Cakestrete				nil
Item from Halywell				1
	Sum		1	5
[*28 November*]				
First Sunday in the Advent of the Lord, from the town			1	1
Item from Westrowe				4
Item from Bek				4
Item from Halywelle				3
	Sum		2	0
[*5 December*]				
Second Sunday in the Advent of the Lord, from the town				11
Item from Westrowe				5
Item from Bek with Cakestrete				2
Item from Halywell				2
	Sum		1	10
[*12 December*]				
Third Sunday, from the town				11
Item from Westrowe				5
Item from Bek				5
Item from Halywell				5
	Sum		2	2
[*19 December*]				
Fourth Sunday, from the town				11
Item from Halywell				3
Item from Westrowe				5
Item from Bek with Cakestrete			0	4
	Sum		1	9
	Sum		10	11

[*fol.15r*]   **[*1451*]**

		£	s.	d.
[*26 December*]				
Sunday in the octave of St Stephen, from the town			2	0
Item from Westrowe				3
Item from Bek with Cakestrete	Nil because nothing collected			
Item from Halywell	Nil here because nothing collected			
	Sum		2	3

[*1452*]

		£	s.	d.
[*2 January*]				
Sunday within the octave of Epiphany, from the town				9
Item from Westrowe				5
Item from Bek with Cakestrete				nil
Item from Halywell				3
	Sum		1	5

		£	s.	d.
[9 January]				
First Sunday after the feast of Epiphany, from the town			1	3
Item from Westrowe				5
Item from Bek with Cakestrete				4
Item from Halywell				5
	Sum		2	5
[16 January]				
Second Sunday, from the town				11
Item from Halywell				4
Item from Bek				4
	Sum		1	7
[23 January]				
Third Sunday, from the town			1	0
Item from Westrowe				6
Item from Bek				3
Item from Halywell				2
	Sum		1	11
[6 February]				
[Septuagesima] Sunday, from the town				11
Item from Westrowe				4
Item from Cakestrete				2
Item from Halywell				2
	Sum		1	9
	Sum		10	2

[fol.15v] [1452]

		£	s.	d.
[13 February]				
[Sexagesima] Sunday, from the town				11
Item from Westrowe				5
Item from Bek				2
Item from Halywell				2
	Sum		1	8
[20 February]				
[Quinquagesima] Sunday, from the town			1	0
Item from Westre				2
Item from Bek				1
Item from Halywell				2
	Sum		1	5
[27 February]				
First Sunday 40 [Quadragesima], from the town				9
Item from Westrowe				3
Item from Bek				3
Item from Halywell				3
	Sum		1	6
[5 March]				
Second Sunday, from the town			1	0
Item from Westrowe				6
Item from Bek				5

		£	s.	d.
Item from Halywell				3
	Sum		2	2
[12 March]				
Third Sunday, from the town				9
Item from Westrowe				5
Item from Bek				2
Item from Halywell				3
	Sum		1	7
[19 March]				
Fourth Sunday, from the town			1	1
Item from Westrowe				4
Item from Bek				4
Item from Halywell				1
	Sum		1	10
	Sum		8	9

[fol.16r]   **[1452]**

		£	s.	d.
[26 March]				
Passion Sunday, from the town				9
Item from Westrowe				2
Item from Bek with Cakestrete				2
Item from Halywell				3
	Sum		1	4
[2 April]				
Palm Sunday, from the town				10
Item from Westrowe				4
Item from Bek				3
Item from Halywell				2
And for the soul of Isabelle Bryghtwell, daughter of Simon Chylderstone[44]			3	4
	Sum		4	11
[16 April]				
Low Sunday [first Sunday after Easter], from the town			1	0
Item from Westrowe				4
Item from Bek				2
Item from Halywell				4
	Sum		1	10
[30 April]				
Third Sunday, from the town			1	3
Item from Westrowe				3
Item from Bek				3
Item from Halywell Nothing because none [collected]				
	Sum		1	9

---

[44] Isabel Bryghtwelle was the step-daughter of Simon Chylderston. He died in 1454 (SROB, IC 500/2/9/230).

		£	s.	d.
[*7 May*]				
Fourth Sunday, from the town				9
Item from Westrowe				4
Item from Bek				2
Item from Halywell				1
	Sum		1	4
[*14 May*]				
Fifth Sunday, from the town			1	0
Item from Westrowe				4
Item from Bek				3
Item from Halywell				5
	Sum		2	0
			10	1

[*fol.16v*] [*1452*]

		£	s.	d.
[*21 May*]				
Sunday within the octave of the Ascension of the Lord, from the town				10
Item from Westrowe				5
Item from Bek				2
Item from <Westrowe> Halywelle				3
	Sum		1	8
The same week received from the town's churchale		1	13	4
[*28 May*]				
Sunday on the day of Pentecost [*Whit Sunday*], from the town			1	1
Item from Westrowe				5
Item from Bek with Cakestrete				3
Item from Halywelle				3
	Sum <*20d.*>		2	0
Sum of this side except 4d. [?]		1	17	0

Total sum received by John Bryan, chaplain, and John Paynet, wardens of the church of Mildenhall at the feast of St. Theodore, the martyr, viz the 9th day of November in the year of the Lord 1449 and in the 28th year of the reign of King Henry VI after the conquest of England up to the 29th day of the month of May in the 30th year of the reign of King Henry VI after the conquest of England and the year of the Lord <*Sum received*> 1452.[45]

	£	s.	d.
Sum total received	12	10	9½

---

[45] Only two of the wardens were present on 29 May 1452. William Sutton, the missing warden, did not die until 1473–74 (SROB, IC 500/2/10/523), and it is unusual that there should be no reference to his absence here.

	£	s.	d.
[*4 June*]			
Sunday in the feast of the Holy Trinity after the reckoning, from the town			10
Item from Westrowe			5
Item from Halywelle			5
Item from Bek with Cakestrete			6
Sum		2	2
[*11 June*]			
First Sunday after the feast of the Holy Trinity, from the town			10
Item from Westrowe			2
Item from Bek			1
Item from Halywell			4
Sum		1	5
[*18 June*]			
Second Sunday, for the soul of John Melmay, the servant of William Cotter			4
Item from the town			10
Item from Westrowe			3
Item from Bek			3
Item from Hallywelle			2
Sum		1	6
[*25 June*]			
Third Sunday, nothing on account of the churchale held at the Westrowe because nothing was collected, except the town's churchale	1	13	4
Sum	1	13	4
[*2 July*]			
Fourth Sunday, from a churchale held at the Westrowe	1	5	4
Sum	1	5	4
Item from the town			9
Item from Westrowe			3
Item from Bek			nil
Item from Halywell			2
Sum		1	2

	£	s.	d.
[*16 July*]			
Sixth Sunday, from the town			11
Item from Westrowe			3
Item from Bek			2
Item from Halywell			2
Item from churchale held in the Bek		18	2½
Sum <18d.>		19	2½
[*23 July*]			
Seventh Sunday, from the town			6
Item from Westrowe			6

	£	s.	d.
Item from Bek with Cakestrete			2
Item from Halywell			3
Item for the soul of Margaret Clars		2	0
Sum		3	5

[*30 July*]

	£	s.	d.
Eighth Sunday, from the town			8
Item from Westrowe			3
Item from Hallywelle			4
Item from Bek with Cakestrete			9
Item for the soul of Agnes Holme, former relict of Robert Federyk		1	8
Sum		3	8

[*6 August*]

	£	s.	d.
Ninth <*eighth*> Sunday no collection on account of the autumn [*harvest*], but for the soul of Margaret, daughter of Thomas Chylderstone[46]		3	4
Sum		3	4

[*13 August*]

	£	s.	d.
Tenth Sunday, for the soul of Isabell, daughter of John Wareyn[47]		1	0

[*27 August*]

	£	s.	d.
Twelfth Sunday, for the soul of William, son of Thomas Chylderstone		2	0

[*10 September*]

	£	s.	d.
Fourteenth Sunday, for the soul of John Chapman, lately of Cakestrete		6	8
Item for the soul of a certain person not named		3	4

[*17 September*]

	£	s.	d.
Fifteenth Sunday, for the soul of Margery Sygo[48]		3	0

[*24 September*]

	£	s.	d.
Sixteenth Sunday, from the town		1	0
Item from Westrowe			3
Item from Bek with Cakestrete			2
Item from Halywell			2
Sum		1	7

---

[46] Thomas Chylderston was a member of the well-known local family. This surname appears not only in the collections, but also in the sixteenth-century accounts, the family having several branches within the parish. Childerstones still farmed land at Holywell Row and Wilde Street in 1840: see White, *Suffolk 1844*, p.597.

[47] Wareyn died in 1461 (SROB, IC 500/2/9/300). He was survived by 3 sons, John the younger, who lived in Mildenhall, John the elder, who lived in Clare, and William, living in Ely. Isabell seems to have been his only daughter. Northeast remarks that 'sons in Clare and Ely show the family spreading away from the ancestral home'. See Northeast, *Wills of Sudbury, 1439–1461*, SRS 44, no.1471, p.510.

[48] Sygo was another well-known name in Mildenhall parish: see Coll. fol.8r above. Robert Sygo was churchwarden 1446–49.

[fol.18r]   **[1452]**

		£	s.	d.
[1 October]				
Seventeenth Sunday, from the town			1	4
Item from Westrowe				3
Item from Bek with Cakestrete				5
Item from Halywell				3
	Sum		2	3
[8 October]				
Eighteenth Sunday, from the town				9
Item from Westrowe				5
Item from Bek with Cakestrete				3
Item from Halywell				5
Item for the soul of John Speed by the hands of John Dobyn in the name of William Thomson, tailor, in part payment of the obligation[49]			6	8
Item the same day for the soul of Richard Sutton paid by William Sutton[50]			6	8
	Sum		15	2
[15 October]				
Nineteenth Sunday, from the town				9
Item from Westrowe				5
Item from Bek				3
Item from Halywell				2
Item from the last churchale of the town a further			1	4
	Sum <19d.>		2	11
[22 October]				
Twentieth <19> Sunday, from the town				8
Item from Westrowe				3
Item from Bek				4
Item from Halywelle				4
	Sum		1	7
[29 October]				
Twenty-first Sunday, from the town				9
Item from Westrowe				3
Item from Bek with Cakestrete				5
Item from Halywell				2
	Sum		1	7

[fol.18v]   **[1452]**

		s.	d.
[5 November]			
Twenty-second Sunday, from the town			10
Item from Westrowe			5
Item from Bek			1

---

49 See Notes on People, pp.202, 210 for Dobyn, Speed and Thomson.
50 Richard Sutton, a member of the household of Sir Thomas Tuddenham of Oxborough, was the brother of William Sutton, glover and churchwarden. See Northeast, *Wills of Sudbury, 1439–1461*, SRS 44, no.489, p.187 and Notes on People, p.210.

	£	s.	d.
Item from Halywell			4
Item for the souls of Thomas Goodale and Agnes, his wife		2	0
Sum		3	8
[*12 November*]			
Twenty-third Sunday, from the town			10
Item from Westrowe			5
Item from Halywell			4
Item from Bek			6
[*19 November*]			
Twenty-fourth Sunday, from the town		1	1
Item from Westrowe			2
Item from the Bek			2
Item from Halywell			3
Sum		1	8
[*26 November*]			
Twenty-fifth Sunday, from the town			11
Item from Westrowe			4
Item from Halywelle			4
Item from Bek			3
Sum		1	10
[*3 December*]			
First Sunday in the Advent of the Lord, from the town			10
Item from Westrowe			3
Item from Bek			4
Item from Halywell			2
Item in money collected for the carriage of lead from Brandon towards Bury[51]		3	6
Sum		5	1
[*10 December*]			
Second Sunday, from the town			8
Item from Bek with Cakestrete			3
Item from Westrowe			2
Item from Halywell			2
Sum		1	3

[*fol.19r*]   **[*1452*]**

[*17 December*]			
Third Sunday, from the town			7
Item from Westrowe			3
Item from Bek			3
Item from Halywell			2
Sum		1	3

---

51   This entry includes water-transport across the fen and overland carriage to Bury. Brandon, sometimes referred to as Brandon Ferry, was a crossing point of the Little Ouse before it entered the fen. It provided a direct water route to Lynn.

	£	s.	d.
[*24 December*]			
Sunday in the Vigil of the Nativity of the Lord in the 31st			
year of the reign of King Henry VI, from the town			9
Item from Westrowe			2
Item from Bek			2
Item from Halywell			4
[*7 January*]			[*1453*]
Sunday in the octave of the Epiphany, for the souls of			
Thomas Lestlathe, Isabel, his wife and Margery Taylor		3	4
Item from the town			8
Item from Westrowe			1
Item from Bek			3
Item from Halywell Nil because none collected			
Sum		4	4
[*14 January*]			
First Sunday after the octave of the Epiphany, from the town			6
Item from Westrowe			4
Item from Bek			2
Item from Halywell			2
Sum		1	2
[*28 January*]			
Sunday in 70 [*Septuagesima*] from part <*of the town*> of			
Halywelle churchale by the hands of John Canvas[52]			
(Cannas) and William Gylbyn	1	4	0
Item from the town			11
Item from Westrowe			3
Item from Bek with Cakestrete			3
Item from Halywell nil on account of the churchale			0
Sum	1	5	5
[*4 February*]			
Sunday in 60 [*Sexagesima*], from the town			10
Item from Westrowe			4
Item from Bek			3
Item from Halywell nothing here because no [*collection*] Sum		1	5

[*fol.19v*] [*1453*]

	£	s.	d.
[*11 February*]			
Quinquagesima Sunday,			5
Item from Westrowe			3
Item from Bek			3
Item from Halywell			5
Sum		1	4
[*25 February*]			
Second Sunday of Lent, from the town			7
Item from Westrowe			2

---

[52]   John Canvas (Cannas) wrote his will in 1473 (SROB, IC 500//2/11/15) and died in the following year.

		£	s.	d.
Item from Bek				4
Item from Halywell				4
	Sum		1	5
[4 March]				
Third Sunday, from the town				8
Item from Westrowe				5
Item from Bek				2
Halywell				2
[11 March]				
Fourth Sunday of Lent, for the soul of John Staloun[53]	[illeg.]	2	0	0
Item on the same day, for the soul of John Punge[54]			6	8
	Sum	1	6	8
[18 March]				
Passion Sunday, from the town				5
Item from Westrowe				2
Item from Bek				4
Item from Halywell				1
	Sum		1	0
[25 March]				
Palm Sunday, from the town churchale		1	19	0
Item for the soul of John Punge			3	4
And from the town				9
Item from Westrowe				4
Item from Bek				2
Item from Halywell				3
Sum		2	3	10
And from John Fuller in part payment by permission				
of Lady Isabel Galyon			3	4
	Sum		3	4

[fol.20r]   **[1453]**

		£	s.	d.
[2 April]				
Monday in the octave of Easter, for the soul of Robert				
Woderys[55]			3	4
	Sum		3	4
[8 April]				
Low Sunday, from the town			1	0
Item from Westrowe				3
Item from Bek				3
Item from Halywell				3
	Sum		1	9

---

53 Staloun's (Stalham) will (Appendix 2:8) shows that he left 40s. to the fabric of Mildenhall church, entered here.

54 Punge's will has not survived, but his bequest to the fabric totalled 10s. He was remembered again with his wife Matilda, and her first husband John Wryghte, on Coll. fol.23r when 6s. 8d. was paid for their souls in the following year. Their wills have not survived.

55 The Wooderys family lived in the parish until at least 1528.

	£	s.	d.
[*15 April*]			
Second Sunday, from the town		1	1
Item from Westrowe			3
Item from Bek			3
Item from Halywell			6
Sum		2	1
[*6 May*]			
Fifth Sunday, from a churchale at the Westrowe		18	7
Item from the town		1	5
Item from Westrowe			4
Item from Bek			4
Item from Halywell			3
Sum	1	2	11
[*13 May*]			
Sixth Sunday, from the town			2
Item from Westrowe			3
Item from Bek			2
Item from Halywell			5
Sum		1	7
And with the permission of Lady Isabel Galyon, by the hand of John Fullere		3	4
Sum		3	4
[*27 May*]			
Sunday in the feast of the Holy Trinity, from the town			10
Item from Westrowe			5
Item from Bek			4
Item from Halywell			3
Sum		1	10

[*fol.20v*]   **[*1453*]**

	£	s.	d.
[*3 June*]			
First Sunday after the feast of the Holy Trinity, from the town			8
Item from Westrowe			5
Item from Bek			3
Item from Halywell			3
Sum		1	7
[*10 June*]			
Second Sunday, from the town			8
Item from Westrowe			3
Item from Bek			4
Item from Halywell			3
Sum		1	6
[*17 June*]			
Third Sunday, from the town			9
Item from Westrowe			4
Item from Bek			2
Item from Halywell			6
Sum		1	9

	£	s.	d.
[24 June]			
Fourth Sunday, for the soul of John Speed from John			
Dobyn in the name of William Taylor		6	8
Item from the town		1	0
Item from Westrowe			3
Item from Bek			7
Item from Halywell			2
Sum <23d.>		8	7
[1 July]			
Fifth Sunday, from the town		1	0
Item from Westrowe			2
Item from Bek			2
Item from Halywell			5
Sum		1	9
[8 July]			
Sixth Sunday, from the town			10
Item from Westrowe			4
Item from Bek			5
Item from Halywell			4
Sum		1	11

[fol.21r]   **[1453]**

	£	s.	d.
[15 July]			
Seventh Sunday, from the town			6
Item from Westrowe			4
Item from Bek			4
Item from Halywell			4
Sum		1	6
[22 July]			
Eighth Sunday, from the town		1	0
Item from Westrowe			4
Item from Bek			3
Item from Halywell			5
Sum		2	0
[29 July]			
Ninth Sunday, from the town			9
Item from Westrowe			3
Item from Bek			3
Item from Halywell			3
Item for the soul of Alice, late wife of Robert Frere[56]		3	4
Sum		4	10
[5 August]			
Tenth Sunday	Nil because nothing collected		
[12 August]			
Eleventh Sunday, from the town			11

---

[56] Alice was the daughter-in-law of John Frere: see CWA, fol.10v.

		£	s.	d.
Item from Westrowe				3
Item from Bek				3
Item from Halywell				3
Item from a churchale at Bek, Cakestrete and Wyldestrete			17	8
	Sum		19	2
[16 September]				
Sixteenth Sunday, from the town				10
Item from Westrowe				2
Item from Bek				3
Item from Halywell				3
	Sum		1	6

[*fol.21v*]   **[*1453*]**

		£	s.	d.
[23 September]				
Seventeenth Sunday, from the town				7
Item from Westrowe				5
Item from Bek				3
Item from Halywell				5
	Sum		1	8
[30 September]				
Eighteenth Sunday, from the town				10
Item from Westrowe				nil
Item from Bek				2
Item from Halywelle				3
	Sum		1	3
[7 October]				
Nineteenth Sunday, from the town			1	1
On the same day, for the soul of Robert Tyd[57]			3	4
Item from Westrowe				5
Item from Bekk				2
Item from Halywelle				4
	Sum <2s.>		5	4
[14 October]				
Twentieth Sunday, from the town			1	0
Item from Westrowe				4
Item from Bek				5
Item from Halywell	<nil because>			3
	Sum <1s. 9d.>		1	11
[21 October]				
Twenty-first Sunday, from the town				10
And for the good estate of Roger Grene			3	4
Item from Westrowe				4
Item from Bek				3
Item from Halywell				4
	Sum <1s. 9d.>		5	1

---

[57] Robert Tyd's will was written 20 August 1452 (SROB, IC 500/2/9/128). In it he bequeathed 3s. 4d.
to the fabric of Mildenhall church. See SRS, 44 no.598.

	£	s.	d.
Item for the soul of William Algood			6

[*2 December*]

First Sunday in the Advent of the Lord, from the town			5
Item from Westrowe			5
Item from Bek			1
Item from Halywell			1
Sum		1	0

[*fol.22r*]   **[*1453*]**

<Item in binding of the books firstly in wages of them for
   15 days at 6d. per day 7s. 6d.>
<And in board for three weeks 3s.>
<Item in silk bought for the same work 1d.>
<Item in the clasps and 8 dowes 5d.>
<Item the pakthred 1d.>
<Item in glue bought with parchment 6d.>

[*9 December*]

Second Sunday in the Advent of the Lord, from the town		1	0
Item from Westrow			5
Item from Halywell			2
Item from Bek			2
Sum		1	9

[*16 December*]

Third Sunday in the Advent of the Lord, from the town			9
Item from Westrowe			1
Item from Bek			4
Item from Halywell			3
Sum		1	5

[*30 December*]

Sunday in the feast of the Epiphany, for the soul of John Tyd[58]	1	0	0

[*6 January*]   **[*1454*]**

Sunday in the octave of the Epiphany, from the town			8
Item from Westrowe			2
Item from Bek			2
Nil item from Halywell	because no collection		
Sum		1	0

[*13 January*]

First Sunday after the octave of the Epiphany, from the town			11
Item from Westrowe			4
Item from Bek			1
Item from Halywell			2
Sum		1	6

---

58   John Tyd's bequest to the church fabric was 20s., as recorded here (SROB, IC 500/2/9/152). See SRS,
     44 no.727.

[*fol.22v*]   **[*1454*]**

		£	s.	d.
[*20 January*]				
Second Sunday [*after the octave of the Epiphany*], from the town				6
Item from Westrowe				3
Item from Bek				3
Item from Halywell				8
	Sum		1	8
[*27January*]				
Third Sunday, from the town				6
Item from Westrowe				5
Item from Bek				3
Item from Halywell	Nil because no collection			
	Sum		1	2
[*3 February*]				
Fourth Sunday, from the town			1	1
Item from Westrowe				3
Item from Bek				3
Item from Halywell				2
	Sum		1	8
[*17 February*]				
[*Septuagesima*] Sunday, from the town				7
Item from Westrowe				2
Item from Bek	Nil because no collection			
Item from Halywell				4
	Sum		1	1
[*24 February*]				
[*Sexagesima*] Sunday, from the town				7
Item from Westrowe				2
Item from Bek				2
Item from Halywell				3
	Sum		1	2
[*3 March*]				
[*Quinquagesima*] Sunday, from the town				3
Item from Westrowe				9
Item from Bek				3
Item from Halywell				2
	Sum			11

[*fol.23r*]   **[*1454*]**

		£	s.	d.
[*10 March*]				
First Sunday of Lent, from the town			1	1
Item from Westrowe				5
Item from Bek				2
Item from Halywell				3
Item from the remaining taxes				8
	Sum		2	7

37

	£	s.	d.
[*17 March*]			
Second Sunday, from the town			10
Item from Westrowe			3
Item from Bek			1
Item from Halywell			2
Sum		1	4
[*24 March*]			
Third Sunday of Lent, from the town			6
Item from Westrowe			2
Item from Halywell			2
Item for the souls of John Punge[59] and John Wryghte,			
husbands of Matilda Punge, relict of the said John and John		6	8
Sum		7	6
[*7 April*]			
Passion Sunday, from a churchale from Halywell	1	3	4
From the town			8
Item from Westrowe			nil
Item from Bek			1
Item from Halywell			nil
And in 2 ropes sold to John Paynet[60]			11
Sum	1	4	4
[*14 April*]			
Palm Sunday, from the town			9
Item from Westrowe			4
Item from Bek			2
Item from Halywell			2
Sum		1	5

[*fol.23v*] **[*1454*]**

	£	s.	d.
[*26 May*]			
Fifth Sunday after Easter, from the town <5d.>			4
Item from Westrowe <5d.>			4
Item from Bek			4
Item from Halywell			4
[*10 June*]			
Monday in <vigil> the octave of Pentecost, from a			
churchale held at the Westrowe	1	4	5
[*14 July*]			
Relic Sunday [*the first Sunday after 7 July*], from the town[61]			11

---

59 See Notes on People, p.208.
60 John Paynet, smith, was elected churchwarden in 1449.
61 G.R. Owst, *Preaching in Medieval England: an Introduction to Sermon Manuscripts of the Period c.1350–1450* (1965), p.350: 'Syrres, than on relike Sonday next commyng we shall reverens, honour, and worship the precius sacrament of the awter, verey Goddis body … and in generall all the reverent relikes of patriackes, prophetes, apostelles, martirs, confessours, and virtuous virgins, and other holy and devoute men and women, whoos blessid bodyes, holy bones, and other relikes th' be left in erth

	£	s.	d.
Item from Westrowe			5
Nil item from Bek	because none		
Item from Halywell			5
Sum		1	9
[*28 July*]			
Sixth Sunday, from the town			8
Item from Westrowe			1
Item from Bek			5
Item from Halywell			5
Sum		1	8
[*15 September*]			
Thirteenth Sunday, from the town			8
Item from Westrowe			4
Item from Bek			5
Item from Halywell			4
Sum		1	9
[*22 September*]			
Fourteenth Sunday, from the town			10
Item from Westrowe			4
Item from Bek			4
Item from Halywell			5
Sum		1	11

---

to christen mannes socour, comfort, and recreacion, and their names be regestrede in the boke of life'. Owst quotes from BL, MS Harley 2247, fol.170b, but refers also to notes of a sermon at Bury St Edmunds in Caius College, Cambridge, MS 35b.

THE CHURCHWARDENS' ACCOUNTS
1503–1553

Suffolk Record Office, Bury St Edmunds
EL 110/5/3

Chyrcherevis: John Heynes, Thomas M[*damaged*], Thomas Mey and Thomas
   B[*damaged*]

**Memorandum what mony the seid Chercherevis have rec' in
the seid 19ᵗʰ yer off Kyng Herry the VIIth.**[1]

	£	s.	d.
Fyrst rec' on Candelmes day for the pardon [*1504*]		4	10
Item rec' on Feluppys and James day[2]		3	1
Item rec' off the quethowrd off William Bray[3]		6	8
Item rec' off the quethowrd off Mawte Goodeall		3	4
Item rec' off the quethowrde off Margaret Browech		1	0
Item rec' with the box in ower entre[4]		1	1
Item rec' on Corpus Christi day for the pardon[5]		5	2
Item rec' off the quethowrd off Robert Fryer		1	0
Item rec' off Thomas Hopper[6] for his yer ferme ended at Myhelmes[7] in the twentieth year of Henry VII	1	1	0
Item rec' on Myhelmes day for the pardon		4	0
Item ressyvyd of Dellykacyonn for pardon[8]		3	8
Item rec' <Edw> off the quethword off Edward a Bery[9]		4	4
Item rec'off the quetheword off Richard Billis		6	8
Item rec' off the quetheword off John Bateman		6	8
Item rec' on Candilmes Day for the pardon [*1505*]		2	0
Item rec' off the quetheword off William Hendy[10]			1
Item rec' off the quetheword off Syr George Geytonby[11]		6	8
Item resseved of Sir Jhon Hausteyn		6	8
Item ressyved of Robard Reve[12]		2	0
Item rec' of the quethword of Jone Wode		1	0

---

1   The 19th year of Henry VII ran from 22 August 1503 to 21 August 1504. The first entry dates from
    Candlemas celebrated on 2 February 1504. The names of the retiring churchwardens appear at the
    top of CWA, fol.1r and the accounts that are presented follow on but they are far from complete.
2   St Philip's and St James's Day was the second of Mildenhall's pardon days, celebrated on 1 May.
    The *Handbook of Dates for Students of English History* (ed. C.R. Cheney, Royal Historical Society,
    1981), p.58, gives 1 May as the appointed saints' day.
3   Appendix 2:27. Bray's quetheword or bequest of 6s. 8d. was for church reparation.
4   This suggests that an offertory box stood at the main door, perhaps within the north porch.
5   Corpus Christi was celebrated on the Thursday after Trinity Sunday. It was the third pardon day in
    Mildenhall.
6   Thomas Hopper appears frequently in these accounts, paying rent to the church at Michaelmas. He
    died in 1524 (see Appendix 2:37).
7   Michaelmas was the culmination of the growing season and, as the fourth pardon of Mildenhall's
    liturgical year, was celebrated on the Feast of St Michael and All Angels, 29 September.
8   Dedication Day was the last pardon day in the liturgical year of St Mary's church, Mildenhall. It may
    have been commemorated on either the feast of the Presentation of the Blessed Virgin Mary on 21
    November or on the feast of her Immaculate Conception, 8 December.
9   Edward Bery wrote his will in 1503 (SROB, IC 500/2/13/141) leaving 3s. 4d. to the high altar. A
    bequest of 3s. 4d. is not mentioned in his will. Its entry in the accounts may be due to an extra-
    testamentary arrangement made between him and his executors.
10 Hendy left 10d. to the high altar (SROB, IC 500/2/12/38).
11 For Gatynbe's will see Appendix 2:29, proved on 7 April 1505. 'Sir' was a courtesy title for a
    non-graduate priest. See the following entry for Sir John Hausteyn (Austin).
12 Robert Reve left 1s. 8d. for church reparation in his will of 1505 (SROB, IC 500/2/15/175).

	£	s.	d.
Item rec' off Herry Blythis queword			0
Item rec' for the pardon on Feloppis and James Day		5	0
Item rec' off the quethword off John Bryon[13]		2	0
Item rec' off the quethword of Thomas Taylor		1	8
Item rec' off the quethword of Robert Gaussaydr			8
Item rec' of Halys Meyer quetheword			8
Item rec' off the quethword off Thomas Cole[14]		3	4
Item rec' off the quethword off Robert Pey		1	0

[fol.1v] [1505]

Item rec' off the quethword off John Chiston[15]		3	4
Item rec' on Corpus Christi day for the pardon		4	0
Item rec' of the queword of Richard Fuller		2	0
Item rec' off the queword off John Fayerwar		3	4
Item rec' on Mihilmes day for the pardon		2	8
<Item payd to John Plummer for >			
Item rec' off for his yers fferme endyde at Mihelmes			
in the 21st year of Herry septem	1	1	0
Item rec' on the Cherch Holy day for the pardon		4	0

Memorandum that the yer off Ower Lorde Gode 1505 on Sent Thomas Day [29 December] the cherchewardenes affor namyd rec' off the profits and gyftes that warn gevyn for a play off Sent Thomas, played that same day and yer in the Hall Yard,[16] all charges deductyed

	7	0	0
Sum total	14	9	2
[deleted]	15	9	3

<Memorandum that with all deductions and allowances there remains>

[deleted]	6	10	0

[Latin] Memorandum that Paul, the vicar of this church, gave for painting the solar of the Holy Rood in the same church[17]

		8	0

Names of the wardens for one year: Symonde Eton,[18] Thomas Gesye, William Ballis, John Dey

---

13 Sir George Gatynby was supervisor to John Bryon's will (SROB, IC 500/2/12/38).

14 Thomas Cole left 3s. 4d. to St Mary's reparation in 1505 (NRO, NCC Garnon 34).

15 John Chiston's will of 1502 (NRO, NCC Popy 230) left 1s. 8d. to the church fabric. John Chyldyrstone's will of 1504 (Appendix 2:28) left 3s. 4d. to church reparation, an instance where the name entered in the will register and the amount bequeathed through the accounts do not tally, making it difficult to be certain of the identity of the testator or of their wishes.

16 Hall Yard was part of the manorial complex which lay beyond the church. The sixteenth-century manor house was demolished in 1934 and the land sold for building; Dymond, *Thetford Priory*, I, p.204. One shilling is entered under 'necessary expenses' paid to the 'pley of Myldenhale'.

17 Master Paul Geyton was vicar at this time. This entry records his payment towards the painting of the solar over the rood loft.

18 Symonde Eton (Etton) was a parish chaplain in Mildenhall; see Appendix 2:34. He was not the first cleric to serve as churchwarden in the parish, the chaplain, John Bryan, being elected in 1449. See Coll. fol.9r.

[*Latin*] Memorandum that the year of the Lord 1505, the 15th day of the month of November, all allowances were delivered in the presence of Paul, the vicar.

	£	s.	d.
[*Latin*] Memorandum Henry Pope and certain other parishioners of the said church and churchwardens written above £6 14s. of which money Dom Paul, the vicar, gave for painting and ornamenting the solar of the Holy Rood of the said church.		8	0

[*fol.2r*] — **[*Undated*]**

\<payd Bansty for 9 dayes worke		12	4\>
\<payd for 400 byndes and wayes\>	\<15\>	\<1	4\>
\<payd a hunderde and a halffe of thache		3	6\>
\<payde for rye strawe		5	4\>
\<payd for a hundred bryckes for the almes houses[19] chymny		1	4\>
\<Item taken owte of the churche for the pore[20]		10	0\>

[*fol. 2v*] — **[*1505–1506*]**

Memorandum of the expensys done of Reparacyons be the hands of the cherchewardens in the 21st year in the reign of King Henry VII.

Fyrst payd on to Master Bakkot for borde to the dore in the vestry		6
Item payd on to John Gardenere, the smyth, for hyngys and hokys and stapylls to seyd dore[21]		11
Item payd on to John Pachet and \<f\> his sone and Wylliam Pachet for makyng of the dore[22]	1	1
Item payd on to Thomas Howton for borde and nayle	1	4
Item payd on to John Screvenere for kepyng of the clok[23]		10
Item payd on to the parysche clerke of the town[24]	2	6
\<Item ressyvyd on Candylmas day for the pardon\>		
Item payd on to Thomas Gesum for \to [2] chestys/		6
Item payd on to Wylliam Pachet and to George Dobyn and for an ob' worthe of nayle		10½
Item payd on to John Sadyler for bawdrykks makyng and for leder[25]		9
Item payd on to the parysche \<\> clerke for Crystemes \<deleted\> on to Hester[26]	2	6

---

19 The founding of almshouses was increasing at this time, some testators leaving property in their wills as accommodation for the deserving poor.

20 This was possibly poor relief which was distributed from the general funds of the churchwardens' account.

21 Later on the same page Gardener was paid for nails and for making the censer in which the incense was burnt.

22 This branch of the large, local family of Pachet (Patchett) were carpenters, here paid for making a new vestry door, the wood supplied by a member of the Mildenhall family of Bakkot [Bagot].

23 John Screvenere was employed to wind the clock. The rate was 10d. but this had been increased to 1s. 3d. a quarter by 1507–08.

24 The clerk's wage of 2s. 6d. a quarter included the playing of the organ. Seldom can he be identified.

25 The name Sadyler, that of a leather worker, was still an occupational surname as is seen in this entry.

26 The clerk's quarterly wage at Christmas and Easter.

	£	s.	d.
Item payd on to John Screvenere			10
Item payd on to John Gardenere for nayle and makyng of the sensere			2
Item payd on to John Pachet for makyng of the sepulker[27]			4
Item payd on to John Sadyler for makyng of bawdrykys			3
Item payd on to the Dene for the almes of Norwych[28]		2	6
Item payd for ryngers at the cumyng of the kyng			4
Item payd on to Agnes Maw for bords			10
Item payd on to the parysche clerke[29]		2	6
Item payd on to John Schrevener for the clok			10
Item payd for 2 belle ropys		2	4
Item payd on to John Pachet for hangyng of the lytyl belle, and to his felow beyng with hym[30]		2	8
Item payd for a borde			4
Item payd for nayle			4
Item payd for stageyng of the rodelofte[31]			7
Item payd on to John Hennys for restys to the lytyl belle		1	6
Item payd to the alybaster man for the rode lofte peytyng[32]	1	6	2
Item payd on to the plumber for sowdyng[33] and for sowed		1	9
Item payd on to Robert Smyth for yryn worke on to \the/ lytell bells		1	4
Item payd on to John Pachet for mendyng of the bells			6
Item payd on to <>John Sadyler for bawdrykys to the bells			4
Item payd for payntyng of the rodelofte[34]	1	10	0
Item payd for 2 belle clappers		5	0
Item payd on to the parysche clerke for Myschellmas terme[35]		2	6
Item payd to John Schrevenere for the cloke			10
Item payd for schoryng of the gutters of \the/ cherche			4

---

27 The sepulchre was a wooden housing on the north of the chancel on which the Host (the bread or wafer representing the body of the crucified Christ) was reserved from Maundy Thursday until Easter Day. Important tombs were often placed in this position so that they might be used as an Easter sepulchre.

28 A payment to the diocese of Norwich for charitable expenses.

29 Another quarterly payment.

30 The previous expenses towards the bells are now explained with the arrival of the little bell.

31 Major refurbishments to the rood-loft were about to begin. Here staging or scaffolding was essential as can be seen by the three openings, one high above the other, on the north side of the chancel arch. The overall cost of making and painting the rood-loft was assisted by the collections gathered by the parishioners. The churchwardens' accounts of Great St Mary's in Cambridge record the building of the rood-loft at the same time as Mildenhall, but at far greater expense making it incomparable. See Foster, *St Mary the Great*, pp.36, 41–3, 46, 48. The Cambridge accounts include a pole for drawing up the veil before the rood, p.88; and in 1534 the churchwardens were still owed money for the gilding of the Trinity, p.77.

32 Carved and painted Nottingham alabaster was one of the chief native products designed and manufactured for the Church in the late medieval period. Churchwardens' accounts from Leverton in Lincolnshire and Bramley in Hampshire reveal that alabaster panels were used to decorate the front of the rood loft. See F. Cheetham, *Alabaster Images of Medieval England* (2003), p.4.

33 Solder is frequently mentioned in churchwardens' accounts, being used by both plumbers and glaziers.

34 Here the wooden members of the roodloft were being painted.

35 'Terme' or 'term' is interchangeable with 'quarter', and here represents the quarterly wage paid to the parish clerk at Michaelmas.

[fol.3r] **[1506–1507]**

	£	s.	d.
Item payd for Romeschot[36]		2	6
Item payd to John Pachet, Wylliam Pachet and Rychard Kerver for staging[37]		2	6
Item payd on to the glase wryth		4	0
Item payd on to the clokke maker		6	6
Item payd for a belle rope		1	2
Item payd <> on to the kerver for the rode lofte kervyng[38]			8
Item payd for thee belle welys for all maner thyngs longyng to them		8	4
Item payd for a foder of lede schotyng		7	4
Item payd on to the parysche clerke of towne		2	6
Item payd on to John Schrevenere for the clokke			10
Item payd on to the peyntors for the rode lofte[39]	1	9	0
Item payd for the <pl> palle cloth and for the makyng	1	6	2
Item payd for to rochetys and the makyng		4	4
Item payd for trussyng of the bellys			4
Item payd for 3 pownde wex to the paschale		1	4
Item payd on to the paryssche clerke at Ester		2	6
Item payd on to John Schrevenere for the clok			10
Item payd for bawdrykys to the bells			9
Item payd for pamentyng of the cherche			6
Item payd for settyng up of the sepukyr[40]			3
Item payd on to John Gardener for mendyng of clok		1	0
Item payd on to Thomas Howton for wex to the rowel and makyng and for nayle[41]		1	10
Item payd for Norwyge almes[42]		2	6
Item payd for making of the cherche gatys		1	3
Item payd for 2 belle ropys		2	2
Item payd for kepyng of the clokke and mendyng		1	3
Item payd for a panne to feche fere in[43] and for sowdyng of the canope[44] and for mendyng of the mattoc			9

---

[36] Otherwise called Peter's Pence, an annual payment made to Rome.

[37] Staging was set up once more as the rood loft was to be carved and painted.

[38] Did Richard Kerver have an occupational surname? See the entry for the rood-loft carving four lines above.

[39] Painting the rood-loft so far had cost over £4, its suggested size being so great. It is likely that there would have been a separate contract for painting the rood-screen.

[40] The Easter sepulchre, now finished, was put in place.

[41] The rowell was the light or lights hanging before the rood, also called the 'common light'.

[42] Another payment to Norwich diocese for charitable expenses. See CWA, fol.2v n.89.

[43] This may refer to the blessing and kindling of the new fire on the vigil of Easter, either in the church or within the porch. This was accompanied by the lighting of the paschal candle, the light and the fire being symbolic of the risen Christ, all of which necessitated the carrying of live fire into the building. Alternatively a pan in which fire was carried would have been necessary during the leading of the roof. Fire was also needed in the church throughout the year to light the censer and to illuminate the church with candles.

[44] 'Sowdyng of the canape' means sewing the canopy.

	£	s.	d.
Item payd on to the browder[45] for mending of the copys and making of the canope		3	8
Item payd for hys borde of 8 dyis and for sylke		1	10
Item payd <of> on to the parysche clerke		2	6
Item payd for 2 belle ropys		2	4
Item payd for 2 ropys for the clokke		1	0

[fol.3v] **[1506–1507]**

	£	s.	d.
Item payd for a plate of yren, a stapyll to the cherche gate			4
Item payd for castyn[46] of a walle and makyng up of the walle at the cherche ende			8
Item payd for a bawdryke making			5
Item payd for a man to goo for a clok smyth			8
Item payd for a rope to the lytyll belle			3
Item payd to the parische clerke for Myschelmas quarter		2	6
Item payd for <for> a lokke to the cherche gate			2
Item payd [deleted] for the [deleted] pullys in the chancel and for the naylyng up[47]			9
Item payd for a brygge makyng, going to Hesewell[48]		1	0
Item payd for 2 hundryd <> pament for the cherche		3	11
Item payd to the clokke smyth for making of the clok and oder thyngs perteynyng there to		1	4
Item payd for trussyng of the belles		1	1½[49]
Item payd for hangyng up of the <> sacry belle			3
Item payd for Romeskot		2	6
Item payd for mendying of a bawdryke			1
Item payd for wassyng of the surplysys		4	0
Item payd for a bawdryke makyng			7
Item payd for the rowell			9
Item payd for a man goyng to the vysytacyon[50]			6

	£	s.	d.
Memorandum that all manner thengs contyd and rekenyd the cherche wardens have deliveryd	1	16	10

[Latin] Item of the same money
Payd to Master Vikery of the whych 8s. Master

	£	s.	d.
Vekery have gevyn 6s. 8d. to the peyntyng of Owr Lady[51]		8	0

---

45 'Broider, browder': to ornament with needlework. Browder may have become an occupational surname for one who sewed or mended cloth, as is suggested in this entry.

46 Casting as in roughcasting.

47 These pulleys were perhaps for the Lenten veil which was lowered during Lent, thus screening the chancel from the body of the church and obscuring the view of the high altar. Until Easter, all statues within the chancel were covered with cloths painted with a red cross, and the rood on the rood-screen was covered with a veil until Easter.

48 Eriswell, the neighbouring parish lying on Mildenhall's north-eastern boundary. See map 1.

49 The odd halfpenny is made up to a full penny in the reckoning below.

50 The annual visitation within the deanery when the archdeacon or dean would receive from churchwardens an account of the church affairs, during which the inventory of church goods would be checked.

51 A further payment from the vicar, Paul Geyton, towards painting the Virgin on the rood-beam.

	£	s.	d.
[*Latin*] Memorandum debts pertaining to the church			
Firstly the wife <of> sumtyme of Thomas Mey owyth	1	0	0
Item Robert Costyne <> be the quetheword of hys moder		6	8
Item Margeria Mot by the quetheworde of here moder		6	8
Item John Donnome by the quetheworde of Issabella Glover		6	8
Item Robert Austyn for the beryyng of hys moder in the cherche[52]		6	8
Item to Thomas Blake <> for the beryyng of hys wife in the cherche[53]		6	8
Item Thomas Clarke for hys qweod of Halywell		2	0
Item Roberd Morley for hys qhueod'word[54]		3	4
	13	0	5

[*fol.47r*][55]

	£	s.	d.
Memorandum that Robert Austen owt onto the church of Myldenhall for beryyng of hys moder in the seyd church		6	8
Item Thomas Blake owt for the berying of hys wyfe in the church		6	8
Item for the qwethod of Robert Morle		3	4
Item John Wyng owt for the quethod of hys fader		<3	4>
Item for the qwethod of Rychard Sparhauke		1	8
Item for the qwethod of John Fynne		1	0
Item for the qwethod of John Morle and pleg Thoms Chiston		1	0
Item Wylliam Place of Lyn gave to the church after the decesse of his wife		15	0
<Item Wylliam Patchet> owt for ocupyeng the church hous		1	0
Item John Bury and Thomas Gesyn owe in led 12 hundred pounds and a quarter			
Item Robert Dyer owt in led an hundred pounds and more			
Receyved of the same one hundred pound and four pounds			
Item Wylliam Swayn and Wylliam Gesyn owe <*illeg.*>in led an hundred pound and 30 <>			
Item Jone Powle owt in led 80 pounds recevyd ther of 15 pounds remayneth 60 li [pounds] 5 pounds			
Item John Bury owt in led an hundred pounds and 15 pounds			
Item Sir Rodger Barford gave to bey a paule cloth	2	0	0

---

52 Austen was a member of the Salters' Company in London, but a native of Mildenhall; see the following folio, the misplaced CWA, fol.47r. He died in 1514, leaving 20s. to St Mary's 'to the intent my soul, my father's soul and all Christian souls may be prayed for there in the bederoll 20s.' (TNA, PCC Holder 29). This entry is duplicated on CWA, fol.47r.

53 This entry is also duplicated on CWA, fol.47r.

54 Robert Morley's will was proved 5 June 1505 leaving 3s. 4d. to the reparation (NRO, NCC Garnon 35). See CWA, fol.47r where this entry is duplicated.

55 When these papers were orginally paginated at the end of the nineteenth or beginning of the twentieth century, this folio received its present number of CWA, fol.47r. It has now been repositioned between CWA, fols 3v and 4r because, despite the repetition of payments made by Austen, Blake and Morley, there are twenty-one other entries which might otherwise be overlooked. Fol.47r seems to be a rough copy of the accounts, as this scribe's handwriting is not found elsewhere in the documentation whereas the hands on the adjoining fols 3v and 4r are the same. It is not possible to be more accurate than this, but Robert Austen, citizen and salter of London and a native of Mildenhall, died in the first weeks of December 1514, requesting that his name and that of his father be recited from the Mildenhall bede-roll, 1514 (TNA, PCC Holder 29). CWA, fol.47r must therefore have been written between 1505 and 1514.

	£	s.	d.
Plege John Dey[56]			
Item Thomas Ffrynge gave to the church	2	0	0
Item for the qwethod of John Smyth		13	4
Item Jone Baker owt for the qwethod of John Smyth		3	4
<Item Moder Schadynhalk owt for the qwethod of hyr			
fader pleg M Chadenhalk		6	8>
Item Symond Halstede owt for qwethod of hys fader		3	4
Item receyvyd of John Bure in led 400 save 6 pund			
Item Wilim Geson owe in lede 22 pounds			
Item Thomas Lane beqwest to the reparacyon of the			
chyrche to be payd by hands of hys wyff the yer of			
Owr Lord a thousand 5 hundreth <XI> XIIII			
Surteys Master Pope and Master Nicholas Bagott			
promysyd befor Master John Wyllkynson[57] vicary	4	0	0

[fol.4r]   *[1505–1506]*

Memorandum of the receytes receyvyd be \the/ hands of the cherchewardens in the twenty-first year of the reign of King Henry VII.

	£	s.	d.
Fyrst receyvd of John Dey and John Bury be the			
quetheword of Sir Roger Barford[58]		10	0
Item receyvyd of the wife of John Curtes be the			
quetheword of the seyd John[59]		3	4
Item receyvyd for the pardon on Candylmas day		6	4
Item receyvyd be the quethewo\r/de of Wylliam Jaketyne			8
Item receyvd for the pardon on Philipe and Iacob day		2	0
Item receyvyd in the feast of Corpus Christi for the pardon		3	10
Item receyvyd on the pardon day at Myschelmas		3	6
Item receyvyd be the qwetheworde of Symon Place		6	8
Item receyvyd be the qwetheworde of Rychard Style		1	4
Item receyvyd for the pardon on the Cherche Holy day[60]		3	8
Item receyvyd be the qwetheworde of John Sadyler		6	8
Item receyvyd be the quetheworde of Katerina Jaketyne		1	0
Item receyvd be the qwetheworde of John Sperhawke		1	8
Item receyvyd be the qwetheworde of Wylliam Beneth		1	0
Item receyvyd \for the pardon/ in the feast of the			
Purificacion of the Blessed Mary [*1506*]		3	4
Item receyvyd be the qwetheworde of <John *illeg.*> Roberd Dey		6	8
Item receyvyd be the qwetheworde of Thomas Makworth		2	0
Item receyvyd be the qwetheworde of Roberd Mey		1	0
Item receyvyd be the qwethe worde of Thomas Mey	1	0	0
Item receyvyd of Wylliam Pechy		10	0

---

56   Roger Barford's will was proved 4 December 1504; see Appendix 2:30.
57   See Wylkynson under Notes on People, p.211.
58   John Dey and John Bury were executors of Roger Barford, the stipendiary priest, Appendix 2:30.
59   John Curteys' will was written on 4 October 1505 and proved a month later (SROB, IC 500/2/12/44).
60   An alternative title for Dedication Day.

	£	s.	d.
Item receyvd on <f> Philipe and Jacob day		3	0
Item receyvyd on Corpus Christi day		4	6
Item receyvyd on Mischelmas day for the pardon		3	4
Item receyvd be the qwetheworde of Wylliam Chystyn		4	4
Item receyvyd on the cherche Holy day		3	4
Item receyvyd for the cherche ale all maner of thyngs cowntyd clerly < >	1	8	8
Item receyvyd of Thomas Hoper	1	1	0
Item receyvyd for a rope			6
Item receyvyd for reysthys in the comyn		1	0
	14	16	4

[fol.4v]   **[1507–1508]**

	£	s.	d.
Delyvered on to the cherche wardens	1	15	6

Wardens: John Gardener, Wylliam Gesyn, Robert Pege, John Place

Memorandum of the expensys done be the hands of the cherche wardens in the year of the Lord the twenty-third year of the reign of King Henry VII

	£	s.	d.
Firstly payd for payntyng of Owr Lady[61]		6	8
Item payd on to the parysche clerke		2	6
Item payd to John Gardener for kepyng of the clok and for were [wire] and for a stapyl		1	8
Item payd to Robert of Bury for scoring of canstykys			1
Item payd for a belrope		1	1
Item payd for a belrope		1	0
Item payd for the clapyr of the bell		3	6
Item payd for the makyn of to [2] bel clapyrs [illeg.]		12	0
Item payd for lyne for the veyle[62]			2½
Item payd for the caryage of the bel clapyrs fro Bury			2
Item payd for the clarke for hys quarter at Owr Lady		2	6
Item payd for the kepyn of the cloke		1	3
Item payd for the mending of an auter cloth and other geyr			3
Item payd to John Pachet for mending of the lytyll bell whell			5
Item payd to John Pachet for hys werke to the paschall[63]			5
Item payd to Thomas Lane for hys werke to the paschal			6
Item payd for the lynys to the paschal			5
Item payd for waks for the paschal and for the makyn		1	4½
Item payd to John Brewer the carver for mendyng of the paschal hede			4
Item payd for setting upe of the herse			3
Item payd to John Sarnyd for yerren wherke			2

---

61   As patron saint of Mildenhall church, St Mary would have been depicted in many places within the building in paintings of her birth, childhood, presentation in the temple, annunciation, visitation and Christ's nativity.

62   This refers to the Lenten veil.

63   John Pachet, a carpenter, may have made the candlestick holding the paschal candle which was lit on Easter eve. It stood to the north of the high altar and burned for forty days.

	£	s.	d.
Item payd to Wylliam Tyler for pathyn in the chyrche			10
Item payd for a lanthorne			6
Item payd to Thomas Hopper for waschyn			2
Item payd to John Pachet			3
The sum	2	0	4
		<3	4>
		<14	6>

[fol.5r] **[1507–1508]**

	£	s.	d.
Item payd for Rumskote		2	3
Item payd for lyme and for Wakman for makyn of the dore goyng in the <f> vestry		1	6
Memorandum that we put owt of the chyrche boxe 4s. 1d. to the makyn of the schyppe[64]		4	1
Item payd for plate to the Rodelofte and mendyng		1	8
Item payd for mendyng of the Belows of the orgawns			8
Item payd for lokyn owte of bylls and for wrytyn			6
Item payd for the losse of illmony in the chyrche box			8
Item payd for the clokepyng [sic]		1	3
Item payd for the horgonns plyer the paresche clarke[65]		2	6
Item payd for the mendyng of the almery longyng to the chyrche boxe			4
Item payd for a rope makyn and mendyng of a ropes			6
Item payd for a stone of hempe			10
Item payd for a drenyn of the paschall waks <for the rowell>			2
Item payd for to loks for coffyrs and for a locke on to the cope dore[66]		1	0
Item payd for the makyn of the sensyr and for the scheppe makyn[67]	1	9	0
Item payd to John Gardinyr for the cloke kepyng		1	3
Item payd to the parsche clarke for Myhelmes quartyr		2	6
Item payd to the glaserys		12	7
Item payd for wachyn		2	0
Item payd for Rumskot		2	6
Item payd for makyn of the locke for the Rodelofte dore			4
Item payd for the plumer for sowde and for warkmanschepe	1	5	5
Item payd for mendyng of the chyrchegate			2
Item payd for mendyng of a schofyll			1½
Item payd for mending of the rowell			1
Item payd for too serplese[68]		4	2

---

64 Incense was kept in an incense boat known as a 'ship' or 'navykyll'.

65 The parish clerk frequently doubled as organ player in the late medieval church.

66 It was now necessary to fit locks to the coffers; seven entries below a lock is fitted to the rood-loft door. On CWA, fol.5v a lock is fitted to the long hutch and a key made for the chancel door. Craig suggests that there was a tendency for iron keys to break and for locks to grow stiff, 'Co-operation and initiatives', p.377.

67 The repair of censers was an annual item in the sacrist rolls of every large church, the carelessness of thurifers being an unending cause of damage: Oman, *English Church Plate*, p.90.

68 Surplices cost 2s. 1d. each. For comparative Suffolk prices see Middleton-Stewart, *Inward Purity*, pp.206–7.

	£	s.	d.
Item payd for cloth for the bakeseyd of the rodelof[69]		1	9
The sum	4	19	9½

[fol.5v]   **[1507–1508]**

		£	s.	d.
Item payd for [?] skuyng of the rodelof to Busch			4	0
Item payd for nayle and lathe <6d.>	<7d.>			7
Item payd for to John Gardnyr for iynr werke				4
Item payd for kepyng of the cloke to John Garnyr			1	0
Item payd for makyn of the chyrche steyll				3
Item payd for rope to Sanctus bell				4
Item payd to the paresche clarke for Cristeme quartyr			2	6
Item payd for a bellrope			1	0
Item payd for the feyerpane makyn[70]				2
Item payd to Roberd Brion for the crowne of Owyr <> Lady[71]			2	8
Item payd for mendynd of the to <crose of> copyr crose			1	8
Item payd for wyr <of> for the latyn sensyr				2
Item payd for mendyng of the same sensyr				1
Item payd <for> to John Gardnyr for the clok kepyng			1	3
Item payd to the clark for the orgonys kepyng			2	6
Item payd for the rowell waks				8
Item payd for waks to the paschal			1	5½
Item payd to Roberd Bryon for mending of the herse				6
Item payd to John Bruer for angelis makyn to the pasc all hed			1	7
Item payd to John Pachet for mending of the lytyll bell wheyll				2
Item payd for takyn downe of the herse \3d./ and for				3
makyn of the inventory 12d.			1	0
Item payd for waschen for the halfe yer			2	0
Item payd for makyn of a locke for the longe hoche[72]				8
Item payd for Norwyche almes			2	3
Item payd for a belrope			1	2
Item payd for makyn of a key to the chawncell dore				2
The sum		1	10	10½
			<12	6>
			<11	2>

[fol.6r]   **[1508–1509]**

	s.	d.
Item receyvyd for bord of Syr Symond[73]		8
Item receyvd for the pardon day <> on Canldylmes	6	8
Item receyvyd of Thomas Hopper[74]	4	0

---

69 A covering for the backside of the rood-loft.
70 See CWA, fol.3r.
71 Images of the Virgin, the queen of heaven, frequently bore a crown. The cost of this item suggests it was made of latten and then gilded.
72 Perhaps this is the very large chest that still remains at the west end of the nave in St Mary's. Sherlock, *Suffolk Chests*, p.83, illus.
73 Here board was paid for a visiting chaplain.
74 Thomas Hopper appears frequently in the accounts. He attended to the washing of the church linen and probably rented a property from the church referred to in the accounts as Hopper's 'kot'. See CWA, fol. 19r.

		£	s.	d.
Item receyvyd for the pardon day <Phylype and Jacob>			3	2
Item receyvyd for Halywell May ale[75]			13	4
Item receyvyd for the town May ale		2	0	0
Item receyvyd for the pardon day on Corpus Christi day			4	0
Item receyvd for the qwhetod of John Fuller			3	4
Item receyvd <for> \on/ Master Bacun		1	0	0
Item receyvyd of Thomas Hopper	< >		16	0
Item receyvyd for the qwethod of Kateryn Pynhorne			6	8
Item receivd for the quheod of Kateryn Costyng[76]			6	8
Item receyvd for the pardon day Micaelys Arcangeli			3	0
Item receyvd for old belropes				4
Item receyvyd on the pardon day of the Dedicacon			6	4
Item receyvyd on the pardon day of Candilmes			3	0
Item receyvyd for the quheod of Thomas Clarke			2	0
Item recevyd of Roberd Cotes for 4 skor pownd leed			3	4
Item receyvyd of Thomas Hopper for the halfe yere ferme			8	0
Item receyvyd of the pardon day on Philypp and Jacobb			3	4
Item receyvyd for the May ale in the Becke weche[77]		2	4	0
Item receyvyd for the qwhetod of Isbell Glover			6	8
Item receyvyd at the gatheryn of Owyr Lady			3	4
Item recevyd for the pardon of Corpus Christi			5	11
Item receyvyd for the Westrowe May [*damaged*]	<xlii>	2	2	0
Item recevyd for the pardon day at Mihelmes			3	6
Item receyvyd of Thomas Hopper for halfe yer ferme			8	0
Item receyvd on Dedicacion day for the pardon			5	0
	The sum	14	0	3
		<13	10	0>

[fol. 6v]

	£	s.	d.
Item payd for an horse heyd		1	6
Item payd for mendyng of 4 baudrykes and hys bordyng			6
Item payd for mendyng of the bellys to Wylliam Pacheth and to George		1	2
Item payd to John Gardnyr, the smyth, for iern werke			6
Item payd for a box for to gathyr in the chyrche			4
Item payd for feyng of the grate to Landdysdale			1
Item payd for the mending of bell clapyrs		4	0
		<6	0>
Item payd for mendyng of the < > chyrche howse[78]		1	6
Item payd to John Gardnyr for the cloke kepyng		1	3
Item payd to the parescherke[79] for the orguns		2	6
Item payd to George for a bed makyn longyn to the chyrche howse			4

---

75 Two churchales held in May in Holywell Row and the High Town raised £2 13s. 4d.
76 The testament of Kathryne Costyng, 1506 (SROB, IC 500/2/13/179).
77 An alternative spelling of 'week', during which Beck Row and West Row held May ales.
78 The church house was used for churchales, entertainments and parish gatherings.
79 See Introduction, 'Priests and Parochial Personnel', for a description of the parish clerk's duties.

	£	s.	d.
Item payd for the makyn of the pycks and the locke			8
Item payd for Rumscote		2	6
Item payd to John Smyth for mendyng of the bokys[80]		9	0
		11	
		<8	8>
Item payd for mending of an awter cloth			2
Item payd for kepyng of the cloke to John Gardinyr		1	3
Item payd for the clarke for hys quartyr		2	6
Item payd to the plumyr		14	8
Item payd for waschyn for the \halfe/ yer[81]		2	0
Item payd for to [2] bellropys		2	1
Item payd to the glacewryeth		2	0
Item payd for to locks and <> to keys		1	10
Item payd to Roberd Bryon for a dore makyn		1	3
Item payd for menddyng of the cloke		2	0
Item payd for a peyr of gemewys to the dore within the <> vestry			6
Item payd for seftyng on the locks and for nayll			3
Item payd for kepyng of the clocke and to the clarke		3	9
		[illeg.]	
The sum	3	0	0

[fol. 7r]   **[1509–1510]**

[Latin] The year of the Lord 1509, 8th day of October, in the first year of the reign of the king, Henry VIII

	£	s.	d.
Remaynyng in the box	3	6	0
The chyrche wardens: Thomas Hopper, Edward Webbe,[82] Thomas Gardnyr, Rychard Holme			
Item payd for the <paschal> Rowell makyn			8
Item payd for the schryvv' stolys makyn			6
Item payd for the clappetts makyn			3
Item payd for the clokkepyng to John Gardner		1	3
Item payd to the paresch clarke at Owyr Lady Day		2	6
Item payd for the paschal makyn[83]		1	5
Item payd for the herse settyng uppe and the takyn doing			4
Item payd for mendyng of Owyr Lady			2
Item payd for Rumskott		2	3
Item payd for an ernest for the mesbok on Owyr Lady schappel[84]		6	8
Item payd for waschyng for the halfe yere		2	0

---

80 John Smith mended books for the church over the next few years; see CWA, fol.7v.
81 Thomas Hopper was here paid for washing the church linen.
82 The will of Edward Clerke, otherwise Webbe, 1528 (IC 500/2/15/214).
83 The paschal candle in 1505 weighed 3 pounds and it cost 1s. 4d. Here it cost 1s. 5d. but must have been much the same weight. In 1538 the candle still weighed 3 pounds but the wax cost 1s. 6d. and to make it cost another 2d.
84 A pledge or down payment on a missal or mass-book for the Lady Chapel.

	£	s.	d.
Item payd for nayll and for the credyll makyn[85]		1	3½
Item payd for to [2] lodes of sond caryage			4
Item payd for helpe to the plumer for costs and charges			5
Item payd to the plumyer for hys wages		4	4
Item payd for hys bordyng		2	0
Item payd to the plumbyr		5	7
Item payd for to lodys of cley, the carage and the having uppe onyt		1	4
Item payd for the muld makyn[86] and for feyrwod		3	1
Item payd for nayll, and for an hors to the plumyr			3
Item payd for hys bord and for hys mans bord		1	8
Item payd to the plumber		3	8
Item payd to John Gardner for nayll and sowd'		1	4
The sum	2	3	8½

[fol. 7v]

	£	s.	d.
Item payd to the plumer and hys man for an wekes werke		3	9
Item payd for bordy<n>g		3	9
<Item payd for sowd' nayll for drayng' of the corte and for talow>		<1	8>
Item payd for the drawyng of the cort		1	5
Item payd for nayll for wod and talow		1	2
Item payd for 4 fanns[87] the s<sic> price		4	0
Item payd to the plumer and hys man		4	8
Item payd for sowd'		5	6
Item payd for rosen and for talow and wood to the pynnakyll and for nayll		5	0
Item payd for the pleyers at the May all[88]		1	1
Item payd to the plumer <> and hys man for hys bordyng		2	5
Item payd for nayll and oyll			6
Item payd to the tabyrar[89] at the May ale			4
Item payd to John Gardner for the clockepyng		1	3
Item payd to the paresche Clarke		2	6
Item payd for gyrdylles and for a loke menddyng the cloke menddyng			5
Item payd for 8 fanns makying		4	4
Item payd mendyng the bokys to John Smyth		1	4
Item payd for Norwyche almes		2	6
Item payd for mendyng of the paymet in the chyrche			6
Item payd for two [2] stone of hempe and for the wyrkyn		2	2

---

85 A 'credyll' or cradle for the men working on the tower.

86 Perhaps this mould was made to fashion the clay entered in the previous entry.

87 A corruption of fane or vane, meaning a pennon or weathercock, which may be a reference to the pinnacle below. See P. Northeast, *Boxford Churchwardens' Accounts 1530–1561*, SRS, 23 (1982), p.98, where vanes are mentioned for the pinnacle which was under construction.

88 A reference to a double entertainment consisting of a churchale and a play with hired players. The players were paid 1s. 1d.

89 A taborer or drummer played the tabor, a small drum usually beaten with one stick, often accompanied by a pipe, the one musician drumming with one hand and piping with the other. This provided an irresistible combination for dancing, the tabor providing the beat and the pipe providing the tune. See *The Luttrell Psalter: a Facsimile*, ed. M.P. Brown (2006), fol.164r.

	£	s.	d.
Item payd for the clokke kepyng to John Gardner		1	3
Item payd to the paresche clarke at Myhelmes		2	6
Item payd to Thomas Hopper for waschyn for the halfe yer at Myhelmes		2	0
Item payd for the rowell makyn for the wax and the makyn			6
The sum	<1	9	10>
	1	4	10

[fol.8r]   *[1510–1511]*

	£	s.	d.
Item payd for to [2] bell clapyrs for the makyn		12	2
Item payd the charyage of them			4
Item payd to John Smyt for menddyng of 3 antyfeners and for a schyn		2	2
Item payd for mending of the leytorn			2
Item payd for mendyng of the clothys for the quere and for the cloth		1	0
Item payd for laces			1
Item payd for mendyng of the credyll to Bryon			3
Item payd for hokys <the> for the quere and yren werke			3
Item payd for the cloke kepyng for Christemes quartyr		1	3
Item payd for the paresche clarke for Crystemesse quartyr		2	6
Item payd for receyvyg of the king for the rengars(t)[90]			10
Item payd to \John/ Mandall of Thy\r/stun for makyn of \a new/ wheyll to the thred bell		7	0
Item payd for mendyng of the secund bell wheyll, and for a pese of tymber for the solyr, and for the leyng ouytt and for hys bordyng		4	0
Item payd for a planke and for the caryage		1	0
Item payd for weyr for the cloke		1	0
Item payd for the cloke kepyng to John Garner		1	3
Iem payd \for/ the mendyng of the cloke to John Gardner			4
Item payd for the clarke wages for the orgawns		2	6
Item payd for washyng to Hopper's wife		2	0
Item payd for mendyng of the gate			5
Item payd for the paschall makyn[91]		1	3
Item payd for setyng uppe of the herse and for the takyn downy ovyt			6
Item payd for the caryage of a pece of tymbyr for Bery			4
Item payd for Norwyche almes		2	3
The sum	2	4	10

[fol.8v]   *[1510–1511]*

	£	s.	d.
Item receyvyd for the pardon at Candellmes		3	4
Item receyvyd of Thomas Hopper for the halfe yere ferme		8	0

---

90   This refers to bells being rung for a royal visit, for which there are several entries in the accounts; see also CWA, fols 11v and 16r. Here it is Henry VIII who passes through, but there is no hint of where he might be going. However, the road from London towards Thetford cut through Mildenhall's sandy heath and bells might well have been rung to mark the occasion.

91   Where there is no other indication, the making of the paschal candle or the setting up of the herse can be taken as the beginning of the Easter celebrations.

	£	s.	d.
Item receyvyd for the pardon day on Phylyppys and Jacobb		5	4
Item receyvyd for the May ale the sum	1	3	4½
Item receyvyd for the pardon day on Corpus Christi day		5	4
Item receyvyd for the qwheod of Roberd Calfe		2	0
Item receyvyd for the pardon day at Myhelmes		3	4
Item receyvyd of Thomas Hopper for half yer feyrme at Myhelmes		8	0
Item receyvyd for the pardon at Dedycacion day		4	0
Item receyvyd for the pardon at Cadylmes day		3	10
Item receyvyd of the coll cartes to the reparacions of the chyrche			8
Item <receyed> receyvyd for the qwheod of John Chapman		6	8
Item receyvyd for the qwheod of Roberd Reve		3	4
Item receyvyd for the qwehod of John <Tyrle> Tyrrell		1	0
Item receyvyd of Thomas Hopper for the half yers ferme			
at Owyr Lady day		8	0
Item receyvyd for the pardon day on Phylyp and Jacobb		3	4
Item receyvyd for the qwheod of Wylliam Weynge		3	4
Item receyvyd for the May ale in the West Rowe	1	17	0
Item receyvyd on <> Corpus Christi day for the pardon		4	0
Item receyvyd on Myhelmes day for the pardon		4	0
Item receyvyd of Thomas Hopper for the halfe yers ferme		8	0
Item receyvyd for the pardon day on Dedicacon		6	6
Item receyvyd for the quethed of Alys Reve			7
Item receyvyd for the pardon at Candellmes		3	0
Item receyvyd for the qwethod of <Thomas> John Morley		1	0
The sum	9	5	0½
		<1	1½>

[fol. 9r]

Item payd to John Smyt for mendyng of the prosecenary	1	0
Item payd for the clarke wages at Mydsomyr for the orguns	2	6
Item payd to John Gardner for the cloke kepyng	1	3
Item payd for the belles halowyng and othyr costs withall[92]	2	4
Item payd for the prystes syrples	4	4
Item payd for Rumskot	2	6
Item payd for the cloc kepyng to John Garder	1	3
Item payd to the paresche clarke for Myhelmesse quartyr	2	6
Item payd for mendyng of the pystyll boke to John Smyth	1	4
Item payd for wasyng to Thomas Hopper	2	0
Item payd for the rowell makyn	1	0
Item payd for sowd for the plumer and for hys labyr and hys bordyng	4	6
Item payd for a ladder payd to John Donome	2	0
Item payd for a bell rope		8
Item payd for 3 baudrckes makyn		5
Item payd for <>1 bell rope		3
Item payd for paymet tyll	3	4

---

[92] The hallowing of the bells was a dedication ceremony not unlike baptism during which the bells received names. For Mildenhall's bell called John see Introduction, 'The Bells and the Clock' (p.liii).

	£	s.	d.
Item payd for the cofyn makyn		1	8
Item payd to John Gardner for the cloke kepyng		1	3
Item payd to the clarke for Myhelmes quartyr		2	6
Item payd to Umfrey Dofeld for the sangrene[93]		8	0
The sum	2	6	7

[fol. 9v]

	£	s.	d.
Remanyng in the box	3<5>4		0

The chyrche werdens: John Clement, Wylliam Costyng,
    Roberd Petche, John Alen

	£	s.	d.
Item payd to the paresche Clarke		2	6
Item payd to John Garner for the cloke kepyng		1	3
Item payd to Margery Hopper for waschyng[94]		2	0
Item payd for mendyng of the westry dore loke, and for tentyr hokys and Bagot's bell			4
Item payd John Pachet for mendyng of the same bell wheyll		1	1½
Item payd for pathyn in the chyrche		1	3
Item for waxe 3 pound for the paschale[95]		1	8½
Item payd for mendyng of the letorne to John Bruer			4
Item payd for a bell rope		1	1
Item payd for skoryng of the canstylls			4
Item payd for the herse setting uppe and for the taking donge[96]			9
Item payd for Rumscot		2	3
Item payd for the hangyn of the halywater stoppe			3
Item payd for <al> a rope for the clocke		1	3
Item payd for the rowell			2
Item payd for the mendyng of the copys and the vestementes			4
Item payd to the parysche clarke for mydsomyr quartyr		2	6
Item payd to John Gardner for the clocke kepyng		1	3
The sum	1	0	8

[fol. 10r]

	£	s.	d.
Item payd for burd		1	7
Item payd for nayll		1	1
Item payd for the casykke		1	4
Item payd to John Pachet for hys werke			8
Item payd for to [2] lodes of sond			8
Item payd to the plumer		4	0
Item payd for hys bordyng		2	0

---

93   In the Suffolk dialect spoken in the west of the county, the word 'sangrede' or 'sangrene' meant a service chanted for the souls of the departed, often sung or said from the pulpit. In the east of the county, similar prayers were called a 'certeyn'. The going-rate for either was between 3s. 4d. and 4s. 4d.

94   Margery was the wife of Thomas Hopper; see Appendix 2:37, a transcription of his will of 1524 (SROB, IC 500/2/14/91–92).

95   The paschal candle, lit on the Saturday of Holy Week, was placed on the Gospel side of the altar where it burned until Ascension Day. See Northeast, *Boxford*, p.100.

96   The herse, bedecked with candles, was set up on the Easter sepulchre. The candles burned here from Maundy Thursday until Easter Day, when the herse was taken down again.

	£	s.	d.
Item payd for hys man for the plumer		1	0
Item pay for 6 days and an halfe to the plumer[97]		4	4
Item payd for sowyd		1	0
Item payd for nayll			10
Item payd for wod		1	0
Item for hyr [sic] bordyng		2	10
Item for bord			3
Item payd for the trusyng of the bells		1	0
Item payd for Norwyhee almes		2	3
Item payd tor [sic] John Gardner		1	3
Item payd to the paresche Clarke		2	6
Item payd for a loke for the mendyng			3
Item payd for a masun and lyme			6
Item payd for gyrdylles			4
Item payd for laces			2
The sum	1	10	8

[fol. 10v] — **[1512–1513]**

	£	s.	d.
Item payd for a copyll asprys			7
Item payd for hempe			3
Item payd for Elys for the ropys			3
Item payd for a key makyn to the chawnsell dore[98]			6
Item payd for a locke and to[2] keys			6
Item for lynyng of the vestry dore		1	2½
Item payd for wascheyn to Hopper		2	0
Item payd for the locke settyng on			1
Item payd for mendyng of the almery			3
Item payd for <to the chyrche> to barres to the dores			4
Item payd to the chymny makyn		5	0
Item payd for the rowell makyn		1	1
Item payd to John Gardner for the clocke kepyn		1	3
Item payd to the clarke for the orguns kepyng		2	6
Item payd for 2 clapyrs makyn		16	0
Item payd for a prosessenary makyn		2	5
Item payd for olys for the ropys			2
Item payd for the taske		1	0
Item payd for the <he> clokke kepyng		1	3
Item payd to the paresche clarke		2	6
Item payd for skuyng of the rodelofte		3	4
The sum	2	2	4½

---

97 The plumber's rate of pay was 4d. a day. He probably came from Bury St Edmunds. His boarding and that of his mate at 4s.10d. was half the cost of the work carried out. It is surprising that so much repair work was carried out by workmen who came from outside the High Town. Perhaps the proximity of Bury St Edmunds encouraged the wardens to employ more expert help, which might be available from the abbey.

98 The second key to be made for the chancel door in a very short time: see CWA, fol.5v.

[fol.11r]   [1513–1514]

	£	s.	d.
Item receyvyd of Thomas Hopper for the halfe yers ferme		8	0
Item receyvd for the pardon day on Phylyppys day and Jacobb		4	0
Item receyvd for the pardon on Corpus Christi day		6	0
Item receyvyd for the chyrche all [ale] makyn	1	16	8
Item recevyd for the pardon day at Myhellmes		4	2
Item receyvyd for the pardon day on Dedycacion		5	0
Item receyvyd of Roberd Baker for leyd		1	1
Item receyvyd of Tomas Hopper for the halfe yere ferme		8	0
Item receyvyd for the pardon day at Candylmesse		6	8
Item receyvyd of Thomas <p> Hopper for the halfe yer ferme		8	0
Item receyvyd for the pardon day of Phylyppe and Jacobb		5	8
Item receyvyd for the qhethod of Thomas Howton[99]		16	4
Item recevyd for the pardon day on Corpus Christi		6	4
Item recevyd of Thomas Hopper for one yer ferme		16	0
Item receyvyd for the pardon day at Myhelmese		3	4
Item rceyvyd for the pardon day on Dedycacion		6	0
Item receyvyd for the pardon day at Candelmesse		6	0
Itemreceyvyd for the halfe yers ferme of Thomas Hopper at <Candelmesse> Myhelmes		8	0
Item receyvyd for the qhethod of Thomas Gardner			8
Item receyvd for the qhwthod of Master Vekery[100]		3	4
Item received by thands of Master Vicar[101]		5	0
Item received of Thomas Hopper for the \first/ half yere ferm paid at the feast of thannunciacion of Owr Lady [in the] 5th year of Henry VIII [1514]		9	6
<The sum	7	19	7>
<The sum	8	14	1>
			5
The sum	11	18	5

[fol.11v]   [1513–1514]

	£	s.	d.
Item payd for the pascale	<illeg.> 1		7
Item payd to the plumer			6
Item payd for Romskot		2	3
Item payd for mendyng of the syrples and aube mendyng			5
Item payd for wasschyng		2	0
Item payd for the setyn uppe of the herse and the takyn downe ovyth			4
Item payd to John Gardner for the clocke kepyng		1	3
Item payd for mendyng of the cloke			2
Item payd to the paresche clarke for the orguns		2	6
Item payd for a glaswreyt		1	0

---

[99] Thomas Howton's widow, Margery, died within the next few years. Her will contained interesting bequests to Mildenhall church, of which Thomas had been a benefactor: Appendix 2:33.
[100] Perhaps this is a reference to the death of Paul Gayton. His incumbency ended in 1511–12 by which time he had been in post for forty-one years.
[101] In 1512 the new vicar appointed was John Wyllkynson.

	£	s.	d.
Item payd for a loke to the chyrche gate			2
Item for swepyng of chyrche		2	0
Item for feyng of the grate[102]			1
Item payd for trusyng of the <lyl> lytyll			6
Item payd for the makyn of the rowell			2
Item payd for mendyng of the copys			2
Item payd to John Gardner for the clocke kepyn		1	3
Item payd to the paresche clarke for orguns		2	6
Item payd for waschen for the halfe yer		2	0
Item payd for laces and nayll			2
Item payd for the receyvyn of the <qe> queyn[103] an the mes boke			9
The sum	1	1	9

[fol. 12r]

	£	s.	d.
Item payd for Romskot		2	3
Item payd for bell ropys		2	8
Item payd for mendyng of the bell wheyll			2
Item payd to John Gardner		1	3
Item payd to the paresche clerke		2	6
Item payd for the stokyn of 2 belles		1	5
Item payd for the rowell makyn [illeg.]		1	3
Item payd for mendyng of the bokys and the pathyn		<1	8>
of the chyrche		2	0
Item payd for waschyng		1	1
Item payd for gyrdylles <and a sentens boke>		2	8
Item payd for the cloke kepyng		1	3
Item payd to the paresche clarke for the orgawns		2	6
Item payd for waschyng at Owyr Lady day		1	0
Item payd for lynen cloth for the syrples			1

Memorandum John Dey hath paide 4 mark for the
quethword of Sir Roger Barford[104]

	£	s.	d.
The sum	1	3	0

[fol. 12v]   **[1515–1516]**
[Latin] The day of the Annunciation of the Blessed
Virgin Mary the 6th year Henry VIII [1515]

	£	s.	d.
Remaynyng in the chirche wardens handes	4	9	8

---

102 References to the 'grate' are frequent: the grating was set at the entrance to the churchyard to discourage animals from wandering on to the hallowed soil.

103 Katherine of Aragon was queen at this time. Katherine and Henry both passed through the parish, but not together. See CWA, fols 8r and 16r. She wrote to Henry on 16 September 1513 that she was going to 'Our Lady at Walsingham that I promised so long ago to see'. See *Letters and Papers Foreign and Domestic of the reign of Henry VIII*, ed. J.S. Brewer *et al.* (1880–1965), I, part 2, p.1016; Dymond, *Thetford Priory*, I, p.308. Katherine was entertained at the priory between June 1513 and June 1514. More expenses for the queen's visit were entered in the following year, referring to the purchase of rabbits and rushes.

104 Barford, the chantry chaplain, died in 1504. See Notes on People, p.199.

The chirch wardens this yere: William Pachet, Nicholas Willes,[105] Thomas Rolff, and John Bradley[106]

	£	s.	d.
Itym for 3 pownd wax for the paschal and the making		1	8
Itym for <tw> 2 surplysse making		4	0
Itym for the settyng up of the herse and takyng downe			8
Itym for swepyng of the glasse wyndow and the bell soler			3
Itym for byndyng of the newe messe boke[107] of the gyfte of Syr Roger Barford		2	6
Itym for a newe albe cloth and makyn			8
Itym payyd for Norwyche ames		2	3
Itym for repracion of the font			10
Itym for the repracion of the lytyll bell for stokkyng and tuining		10	2
Itym payd to the parysche klerke for the organs kepyng		2	6
Itym for the kepyng of the klocke		1	3
Itym payd for the cherche clothys waschyng		1	0
Itym payd for makyn clene of the cherche yard		< >	4
Itym payd for the halowyng of a peyr of chalys			6
Itym payd for the <go> cherche reveys \costys/ goyng to the visitacyon to Branne Fery[108]		< >	8
Itym payd to the repracion of the cherche walles			3
Itym payyd for the lytyl bell \whele/ making		3	4
Itym payyd for wax to the rowell		1	2
Itym payyd to the parysche clerke on Myhylmas day		2	6
Itym payyd for wascheyng		1	0
Itym payyd for clokke kepyng		1	3
Itym payyd for a fyre panne making[109]			1
Itym payyd for the lytell bell clapyr making		1	0
Itym payd for making clene of the stepyll			2
Itym payyd for the wryghtyng owt of the wyll			5
Itym payyd for 3 bellropys making	<5>	2	6
Itym payyd for 2 clapyrs making		9	10
Itym payyd for gyrdyllys for the vestmentys			6
Itym payd to the paresche Clarke		2	6
Itym payd to John Gardner for the clok kypeyng		1	3
Itym payd for waschyn to Wylliam Costyng[110]		1	0
Wylliam Costyng had 9d. of the cherche mony, the wyche was borne howt of the vestry		–	–
Itym for charke laying in the cherche \yerde/ <herde>		1	8
Itym for a cace makyn for the lectorne		2	0
Itym payyd for waxe for the paschal at Ester		1	10

---

105 Perhaps the same Nicholas Willes, 'tayler', who wrote his will in 1536, leaving 3s. 4d. to the repair of the church (SROB, IC 500/2/19/229).

106 Possibly John Bradley, who wrote his will in 1525 (SROB, IC 500/2/17/119).

107 Barforth made no mention of the gift of a mass-book in his will (Appendix 2:30).

108 Here Brandon was to be the meeting point for the archdeacon's visitation, to be attended by the churchwardens within the deanery.

109 The pan in which fire was carried in to the church, either for fabric repairs or for use during various services.

110 Costyn took over the laundering of the church linen at this point.

	£	s.	d.
	< 3	1	5>
		<illeg.>	
<sum> The Sum	3	3	4

[fol. 13r]

	£	s.	d.
Itym payyd to Rychard Nores for a bawdrycke making			2
Itym payyd for klapers caryyng from Bury			2
Itym payyd for <let> lectorne and a lyne for the veyll			2
Itym payyd for two strakys of the rodelofte			3
Itym payd to the parysche clerke		2	<>6
Itym payyd for wascheyng of the cherche clothys		1	0
Itym payyd to John Gardener, smythe, for kepyng of the clokke		1	3
Itym payyd for waxe for the pascall		1	10
Itym payyd for Romeskot		2	6
Itym payd for Norwyche almes		2	3
Itym payd for Romeskot		2	6
Itym payd for Norwyche almes		2	3
Itym payd for hyll mony that is put to the sensyr makyn		13	4
Itym payd for 2 lodes of sond caryin			4
Itym payd for the herse settyng uppe and the takyn down			6
Itym pay for 2 lodes of wode		2	8
Itym payd for the lenthyn of the mowld and the wall			6
Itym payd for a bord to Thomas Hopper			6
Itym payd for a syrples		2	6
Itym payd for the mendyng of the lytell clapyr		1	0
Itym payyd for 2 belle ropes		2	6
Itym payyd for bawdrykys for the belles			8
Itym payyd for <the> the rowell makyng		1	3
Itym payyd for the senser makyng[111]	1	0	8
Itym payyd for sylvyr that the goldsmyth put in the senser 2 ownce and half. Also for faschynyng		10	5
Itym payyd to the plummer for a eleven fothyer of leed leyyng on the cherche	2	4	0
Itym payyd for hys burd and hys man		14	8
Itym payyd for a hundryth leed		4	0
Itym payyd for tryyng of the aschys[112]		6	8
Itym payyd for 5 hundryth of leed nayll		2	1
Itym payyd for a broydrer for copes and vestmentes mendyng and for sylke and his burd		8	4
Itym payyd for lentyn crosse[113]			2
Itym payyd for a man goyng for a clarke			8
Itym the wages of the plomer and hys servant 3 days		2	0
Itym for ther bordyng		1	0

[111] In this entry and the one below, the church had a new silver censer made to a new design weighing 2½ ounces troy. It cost £1 11s. 1d.

[112] Trying was the act of sifting or separating the ashes left from the process of lead manufacture.

[113] During Lent a wooden cross painted red was used. This would account for the very reasonable cost of 2d.

	£	s.	d.
Itym to the parysche clarke for mydsomer quarter		2	6
Itym John Gardener for the clokes		1	3
Itym for 2 storopes for the spowtes			3
Itym for waschyng to William Costyn		1	0
< Sum	8	0	11>
<		13	10>
<	1	16	0>
<	1	18	2>
Sum	8	2	3
Sum	8	0	6

[fol.13v]   **[1515]**

	s.	d.
Item receyvyd for the quethe wurd of Thomas Gardener of Cake Strete[114]	3	4
Item receyvyd for the quethe wurd of Elsabeth Makwurthe		6
Item receyvyd for the quethe wurde of Symond Gardener		8
Item receyvyd for the pasturynge of Ely bullokks in Myldenall fenne[115]	2	4
Item receyvyd for the pardon day of Phylyp and Jacob	3	8
Item receyvyd for the quethe wurd of Robert Warren	1	0
Item receyvyd for the quethe wurd of Mothyr Boltton	1	0
Item receyvyd of the quethe wurde of John Morley	4	0
Item receyvyd for the pardon day of Corporis Christi	7	0
Item receyvyd for the cherche ale	4 marks	
Item receyvyd of the pardon day of Myhylmas day	3	0
Item receyvyd of Thomas Hopper on Myhylmas day	9	6
Item receyvyd for the pardon of Dedicacon day	4	8
Item recevyd for the pardon day of Candylmas day	5	0
Item receyvyd of Thomas Hopper for the ferme of the half yere for the londes that he hold dan at the Annuncyacon of Owr Lady 1515	9	6
Item receyvyd for the quetheword of George Symond	1	0
Item receyvyd for the pardon day of Corporis Christi	6	0
Item resavyd of wyll of Robert Symonds[116]	1	8
Item receyvyd of John Lynnde	1	0
Item receyvyd for the quethewurd of Rychard Tydde		6
Item receyvyd for the quethe wurd of <Symo> Mawte Halstede	3	4
Item receyvyd for the quethe wurd of Emme Burgayne		4
Item receyvyd of Myhilmas for the pardon	3	0
Item receyvyd of Thomas Hopper at Myhilmas	9	6
Item receyvyd for the pardon day of Dedicacon <10>	5	4
Item receyvyd of Thomas Lany's wyll	12	8
Item receyvyd of Donom's quethword	3	4
Item receyvyd of the gyft of Annes Emson	3	4
Item receyvyd of William Geson	a nobyll	
The sum	7 19 6	

---

114 The will of Thomas Gardener of Cake Street, 1513 (SROB, IC 500/2/13/187).
115 A substantial payment was received here by the churchwardens for renting out pasture.
116 The will of Robert Symonds, 1514 (SROB, IC 500/2/12/126).

	£	s.	d.
Item receyvyd in the fest of the Purificacion for the pardon day		5	0
Item receyvyd for the qwethwurd of George Halstead		1	8
Item receyvyd of Thomas Hopper of Owr Lady day		9	6
Item receyvyd of Philipys day and Jacob for the pardon		4	0
Item receyvyd of the quethewurd of Mawte Holme		1	0
Sum total received	13	8	0

[fol. 14r] [1516–1517]

	£	s.	d.
<Item for mendyng of the chyrche gate		<3	>
<Item payd for a bell whelle makyng		<	>
<Item payd for twyn bell ropes makyng		<2	4>
<Item payd for trusyng of 2 belles		<1	1>
Item payyd for a sanggered[117] payyd to Master Vicar		8	0
Item payyd to Jhon Screvyner for mendyng of bookes			6
Item payd for wax for the rowell		2	1
Item payd for a rope \for the paschal/			4
Item payd for Romeskot at Ester		2	3
Item payd to John Gardener, smythe, for clokk kepyng		1	3
Also to the same John for makyng of 2 lokkys			6
Item payd to William Costen for waschyng		1	0
Item payd for swepyng of the rode loft			8
Item payd for the sepulture <sep> setyng up and takyng downne[118]			6
Item paid for wax to the rowell			4
Item paid for the pascall[119]		1	9½
<Sum total received	13	8	0>

	£	s.	d.
Item \payd/ John Garner for the cloke kepyng		5	0
Item Wylliam Costyng for wassyng		4	0
Item payd to the parys clarke for [illeg.] \organ/ kepyng[120]		10	0
Item payd for the clerks costs of yngom to Master Tawmage		1	5
Item payde for grett bell clapper makyng		4	2
Item payd for a mason and hys man and for lyme and sond and for ther mett and <> drynke		4	1
Item payd for 2 bell ropys		2	6
The sum	2	10	4

[Latin] The year of Our Lord 1516 [illeg.] the churchwardens of blessed Mary of Mildenhall [illeg.] nominated by the town <Ralph> Humfrey Duffyld[121] and William Langham[122] and they received

---

117 An un-named parishioner left 8s. for short-term commemorative prayers: see Glossary p.194.
118 This refers to the Easter sepulchre.
119 The paschal candle, which would burn for forty days.
120 This payment must represent the wage for twelve months.
121 Humfrey Duffyld and William Langham were nominated as churchwardens for the High Town. In his will of 1530 (NRO, NCC Attmere 120) Duffyld left William Langham 3s. 4d. and made him an executor, which Langham renounced. See Apendix 2:38.
122 William Langham's will was written in 1532 (SROB, IC 500/2/19/89). The second of his two sons was called Umfrey, no doubt after Humfrey Duffyld.

in advance in the pyx £3 5s. For the towns George Plase and
John Dokyng named.[123]

Memorandum that Jone Gardner owes 6s. through a will.

	By hand	£3	5	0

[fol.14v]	£	s.	d.
Rec' Thomas Hopper		9	6
Memorandum Receved in the fest of Sent Meichall the pardon day		4	6
Item rec' of the laste wyll of Sir Andru Place	2	0	0
Item rec' of the laste wyll Symonde Broweht			8
Item rec' of the laste wyll of Rychard Place[124]		5	0
Item rec' up on Dedicacion day for the pardon		6	4
Item rec' of the laste wyll of Wylliam Peche		6	8
Item rec' of the last wyll of John Basset		1	8
Item rec' Thomas Hopper			6
Item rec' Thomas Hopper		9	6
Item rec' up on Candelmas day for the pardon		4	4
Item rec' in the fest of Phelup and Jacob for the pardon		4	0
Item rec' of the wache of Halywell for an drynkyng[125]		13	4
Item rec' for the pardon up on Corpus Christi day		3	4
Item rec' of the qwethe word of Wylliam Warde		6	8
Item rec' for the pardon in the feste of Sent Michaell Archangell		3	0
Item rec' for the pardon up on Dedicacion day		4	4
Item rec' for the pardon up on Candellmas day		5	0
Item rec' of the qwethe worde of Margery Howtton[126]	1	0	0
Item the qwtheworde of John Clemend		6	8
Item received from Thomas Hopper		9	6
Item received Thomas Hopper		9	6
Memorandum <illeg. For Joan Lane wedu>		12	1
Item received <John Lane>		6	8
Item rec' in the feste of Phelyp and Jacob of the pardon		3	8
Item rec' in the fest of Corperys Christi		4	0
Item rec'in the fest of Sent Mychell the Archangell		4	4
Item rec'of the beqweste of Mastres Margarete		6	8
Item rec' in the fest of Dydycacon		4	8
Item rec' of the qwethe worde of John Mansell		2	0
Item rec' in the Puryfycacon of Wer Lady		3	4
Item rec' Thomas Hopper		9	6
Item rec' of the qwethe of Thomas Symonde		1	0
Item rec' of the qwethe of Wylliam Flawner			4
Item rec' of the qwethe of Wylliam Rawlyng		1	0
Item rec' of the qwe[theword] of John Hadnham			8
Item received in the fest of Sent Miell the Arcangel for the pardon		2	8

---

123 George Place and John Dokyng were nominated as wardens representing the Rows.
124 Richard Place left 5s. to the reparation of St Mary's church in 1516 (SROB, IC 500/2/13/221).
125 This refers to a churchale held at Holywell Row.
126 See Appendix 2:33.

	£	s.	d.
Receved Thomas Hopper[127]		9	6
[Latin] Sum Sum of this side	12	8	5
Item by hands	3	5	0
The Sum total	15	13	5

[fol.15r]   [1516–1517]

	£	s.	d.
Item payd for sute of the courte[128] for the cherche		2	4
Item payyd for scheers makyng			6
Item payyd for Norwyche almes		2	6
Item payyd to the parysche clerke for waschyng		1	0
Item payyd to John Garner for kepyng of the cloke		1	3
Item for mendyng of a sorplese			1
Item payyd for trusyng of twayn belles		1	0
Item for mending of the cherche gate			3
Item payd for a bell wele makyng		2	0
Item payd for 2 bel roppys		2	4
Item payd <p><> for trussyn of 2 belles		1	1
Item payd to John Gerner for kepyng of the kloke		1	3
Item payd for wassyng of the cherche clothys		1	0
Item payd to the parise klerke for kepyng of the ordles		10	0
Item payd for glasyng in the cherche		3	7
Item payd for mendyng the pamentyn of the cherche			6
The Sum	1	10	8

	£	s.	d.
Item payd for the clerkes costes		1	6
Item payd a loke for the cherch gate			2
Item payd for mendyng of the vestemens		2	4
Item payd for hys bord		1	0

[fol.15v]

Costes and expens

	£	s.	d.
Item payd for sqworyng of the hernes[129]		2	0
Item payde for 2 bell roppis		1	6
Item payd for 9ᶜ 5ˣˣ and 6lb led		19	5
Item for <> caryage of the same led		1	1
Item for reparyng of the cherche howse		1	0
Item payd to the dene for Romeskot		2	6
Item for 2 crwttes[130]		1	0
Item for mendyng of the cherche gattes		2	2
Item for mendyng of the peyxte		4	0
Item for 2 <bellys> bell ropys		2	6
Item to the parys Clarke		2	6

---

127   This is the final reference to Thomas Hopper in the churchwardens' accounts. His will was proved at Bury St Edmunds in 1524 (SROB, IC 500/2/14/91). See Appendix 2:37.

128   A suit of court was an obligation for a tenant to attend the court of his lord. There is no indication of the identity of this court, but as the church was involved it must refer to an ecclesiastical court.

129   This refers to scouring a harness, but what type of harness is not known.

130   Cruets or flasks came in pairs, one holding the wine, the other water for the mass.

	£	s.	d.
Item for wassyng of the cherche clothys			2
Item to John Gardener for the cloke		1	3
Item for 3 bokelles for the belles			6
Item for wytte lether for the belles		1	3
Item payd to Roberd Breon for mending the schrewyng pew		2	0
Item payd for kewerynges of the 3 auteres 12 yerdes canwas[131]		3	7
Item payd for 3 yerdes and a halffe of heyer			8
Item payd to the plomer for sowdyng <1s. 8d.>		1	0
Item payd for the rowell 3lb wax and for makyng		2	1
Item payd for 4 swrpelyse		6	8
Item for mending of an albe			8½
Item<for> payd to John Gardener for kepyng of the cloke		1	3
Item payd to the clarke for the horganes		2	6
Item payd to Wylliam Costyn for wassyng[132]		1	0
Item for mend of 2 bel clapyrs		6	0
Item for the wages of the clarke for kepyng the horganys		2	6
Item payd to J Gardener for kepyng of the cloke		1	3
Item for wassyng of the cherche gere		1	0
Item for mendyng of the chalys		2	0
Item for wyt lethyr for bawdrykys of the belles		2	0
Item for swepyng of the bel soler[133]			3
Item for mending of the pulpet ladder[134]			6
The Sum	4	17	9½

[fol.16r]

	£	s.	d.
Item payd to the clarke for kepyng of the organys		2	6
Item to John Gardener for kepyng of the cloke		1	3
Item for wassyng of the cherch ger		1	0
Item for 3lb and ½ of sowdyr		1	2
Item payd to the plomer		1	1
Item for feryng			2
Item payd to the Norwyche alms		2	3
Item for makyng of 4 bawdryces			8
Item for mendyng of the bellys			4
Item for 1 belrop the price		1	4
Item for drawing of the lake betwyx Ely comun and owr comun[135]			9
Item for 3lb wax for the rowell and for makyng		2	0

---

[131] Canvas and hair cloth were used as under coverings on the altars. The reference to 'the three altars' suggests that the chancel, the vestry and the south aisle were the responsibility of the churchwardens. Other altars, of which St John's altar was one and there may have been more, would have been adorned by those who had endowed them for commemorative practices, e.g. gild and chantry foundations. These were financed by feoffees, families and friends of the departed.

[132] William Costyn now becomes the official launderer to the church.

[133] The bell-ringing chamber.

[134] Pulpits were already in place in many churches before the Reformation. Southwold church has a pulpit of c.1470. See Cautley, *Suffolk Churches* (1975), p.348.

[135] 'Drawing' is a mis-reading of draining which would have been entered in the rough copy of the accounts. The entry refers to the draining of the expanse of water between Ely and Mildenhall commons.

	£	s.	d.
Item for thache and thachyng of the cherche howse		1	2
Item for kepyng of the organys onto the clarke		2	6
Item to John Gardener for kepyng of the cloke[136]		1	3
Item for wassyng of the cherche clothys		1	0
Item for 4 bowrds for the lates for the stepyl wyndos		1	4
Item for tymber for the sayd lates			8
Item for sawyng of the bowrdes			6
Item for <fa> naylys for the sayd wyndos		1	0
Item for makyng of the sayd lates		1	9
Item for 2 yerdes of clothe for albys and makying		1	2
Item for 1 roope for the lekyll bell			3
Item for mendyng of the cherche clothys			6
Item for rengyng for the qwene's grace comyng throw towne[137]			4
Item for half 1 horse hyde of wetlether[138]		1	1
Item for 7 gardelys for to towe			3
Item for 1 bowrde for the cherche howse			4
Item for 2lb wax and for the paskal and for makyng		1	4
Item for makyn of 1 belrope		1	10
Item for mendyng of 1 bawderek			2
Item for setyng up and takyng down of the sepulture			4
Item for Norwyhe almese		2	3
Item for makyng of the sencer			2
Item for mendyng of 2 bokys[139]			7
The sum	1	16	5

[fol.16v]

	£	s.	d.
Item for 2 skennys for to cower the bokys			6
Item for makeng of 1 bawdryc			2
Item for masonys warke in the cherche			3½
Item for mendyng of copys and vestments		7	0
Item for selke threde and rebon price		1	7
Item 2 yerdys of bokerham			8
Item to the clarke for kepyng the horganys		2	6
Item to kepe the cloke		1	3
Item for wassyng the cherche clothys		1	0
Item for mending of the pa<y>mente in the cherche			5
Item for mendyng of 1 loke			2
Item payd to the clarke for the horgans		2	6
Item for wassyng the cherche clothys		1	0
Item for kepyng of the cloke		1	3
Item for 3lb wax and the makyng of the paskall		2	2

---

136 John Gardener, the smith and keeper of the church clock, wrote his will in 1519 (SROB, IC 500/2/12/26). It is damaged and has no probate.

137 This records ringing of church bells when royalty passed through the parish. See CWA, fols 8r, 11v and n.103.

138 This white leather was used to cover the baldricks or the books in the following entry. See also n.156.

139 The expenses for mending two liturgical books are carried over to the next folio.

	£	s.	d.
Item for mendyng of 3 sorplyse			3
Item for mendyng of a grawe[140] in the cherche			4
Item for the wages to the paryche Clarke		2	6
Item for 3 quarters clothe for 1 albe			5
Item for mendyng of the paskall hed			2
Item for seftyng up the sepulker and takyng downe[141]			6
Item payd to Norwyche almes		2	3
Item for mendyng a bell weyll			5
Item for mendyng a loke for the <>[deletion] stepyll dore			4
Item for mendyng of the pawle and for pynnys and stawys			3
Item payd for wasyng of the cherche ger		1	0
Item payd kepyng of the cloke		1	3
Item for kepyng of the organys		2	6
Item for mendyng of bokes and for claspys[142]		1	9
Item to the plomer for sowde and warkemansche		2	1
Item for sangredys to Mastyr Weker			8
Item for skoryng of the candylstykes			2
The sum		<6	8½>
	2	6	8½

[fol. 17r]   [1528]

Allocacons to be allowed unto the new churchewardens, that ys to sey
   Nicholas Palton, Thomas <Quasshe> Cotes, Thomas Wederes and
   John Peche of Beck, at Ester quarter the 20th year of Henry VIII.

	£	s.	d.
Fyrst to Romeskott <quarter> at Ester quarter, the 20th year of Henry VIII		2	3
Item for Quasshe wages dew at Mydsomer, the 20th year of Henry VIII[143]		3	4
Item paid to one for polysshyng and burnesshyng of the laten crosse and the laten sencers with a shypp, 1 peyr <candykkes> candelstykes coper and gylt, and to <1> other laten candelstykes		3	8
Item for botemyng of the latent sencers and sowderyng of one of the laten candelstykes			6
Item payd to greate wyer for to mende the clock			6
Item paid to Polyngton for mendyng of the belowe of the greate orgaynes			2
Item for 1 lb of wax 6d. and makyng of the ruell at genst Wytsond,[144] the 20th year of Henry VIII			10

---

140 Grawe is a mis-spelling of grave.
141 Seftyng is a mis-spelling of setting.
142 Books written on parchment and not having board covers were apt to have buckled leaves. Clasps kept the leaves straight and together. Books were shelved with the fore-edge facing out, but clasps might be damaged by being used as handles for pulling the book off the shelf. A visitation at York Minster reported that 'we fynde grete neclygense of the deacons and clerkis of the vestry that the mesbuke is not clasped, wherby a fayre boke is nye lost'. See Wordsworth, *Old Service Books*, p.274.
143 The wage of the parish clerk and organ player is raised to 3s. 4d. a quarter. Perhaps Thomas Quasshe was the clerk at this time.
144 Whit Sunday.

	£	s.	d.
Item paid for the heyre that lyeth upon the vestre auter[145]			7
Item payd to Polyngton for kepyng of the clock in Ester terme		1	3
Item payd for wasshyng <> of the church gere the same Ester terme		1	0

Mydsomer quarter, the 20th year of Henry VIII

	£	s.	d.
Item for 2 bell ropys, that is to say for the forebell and the thyrd belle		3	6
Item for skowryng of the oldest coper crosse and 2 the lest laten candelstykes			10
Item for Bagott's bell ropys[7d.] and for laces[1d.] to mend copys			8
Item for glasyng of the churche wyndows in every place		3	6
Item for this clerke's quarterage of the half quarter			10
Item for waschyng the chyrch stuff this quarter			2
Item for mending[1d] and kepyng of the clock this quarter[15d]		1	4

Michelmasse quarter

	£	s.	d.
Item paid for 6 unnces of Reband sylk		6	0
Item paied for Romeskott		2	3
Item for 2 <> bell clappers [6s.] new making, and 6 mendyng [6s.] and [illeg.]	1	3	0
Item for a new lantern bought for the chyrche			9
Item for 2 laches of the belles			4
Item for the orgeyn player quarterage[146]		3	4
Item for wasshyng of the chyrch gere this quarter		1	0
Item for kepyng of the clock this Michel quarter		1	3
Item for mendyng of the clock ropis and for papur for clerke			2
Item for mendyng of the paryshe surplesse			3
The Sum part	–	–	–

Crystmasse Quarter in the 20th year of Henry 8 <>

	£	s.	d.
Item for the sangrede of Thomas Sherd and his frends overpaid on the ffest of the Puryficacon of Oure Lady		4	0
Item for the skowryng of the lamp bason		1	1
Item for the greate bell rope		1	6
Item for yron werk of the market gate[147]			2
Item for mendyng of the lock of the over stepell dore <mendyng>			1
Item for tymbre of the west <church> gate of the church			4
Item for yron and nayle to the \same/			2
Item for a carpenter for 2 daies mendyng therof, and in the stepyll, with mete the same 2 daies		1	2
Item for a bawdre makyng			2
Item for wax for the ruell 2lb and makyng therof and candell		1	3
Item for mendyng of the sylver pyx at Bury		1	8

---

145 The vestry was housed in the thirteenth-century north chancel chapel, the oldest part of the church. The 'heyre' in this entry refers to haircloth used as an underlay.

146 The organ player received a pay rise from 2s. 6d. to 3s. 4d. a quarter.

147 The market gate, leading to the market place, was the east gate of the churchyard. The following four entries show that the carpenter worked on the market gate, the west gate and the steeple for two days, receiving 1s. 2d. and board without lodging.

	£	s.	d.
Item for the ◇ clerkes wages and the orgeyns pleyeng[148]		3	4
Item for wassyng of chyrch <ceg> gere			11
Item for the clock kepyng quarterly		1	3
Item for mendyng of the same clock			2
Item for oyle spent this quarter for the lamp			6
Item for lyme spent abowt the payment[149] of the church			8
Item for pavyng of the same payments in a greate			10
Item for a lache and other gynnes[150] mendyng abowt the greate<byl> bell			4
Item for a lyne to draw up the cloth ◇ before the rode on Palme Sonday[151]			1½
Item for a lod of sonde to the same werk			3

[1528–1529]

Ester Quarter the 20th year of Henry VIII

	£	s.	d.
Item for settyng up the sepulture and drynks 2d for the same folks			8
Item for 3lb wax for the wax of the paschall \after 5½d. of the pound/		1	4½
Item for makyng of the same pascall			2
Item for mendyng of the whele of the Sanntes bell			2
Item for mendyng of the clock wele			6
Item for Norwyche almes		2	3
Item paid to prystes and clerkes for the obyte of Thomas Sherd and his wyffes		4	8
Item for mendyng of the quere say clothys and curteyns			2
Item for the clerkes wages for pleyng at the orgeyns		3	4
Sum part			

[fol.18r] **[?1529]**

	£	s.	d.
Item pay to the plomer for casting 1000 lb leeds in webbys[152]		5	0
Item for wood for to melt the same leed			10
Item to John Lane for 700 leed nayle and half		3	9
Item boords for the pentyse and the dore \makyng/ for the lanter[153]		1	0
Item to John Lane for nayle for the same dore and pentyse			2½
Item for mendyng the lectorn, the lawer and the weyll for the clok			5

---

148 The parish clerk was now on a steady income of 3s. 4d. per quarter.
149 Lime mortar was used here where paving was being replaced.
150 The principle on which 'gynnes' worked was by a rope which ran over a wheel or pulley fixed to a point above the position to which the stone, wood or, as here, the great bell was being moved. The rope had a hook at one end, the other end passing round an axle rotated by a wheel. Salzman, *Building in England*, pp.324, 329 and 565.
151 A reference to the Lenten veil which hung across the chancel arch during Lent, shrouding the chancel.
152 The lantern was constructed by John Lane, the carpenter, while Poule, the plumber, laid the lead on the roof.
153 Many of the entries on this folio refer to the leading of the lantern. Poule received wages totalling £2 overall, with 6s. 8d. and two part-payments of 10s., each on the present folio and the balance on CWA, fol.18v.

	£	s.	d.
Item [*illeg.*] hemp and leyng the same and mendyng the roop for the gret bell			6
Item payd to Master Wekery for the sangred for Scherd		4	0
Item payd to the plomer in parte of his payment		6	8
Sum	1	13	2½

The 5th Quarter

	£	s.	d.
Item for the clarkes wages for the organis		3	4
Item payd to the sexten for kepyng the clok		1	3
Item for waysyng the clothis of the cherche		1	0
Item to John Lane for halffe a hundred leed nayle			3
Item to the plomer for castyng and schotyng 1600 leed in webbys		8	0
Item for wood to melt the same leed			10
Item for setyng hup of the sepulter and takyng down of the same			8
Item wax for the pascall and for making of the same		1	2
Item to the clarks of the regester at London for the cherche londes serching[154]		2	0
Item payd to the prystes and clerkes and poore pepyll up on the anniverser of Thomas Scherd, Anabyll and Alys, his wyefys		4	0
Item payd on to Norwyche almes		2	3
Item payd to John Lane for a hundred led nayle and trosyng of the therd bell		2	0
Item payd to Poule the plomer for hys wage		10	0
Item payd to John Lane for led nayle and other nayle			3
Item payd to Poule the plomer for his wagys		10	0
Item payd to Poule the plomer for 11lb sond		3	8
Item for wood for to meke the same leed[155]	—	—	

[*fol. 18v*]	[*?1529*]		
Item payd for 1 lood of sond			2
Item for <halffe> a heyd of wyht lether[156]		1	8
Item for makyng a bawdryc for the lekyll bell			4
Sum	2	12	10

The 6th Quarter

	£	s.	d.
Item the clarkes wagys for kepyng the organes		3	4
Item payd to the sexten for kepyng of the cloke		1	3
Item payd for wayssyng the clothys of the cherche		1	0
Item for makyng the lyte of the rowell and expensis at the vesitacion[157]			10
Item payd to the goldesmyth for mendyng the crost and the senceres and the schepe, and the gyldyng of thos same		12	0
Item payd to the masonys for boord and wagys		3	0
Item payd for for lyme and sond and careng		3	6

---

154 This entry is too early to be a reference to *Valor Ecclesiasticus*. It could concern glebe land or even land bequeathed for commemorative purposes, such as the entry immediately below in which the monetary return from land left by Sherd supported his anniversary and that of his wives.

155 There is no amount entered here in the accounts.

156 Leather would be used to cover the baldrick of the little bell in the entry following. See also n.138 above.

157 This would be the visitation of some important cleric, such as the archdeacon.

	£	s.	d.
Item payd to the glaswryht		6	0
Item payd to the smyht for settyng the lok on the cherche dore and for trussyng of Bakot's bell		4	0
Item payd for the Romskot		2	3
Sum	1	13	6

The 7th Quarter

Item the clarkes wagys for kepyng the organs		3	4
Item to Rychard Politon for kepyng the clok		1	3
Item for wayssyng the clothys of the cherche		1	0
Item payd to Poule the plomer forte schelynges in a full payment of his wages for the lanter		13	4
Item to the carpenter for makeng the third bell whell, for his boord and his wagys		4	8
Item for nayle and a sole for the same wheyll			6
Item to Nycholas Mey for tymber and Umfrey for [illeg.]		1	2
Item a new roop for the therd bell		1	8

[fol.19r] **[?1529]**

Item for 1 bolt of eren for the gret bell			6
Item payd for halfe 100 leeds on schet		2	6
Item for a new belroop for the thyrd bell		2	4
Item to the boke bynder for mendyng the bokes		5	8
Item for mendyng of and sondyng of 2 crossys			7
Item payd to the clarkes wages, the sexten and waysyng[158]		5	7
Sum	2	4	1

The 8th Quarter

Item the clarkes wages for kepyng the organs		3	4
Item payd to the sexten for kepyng of the cloke		1	3
Item payd for wayssyng the clothis longyng to the cherche		1	0
Item 3lb wex for the pascal and for makyng of the same		1	9
Item settyng up the sepulcer and taking don agen			8
Item for a lok and settyng upon a coffer			10
Item for mendyng the albys and the vestementes			4
Item payd to prystes, clarkes and to poore pepyll on the anniverser of Thomas Scherd, Anabell and Alys, his weyeffys		5	0
Item for a bolt of eren and 5 staplys and 2 loks for the cherche gates			7
Item for makyng 1 bawdryk for the bell			2
Item to Master Wekery for the sangerd of Scherd and his weyfys		4	0
Item for makyng of the deed for the land of Scherd		1	0
		19	11

The 9th Quarter

Item Receyved of Herry Morley for a howse is in the common callyd Hopperys cotte[159] for the ferme of 4 yerys past at the fest of Sent Mihell last past		3	0

---

[158] A breakdown of this entry would be 3s. 4d. to the clerk for playing the organ, 1s. 3d. paid to the sexton for keeping the clock and 1s. to the 'official' launderer to the church.

[159] This property had presumably been rented by Thomas Hopper, the parishioner previously in charge of the church laundry, who had died in 1524. See above, notes 74, 127.

Memorandum her ys renayneng in the cherche 400 lb and ½ in leed, redy schet in webbys.
< *illeg.*>

[*fol. 19v*]   [*1528–1529*]
Myldenhale

[*Latin*] **Memorandum that on St George's day in the <19> 20ᵗʰ year of Henry VIII, William Reve,[160] chaplain of the carn[ary], Thomas Gyson,[161] William Peche[162] of Wilde Street and John Chyston of West Row, churchwardens of the parish church of Mildenhall aforesaid, came into the presence of all the parishioners aforesaid and made their account of the church aforesaid and made their account of which all things that have been charged and are to be charged and all things allowed, William Reve, Thomas Gyson, William Peche and John Chyston on the said day and year and place came again and quit their account. And they are quit.** [*1528*]

Memorandum that on the same St George's day in the 20ᵗʰ year of King Henry VIII, the said parishioners elected to the office of churchwarden of the aforesaid church: Nicholas Palton, Thomas Cotes, Thomas Wederys and John Peche, and they received in counted money as follows:

	£	s.	d.
Firstly they received from the old churchwardens on the said day and year	1	9	6
Item they received from the same wardens for lead sold		1	6
Item in collection[163] for Mildenhall church on the day of <the Finding of the Holy Cross> the apostles, Philip and James, in the 20ᵗʰ year of Henry VIII [*1 May 1528*]		2	2
<For the burnysshyng and polysshyng of the coper crosse and the laten sencers and the <> peyre of candelstykes of coper gylt and the laten candelstykes and the laten shypp		3	8
Item for botemyng of the laten sencers and sowderyng of the laten candestykes			6>

[*Latin*]
Item received from the bequest of William Balles, deceased		10	0

---

160   William Reve's will was proved in 1545/6 (SROB, IC 500/2/21/184).
161   Thomas Gyson (Gesyn, Geson) must have died soon after relinquishing the post of churchwarden in 1528 (SROB, IC 500/2/15/217).
162   See Appendix 2:42.
163   The finding of the Holy Cross by St Helena was celebrated on 3 May, three days after St Philip and St James's Day which was one of the pardon days in Mildenhall. Moneys gathered in this entry are now referred to as 'collections'. On Corpus Christi Day four entries below, the word 'indulgence' is used for the last time; but money continues to be gathered on the former pardon days.

	£	s.	d.
Item received from the donations of the parish on Corpus Christi day, from the indulgences yielded this day			10
Item received from the gift of John Place for <church> the chapel of the Blessed Mary[164]			8
Item received from the same John a donation towards the reparation of Mildenhall church		5	0
Item received from the donation of Thomas Docking of Le Beck[165]			12
Item received from the bequest of Thomas Woderys, deceased	1	0	0
Item received from the collection of the whole parish on the day of St Michael the Archangel		2	0
Item received from the collection of the whole parish on the Dedication day of Myldenhall church		5	0
Item received from the bequest of Richard Norrys, on the day of his death as in the last will		2	0
Item received from the collection of the whole parish of Myldenhall on the day of the Purification of Blessed Mary		4	3
Item received from the donation of Thomas Chyston of Eryswell		3	4
Item received from the collection of the parishioners on Philip and James' day		4	3
Sum part			

[fol.20r]   **[1528–1530]**

[Latin]

	£	s.	d.
Item received of Seyman of <Sphep> Shephey[166] from his payment for the overstocking of the common pasture or marsh between the common of Ely and Mildenhall going out with cattle to the common of Ely called The Sheld, pasturing in the <> Sedgefenne of Mildenhall		6	8
Item received from the collection of the parishioners on Corpus Christi day		4	5
Item received from the donation of Robert Baker for the chapel of the Blessed Mary in Mildenhall		1	8
Item received from the same Robert for Mildenhall church to the reparation of the same		13	4
Item received from the land of Ralph Sherd owed to Mildenhall church to the feast of the Annunciation of the Blessed Virgin Mary last past, viz <> in the 20th year of Henry VIII [25 March 1529]		9	6
Item received from the collection on St Michael's day in the 21th year of Henry VIII [29 September 1529]		6	2
Item received from the collection on Dedication day of Mildenhall church		4	0

---

164 John Place's will was proved in 1527 (SROB, IC 500/2/17/259). The chapel referred to is the Lady Chapel.
165 Dockinge left 12d. to church reparation in 1527 (SROB, IC 500/2/17/236).
166 Shippea Hill, originally 'Sheep Isle', lies north of Mildenhall parish.

	£	s.	d.
Item received from Westrow from a collection by Thomas Skott,[167] the Lord of Misrule, at the Nativity of the Lord, the 20th year of Henry VIII [*1528*]		7	4
Item received from the bequest of Thomas Holme, deceased		1	8
Item received from the donation of Agnes Coke and 1 cloth			4
Item received for the rent of Le Fysch Cote[168] lately Hoppers, for 2 years to the feast of St Michael the 21st year of Henry VIII [*1529*]		2	0
Item received from the collection of Mildenhale parish on the day of the Purification of the Blessed Virgin Mary		5	6
Item received from Joanna Gardener from her own donation[169]			8
Item received from the collections on Philip and James's day the 22nd year of Henry VIII [*1530*]		3	8
Item received from the bequest of Thomas Chyston of Westrow, deceased	1	0	0
Item received <>from land of Thomas Sherd[170] owed from the feast of the Annunciation of the Blessed Virgin Mary last past for \a half/ part to Humfrey Duffield		9	6
Item received from the hand of James Salter[171] for 2 acres of land of Lampland for two years similarly at the feast of the Annunciation of the Blessed Virgin Mary last past namely in the 21st year of Henry VIII namely at 21d. an acre a year [*1530*]		3	6
Item received from Henry Pope[172] for rent of 5 rods of land in his hands from the Lampland at 20d. a year for 2 years namely to the feast of St Michael, Archangel, the 21st year of Henry VIII [*1529*]		3	4
Item received from John Dobson for rent of 5 rods of land from the Lampland at 12d. a year <> namely for 4 years similarly to the feast of St Michael, the Archangel, the 21st year of Henry VIII [*1529*]			

Sum part

[fol.20v]
[Latin]

[1529–1530]

Received from the donation of Chyston <>for the reparation of the chapel of the Blessed Virgin Mary		1	8

---

167 Thomas Scott lived in West Row where in 1528 he was chosen as the Lord of Misrule to oversee the Christmas games and revels. He died in 1545 (SROB, IC 500/2/19/522). In his will he asked that 'if my wife, Agnes, have perfect knowledge that I be dead, then I will my said wife do bestowe a lay out amongst priests, clerks and other poor people, my neighbours, for masses and dirige to be done within Myldenhall church immediately after her perfect knowledge to pray for my soul and all my benefactors' and friends' souls'.

168 A small cottage by the water, previously rented by Thomas Hopper.

169 Joanna Gardener, the widow of John, the smith. She specified 8d. in her will to 'the reparations of the church' (SROB, IC 500/2/17/136).

170 For Thomas Sherd see Notes on People, p.209.

171 Salter died in 1547 leaving 1s. 4d. to the reparation of Mildenhall church (SROB, IC 500/2/21/290).

172 Henry Pope died in 1537 (SROB, IC 500/2/20/51). His bequest of £5 to St Mary's reparation was to be paid over five years and a payment of 30s. to the high altar over three years. A further £3 10s. was to be paid towards the making of the great bell.

	£	s.	d.
Received from the collection on Corpus ◇ Christi day in the 22nd year of Henry VIII [*1530*]		4	8

Received from the collection on Corpus ◇ Christi day in
    the 22nd year of Henry VIII [*1530*]   4   8

Item received from the collection of Mildenhall town by
    the hand of John Lane collected at the season of the
    Nativity of the Lord in the 19th year of Henry VIII in
    part payment of 8s then owed [*1527*]   3   4

Item received from several parishioners in the month of
    May last past for the game called Maygame[173]   2   4   0

                             Sum part

[*fol. 21r*][174]   **[*1536–1537*]**

The 3rd Quarter from <May Day> Lammas to Halowmasse,
    the 28th year of Henry VIII [*1536*]

	£	s.	d.
Item payd for beere at the second belfounders comyng			2
Item payd an ernest upon the bargeyn makyng with the same belfounder			4
Item for a comb of charkcoles^{8d.} and for caryeng of theym ^{4d.}		1	0
Item for nayles^{3d.} to the stock of the bell and mendyng the stepyll doore ^{2d.}			5
Item for a plate to the greate bell wheele			2
Item for an oblygacon makyng for the second belfounder			4
Item for a nother plate to the same greate bell whele			4
Item to Lane for a greate stapyll and other yron werk for the same bell		2	10
Item to the second belfounder for hys makyng of the same bell	1	13	4
Item payed for the soper of the same second belfounder at the new ryngyng after the mendyng and other with hym		1	0
Item for his brekefast and other uppon his departing of the same belfounder			9
Item spent in beere aloft in the stepyll vewyng the sayd werk			4
Item geven by the commanndement of the parysshners in the rewardes to the same second belfounder at his departyng		3	4
Item payd this quarter for wasshyng of the chyrch napre		1	0
Item payd for wood for the same greate bell to John Polyngton		1	0
Item payed to Browet for makyng clene the grate hole			1
Item payed for the clock kepyng this quarter		1	3
Item for pleyeng on the orgayns this quarter		3	4
Item for a bokyll tong for the greate bell			1
Item for kepyng of the belles to Pachet and Polyngton			4
Item for a bawdryk makyng for the greate bell			5
Item for spykens for the stepyll doore			3

---

173   May Day was regarded as the beginning of summer. It was followed by much parochial activity
    until harvest. Maygame is another name for a performance, probably a folk play, accompanied by
    eating and drinking, one of the most profitable, enjoyable and sociable ways of raising funds for the
    church.
174   The churchwardens' accounts between 1530 and 1536 have not survived.

79

	£	s.	d.
Item for costs to Bury at the bysshoppys vysytacon[175]			8
Item for a rope for the greate bell		2	1
Sum	2	14	11

[fol.21v] [1536–1537]

The 4th Quarter from \<Lammas to\> Halowmasse \to
   Candelmasse/, the 28th year of Henry VIII [1536]

	£	s.	d.
Item payed for a key for the round chyst			4
Item for for lokyng and other werk abowt the belles		1	4
Item for \<forelokyng\> forelocks for the same belles			4
Item for mending of the fore bell whele			3
Item for a shovel shoyng			6
Item for small nayles for bell \whelys/			2
Item for paving of the churche aley			8
Item for makyng clene of the stypyll		1	0
Item for wasshyng this quarter of the church napre		1	0
Item for the orgeyn player wages this quarter		3	4
Item for kepyng the clock this quarter		3	3
Item for gluyeng of the belows of the greate orgayns		1	1
Item for shotyng of the bell ropeis			2
Item for money to Pachet and Polyngton kepyng the belles			4
Item for the glasyars werk of the nether storys a greate		4	4
Item for wood to melt lede and for the glasyars occupyeng			4
Item for a stey to the fyrst bell to Pachet			2
Item for a mason werk at the grate 3 dayes a greate		1	6
Item for 3 servers 3 deys for the same werk a greate		1	8
Item for 3 combs lyme for the same grate		1	6
Item for 1c and 1 quarter of bryks for the same grate		1	3
Item for mending of the ffyre panne for the church			8
Item for a rope for the thyrde bell		1	6
Sum	1	3	8
Sum total this year	9	10	3

[fol.22r] [1536]

The Fyste Quarter begynnyng \<from Halowmasse\>
   Candelmasse to \May Day/, the 28th year of Henry VIII [1536]

	£	s.	d.
Item payd to John Smyth for mendyng the church gate			3
Item for a lock mendyng of the scole howse[176] doore			2
Item for \<flassyng\> flasshyng of the church walles a loft and			
fastenyng certeyn stonys of the batylment		1	9

---

175   It was customary for parishes to pay costs towards the visitiation of bishops and archdeacons. There had long been bitter rivalry between the bishops of Norwich and the abbots of Bury and it is not known whether the bishop's visit included the town of Bury or just the surrounding parishes. The bishop, William Rugg, had been appointed to the Norwich see in 1536 but had formerly been abbot of St Benet at Hulme. His relationship with the abbot of Bury, John Reeve, may therefore have been quite cordial.

176   This is the first mention of the school house. See Introduction, 'The Parish Clerk' under 'Priests and Parochial Personnel' (p.xxxvii).

	£	s.	d.
Item for laborers 3 deys werk to the same with mete		3	0
Item for sond to the same werk			1
Item for 6 bushells lyme to the same			9
Item for making the holy water stock[177] on the north side		2	0
Item for 2 galons ale for the seyd fflasshyng			2
Item for a comb of smythes colme[178] for the same fflasshyng		1	4
Item for wasshyng the lynen this quarter		1	0
Item for the orgayn player wages this quarter		3	4
Item for the clock kepyng this quarter		1	3
Item for paving of certeyn plottes in the church			6
Item for yron werk for the church gate			2
Item for mendyng of one of the quere cheyres			2
Item for 4 deys werk of a plumer		2	0
Item for 10lb of sowder to the same		3	4
Item for 4 deys werk of the plumers man		1	4
Item for 8 deys bourdyng of theym both		2	0
Item for shotyng[179] of the holy water stook and sowderyng a loft uppon the spyre of the stepyll		2	0
Item for mendyng of the veyle cloth to Alexaunder[180]			4
Item for carpentre werk to Patchet among the belles			4
Sum	<1	19	1>
	1	7	2

The Syxte quarter begynnyng <at Candelmasse and
   ending> at May Dey to \Lammas/ in the 29th year of
   Henry VIII [1537]

	£	s.	d.
Item for settyng up and down of the sepulture			8
Item for the orgayn pleyers wages this quarter		3	4
Item for the clock kepyng		1	3
Item for wasshyng the lynen of the church this quarter		1	0
Item for mendyng books and wrytyng[181] where neede requyred by 9 dayes werk at		4	2
Item for 4 peyre of bourdeyns for certeyn bookes			8
Item for lether for bookyls to certeyn bookes			4
Item for 2 red lether skynnes for lynynges to bookes			8
Item for 10 deys werk agen byndyng and mendyng bookes		3	2

---

177   This is a mis-spelling of 'stoup'.
178   Coal dust used to heat lead for the flashing.
179   Lining the holy water stoup with lead.
180   The veil was sometimes painted with religious figures or scenes. In 1554, when the church was
    being refurbished for the Catholic liturgy under Mary Tudor, the sexton was paid 10s. for 'staynyng
    of the vayll'. This reference comes from an extract in Mildenhall's Marian accounts reprinted below
    as Appendix 1, (p.133).
181   This entry marks the beginning of an expensive period for Mildenhall church at a cost of £1 12s. 5d.
    Various books were repaired by the bookbinder and the materials he used make interesting reading.
    He received 14s. for his labour and his board, at 3d. a day, cost 10s. The materials cost a further
    8s. 5d.

	£	s.	d.
Item for whyte threde for the same bookes			2
Item for \red/ ynk for bookes			2
Item for 3 skynnes of red lether		1	0
Item for 2 cople of burdeyns <for burdens> for bookes			4
Item for blue threde and red threde for bookes			3
Item for 7 dayes werk of the booke bynder agen		2	11
Item for parchement for the reparyng of the same bookes			4
Item for 2 calf skynnes for lynyng for bookes		2	0
Item for greate threde to bynd bookes			2
Item for ynk for the bookes			4
Item for 9 deys werk a gen of the bokebynder		3	9
Item for more parchement \and velym/ for the sayd bookes			8
Item for a skynne of red lether			4
Item for whyte threde and red threde to the same			4
Item for mouth glue⁴ᵈ· agen and flowre³ᵈ· and blue threde¹ᵈ·			8
Item for bourdyng of the booke bynder by 40 deys at 3d. the dey, holy dey and werkyng dey		10	0
Sum	1	19	8

\ illeg./

The 7ᵗʰ Quarter from <May Dey ending at > Lammas <>
   \Halowmasse/, the 29ᵗʰ year of Henry VIII [1537]

	£	s.	d.
Item for the orgayn pleyers wages thys quarter		3	4
Item for kepyng of the clock this quarter		1	3
Item for wasshyng the lynen this quarter		1	0
Item for 2 deys werk of a carpynter mendyng Bagott's bell frame			10
Item for greate nayles for the same and small nayle			5
Item for tymbre to the same bell			2
Item for hornyng of a lanterne			5
Item for 3 queyres of the Masse of John and mendyng other bookes of the fest of John		5	0
Item for makyng the not of the clock to John Smyth¹⁸²		1	4
Item for a new lanterne for the church			8
Item for mendyng of the church gates			2
Item for 3lb wax for the ruell		1	4½
Item for mendyng of old surpleces			2
Item for mendyng of the fyrst bell whele			3
Item for makyng the same ruell			4
Item for mendyng the west window in mason werk		1	4
Sum		18	0½

The 8ᵗʰ Quarter from <Lammas to> Halowmasse \to
   Candelmasse/, the 29ᵗʰ year of Henry VIII [1538]

	£	s.	d.
Item for 6 deys werk of a glasyer ²ˢ· ⁴ᵈ· and his bourdyng ¹ˢ· ⁴ᵈ·		3	8

---

182 The knot of the clock was the iron ring which connected the chain to the weight. 1s. 4d. would represent the cost of the material and work for a day and a half at the least.

	£	s.	d.

Item for <his servers wages and mete ¹ˢ· ³ᵈ·> 3½lb of sowder
  therto / 1 / 4

Item for glasse the same tyme / 1 / 8

Item for wages and mete of a mason for 2½ deys, mendyng
  church walles and paving broken plottes¹⁸³ ther / 1 / 3

Item for his server mete and wages / 10

Item for 6 bushells lyme for the same werk / 7

Item in rewardes to a clerk / 2 / 0

Item for kepyng the clock ¹ˢ· ³ᵈ· and wasshyng ¹ˢ· this quarter / 2 / 3

Sum / 13 / 7

[fol.23v] — *[1538–1539]*

The 9ᵗʰ Quarter from Candellmasse to May Day, in the 30ᵗʰ year
  of Henry VIII [1538]

Fyrst for the orgeyn pleyer wages this quarter / 3 / 4

Item for the clock kepyng ¹ˢ· ³ᵈ· and wassyng lynyn ¹ˢ· this quarter / 2 / 3

Item for an auter dext mending / 2

Item for mendyng the greate organys and nayles to the same / 2½

Item for 1lb wyer for the clock / 5

Item for setting up and down the sepulture / 8

Item for 3lb wax to the pascall¹ˢ· ⁶ᵈ· and the makyng of yt ²ᵈ / 1 / 8

Item for lyne for the pascall / 1½

Item for makyng off a new keye for the cheyst yn the vest\r/y
  and other yeorn warke for the same cheist / 1 / 0

Sum / 9 / 10

Sum total of 1 yere and 1 quarter / 5 / 8 / 3½

Sum of 2 yers and 1 quarter ended at May Day, in the
  30ᵗʰ year of Henry VIII [1538] / 14 / 18 / 6½

And thus they owe / 3 / 17 / 6

[Latin]

And they seek allowance for the cross newly made in the
  market place as appears in the bill here shown, made by
  the hands of the churchwardens aforesaid / 2 / 17 / 7

And furthermore they owe £1 0s. 11d. which the aforesaid
  churchwardens made paid on account <in foro>.

And they are discharged

[fol.24r] — *[1538–1539]*

**Memorandum that the paryssheners have elected for the new
churwardens Pawle Duffeld, John Lane, Thomas Skott and
Robert Peche, the yonger, and the same church wardens
have receyved the day of theyr entre** / 19 / 9

---

¹⁸³ A reference to making good the ground after bodies had been interred and re-paving where necessary.

**Memorandum that the chyrch wardons have reseyvyd in the
fyrst quarter, that ys to sey from the last day of May on to
Seynt Petyr ad vincula,**[184] **the 30th year of Henry VIII** [*1538*]

	£	s.	d.
Firstly reseyvyd at ther entteryng in to the offyce in the chyrch box		19	9
Item for the gatheryng on Corpus Christy day in the chyrch[185]		11	0
Item for the gatheryng in the chyrch on Myhelmesse day		4	1
Item for the gatheryng on Candyllmesse day		4	8
Item for the gatheryng on Corpus Christi day, the 31st year of Henry VIII [*1539*]		8	0
[*illeg.*]			
Sum	2	7	6

	£	s.	d.
Item reseyvyd of Antony Yorewly of Cambryge, \goldsmyth/, for 9 unce of sylver	1	10	8
Item reseyvyd for 7 skore pounde of olde laten		17	6
Item res' for 5 skore pounde of old iyren		4	2
Sum	2	12	4
Sum total	<4	11	10>
	4	19	10

**Memorandum that the chyrch wardens have payd for the fyrst
quarter, that ys to sey from May Day on to Lamesse, on to the
clark for the orgens**

	£	s.	d.
		3	4
Item to Richard Polyng for the cloke		1	3
Item for 2 keys for the coffyrs for the Kyng's injunctions[186]			6
Item to the plomer for 3 days werk of hym and his man		2	11
Item for ther borde		1	5
Item for <*illeg.*> 40 lb and a half of sowde		1	4
Item for thatchyng of the chyrch hows and for the thatch		2	8
Sum	1	8	1

[*fol.24v*]   [*1538–1539*]

The quarter from Lamesse to Hawlowmesse		
Item payd to the clark for the orgons	3	4
Item to Richard Polyngton for the cloke	1	3
Item to the carpenterr for the grounsellyng of the skole hows	1	6
Item to the carpentter that came fore Hawley[187] for to se the stepyll for 2 tymys comyng	1	8

---

184 St Peter in Chains was celebrated on 1 August.

185 An alternative name for a collection, but these gatherings were now taking place on the same date
as the pardon days in the past. Hence the terminology has changed, but not the intention.

186 The injunctions of 1538 had ordered the removal of images. See Duffy, *Stripping of the Altars*,
pp.392–95. These injunctions were kept in a locked chest which would have had three keys, one
for the priest and one for each of the churchwardens.

187 Haughley, between Bury St Edmunds and Stowmarket.

	£	s.	d.
Item for the pynnyng and cleyyng of the skole hows[188]			4
Item for mercyment of the toun for the buttes[189]			3
Item to the carpenter that came fro Dommnow[190] the [sic] se the stepyll		3	4
Item for the lokke for the hotch in the chyrch for the cristyng and berryng[191]			8
Sum		12	4

The quarter from \<Lamesse\> \Halumesse/ to Candylmesse [1538]			
Item payd to the clark for the orgons		3	4
Item to Richard Polyngton for the clokke		1	3
Sum		4	7

The quarter from Candylmesse to Crouchmesse [1539]			
It payd to the clark for the orgons		3	4
It to Richard Polyngton for the clokk		1	3
Item for pament for the chyrch		3	4
Item to the masson for the leyyng of the pament and the rassyng owht of the bysschoppys of Rome pardon on the wall[192]		2	6
Item for 6 bosschelles of lyme			9
Item for rassyng of the bokes of Thomas Bekett[193]		2	0
Item for lyne for the rodlofft			3
Item for reparacion of the chyrch gate		1	8
Item for 1 lode of sonde and for cley			4

[fol.30r][194]   **[1540–1541]**

The resseytes of the chyrch of \Myldenhale/ legaces in the 32nd yer of the reyne of our soveryn lorde kynge Henry the VIII as her after folwyth.

Firstly of Agnes Hay for hyr husbondes legaces		6	8
Item for the legaces of Jaffrey Knyht		3	4

---

188 The timber-framed school house had laths, fixed with pin-nails and plastered with clay.
189 Henry VIII's statute of 1515 had ordered archery butts to be made in every city, town and place to maintain archery as the preferred sport, a fine or amercement to be imposed if this was not implemented.
190 Dunmow in Essex.
191 The injunctions of 1538 meant that a record of marriages, christenings and burials was written in a register and, in Mildenhall, it was kept in a locked chest.
192 The break with Rome in 1534, followed by the Act of Royal Supremacy, rendered indulgences and pardons useless. Of Mildenhall's five pardons, none survived. Mildenhall's pardon from the Pope was in written form, painted or perhaps carved on the wall, as it was a mason who was paid to remove it.
193 In November 1538 Henry VIII proscribed Thomas Becket for his opposition to Henry II. Becket's name and his saint's day, 29 December, were erased from calendars of liturgical books and his image obliterated. See Duggan, *Thomas Becket* (2004), pp.109–10 and Duffy, *Stripping of the Altars*, p.412.
194 This folio and the subsequent folios as far as CWA, fol.32v have been incorrectly paginated. Here I have retained their folio numbers, but have placed them in their original and correct position. This folio contains entries which are a mixture of general income from legacies and receipts.

	£	s.	d.
Item for the gatheryng on Candilmesse day[195]		8	0
Item for the legaces of Rosse [sic] Mortmer[196]			8
Item for the gathryng on May daye		7	4
Item for the qwethword of Robert Couper		1	8
Item for the qwethword of Margett Charnok[197]		3	4
Item of the gatheryng on Corpus Cersty day		7	0
Item of the gatheryng mony for the pley \or chyrchall/	1	1	0
Item rec' of the odmony for the ower weyht off our belles		15	6
Item rec' for the overwhyt of the brassys		2	0
Item rec' for the owereyht of the belles	12	0	0
Item rec' of Richard Tabard		1	0
<Item rec' for the exchaunge of the belles	12	0	0>
Item rec' of John Dey of Worlyngtun for the olde coote in the fen		2	8
Item rec' of the chyrch all made the Sunday befor Seynt James day	5	5	0
Item rec' of the gatheryng on the annciacion of Our Lady [25 March]		8	4
Item rec' John Lane for the comyn at the ffeyr spott		4	0
Item receyvyd of the same John <> for yyern		12	6
Item rec' of Richard Halsted for 2 belstokes			8
Item receyvyd of the gatheryng at Myhelmelmesse		13	4
Item receyvyd of Master Vicar for a surplys and 2 purssis		4	4
Item rec' off the drovers for ther bullocks ffedyng beyond the bryges on the Comon		1	0
Item rec' of Richard Coolle for Mr Sydle	1	0	0
Item rec' of Robert Pettche for 11 lbs off lede			8
Item rec' of John Egyll for 1 belstok			3
Item rec' of Thomas Hart for lede and ther		10	0
<illeg.> for led		<illeg.>	

[fol.30v]   [1540–1541]
[in the margin] Sum £30 5s. 5d.

In the 32nd year of King Henry VIII

The fyrst quarter fro Halamesse to Candylmesse of this present yer
The cosstes

In payd to John Browett for goyng to Yxworth			8
Item to Wylliam the barber for a processionary boke			8
Item to Robert Coole for makyng of the chyrch gate		4	0
Item for <> iyernwork and the costes at the settyng up of the same gatte		1	6

---

195 In 1539, Henry VIII still supported some of the ceremonies of the old church, including Candlemas.
196 Rose Mortymer was the wife of Robert Mortymer. He was described as a 'rough mason'. He left 8d. to the high altar in 1539 (SROB, IC 500/2/19/294).
197 This is the last 'quetheword' to be entered in the accounts, prayers for the soul being unacceptable to the new regime.

	£	s.	d.
Item to John Polyngtun for caryyng the tymbyr fro the feyrspott[198]			6
Item for mendyng of the hutgche dor in the vestry that tyhevis dyd brek[199]			6
Item for mendyng of the ssurplyces			6
Item for mend of the stole for the rector cor'[200]			8
Item for 1 bell rope		1	4
Item for mendyng of the pament in the chyrch porche and in the chyrch		1	8
Item to the glasseres for mendyng of chyrch wyndows, for mett and drynk and wages, lede and sond		2	3
Item mendyng of the lectron at the alter ende			6
Item for the lectronn for the bybyll[201]		1	3
Item for mendyng of the stepyll window and other fauttes in the chyrch			11
Item for a mercyment for the comyn water			6
Item for the bordes for the chyrch gatte			8
Item for the skoryng of the lectron in chanssell		2	8
Item for 1 ladder pece for the cloke			6
Item to Richard Polyngtun for the cloke		1	3
Item to William Lovnesse for mendyng of the watch whell			2
Item for wasschyng of the chyrch clothis		1	0

[fol.31r] [1540–1541]

	£	s.	d.
Item for mendyng of the lok on the vestry dore			8
Item for the lytyll bell whell iyern tymbyr and workmachip		5	0
Item for mendyng the lethyr closer for the lectron			3
Item for 1 lyne for the sacry bell			1
Sum	£1	9	10

The second quarter [1540–1541]

	£	s.	d.
Firstly to the clarke for the organs		3	4
Item to Robert Coole for the makyng of the bere and the skole ho\w/sse wynd and the leddar for the stepyll		4	8
Item to Lovenesse for naylles and iyernes to the same bere			11
Item to John Polyngtun for bordes to the same		1	1
Item for thyrtty pound lede		1	2

---

[198] This refers to the Fair Spot, the land on which the local fair was celebrated.

[199] The door on the vestry hutch had been broken by thieves. Over the next few months there are references to the repairs undertaken in the vestry. The lock on the vestry door was mended and the vestry windows renewed at a cost of £3 2s. 7d. on CWA, fols 30v and 31r. Further repairs to the door lock, providing locks for the hutch and the door to the solar and making the wall above the vestry cost a further 9s. 8d. on CWA, fols 31v, 32r, 32v, 25r and 25v.

[200] Probably the choir master's stall or stool, since only a priest could wear a stole.

[201] The injunctions to the parish clergy in 1538 had ordered curates and parishioners to provide 'one book of the whole Bible of the largest volume ... the charge of which shall be ratably borne ... the one half by you and the other half by them (the parishioners)'. See C.H. Williams, ed., *English Historical Documents, 1485–1558* (1967), p.811 and Duffy, *Stripping of the Altars*, p.406. Not all parishes responded immediately and Mildenhall's accounts at this time are incomplete. Nevertheless, the payment for the lectern suggests that the bible had already been purchased.

	£	s.	d.
Item for the reparyng of the glasse in the vesstry wyndows and for 3 lb of sowed		1	4
Item for mendyng of \the/ pewe for schryfft			1
Item for mendyng of the lentun crosse			1
Item to Wylliam Lovenes for 22 skore pounde of iyern to the vestry wyndows at 1½d. the pounde	2	15	5
Item for the workmanchyp of 44 lbs of our olde iyern to the same wyndow at a ½d. the pounde		1	10
Item for the hewyng of the wyndows and lyme and massons worke for the same windows		4	0
Item for wasschyn of the chyrch clothis		1	0
Item to Richard Polyntun for steynyng of the aulter clothis		1	8
Item to Richard Polyngtun for kepyng of the cloke		1	3
Item for 1 bell rope		1	0
Item for carryng off the stone			2
Item for mendyng of the glasse wyndow			2
Item for 1 rop for Bagotts bell			6
Item for settyng up of the hersse[202]			4

[fol.31v] [1541]

	£	s.	d.
Item for the passcall wex and makyng		1	1
Item for the sawyng of 1 bordstoke 114 fett		1	1
Sum	4	1	9

The third quarter [1541]

	£	s.	d.
Item to the clarkes wages for the orgons		3	4
Item for makyng of the doore fore the skole hous, nayll and workmanchyp			4
Item for the hewyng of the stoke for the loke of the vestry doore			2
Item for the kepyng of the clok		1	3
Item for wasschyng of the chyrch clothys		1	0
Item for mendyng of the towelles that serve for to bere the cressmetores			1
Item for takyng down of the hers affter Ester			4
Item for the hewyng of the stoke for the lokk of the vestry dore			2
Item for the makyng of the wall over the same dore		1	2
Item for lyme to the same wall			8
Item for sowdyng and amendyng of 2 peyr of challes		1	4
Item for sowdyng of the ffonte		1	1
Item for the costes at Burry for ther belles at the takyng down and weyyng, tarryng there 3 days[203]		7	0

---

[202] At Easter, the herse was placed on the Easter sepulchre, its frame filled with candles. During funerals, the herse holding lighted candles was placed on the coffin.

[203] This entry marks the beginning of an expensive period for the churchwardens, £4 18s.11d. expended on this folio alone in taking the bells to Bury to be weighed. The board, lodging and travel expenses of those involved are included. Palmer appears to be an outsider, perhaps from Bury, but had the essential knowledge for the removal of the bells and their carriage. It is not known why 'the court' was involved or what this entailed. This episode continues on the following fol.32r.

	£	s.	d.
Item for the costes when we ssett hom the same belles to Myldenalle		6	0
Item for the costes at Burry when we ledd forth our belles for weyyng and othyr charges	1	5	3
Item to Kateryne Terrell for costes off mete and drynk for the helpers and to the carryas of both the rynges of belles		10	0
Item to Palmer for the belstokkes and whelles and takyng doun of our belles	2	0	0
Item to Palmeres servant for the bryngyng of the taklyng		1	0
Item for ther bordyng off Palmer and his sarvaunt 1 day and halff and supper over nyht		1	3
Item for the costes off the cort <> at Burry for the dysstryngs for the belles			4
Item to the porter at Burry to sserve the same distryngs		2	0
Item for costes off < > Nicholas Paltun and Richard Halsted and John Oxford horsse and man		3	2
Item for 2 carpenters when they cam to se the work <when> for to hang the belles		1	0
Item for ther costes			10
Item Thomas Kyng for hyryng of a man to bryng worde from Burry that Herry Evrod[204] was come and Palmer to delyver the belles	1	1	

[fol.32r]		[1541]	
Item for the ledyng of the iyern and the taklyng to Thetfford for Palmer		1	0
Item for the costes at Burry to know the answer at the court		1	0
<Item to John Wotun for the lok of the vestry dore>		–	–
Item for a copyll of jaketts to Master Holt for his peynes takyng at the courte to answer for this toun			9
Item to John Wylson for caryyng of the gret bell to Burry		2	0
Item to the same John for tarryng ther to help wey the belles			4
Item to Robert Coole for rydyng to Burry for to spek to Newman			6
Item for the costes at Burry when we sowht for the carpenters		1	4
Item for ssettyng of the taklyng at Burry to hyusse up our belles			8
Item to Newman, the carpentter, for 12 days worke for the belles frame at 8d. the day[205]		8	0
Item John Chapman, carpentter, for 12 days lyk wages		8	0
Item Robert Coole, carpentter, for 10 days at 6d. a day		5	0
Item to John Mey for 2 days work			6
Item to Richard Coole for 22 \fote/ and a half of tymbyr, price 3d. a foote		5	7½
Item to John Garard for 22 foote of tymbyr, price 2¼d. a foote		4	1½
Item for 2 bell roopys		1	10
Item for makyng clene of the vesstry			2

---

204 For Evrod read Everard.
205 A new timber bell frame is constructed in the tower by three carpenters, the two master carpenters being paid at a higher rate than the third. The costs on this folio come to £3 15s. 2d., board again being provided by Katherine Tyrrel.

	£	s.	d.
Item for 1 bell roope			9
Item to Katerryn Terrell for bordyng of the carpenteres and of ther helpers when they made the bellfffram and the hanging of the belles	1	2	6
Item to John Lane for the mendyng of 3 bell clapyrs		3	0
Item to the same John for makyn othyr iyern work to the bell frame		–	–
Item for sawyng of the fre ston for the wall of the vestry dore			2
Item for the makyng of the same wall			8
Item to William Lovenesse for stapylles and othyr iyernes or the belles			6
Item for the 2 carpenterres <wel> when they dyd tary to make the bargeyn for to repare the stepyll for ther day work			8
Item for ther borde			6
Item the ernest for the same bargeyn			4
Item to Kateryn Terrell for ther bord of them and ther helpers when they be gane ther work to reve the ledes and <sch> cerchyng the stepyll		3	2
Item John Chapman for 2 days wok for to reve[206] the lede \and cherchyng/		1	4
Item to John Mey for a day work			4
Item for bordyng them and ther helpers		2	0

		[1541]	
[fol.32v]			
Item to John Newman for to bye tymbyr for the stepyll	1	0	0
Item for pottes for the churchall		2	2
Item for mendyng of the stepyl dore and for nayles to the same			2
Item for 3 keys to the lok of the stepyll dore			6
Item <for> to Newman		3	9
Item to Newman		2	11
Item to Poull the plomer when he cam to se the work on the stepyll for his labur and for his costes		1	0
Item <for> a nayll			2
Item to John Newman and to Chapman	1	10	0
Sum[207]	12	7	3

The fourth quarter [1541]			
Item to the clark[e] for the organs		3	4
Item to James the talyor for his helpyng to Bery with the belles			8
Item to Thomas Hart for caryage of the lyttyll bell to Burry		1	4
Item to Wylliam Lovenesse for 1 mendyng of the cloke			4
Item for naylles for the stage on the stepyll			6
Item to Newman and Chapman	1	3	4
Item to John Wotunn for the lokk of the vest\r/y dore		5	4
Item for lyne for to woole the stage on the stepyll		1	1

---

206 To 'reve' is to pull or tear the thatch or the covering of a house. Here the lead from the steeple is removed and the steeple repaired and re-leaded. See also fol.32v.

207 The overall cost for the work involving the bells, the bell frame and the repairs to the steeple is entered here.

	£	s.	d.
Item for ynkyll gyrdylles ffo the vestmentes			7
Item to Thomas Hart for 2 asschen polles			2
Item to Thomas Busch for a lader		2	2
Item for the costes at the comying of the plomer		1	0
Item for nayles to the stepyll			7
Item to Newman <> and Chapman	1	6	8
Item to Lovenes for 44 lbs of yyern at 2d. the pound		7	4
Item for the removyng of the lok on the vestry dore			8

[fol. 25r][208]   *[1542–1543]*

Item delyverd unto Bassett the myller 400lb off led uncast to be
   delivered aggyn unto the chirchis use when it schalbe reqweryd
   be the chyrchwardens[209]

The Fyrst Quarter ffrom Candilmesse un to Crwchmesse,
   in the 33rd year of King Henry VIII [*1542*]

	£	s.	d.
Firstly payd for a hundred fowr peny nayll to the stepill			4
Item to the clark for the orgonys		3	4
Item for 1 lode of cley to the stepill			4
Item to the plomer for 8 days borde and wages		6	10
Item for his servardes 9 days of 1 man at 5d. a day borde and wages		3	10
Item for the castyng of the bank ageynst the chyrche wall			8
Item for 2lb wax for the passkall and the makyng[210]		1	1
Item for fyve skore lede nayll			5
Item for iyern and nayll for the chyrch gattes			3
Item for the mendyng of the same gaates		3	4
Item to Polyngton for the cloke		1	3
Item for wasschyng of the chyrch clothys		1	0
Item for mendyng of the lokke off the grett hutche in the vestry			2
Item Item for 1 key to the chapell dore over the porch			4
Item to John Lane for makyng of the claper for Bagott's bell		1	0
Item for 1 bawdrykk to the same bell			1
Item for settyng up and takyng down of the hersse			8
Item for skoryng off 3 peyr of \grett/ canstykkes		2	0
Item for nayll and mendyng of the mydill soler on the stepill			2½
Item delivered to Robert Ston, the goldesmyth, for the pax \in brok mony/		2	3
Item for the coper cressmatory to Chyllwhaytt		1	4
Item Lonesse for 1 lok for the chyrch gate			4

---

208 Here normal pagination resumes, after a misplaced section, fols 30 to 32, has been restored to its correct position in the text. See n.194 above.

209 Building, or even repair work, must have stopped at this point. The abbey at Bury St Edmunds had been dissolved the previous year and, apart from those in the position to profit from the dissolution, the parishioners perhaps had little appetite to continue building and repairing.

210 The paschal candle in 1505 weighed 3 pounds and cost 1s. The entry here shows the candle was now lighter by a pound but the cost was roughly the same as in 1506–07 because the current price included the making.

	£	s.	d.
<Item fro for enteryn of the pleynt in the dirtryngs for the lede that the olde vicar dyd owe to the chyrch 5d.>[211]			
Sum	1	13	8½

[fol.25v]
The 2nd Quarter from Cruchmesse to Lamesse [1542]

	£	s.	d.
Firstly payde to the clark for the orgons		3	4
Item to Sir Rycharde for byndyng off a prosessioner boke			6
Item for a key to the vestry soler dore[212]			2
Item for wasshyng of the chyrch clothys		1	0
Item for mendyng off the clapyr off the lytyll bell to John Lane			8
Item for mendyng off the bawderyk off the same bell			2
Item for the sylver pax unto the goldssmyth for over weyht		1	9
Item for the makyng ther off and the ssettyng off the stone in the best pax[213]		5	4
Item for mendyng off 10 aubres and 10 amys that were in decay[214]			8
Item for 100 threepeny nayll			3
Item for half a hundred off fourpeny nayll			2
Item for for helpers to wynd up lede			2
Item for the hewyng of the dormanttes for the bellropys to goo			2
Item for woode to melt lede			4
Item for 5 skore lednayll			5
<Item to the plomer for 6 days bord and wages		5	6>
<Item for his servers 7 days of a man bord and wages		2	11>
<Item for wyr for the cloke			4>
Item for woode for to melt lede			4
Item for stopys for the crismatori		1	0
Item lathis for the stepill roffe			3
Item for 100 threepeny nayll			3
Item for 1 fagett of wood to melt lede			1
Item for 2 bosschell of lyme			3

[fol.26r]

	[1542]		
Item to the plomer for 22 days bord and wages	1	0	2
Item for his servers 27 day off a man bord and wages		10	7
Item to Lonesse for 8 skore lede nayll			8
Item for the key within the vestry for the dore			2
Item for wood to melt lede		1	1
Item for sowd			10
Item for helpers to draw up lede			2

---

211 The reference to the 'old vicar' was to John Wilkinson who had recently died. The new vicar was Thomas Scott and, overleaf, small expenses for improvements and replacements are entered, suggesting that church furnishings were in need of care and attention. See Notes on People, p.211.

212 The staircase that led up to the sanctus bell-tower.

213 A silver pax had been made, perhaps at Bury, with a stone set in the surface. A pax of c.1400 is in Moyse's Hall Museum, Bury St Edmunds. See J. Alexander and P. Binski, Age of Chivalry (1987), no.120.

214 Ten albs and amices suggest that there were at least ten choristers in the choir at this time.

	£	s.	d.
Item for lyme			4
Item for mendyng off the chyrch gatte			2
Item to Richard Polyngton for weyr and for the distryngs for Master \<Master\> Vicar's stone[215]			11
Item for 2 hundred threepeny nayll			6
Item to Richard Polyngton for the clok		1	3
Item to Robert Clark for cottyng of certeyn pecys of tymber that we borud for the staging for the stepyll			2
Item to the glasser for led and sowed		1	4
Item for 5 ffootte off glasse		1	8
Item for his bord and his servants borde		1	4
Item for woode to melte and hete the iyernes			1
Item for the glaser and his servant 2 days and a halfe, his wages		1	2
Item for the plomer 6 days bord and wages		5	6
Item for 8lb off sowde \and half/		2	10
Item for woode to hete the iyernes			2
Item for a mending off the loke for the font			1
Item for the recordyng of the declaracion for the vicar's stone			4
Item for server for the plomer 6 days bord and wages		2	6
Sum for the quarter	3	11	4

[fol.26v]   **[1543]**

The 3rd quarter fro Lamesse to Halummesse [1543]

	£	s.	d.
Firstly paid to the clark for the orgons		3	4
Item to William Lonesse for mendyng of the clokwarke			1
Item for mendyng iyern barrys for the glas window			1
Item for a rope for Bagott's bell			6
Item to Richard Polyngtun for the cloke		1	3
Item for wasschyn of the chyrch clothis		1	0
Item for the voydyng off the erth in the grat at the chirch gate			2
Item \<the\> to Thomas Hart for 30lb off lede		1	3
Item for wyr for the clokk		1	8
Item for 2 lodes of gravell in to the town hous yeard[216]			6
Item to the clark for the orgons		3	4
Item to James Alexzander for notyng the processionary			2
Item for the charges of the makyng off the wey at the mylles		2	8
[Latin] Sum of the third quarter		16	0

	£	s.	d.
Sum received	7	2	11
Sum of all allocacions	6	1	0½
And thus they owe	1	1	10½

---

215 This entry and another, second from the bottom of this folio, refer to the gravestone of the late vicar, John Wilkinson, who died in 1541. Another reference to this follows on CWA, fol.27r. See Notes on People, p.211.

216 This is the first mention of the town house which may have formerly been the church house, now renamed, or perhaps the Holy Trinity gild hall, the gild having been disbanded in 1535 ('A Release of the Bretherne of Trynyte gyellde', 14 March 1535, SROB, E18/400/1.1a).

	£	s.	d.

[*Latin*] Item they elected to the office <to the office> of churchwarden for Mildenhall church, for Mildenhall town [*High Town*] aforesaid Thomas Venall and John Gerold;[217] and for Westrow Richard Clyff, and Thomas Dockyng for Beck.

And they received on the day of entry to the office aforesaid <21s. 10d.>, that is to say on the day of the commemoration of All Souls [*2nd November*] the 34th year of Henry VIII [*1542*] 1 1 10
And thus they retire and are quit.
And they are quit.

[*fol. 27r*]   [*1543–1544*]
The yer of Owyr Lord 1543
   The fyrst day of the monyth November
   John Jerold, Thomas Fenall, Thomas Dockyng and Rychard
   Clyfte, cherchewardeyns

[*notes in the margin*]
Sum for the reseytes of 2 yers of the cherchewardyns being
   amownte to the figure of <> £6 5s. 10d.

Item receyvyd of Richard Pollyngton for a grave stone sold and
   prysyd be four honest men whiche somtyme was John
   Wylkynsonys, vicar of Myldenhall, 8s. and all chargys payd[218]   8   0

Item receyvyd of Robert Salste		2	6
Firstly receyvyd at the cherche ale clere	1	1	8
Item at the Purfycacion of Owyr Lady \rec'/ next folowyng		8	8
Item receyvyd of men of Stontney for dryvyng catell throwe the Comon[219]		1	0
Item receyvyd clerly at the churche ale	1	17	4
Item receyvyd <of> att the gatheryng day beyng May day[220]		6	2
Item receyvyd at the gatheryng day on Corpys Crysty day		3	4
Item receyvyd at Myhellmasse		4	0
Item receyvyd of John Lane		4	0
Sum for the first yere	4	16	8

Yn the second yere receyvyd of the gatheryng on Candellmesse day [*1544*]		3	9
Item for the gatheryng on May day		6	4
Item for the gatheryd day on Corpys Crysty day		3	0

217 Will of John Jerolde, 1545 (SROB, IC 500/2/19/548).
218 Richard Pollington paid the churchwardens 8s. which he had received on the appraisal of Wilkinson's gravestone. Wilkinson had died two or three years previously. See Notes on People, p.211.
219 Stuntney was across the fens in Cambridgeshire. This payment was due for driving cattle over Mildenhall's common land, the cattle grazing on the way through.
220 A gathering was the new name for what formerly would have been called a pardon day, but money was still collected on the same feast days as before.

	£	s.	d.
Item receyvyd for the beqweth of Jone Dobeson[221]		1	8
Item receyvyd of Reyngnold Meyrer for the beqweth of			
Had<>\nam/		6	8
Item receyvyd <> for the gatheryng of Myhellmesse day		3	9
Item receyvyd of John Lane		4	0
First quarter for the second year <illeg.>	1	9	2
Firstly payd to John Tydde			2
Item payd to Rychard Polyngton for mendyng of the organs			4
Item payd to Rychard Polyngton for the clocke		1	3
Item payd for too keyes makyng		1	1
Item for mendyng of the cherche gate			2
Item for mendyng of the pewe and of a tabernakyll			7
Item for a bell rope		1	2
Item payd to the Clarke		3	4
Item payd for the waschyng		1	0
Item payd for the mendyng of the belle whele			1
Sum		9	2

[fol. 27v]   **[1544]**

The second quarter

		£	s.	d.
Item for a locke for the fonte[222]				2
Item for tyle for the chyrche	<>		3	0
Item for expences rydyng to Lynne to bye the sayd tyle[223]				8
Item for caryage of the same tyle			2	0
Item for 6 bushelles of lyme			1	2
Item for masons worke to lay the sayd tyle			1	2
Item for burdyng of 2 men a day and a halffe			2	1
Item for the clocke			1	3
Item for wasshyng and mendyng of surplyces			1	2
Item for a belle rope				1
Item for the pascall light			1	1
Item for setting uppe and takyng downe of the sepulture				8
Item for a claspe of yoron for the sepulture				½
Item for a locke for the chyrch gate				2
Item to the clerke for the organs			3	4
Sum		18	8½

The thyrd quarter [1544]

	s.	d.
Firstly a rope for the clocke		10
Item for skoryng of \the candelstykes/ on the rode loft and		
in the cherche		10

---

[221] Joan Dobson bequeathed 1s. 8d. for repairs to the church, entered here. Her will of 1543 has no probate (SROB, IC 500/2/19/395).

[222] Since 1236 it had been required for fonts to be locked to deny access to the hallowed water by any undesirable being. Many fonts bear scars of the locks which were attached to their rims and padlocked; see F. Bond, *Fonts and Font Covers* (Oxford 1908; reprinted London 1985), p.281.

[223] Lynn was easily accessible from Mildenhall by water or land, as suggested here. At Lynn there was a 'kontor', a warehouse of the Hanseatic traders, which would have given a great choice of commodities to a purchaser.

	£	s.	d.
Item for expensys on the mason			2
Item for waschyng		1	0
Item for the clocke kepyng		1	3
Item for the ston and caryage		3	2
Item for the clarke		3	4
Item for mending of albys			2
Sum		10	9

The forth quarter [*1544*]

	£	s.	d.
Firstly to Polyngton for the clocke kepyng		1	3
Item to John Wotton for medyng of Bagottes belle			4
Item for waschyng		1	0
Item to the clarke for the organs		3	4
Item to John Wotton for a keye			4
Item for mendyng of the cherche gate			4
Item for a locke for the same gate			2
Item for mendyng of a certeyne yerne			1

[*fol. 28r*] [*1544–1545*]

	£	s.	d.
Item for mendyng in the slole <*sic*> howse and for the mendyng of the pament in the cherche			6
Item payd for makyng clene of the skole howse			1
Item payde to Rychard Pollyntun and John Oxfford at the commaundement of Mr Pope at the corte day for the fenne		10	3
Sum		17	8

The fifth quarter
<Receyvyd on Candellmes day>

	£	s.	d.
Firstly for waschyng		1	0
Item for mending of the preystes syrplyces			2
Item for mending of the albeys			1
Item for cloth for the syrplyce and albys			4½
Item for the clocke kepyng		1	3
Item for the Clarke		3	4
Sum		6	2½

The sixth quarter

	£	s.	d.
Firstly for mendyng of the whele of Baggottes bell			4
Item for a bell rope		1	1
Item for halfe a whyght lether hyde		1	0
Item for ierne werke to the clocke			3
Item for mendyng of the locke to the rode loft			3
Item for a key to the almery in the vestre			3
Item for the clocke kepyng		1	3
Item for waschyng		1	0
Item for a key to the cherche dore			3
Item payd to Kyd[224] for mendyng of the schryvyng pue			3

---

[224] Kyd, also spelt as Kyde, takes over the general carpentry repairs. See CWA, fols 41r, 41v, 42v.

	£	s.	d.
Item payd for the settyng up and havyng downe of the sepultur			8
Item payd for the paskall		1	0
Item payd for the mendyng and naylys for the bell whele			2
Item payd to the clarke for the organs		3	4
Sum		10	11

[fol. 28v]   **[1544–1545]**

On the third qwarter in the secund yere

Firstly payd for the mendyng of the clocke	2	0
Item mendyng of the organs and for lynnen cloth to the same		2
Item for mendyng the wyndow on the clerestory and the stuffe to the same	7 and <illeg.>	
Item to the clarke for the organs	3	4
Item payd to the plommer for mendyng of the lede on the cherche	1	0
Item payd for mendyng of coapys albys[225]	1	4
Item payd for cloke kepyng	1	3
Item payd for mendyng of a crosse to Rychard Polyngton		4
Item payd for waschyng	1	0
Sum	17	7

In the forthe qwarter of the secund yere

	£	s.	d.
Firstly payd for the prosessyners[226]		1	8
Item payd to the classe wrygtte		8	2
Item payd for the mendyng and settyng up of the crost at Jesus alter[227]			10
Item for the makyng clene of the grate at the cherche gate			2
Item payd to the clarke for the organns		3	4
Item payd for waschyng		1	0
Item for mendyng of an albe and syrplyce			2
Item for the remevyng of the ladder for the glasse wryte			2
Item for the clocke kepyng		1	3
Item for the gate at the west syde for tymbyr			9
Item for the makyng			8
Item for a bell rope		1	4
Item for mendyng of the thyrde bell			3
Item for wrytyng for the tou yeres[228]			6
Rest to the cherche and all thynges payd and conted and browght <brought> in by the sherche wardyns	1	0	3
then being for the 2 yerys	2	3	2
Item reseyvyd of the sayd sheche wardyns of the goodys off Mother Thetford			6

---

[225] Copes and albs.

[226] The new processioner of 1544 was printed in English. See Introduction, p.xxxii.

[227] The Jesus altar was a side altar probably standing in the width of the aisles, used for celebrating the mass of Jesus or the Holy Name of Jesus on a Friday, the feast of the Holy Name having been adopted first in 1457. See E.G.F. Cuthbert and F. Atchley, 'Jesus Mass and Anthem', *Transactions of the St Paul's Ecclesiological Society*, 5 (1905), pp.163–69; Middleton-Stewart, *Inward Purity*, p.124. At Holy Trinity church, Long Melford, there was a Jesus aisle with the image of Jesus at the north end of the altar and Our Lady of Pity at the south. See Dymond and Paine, *Spoil of Melford*, p.2.

[228] Money paid to the scribe for writing the accounts for two years.

[fol. 29r]   **[1545]**
[in the margin]
£12 2s. 0½d. church ale £4 ◇ 3s. 10d.

[Latin]	**£**	**s.**	**d.**
Total sum received this year	16	5	10½
		[from which allowed]	
The first quarter from Halow to Candellmes			
Item for tapr' for gerdelles			8
Item paid to a plomher for 2 dais worke and for his borde		1	4
Item paid for 6 lbs soder		2	0
Item for naille			1
Item for a hundred and a hallfe of lede		6	2
<Item for a belle rope			10>
Item for the marsementt of the buttes[229]			6
Item for 4 yerdes and a hallfe of blew bokerum for the best copes[230]		3	0
Item for 2 skains of blew therde for the same			2
Item for 2 yerdes of canvas for the same			10
Item paid to the workeman for 5 daise		2	6
Item paid to him for therde of divers colers			4
Item paid for his borde		1	8
Item paid to Polington for the cloke		1	3
Item paid for the mending of the beloss of the grett orgenes			2
Item paid for 3 ownssis of lasse of sillke and gollde for the copes		4	0
Item paid for a pound of fine therde of divers colres		2	4
Item paid for wasshing of the clothis		1	0
Item paid to the clarke for the orgens		3	4
Sum of this quarter	1	11	◇4

[fol. 29v]   **[1545–1546]**

The second quarter			
Item for the mending of the silver candillstike and a paiar of the sensers and a shepe		3	0
Item for the costes that wentt to se the belles at Bery		1	8
Item paid to the plomer for 20 lbs soder		6	8
Item paid to him for a daye worke and a hallffe			8
Item for line and nailles for the quere			2
Item paid for a daye worke of a man and for his borde to sarve the plomer			4
Item to the glaysair for 5 lbs of sodr[231]		1	8
Item paid to him for his wagis		2	6
Item paid for his borde		2	0

---

[229] An amercement of 6d. was paid for the butts. In archery there would be a butt at either end of the range which was used for shooting practice. See CWA, fol.24v.

[230] The following eight entries refer to the making and decorating of new copes. The cope maker's wage was 6d. per day, but as he probably came from Bury St Edmunds, there was also his board to find at 1s. 8d.

[231] The glazier returned to attend to the windows. Subsequently, 4s. was paid for 12 feet of coloured glass.

	£	s.	d.
Item paid for the cloke keeping		1	3
Item paid for the mending of the churche gate			8
Item paid for the mending of the hoche			8
Item paid for the seting up of the sepulker			8
Item paid for a loke for the chapell dore			4
Item paid for the mending of the pamentt of the churche			2
Item paid to the clarke for the orgins		3	4
Item paid for the wasshing of the clothis		1	0
Item paid for a dossen peses of lasse for the copis[232]		4	6
Item for a pesse of blew bokerum		3	4
Item to a man that came to rasse the bokes for a reward[233]			4
Item for 2 hownssis of lasse of sillke and gowlld		3	0
Item for 2 dosen of crewel lasse		2	0
Item for 12 fotte of colerd glasse		4	0
Item for making clene of the grate			2
Item paid to the broiderer for a monethis worke		1	8
Item for his borde		10	0
Item paid for the <bibull> bibill[234]		18	0
Item for the bossing of the bibill		1	4
Item for the careage of the bibill			6
Item for making of the paskall			2
Item for charges concernyng the church drynkyng		14	6
Sum < deleted >			
	5	8	7

[fol. 33r]	[1546–1547]		
Item to Rychard Pollyntun for the dete of Mother Dyer			5
Item for nayle			1
Item to Willem Innes for mendyng of the cloke			6
Sum	1	1	7
Sum total	10	15	11

Memorandum that Thomas Webb have payd of the gylde of
**   <Sant> Thomas Becket of the dett due unto the sayd gylde**   1 8 0

Item receyvyd of Thomas Mann by the handes of the
    <shurche> cherche wardens for the dett of Marten
    Siddley, gentyllman   2 0 0

---

[232] This purchase of lace, with a further two entries below, reveals the enormous expense laid out for vestments.

[233] Payment made to the man who erased the name of St Thomas Becket from service books in the church.

[234] Clergy and parishioners had been ordered to buy the Bible in 1538. Although few rural parishes had purchased the Bible by 1540, most had acquired it within five years; see J. Guy, *Tudor England* (1988, paperback 1990), p.182; Mildenhall's purchase may not have been its first, see CWA, fol.30v. At Morebath, the earlier Bible was replaced by one with bosses in 1542, as it lay 'available for public reading, chained to its desk in the church', E. Duffy, *The Voices of Morebath* (2001), pp.100, 107. This may have been the case at Mildenhall also.

Memorandum that Thomas Quasshe and Wylliam Clerke, Henry Morby, fysshers, and Thomas Jacobe are elected to be cherche wardens and they have receyvyd in money £1 15s 8d. the 6 daye of December in the 38th yere of Kynge Henry the eyght [1546]

	£	s.	d.
Firstly receyvyd of the legace of John Chyston of Bek		1	8
Item receyvyd of the legacy of John Prat		1	4
Item recyvyd for gatheryng of May daye [1547]		15	2
Item recyvyd of William Garnar for a pan		1	9
Item receyvyd for the legace of John Man		1	0
Item receyvyd for the legace of Robert of Lynkoln		1	0

[fol.33v]

	£	s.	d.
Item in other small thynges		14	0
Item rec' of John Lane for selyng bord		4	0
Item rec' of the legace of Robert Cheston[235]		1	8
Item rec' for the gatheryng at Myhelmes[236]		9	10
Item rec' of Robert Clerk for yron		5	10
Item rec' of John Lane for yron		9	4
Item rec' of Wylliam Cage for clothe[237]		3	4
Item rec' of Mason hys wyffe for lyke		1	5
Item of Coper for clothe		2	2
Item for the banner clothys 6[238]		4	8
Item of William Clerke for a pott		5	0
Item of Kyd for bordes and candylstykes, tymber		3	8

The first quarter [1547]

	£	s.	d.
Firstly to Pollyngton for the clok kepyng at Crystemas		1	3
Item to Lytyll Johns wyff for the boy kepyng[239]		1	8
Item to Kyd for the lokes for the belropes			11
Item to John Wotton for nayles			5
Item payde to lytyll Johns wyffe on New Yeris day at nyght for the boy kepyng		1	8
Item payde to the roper of Thetford for bell ropis		5	0
Item payde to lytyll Johns wyffe for the boy kepyng on Candylmes day[240]		1	8

---

235 Robert Cheston left 20d. to the high altar and 3s. 4d. to church repairs in 1546 (SROB, IC 500/2/21/202).

236 The Michaelmas gathering brought in 9s. 10d.

237 This reference and those following must refer to the sale of materials such as the contents of the inventories. CWA, fols 50r and 50v.

238 This suggests that six church banners had been sold. Formerly they would have been carried on the feast days of certain saints, but the religious climate of the time makes their sale probable.

239 The name or provenance of the child who appears frequently in the following pages is never revealed, but payments were made for his upkeep for eighteen months until 1548–49. See Northeast, *Boxford Churchwardens' Accounts 1530–1561*, SRS, 23 (1982), pp.68–69, 74. See also L.A. Bothelo, ed., *Churchwardens' Accounts of Cratfield 1640–1660*, SRS, 42 (1999), pp.7, 83.

240 The last time Candlemas was entered in the accounts occurs in this entry and the one following. One of the great feasts of the pre-Reformation Church, it was abrogated on 6 February 1548.

	£	s.	d.
Item payde to Potter for the organs on Candilmes day[241]		3	4
Item payd to John Wotton for mendyng of the clok whele			7
Item payde to John Mason for the supplicacion		5	0
Item payde to lytyll John wyffe for the boy on the fyrst Sunday in Lent		1	8
Item on Palme Sonday for the same		1	8
Sum	1	4	10

The second quarter on Owr Ladys day [*1547*]

	£	s.	d.
Firstly to Pollyngton for the clok		1	3
Item payde to the norse of the boy on May day		1	8
Item to Alysander for Backhottes bell mendyng		2	6
Item payde to the norse of the boy the Sunday next th'Assencion		1	8
Item payd to Potter for the organnis		3	4
Item payde for setting up and taking down the sepulchre			8

[*fol.34r*] [*1547*]

	£	s.	d.
Item payde to the belman for fying of the grate			2
Item payde to Oxfor for making of the pascall[242]			2
Item payde for paper			1
Item payde to the norys of the boy		1	8

[*in the margin 13s 2d*]

The third quarter at Mydsomer 1547[243]

	£	s.	d.
Item to Pollyngton for the clok		1	3
Item to the norys of the boy		1	8
Item to Potter for the organce		3	4
Item for a rope for the lytyll bell			1
Item payde the Sunday before Holy Rode day[244] to the norys of the boy for 2 monethys		3	4

[*Item for the norys*]
[*in the margin 10s 6d*]

The fourth quarter at Myhelmes 1547

	£	s.	d.
Firstly to Pollynton for the clok kepyng		1	3
Item to the noris of the boy		1	8

---

241 The parish clerk and organist is named here as Thomas Potter.
242 This is the last entry to mention the paschal candle. John Oxford charged 2d. for making it, but there was no charge for wax.
243 On 31 July 1547 a new set of injunctions for religious reform was announced: see Duffy, *Morebath*, p.117. Processions, 'praying upon beads', statues, shrines and glazed images were forbidden and all candles except two on the altar were to be snuffed out. A coffer with three locks was to be provided for use as the poor man's box (see also n.256) and in the following February there was a total ban on all imagery.
244 14 September.

	£	s.	d.
Item at Bury to the vysytors scrybis[245]			6
Item the bel man for hys table setting at the receyvyng day			2
Item to the smyth for 2 tethe for the clok			2
Item payde to Jamys Alysander for the belles kepyng		1	0
Item payde to the norys of the boy		1	8
Item at Bury at the second vicitation to Mr Bodyes and to his clerk for making ower boke perfyte		2	4
Item payde for ower chargys that were at Bury then[246]		4	8
Item payde for the stole making be fore Saynte Crystofer[247]			10
Item payde to the norys of the boye		1	8
Item payde to Potter for Halomes quarter		3	4
Item payde to the plummer for sodre and hys wagys and hys man and ther bord		4	3
Item payd at William Clerk when the obligacion was made for the bond of the plate[248]		1	0

[in the margin £1 4s. 6d.]

[fol.34v]
The year of Our Lord 1547[249]

	£	s.	d.
Item rec' at Myhellmesse of Thomas Man for Master Sydleye[250]	1	0	0
Item rec' for a brasse pan of John Sparhauk		4	6
Item rec' of William Clerk for 3 brasse pottes	1	0	0
Item rec' of Robert Hawlsted for the gylde hall[251]		10	0
Item rec' of John Peche for a hutche that stode on the rode loft[252]			6
Item rec' of Nycholas Pollyngton for one other Hutche		1	0
Item rec' of John Lane for the comon plott		4	0
Item rec' of John Jonson for an old rope			6
Item rec' of Umfray Jhonsin for one other rope			9
Item rec' of Thomas Hert for one busshell lyme			3

---

245 The visitation of the commissioners caused the wardens to travel to Bury for the presentation of their returns of church plate, for which they were charged 6d. The presentation of the Boxford church-wardens' returns was also charged at 6d., but when the Mildenhall churchwardens returned to Bury some time later, their charges came to 4s. 8d. while those for Boxford were 1s. 1d. See Northeast, *Boxford*, p.51.

246 These are incidental expenses for the churchwardens' second visit to Bury St Edmunds. The expense to the parish officers at this period, both in time and in loss of property, was immeasureable.

247 This seems an unlikely entry. Would a stall – or even a stool – have been made before St Christopher at this time, or does this refer to a wall-painting that had not yet been whitewashed?

248 Money paid as a pledge for the sale of church plate. William Clerk was churchwarden at the time.

249 Henry VIII died 28 January 1547. These are the first accounts entered under the new king, Edward VI. In Henry VIII's last injunctions of 1547, injunction 28 had ordered the destruction of mural images as well as images 'in glass windows'. See Duffy, *Stripping of the Altars*, pp.451–478.

250 Master Sydleye (Sidley) appears several times in the accounts at this time, but cannot be identified.

251 The last entry in which the gild hall appears, but to which gild had this hall belonged?

252 The hutch on the rood-loft was sold and, in the following entry, another church hutch was sold marking a steady disposal of church goods. John Peche had been churchwarden in 1528. This is more likely to be his son, also known as John Peche, a surname today spelt as Peachey and still found in the Mildenhall area.

[fol.35r][253]   **[1547]**

	£	s.	d.
Memorandum rec' of Roger Langham	1	0	0
Item rec' of Quasshe for clothys[254]		12	0
Item rec' of John Lane for 2 panns		6	0

Sum totalls of all the reseytes *<illeg.>*   0   0

**Item Roger Langham <> and Robert Suckerman hathe receyvyd
in plate of the townshyp of Myldehall 280 unsis and a levyn
price the ounce five shyllynges**[255]   60   0   0

                                                    12   15   0

**Memorandum delyvered to the chyrche wardens the 12 daye
of Auguste in the seconde yere of Kyng Edwarde the syxte
8 oblygacyons [1548]**

**Item alowed to Robert Sokerman and Roger Langham the
12th daye of Auguste in the second yere of Kynge Edwarde
the syxte 25 shillings for that they lakked wayte of serten
plate sold unto <missing>**

**Also delyvered the sayd daye \and yere/ to Thomas Potter,
Edmund Wryght and John Froste 10 ownses and 3 quarters
of broken sylver**

Memorandum payde to John Lane for one lok and 2 keyes for the hutche <> for the pore and the hutche for the regestre[256]	1	2
Item payde to John Ffrost for a chalder of lyme and caryage of the same	5	4
Item payde to Mother Haye for a lode sande	<6> 4	
Item payd to Pollyngton for Crystemas quarter for the clok	1	3
Item payde to the norys for the boy	1	8
Item payde to Mother Tylney for bordyng of the masons and the glaser[257]	18	6
Item payde to the mason for whytyng the churche[258]	17	6
Item payde to the glaser for glasse, sowder, < > leade and for 11 dayes work[259]	6	5

---

253   Several folios are missing here.
254   The substantial payment received suggests that these were altar hangings or vestments.
255   This bald entry states the amount of money received for the church plate sold under the new protestant regime.
256   The hutch with one lock and two separate keys contained alms for the poor, the first time poor relief is so mentioned in the accounts. It was normal practice to have three keys, one for the priest and the other two for the churchwardens, so that three people had to be present at the opening. A second hutch housed the church register, the latter having been introduced during Henry VIII's reign.
257   This payment refers to board for the mason and glazier who came to whitewash the walls and remove the stained glass from the windows. See the following entries.
258   The church walls were whitewashed, obscuring any mural painting or written tracts.
259   Even though the glass was a replacement for painted glazing, this seems a modest sum to pay. Nevertheless, the overall changes wrought in the church were accomplished dearly.

	£	s.	d.
Item payde to the norys for 2 monethys		3	4
Item payd to Potter for Candylmas quarter [1548]		3	4
Item payde to the norys for 2 monthys		3	4
Item payde to Innes			8
Item for candyll when they whytyd the churche[260]			4
Item for a lyne for Backottes bell			3
Item for besomys			1
[Sum]	3	3	6

[fol.35v]   [1548]

	£	s.	d.
Item payde to Purdy for the stock and to the smythe for the same		9	0
Item for expenses at Bury before the vysitors of chaunterys[261]		2	8
Item to Potter for Crowchemese quarter		3	4
Item to the norys		1	8
Item payde to Pollyngton for Our Lady day quarter		1	3
Item payde to Potter for a lok whyche is on the pore mans hutche			6
Item payde <> for five hundryth thatche[262]		5	0
Item payde to Alysander for mendyng the grete organs			4
Item payde for byndes and swayes		1	4
Item payde to Thomas Pollyngton for thatching		7	0
Item payde to John Dockyng for sways			4
Item payde to Innes for the fount mending			8
Item payde to Pollyngton for Mydsomer quarter		1	3
Item payde fro wasshyng for one yere and three quarters		7	0
Item payde for clothe to mend surples			4
Item payde to the norys			10
Item payde for mendyng of the clok			2
Item payde to John Pollyngton for <> roddys			4
Item to Rycherd Pollyngton for wythys			1
Item payde to Jacob for three quarters thatche			9
Item to Lane for carying of the hutche			2
Item payde for a badryk of a bell			2
Item for removing of the byble			1
Item for makyng cleane the scole howse			1
Item payde to Thomas Potter for Lammas quarter		3	4
<Sum illeg.>			
	1	19	6
Sum the gross annual sum	11	5	0

---

260 This entry suggests that candles were used to extend the working hours in the Candlemas quarter.

261 The chantry commissioners gathered information about the foundation of chantries, colleges, religious gilds, obits, lights, free chapels and hospitals. Their investigation subsequently led to the suppression of these foundations, although some hospitals were reprieved. On Easter Day 1548 all intercessory institutions became the possessions of the Crown.

262 Terms such as 'byndes' and 'sways' suggest that a thatching programme was underway.

[*fol.36r*][263]   [*1548*]

	£	s.	d.

Memorandum that there dothe remayne the 6 day of Auguste
In the second yere of the reyne of Kynge Edwarde the VI
[*1548*] £2 4s. 8d. of the stoke of the waxe and thys day gatheryd
to the use of the pore wherof ys dystrybuted the same daye
to thes persons folowynge by the assente and consente of all
the hole pariche   2   7

Item to Johane Clement and to Wylliam Clement and to
   Pantelles wyffe for to kepe them   1   0
Item to Mother Worde 6d Margerey Conyers and to Alys Barker   8
Item to the pore boye   5

Item payde out of the mony before specyfyd, whyche ys £2 4s. 8d.,
12s. save 2d. layde oout to the pore pepll at tyme whan they
dyd call for yt

Item layd out of the sayd mony for one payer off shooes for the chylde   6
Item payd for one moneth for the chylde 14 dayes before Chrystmes   1   8
Item payd for the chyldes coote and for the makynge to Thomas Cootes   2   8
Item payd to great Besse   4
Item payd for a moneth for the chylde \to Besse/ <for a moneth>   1   8
Item payd to Margery Wryte for the chylde \for a moneth/   1   8
Item payd for a moneth for <>the chylde \to Margery Wryte/   1   8
Item payd to Harry Wrytte for the pore chylde at the receayte
   of the sayde \chylde/   12   0
Item payd to the pore pepyll whan they dyd not gather
\at the/ fyrst <tyme>   2   8
and agayne at another tyme than   8

[*fol.36v*]
Item payde to hym that make the slewsse in hand[264]   5   0   0
Item to the plummer   1   0   0
Item receayvyd off Wylliem Clarke for sylver plate[265]   23 10   0
< *illeg.*>
Item payd for capons and chekens with pegyons   12   8
Item payde to the four men that sarvyd the King and
   for mendynge of harness   1 10   0
Item payd at the seconde tyme settynge forth of the
   men for the King   15   0

Remaynyng £23 4s. 3d.   23   4   3

---

263   This folio is unusual and interesting in that it deals solely with distributions to the poor resulting from the ban on the use of candles. The child in the churchwardens' care received a pair of shoes and a coat from the profits of the redundant wax as well as his keep, but his identity is never revealed.

264   The sluice would have been on the river Lark between Worlington and Mildenhall mill.

265   A further payment to the churchwardens for the sale of plate.

<of all thynges deductyd and alowyd ther remaynythe
they do ow upon ther acownt 16s. 11d.> 10s. 5d.

**Memorandum ther reamaynythe of the profetts that cummythe
of the lone munny £4 11s. 8d.**[266]

[*fol.37r*]
Ornamentes belongynge to the chyrche AD 1547
Item one auter clothe of dyaper in length 7 yerdes in brede a yerde and a half
      And a nother in length 2 yerdes and in brede <>
Fyrst an auter clothe of dyaper 6 yerdes in length and in brede one yerde
And a nother of dyaper 6 yerdes yn <> length and brede one elle
And a nother of dyaper in length 3 yerdes and a quarter in brede a yerde
And a nother of dyaper in length 4 yerdes in brede a yerde
And a nother of dyaper in length 4 yerdes in brede a yerde
And a nother dyaper auter cloth in length 12 yerdes in brede 2 yerdes

And an auter clothe of playne clothe in length 2 yerdes and a halffe
And a nother playne clothe in length 3 yerdes and brede a yerde
And a nother of playne clothe in length 5 yerdes in brede a yerde
And a nother in length 3 yerdes and a half in brede an elle
And a nother in length 5 yerdes in brede scante a yerde
And a nother in length 5 yerdes in brede a yerde
And a nother in length 4 yerdes in brede a yerde
And a nother in length 2 yerdes in brede a yerde
And a nother in length 3 yerdes and a half in brede an elle
And another in length 5 yerdes and a half in brede a yerde with bbwyndes
And a nother in length 3 yerdes and a quarter in brede a yerde

Item a towell of dyaper in length 4 yerdes in brede 3 quarters
And a nother yn length 5 yerdes in brede 3 quarters
And a nother in <bred> length15 yerdes in brede scante 3 quarters
And a nother in length 5 yerdes and a halffe in brede halffe a yerde
And a nother in length 3 yerdes and a half in brede halffe a yerde
And a nother in length 3 yerdes and a half in brede half yerde
And a nother in length 6 yerdes and a half in brede half yerde
And a nother in length 6 yerdes in brede halfe yerde
And a nother in length 4 yerdes in brede 3 quarters
And a nother in length 4 yerdes in brede halfe yerde
And a nother in length 4 yerdes in brede half yerde

Item a towel of playne clothe in length 4 yerdes in brede 3 quarters
And a nother in length 5 yerdes and a quarter in brede half yerde
And a nother in lengthe 3 yerdes a quarter in brede half yerde
And a nother in length 2 yerdes in brede half yerde

---

[266] This suggests that loans had been agreed between the churchwardens and various parishioners, and
      that this entry refers to interest paid by the latter. This unaccustomed wealth of the churchwardens
      could have accrued from the sale of plate and church goods. See CWA, fols 35r, 37v and 42v.

[*fol.37v*]

	£	s.	d.
Thes be the resaytes			
Firstly receayvyd for 9 ownces \and halfe/ of broke sylver[267]	2	5	7
Item receayvyd for 4 hunderde \pounde/ of laten and copper[268]	3	7	0
Item receayvyd of Thomas Mann for Mr Sedley	1	0	0
Item of Robart Halsted for the towne howsse[269]		10	0
Item receayvyd of John Lane for the comunion plate		2	5
Item receayvyd of Robart Halstede for halffe yeare fearme		5	0
Item receayvyd for the olde <olde> bokes of the churche[270]		19	0
The Seconde Yeare			
Item receayvyd of Thomas Man for Mr Sydley	1	0	0
Item receavyd for the testament of Gorge Place		3	4
Item receayvyd of Robert Halsted for the towne howsse		8	0
Item one old hoche[271]		2	0
Item one broken hoche			8
Item 2 payer of candylstykes		2	0
Sum	11	<18	4>
			<3>
	13	7	7

[*fol.38r*]   [*1548–1549*]

Memorandum thatt Thomas Potter and Edmund Wryght,
    John Froste and Wylliam Pechey are elected to be chyrche
    wardens and they have rec' the 6 daye of Auguste in the
    seconde yere of Kynge Edwarde the Syxte £2 11s. 8d. and they
    do gyffe ther accompte the Sonday before the Assumpcyon[272]
    of Our Ladye whyche shal be the yere of our Lorde God 1549

The fyrste quarter		
Firstly payde to Rychard Pollyntun for the cloke	1	3
Item payde to the plummer for hys wagys and hys borde	7	8
Item payd for a bosshell of lyme		3
Item payde to the clarke	3	4
Item payde to Chrystoner Fuller for dabebynge[273] of the skolle hous		2
Item payde for marcyment[274] to Ely	1	0

---

267 Broken silver was a saleable commodity, fetching £2 5s. 7d.
268 Latten was a copper alloy which, when gilded or burnished, looked like gold. Latten and copper had been widely used for candlesticks, censers, chrismatories and cruets, but these items were proscribed in the reformed liturgy.
269 Halsted paid 10s. rent per annum for the town house. In the following year his rent is reduced.
270 Among the old service books of the pre-Reformation church, psalters were spared, but missals, graduals, antiphoners, breviaries and processioners were sold, the latter only recently translated into the vernacular. The use of these service books and their fate are described in the Introduction, pp.xxxiff.
271 This entry and the following two entries refer to redundant items no longer required in the reformed church.
272 The Assumption was celebrated on 15 August.
273 Daubing with a mixture of hair and clay.
274 The reason for this amercement is unknown.

	£	s.	d.
Item to Wyllem Tyrrell, the netheard, for kepying of Eryswell bollockes[275]		1	8
Item payd to Rychard Shyrloke for kepyng of the gryndyll		3	0
Item payd for the parafraces of Erasmus for the halffe of yt[276]		5	4
Item payd for nayles			5
Item payd for a pece of tymber			3
Item payd to the carpenter for 8 days warke hys wagys and hys bord		5	0
Item payd to the smythe for settynge upp of the parafracys		3	0
Item for lynnynge cloth			1
Item payd for paper			2
Item payd for the mercyment in West Ende			6
Item payd for wasshynge <12d.>		1	0
Item for makynge of 3 prestes syrplesse[277]		4	7
Sum	1	15	11

[fol.38v]	*[1548–1549]*		
Item payd to Pollytun for the cloke		1	3
Item payd to the Clarke		3	4
Item payd for two \hundreth/ nayels			8
Item for nayeles for the skollehousse			2
Item payd to a ◇ carpenter for mendynge of the great wynddowndes uppon the stepyll for hys wages and hys borde		4	4
Item for a lache \for a bell/			1
Item for a pyne of yrone			1
Item payd to Rychard Pollyntun for a great plancke and for bord		1	10
Item payd to Shyrloke for the gryndyll kepynge		1	0
Item payd for settynge up of the clothe uppon the rode loft[278]		1	6
Item payd for the kepynge of the cloke		1	3
Item payd for askynge of cowncell at Mr Hygham		1	0
Item payd to the Clarke		3	4
Item payd for makynge of the great bell clapper		3	4
Item for a cleate for the pullpet			4
Item payd for the yrerns for the skollehowsse dore			4
Item payde for the first day at Bury costes and charges layde out ther for 10 parsones[279]		6	1
Item payde for makynge off a new invytory indentyd the fyrst tyme[280]		1	0
Item payde the seconde day agayne at Bury for costes ther		4	8

---

275 Tyrrell was the keeper of the Eriswell herd on Mildenhall fen, and the churchwardens paid out 1s. 8d. in wages.

276 The 1547 injunctions of Edward VI ordered the paraphrases of the gospels by Erasmus to be set up 'in some convenient place' in every church. The smith sets them up four entries lower down.

277 The surplice was now the order of clothing for the clergy.

278 This is the last mention of the Lenten veil.

279 The various expenses incurred due to the making of the new inventories recorded on this page came to 14s. 3d. These were extraordinary payments paid to individuals for work done which lay beyond the duties of the parish clerk.

280 This entry suggests that a scribe at Bury was writing the inventory.

	£	s.	d.
Item payd to the scrybe for new wrytynge of the invytores at the last tyme		1	8
Item for paper[281]			2
Item for wasshynge		1	0
Item payd for \<makynge\> wrytynge of 2 invyntores at home			10
\<Item payde for Syr Thomas for makynge of bokes for the towne\>		1	0
Item payd to Gorge Bassett for a boke of the new order[282]		6	0
Item payd to a carpenter for 2 dayes worke, hys bord and wages		1	0
Sum	£2	7	6

[fol.39r]   [1549]

	£	s.	d.
Item for a ledder for the cloke and for nayeles			6
Item for Rychard Pollyntun for the cloke		1	3
Item payd to Syr Thomas for makynge and wrytyng of bokes for the towne[283]		3	4
Item payd to the Clarke		3	4
Item payd for 4 salters 2 bokes of the new order		15	4
Item payd to John Turner for brede sent to the campe to Bury[284]		3	8
Item payd to Hynd that dyd mend the cloke, hys wagys and borde		13	4
Item payd to Nycholas Pollytun for kepynge of the cloke		1	3
Item payd to the Clarke		3	4
Item payd for sawynge off stone for payment[285] for the church		1	4
Item for a sawe and to \a/ smythe fylynge of the sayd sawe			10
Item payd to a glaser and for glasse, wages and borde[286]		8	0
Item payd for 5 bussheles of lyme		1	4
Item payd to a masun for 6 dayes worke, his man v[d.] and he and ther borde		3	4
Item payd for nayeles			2
Item payd to a carpenter			2
Item payd to the campe at Bury[287]	2	0	0

---

281   The charge for paper must be associated with the entry two lines below, where two inventories are made in the parish. Neither the paper nor the writing of these new inventories came within the remit of the parish clerk.

282   This would have been the First Prayer Book of Edward VI, published in 1549.

283   Possibly new adjuncts to the Book of Common Prayer. This entry and the entry after next give some idea of the additional expenses of the time, a total of 18s. 8d. being spent on new books.

284   There are three important entries in the accounts relating to 1549 and 1550 which are a community rather than an ecclesiastical concern. The entries have no direct association with Mildenhall church except that the church through its representatives, the churchwardens, is seen as a contributor to the Bury stirs which occurred in 1549. This reference is to the camp at Bury St Edmunds during the 1549 rebellions over the enclosure of common land and rising rents. John Turner's name does not recur in contemporary documentation. See also n.287. For an overview of the widespread rebellions of 1549 see MacCulloch, *Suffolk and the Tudors*, pp.301–7, Guy, *Tudor England*, pp.208–10, Duffy, *Morebath*, pp.127–41, and A. Wood, *The 1549 Rebellions and the Making of Early Modern England* (2007), pp.47–69.

285   Pavement or pamment.

286   The coloured glass in the glazed windows was still being removed and plain glass inserted in its place.

287   A substantial amount of money is here sent by the churchwardens in support of the campers at Bury. Not only did these 'rebels' seek to recall their social superiors to their shared duty and to a shared sense of justice and 'remedy', but they felt that they represented the Crown in their actions against

	£	s.	d.

The Seconde Yeare

Item payd to Nycholas Pollyntun for the cloke		1	3
Item payd for wasshynge			8
Item payd to the Clarke		3	4
Item payd for a bell rope		2	0
Item payd to John Pollyngton for thathchynge of of [sic] the towne howsse		13	4
Item payd to John Meye the yownger of the Becke for 700 thathe and to Frances Wenge for 300 thathe for the towne howsse (folded margin)		18	4

Sum <£7 0s. 5d.>

	6 <9>	19	5

[fol.39v]

Item payd to Hynd that take downe the rode lofte[288]		5	0
Item payd to a man for 3 dayes worke for pullynge downe off the altores and other worke in the church, hys wages and borde[289]		1	9
Item payd to the bellman for makynge clene of the church			4
Item payd to the masun for pavynge of the churche and other worke there[290]		2	8
Item payd for lyme and sande		2	2
Item payd for bearynge awaye of the stone and menor[291] in the church and making clene of the stone		1	8
Item payd to a carpenter for makynge off stoles and worke in the church, his wages and borde		2	2
Item payd for the kepynge of the clocke		1	3
Item for nayles for the cloke			2
Item to a plommer for 3 pownde of sowder, for hys wages and hys borde		1	6
		1	0
Item to the clarke for hys quarter		3	4
Item for myndynge of the great bell <whele> badryke			2
Item payd for the cloke kepynge		1	3
Item for wasshynge			8

Sum	1	5	1
Sum total	12	7	11

**All thynge reckynyd they have dyshargyd ther cowntes and
have ther quytus before the paryshe on the fyst daye of
October in the yere of Owr Lorde God the year 1551.**

[fol.40r]   **[12 October 1550]**
**Memorandum that John Lane < > owe for thys
<tyme> halfe yere <2s.> 4s.**

---

the misdeeds of the magisterial class; there was therefore no scandal in officers like constables or
churchwardens joining the East Anglian 'stirs' (MacCulloch, *Suffolk and the Tudors*, p.307).

288 The rood-loft was destroyed, barely forty years after its construction.
289 The stone altars were smashed and replaced by wooden tables.
290 This entry refers to repairing the floor after the removal of the altars.
291 'Manure' here means rubbish or dirt.

	£	s.	d.
<illeg> Item Robert Hawstede		8	0
Item Quashe owe		3	4

An inventory of all ornamentes in the <c> chyrche of Myldenhall over and besyde the ornamentes in the Kynges inventorye made the 12 day of October in the fourth yere of Kynge <he> Edwarde the Syxte.[292]

Item one corporasse <cloth of> case of cloth of tyssew with the corporasse cloth and a red sylke diaper rebond Item 2 yerds <of> and a halfe of grene chamlett and a corporas case of cloth of gold wyth serten pycters theron

Item 2 clothes of whyght dyaper sylke lined with lynnen and one cloth of blew damaske with peckockes of golde inbrodered upon the same and one stayned cloth of the resurreccyon

Item 4 small belles 1 coverlett with lyons wrowght on the same one cloth with <gl> clowdes

Item one cloth of wyght sterched conteynynge the <bagth> brede of the quere

Item one cope of cloth of tyssewe one cope of blew welvett 2 \copes/ of whyght damaske

Item 2 copes of old cloth of tyssewe 1 cope of mottely welvet 2 copes of whyght fustyan with garters 1 cope of dornyxe

Item one alter cloth of whyght lynnen with barres of blew contenynynge 5 yerdes 1 towyll of diaper 4 yerdes longe and a halfe 1 alter cloth of diaper 3 yerdes and a halffe longe and one alter cloth of dyaper in length 5 yerdes and three quarters in breyd 2 yerdes and a quarter 1 alter cloth of dyaper in lengyth 5 yerdes 1 other dyaper cloth of 7 yerdes and a quarter 1 other cloth of dyaper 5 yerdes in lengyth and a yerde and more in breyd. 1 other cloth of dyaper 4 yerdes and a quarter in lengyth

Item one other dyaper cloth 3 yerdes and a quarter of lengyth and one other olde dyaper cloth [?]2 yerdes and a halfe in lengyth Item 1 playne cloth of lynnen in lengyth 3 yerdes and a quarter Item one <cloth> playne clothe 2 yerdes and halfe a quarter 1 other playne cloth 5 yerdes in lengyth Item 1 towell of playne cloth 2 yerdes in lengyth

Item 1 towell of fine dyaper 6 yerdes and a halffe in lengyth 1 other dyaper towel [?]16 yerdes longe 1 other dyaper towel 15 yerdes longe 1 other towel of dyaper 4 yerdes a quarter longe 1 other towell of dyaper 6 yerdes longe 1 other dyaper towel 3 yerdes longe

1 towell playn cloth 5 yerdes long 1 towell playne clothe 2 yerdes longe 1 other dyaper towel 6 yerdes longe and a quarter 1 other towel of diaper 3 yerdes and a halfe longe 1 other dyaper towel 5 yerdes and a halfe longe 1 other diaper towel 4 yerdes longe 1 other towel playne cloth 3 yerdes 3 quarters longe 1 towel of diaper 4 yerdes longe 1 alter cloth 3 yerdes and a quarter longe 1 <alte l> alter cloth 4 yerdes longe 6 olde alter clothes 9 albys, 6 amysys 4 corporas cases and 4 clothes in them 2 lytell belles

---

[292] In this inventory copes have survived as well as various cloths, mostly linen, and it reveals the wealth of hangings and coverings which continued in use for a time. There was little destruction of these items until the reign of Elizabeth. See E. Peacock, ed., *English Church Furniture, Ornaments and Decorations at the period of the Reformation: as Exhibited in a List of Goods destroyed in certain Lincolnshire Churches AD 1566* (1866).

[fol.40v]   **[1550–1551]**

Memorandum that Robert Thurston, George Bassett, Humfery
  Currey[293] and Wylliam Chylderston are elected to be chyrche
  wardens and they have receyvyd the 13 daye of October in the
  fourth yere of Kynge Edward the Syxte £31 15s. 8d. and they
  to geyfe there accompte the Sonday after Alseyntes daye
  In the year of Our Lorde God 1551.

	£	s.	d.
Item rec' of Thomas Man for the dett of Martyn Sydley, gentylman		13	4
Item rec' of Thomas Bowthe at Hallomas[294]	5	0	0
Item rec' of Lanne at Our Ladysday[295] in Lentte	5	5	0

[fol.41r]   **[1550]**

The first quarter

	£	s.	d.
Firstly payd to Antony Steppney for 18 barrylls of bere	1	10	0
Item payd to Roberd Sukkerman that he layd owght at the camp[296]		5	0
Item at the coman day worke for bred		1	8
Item payd to Nygles Pollyngtun for a quarter kepyng the cloke	1	3	3
Item payd to Thomas Potter for one quarter of malte		5	4
Item payd to Potter for hys quarter past at Myhyllmas		3	4
Item payd to Coolles wyffe[297]		3	8
Item payd for 2 carpenders bord 3 days whene theye removyd the organs and the qwyeres[298]		2	0
Item for there wagus		2	6
Item for drynk in to the churche the same tyme			4
Item for naylles			5
Item for a masone and hys manne 2 days for there bord and wagis		2	6
Item payd to the masone for mendyng of the chymney at the gylld halle[299]		4	0

---

293 Humphrey Currey was the son of Thomas Curry who died in 1544 (SROB, IC 500/2/19/483).

294 Hallowmass was soon to change its name to All Saints' Day, 1 November.

295 25 March maintained its importance in the reformed church as a quarter-day in popular and legal reckoning.

296 This entry suggests that Robert Sukkerman was not only a supporter but also one of the campers at Bury in the previous year. Of yeoman stock, he would have been typical of those leaders protesting against enclosures and rising prices. Although the southern half of England was in turmoil at the time, the difference between the uprisings in the south-west of the country and East Anglia has been succinctly described by Diarmaid MacCulloch: 'In contrast to the unambiguous rebellion in the west country, where Edwardian religious changes were the major proclaimed grievance, the East Anglian rebels showed little sign of religious discontent and a good deal of approval of the evangelical programme; their anger was directed at gentry greed and maladministration in local and national government.' See MacCulloch, 'A reformation in the balance: power struggles in the diocese of Norwich, 1533–1553' in *Counties and Communities: Essays on East Anglian History presented to A. Hassell Smith*, ed. C. Rawcliffe, R. Virgoe and R. Wilson (1996), p.108.

297 Coolle's wife provided board and lodging for visiting workmen.

298 The destruction was not yet complete. The organ was dismantled and the choir stalls moved at the same time. There are several references here to 'the organ' which are misleading, and it is likely that in a church of this size there would have been a great organ and a positive organ, which may have been used in the south aisle near St Margaret's altar, in St John's chapel in the north chancel aisle or in the Lady Chapel.

299 Although the gilds had been suppressed by now, the old name lived on. There is a reference to the burning of the gild hall in the 1560s.

	£	s.	d.
Item payd to Hubert Costyne for lyme spentt there and in the churche		6	8
Item for a loyd of sand fechyng			8
Item payd to Kyd for mending of the seytt of the organs			8
Item payd to the orgonmaker[300]	2	0	0
Item payd to Colles wyffe for there bord		8	0
Item payd to Nyglos Pollyngton for hys quarter kepyng of cloke endyd att Chrysmas		1	3

[fol.41v]

	£	s.	d.
Item for wyer for the clok			6
Item payd for making of the churche gaytt next the streytt[301]		1	10
Item payd to Huberd Flanner for yernes for the same gaytt		2	3
Item for naylls			1
Item for a keye of the orgones			3
Item payd for 2 keys for the stepull dore			8
Item for yernes for the qwyer			8
Item for a sawlter[302]			2
Item for settyng uppe agayne of the qwyer[303]		10	2
Item payd to Potter for hys quarter endyd att Crysmas		3	4
Item payd to the carpendars for makyng of the <ff> fylld gayttes		1	8
Item for yerns <> \to/ Flawner for the same gayttes		4	0
Item payd to Potter for his quarter endyd at Our Ladye day[304]		3	4
Item paid to Nyglos Pollyngton for his quarter endyd at Our Ladys day		1	8
Item payd to Potter for his quarter at Midsomer		3	4
Item to Nyglos Pollyngton for hys quarter endyd then		1	8
Item payd to Mr Hollt	1	3	4
Item for 3 payer of challys[305]		10	4
Item payd to Potter for hys quarter at Mykyllmas		6	8

[fol.42r] **[1551]**

	£	s.	d.
Item payd to Nygles Pollyngton for his quarter to Mykellmas[306]		3	4

---

300 The organ might be undergoing extensive repairs, but as it was not destined to remain in the church much longer, perhaps the organmaker was here dismantling the instrument. See Coll. fol.42v.

301 This gate was at the east end of the church towards the High Street.

302 The psalter was the one book of the old service retained in the reformed liturgy.

303 The choir stalls, having undergone repair, are replaced.

304 This entry and that following are the last to use the term Lady Day.

305 Although the plate sold by Langham and Suckerman is not itemized on CWA, fol.35v, it is unlikely that the chalices would have survived. The new liturgy required communion cups rather than chalices, which had probably been sold by this time. Communion cups followed a new design, the cup being taller and deeper, the stem having no knop. See Oman, *English Church Plate*, pp.191–93 (pls 49–52). The churchwardens may still use the old terminology in this entry, but why are three chalices being purchased on CWA, fol.41v if they were not replacements? Their cost suggests that they were made of base metal. The design of the paten had hardly changed, this integral part still fitting the width of the cup's rim. The purchase of three chalices, however, suggests that the two side altars were still in use.

306 The feast of St Michael and All Angels, still known as Michaelmas and as a quarter day, had been another feast day of prime importance and still is, particularly in legal matters.

	£	s.	d.
Item payd for makyng of the clok `<19s.>`		17	0
Item payd to the Kyng for `<sub>` subsedy	10	0	0
Item for bokes[307]		4	0
Item for \200/ thache		3	8
Item of Robert Halsted for the halffe yere dew att Myhelmesse		8	0
`<Sum`	11	1	1`>`
Sum	13	7	1
Item receyvyd of Robert Webbe		5	0	0
Item `<of>` receyvyd of John Petchey the yonger		5	10	0
Item receyvyd of John Sparhawke		5	10	0

**Memorandum ther doth remayne in the handes of
Peter Porye an obligacyon `<of>` wherys Nycholas
May doth stand bounden to the chyrche wardens
and other of the inhabytance of the towne.**

Item ther doth remayne in the handes of Thomas Quasshe	5	0	0

**Memorandum that the 15 day of November in the 5th yere of our
sovereyn Lorde Kynge Edwarde the syxte George Bassett,
Robert Thurston, Humfery Curren [*Currey*] and Wylliam
Chylderston, chyrche wardens of the cherche of Myldenhall,
have made a full and a perfyte accompte to the towneshypp
of Myldenhall at all suche summes of money as they receved
of the `<illeg.>` and so all thyngs receved and acommpted
they be gone from ther frely `<illeg.>` and have their quytest.**

[*fol. 42v*]

Receytes[308]

	£	s.	d.
Receyved of Robart Webbe		10	0
Receyved of Robart Flanner		5	0
Receyved of Edward Kynght		10	0
Receyved of John Clarke		10	0
Receyved of Thomas Manne		10	0
Receyved of Wylleam Lonnes		6	0
Receyved of Paul Lupkynne		10	0
Receyved of Annabble of Bere for the lectorne waynge 208 pound[309]	3	2	0

---

[307] This entry for books, coming so soon afrer the purchase of a psalter, suggests that these books may have been the new order of Common Prayer, known as the 'Second Prayer Book of Edward VI'. See F.L. Cross, ed., *The Oxford Dictonary of the Christian Church* (1957), p.318. The First Prayer Book of Edward VI, published in 1549, had failed to please, being regarded as too much of a compromise. The second Book of Common Prayer was authorized in April 1552, printed the following September and in use at the beginning of November later that year. See Duffy, *Stripping of the Altars*, pp.472–76.

[308] Obligations were bonds issued to secure repayment of money which had been lent out. See CWA, fols 42r, 45v and 48r where obligations had been delivered to some parishioners.

[309] Mildenhall's lectern was sold for roughly 3½d. per pound of brass. In the following entry, copper was sold for 5d. per pound.

	£	s.	d.
Item sowlde to the sayd Annabble 8 pound copper		3	4
Item sowlde Thomas Colles the sepulcker and the housse, the sutte of the organes wythe other thinges belongyng therto[310]		17	2
Sowlde unto John Lane 500 save 8 pound \of yron/ for[311]	2	9	4
Receyved of Water Day	5	0	0
Receyved of John Marshall in parte of payment of his oblygacyons	4	0	0
Receyved of Steven Colle of gyfte of Rychard Coll	2	0	0
Receyved of Wylleam Lonnes in parte of payment of his oblygacyon[312]	1	10	0
Receyved of Robart Haustede for the rent of the Towne House		16	0
Receyved of John Marshall for his obligacyon	1	0	0
Receyved of John Lane for the comond land		4	0
Receyved of Jamys Alexandre in parte of payment of his obligacyonn[313]	1	0	0
Receyved of Wylleam Fynche for his oblygacion		10	0
Received for 6 albes[314]		8	0
Receyved of Kyde for bourd and poustes		2	8
Receyved of Thomas Harte for \parte of the tymber/ gere of the sepulker[315]			9
Receyved of Wylleam Gage	3	0	0
Receyved of Thomas Brygman of his obligacyonn	2	10	0
Receyved of the geare of Ales Barber		3	0
Receyved of Mother Pare and Mother Gosse for there stofe		5	8
Receyved for 8 albes		8	0
Item rec' of Robert Hawsted for the hole yere ferme of the Towne House[316]		16	0
Item payd to Geo\r/ge Basset		1	8
Payd to Robart Thurstann		1	0
Payd to Buntynge			8
Payd to Steven Colle for two tresse for plankes	1	0	0
Sum	33	11	11

[fol.43r]

	£	s.	d.
Item payd for sawynge of them		18	8
Item for a baddrad [sic] for one of the belles			4
Item for a surpples mendynge			2
Item to the belmann for castynge gravel			2
Item payd to Wylleam Clarke		4	4

310 The organ 'with other things belonging' was sold to Thomas Colles. He was probably a lumber merchant as he also bought part of the Easter sepulchre and the 'housse' or herse; see Introduction, p.xxxiii.
311 The receipt is written here in a mixture of Arabic and Roman numerals, i.e. 49s. iiijd.
312 Here the receipt is written as an Arabic 30s., rather than the customary xxxs.
313 See Appendix 2:47.
314 Redundant albs of fine white linen were sold for roughly 1s. 4d. each. In a further entry below they were sold for even less.
315 Wood from the Easter sepulchre, newly destroyed, fetched 9d.
316 The town house rent paid by Hawsted or Haustede, had increased.

	£	s.	d.
Item payd to Thomas Potter for his wages		3	4
Item payd to Nycolas Poullingtonn for his wages		1	8
Item payd to John Pollingtonn 2 hundreth thakke		1	8
Item payd for wasshinge of the lynin and mendyng		4	0
Item payd to Kyde for mendyng of the stoles			8
Item payd to Mayster Pope for the labborous at fyre <4s>	2	0	0
Item payd a hundredth thake		2	4
Item payd to Jamys Alexandre[317] for mendyinnge of byble			6
Item payd for a lowd of wode to melt the ledde		6	0
Item for the relyffe		15	0
Item payd to Symon Cadge of Bere for lead	5	10	0
Item payd to Thomas Lane for helping the plummer		1	0
Item for takyng downe of roufe of the vestre		5	6
Item for Red for Sainte Johnnes hall[318]			8
Item for Rodde and workmanshipe of the same hall		8	8
Item for makynge of the molde and the panne and nayles for the plommer		3	4
Item for burdes and plates		2	8
Item for 2 loddes of saunde		1	0
Item for great nayles			2
Item Poter his wages		3	4
Item for sawdde for the glasser		2	0
Item for rosson and nayles			2
Item for bread and drynke			4
Item for 4 days of the laborers		2	4
Item for 6 pownde of sodder		4	0
Item for careyng of the lead			4
Item for pullinge downe of the bordes of the cross and the nayleng of them up agayne		6	8
Item payd to the glasere for his wages		3	0
Item payd for his bourd		2	8
Item for hewynge a pese of tembre			8
Item for glasse and lead		12	6
Item for glassers wages		3	1
Item for 4 lowdes of sand		2	0
Item for sodder		1	6
Item for 3 lowddes of lyme careynge		1	0
Item for careyng of tembre			6
Item for careynge of lead			6
Item for 2 hundreth of lead nayles		2	6
Item for 3 days worke of a man		2	0
Item 5 days and a halfe of the cheffe massoun		3	4

[317] See Notes on People, p.199.
[318] In the previous entry the vestry roof had been removed. As the gild chapel of St John was adjacent to the vestry, might 'Sainte Johnnes hall' be a reference to the former gild chapel or even to its gild hall?

116

	£	s.	d.
[fol.43v]			
Item for 4 days worke of his manne		2	0
Item for 3 days of hys fermer		1	0
Item for a laberar 2 days		1	4
Item for a daye worke of a woman			4
Item payde for meatt and drynke for the massons and the glassers unto the Goodwyffe Cole		9	8
Item payd for towe chaldes of lyme		15	0
Item to Thomas Potter for his vadges		3	4
Item to Nycolas Pollyngtonn for his wadges		1	8
Item for nayles			6
Item payd to to Wylleam Brede		1	0
<Sum	16	18	11>
Sum	17	4	10
Item for lead of Mestrys Bachote		10	0
Item for sande and lead careyinge			10
Item for nayles		3	4
Item for lead boughte of Nycolas Pollington		5	7
Item payd Bountynge for pullinge out of the yernes in the wendowes and hallowater stoppe[319]		1	2
Item payd for lyme		10	4
Item for lead payd			8
Item for 2 days worke of two men		4	0
Item for 3 days worke 1 man		1	6
Item for 3 dayes worke of a man		1	0
Item payd for ther borde		7	0
Item payd for ther holy days bourd		1	8
Item for 4 days of a labourer		2	6
Item payd for sande			6
Item for eighte pownd lead			8
Item for a horsse a day to Beare			6
Item for 5 coppell of geyste		4	6
Item for careyng of the lead upon uppon the vestre and drynke			11
Item for a pese of tember		6	8
Item for 2 day work of a laborar		1	4
Item for a man two days		1	0
Item for a lode of claye			8
Item to a labourer			8
Item for drynke			2
[fol.44r]			
Item to the carpenter <> for the vestre roffe settynge yt uppe[320]		6	8
Item for lyme		1	0
Item for careynge the lead from Bere		5	0

---

[319] This entry suggests re-glazing the windows after the removal of the medieval painted glass.

[320] In addition to extra expense incurred in rearranging the setting for the new form of services, the re-roofing of the vestry cost over £9, £7 of which was paid to the plumber for his work and the materials.

	£	s.	d.
Item for lead nayles			8
Item payd to the plommer for laynge of the lead	7	0	0
Item payd to the plommer for shottyng of the same lead		13	4
Item payd to the same plomer for soder	1	1	0
Item for two surplesses mendyng			4
Item payd for 4 surplesses washinge			4
Item for stepill making cleane and mendynnge of wenndowes		1	0
Item payd for vouster[321] makenge cleane			2
Item for chapel makeng clean			2
Item for mendyng of Buntynges mattoke			8
Item for Potter his wadges		3	4
Item for coppiinge of out of Busshoppes Invitory		1	0
Item payd at the vicytation to the Deane			4
Item payd Robert Cosyng for 3 busshells lyme			9
Item payd Nycolas Pollington for the cloke		3	3
Item payd for a new boke of service[322]		5	0
Item for two surplesses wasshinge			2
Item to John Lane for laynge of the bellsman his mattock			8
Item to John Lane for a bolte for the churche gate			4
Item for a sayvype			2
Item for crotchets and rafte for pooer almes howse		1	4
Item for settyng up of the same lodge[323]			6
Item for a hundredth sedge		2	0
Item for lyme		1	2
Item for 3 loudes of dead lyme and careyng the same		2	6
Item for mendynge of the pooer menes chymnes		7	0
Item for bread and wyne to the comunecantes[324]			6
Item to Pollingtonn for his wages		1	8
Sum	14	9	2

[fol.44v]

	£	s.	d.
Item for the comunyon table[325]		18	0
Item for stapple unto the stepple dower			2
Item for mendynge of the glasse wendowes		3	4
Item for locke mendynge to the stepple			2
Item to Potter for his wages		3	4
Item payd to Symon Cadge of Bere for lead	5	0	0
Item payd for knytes meatte	2	0	0

---

321 The word 'vouster' is unknown. It may possibly be a surname.

322 The Second Prayer Book of Edward VI of 1552, Duffy, *Stripping of the Altars*, pp.472–76. All references to mass and altar had been removed, the surplice replaced the previous vestments and the Office of Holy Communion was re-thought and re-constructed. The new book cost 5s.

323 Lodge describes a temporary shelter for the men working on the almshouse in the previous entry.

324 The communicants were now offered bread and also wine.

325 A wooden table replaced the stone altar. During the reign of Mary Tudor, many old altar slabs which had not been destroyed during the reign of Edward VI were brought back into the churches as she sought to re-establish the Roman rites. The stone altar in the south aisle chapel in Mildenhall church dates from before the Reformation. It can be identified by the five consecration crosses on the upper surface.

	£	s.	d.
Item for a lowd of sande and a busshell of collme		1	0
Item payd for bread and drynke at the fyre		2	6
Item to Pollingtonn for his wadges		1	8
Item payd for wasshing of surplesses			8
Item payd to the clarke of Mr Loth		6	8
Item for bread and <drynke> wyne to communecant		4	4
Item for 2 days worke of a massonn		1	8
Item for 2 days worke of his server		1	4
Item to Potter for his wadges		3	4
Item for lyme and a lye makenge		3	0
Item for bread and wyne to comunecant		2	1
Item for a bell rope		1	8
Item for making of cloke howse		1	0
Item for a pece tembre			4
Item to the fene reve and for brynginge up of catell		1	4
Item thakeng of an almes howse[326]			6
Item at Bere expenses when whe delyvered churche goodes[327]		3	0
Item for wyne and bread to communicant		2	7
Item to Pollington for his wadges		1	8
Item to the carpenters for pulling downe of burnet tember in the stepple		3	0
Item to a laborer for makenge cleane of the stepple		1	1
Item to the clokesmyth for makenge the cloke		15	0
Item to Potter for wadges		3	4
Item nayles			2
Item for pullyng downe of lead of the steppell		4	0

[fol.45r]	[1553]		
Item gyven to hym that boughte the bell		1	0
Item for a bell rope		1	8
Item for pesenge of a bell rope			8
Item for pecenge of the bell wele			7
Item for mendynnge of church gate			2
Item for a locke for the churche gate			4
Item for bread and wyne to communecant		2	4
Item to Pollingtonn for wadges		1	8
Item to the organs at Beare the comesseneres		1	8
Item for new saulter for the churche		2	0
Item for paper			1
Sum	13	2	6

The holle somme of all the charges belongynge to towneshippe of Mylden-hall to the use of the churche layd out by ous churchewardenges Thomas Cottes John Layne John Shene and Symon Clarke.

---

[326] 'An' almshouse was thatched, suggesting there was more than one in the town.
[327] It is not known what these church goods were, but as such they were now regarded as chattels of the state, not of the parish. The expenses charged for delivery are high and the 'churche goodes' were probably the remnants from the once rich and well equipped church, now stripped of its treasures.

Memorandum that the firste day of the monyth of November In the fyrste yere of our sovereyn ladey Quene Marey, Thomas Cotes, John Lane, Symond Clarke and John Schene, chyrchwardens of the chyrche of Myldenhall, have made ther acounte.

In the presence of the Inhabitance of the same towne and all thynges to them accounted they be freely gone from ther accounte and have ther quittance.

[*fol.45v*]   [*1553*]
◇ Newe chyrche wardens chosen the 6 day of November in the fyrste yere of our sovereyn lady Quene Mary

Stephen Cook
Myles Hulle[328]
John Sparhawke
<Robert Blome>
Peter Petchey
and they have received of the townshyppe the day and yere above wryten 16s and 12 oblygacyons[329]

Quene Marye the second
    Symon Sukerman
    Symon Sukerman
    remembraunce
    understandinge

[*fol.46r*]
EXTRACT FROM MILDENHALL CHURCHWARDENS' ACCOUNTS (undated).

[*Latin*]
THE GILD OF ST THOMAS
The aldermen and brothers of the gild of St Thomas hold, formerly Robert Halsted and afterwards John Playford held, one messuage facing the church of Mildenhall between the messuage of Nicholas Bagot on the north part and the messuage of Thomas Houghton on the south part and abuts on the east on the messuage of Thomas Hopper and towards the west on the King's highway. And pay therefore 2s. 8d. for the year.

And the same [*the aldermen and brothers of the gild*] hold one piece of land, formerly of John Savage, containing 4 acres at the east fen and 12 acres of field and marsh and pasture lying at the end of the same, formerly of William Saddeler and formerly of John Sly, lying between the land of Nicholas Bagot on both parts and it abuts against the south on the river bank of Berton and towards the north on the way leading towards Curles. And therefore pay 7s. 4d. for the year.

---

[328]   Miles was the third son of Thomas Hull (d.1524). He inherited his father's land in Mildenhall. See Appendix 2:36.
[329]   See CWA, fol.48r.

And the same [*the aldermen and brothers of the gild*] hold land, formerly of John Halstead, one and half a rod of land lately of Robert Halsted lying at Forkes Fen crouch near the common way next to the land of the church on the part of the east and <land of Henry Poope> abutting on both heads on the common ways. And pays therefore 1d. for the year. And the same hold 2 acres of land in Millfield next to the land of the hall on the east and land of Henry Poope on part of the west and pays 1 shilling for the year as appears in the court held here on Tuesday before the feast of St Luke, the evangelist, and the aforesaid 2 acres lately were of John Drax and Ralph Symonds.

And the same hold land of half an acre, formerly of John Gregory in Wyndesmyllafeld and lying between land of the manor on the west and abutting towards the north on Styway and towards the south on Old Way and pay 2d. for the year. And the same hold, formerly of Robert Harngham, one messuage lying between the pertinences formerly of John Sly, now of Robert Wyset on the part of the north and fields formerly Thomas Makworth on the part of the south, the west head abutting on the pertinences of the aforesaid Robert Wayset and the other head on the common way. And pay 3d. for one year.

And the same hold, formerly of Thomas Makworth, lately held 1 acre of meadow, formerly of Alice Everard, lying between the messuage of Thomas Tydd on the part of the north and the messuage lately Robert Pratte on the part of the south, the west head abutting on the west and the other head on the stone cross. And pay therefore 8d. for the year.

Item paid to Docking 12s. 4d.

£17 12s. 9d.

[*fol.46v*]
AN UNDATED RECORD OF LAND HOLDINGS *c.*1516–1519

[*Latin*]
5 rods of land lying in Almyscroft fields between the land of Henry Poope,[330] esquire, on both sides, the north head abutting on Charnock Way and the south head abuts on the pightle called Almyscroft.

Half an acre of land lying in Twamell fields with land of the manor on both sides, the south head abuts on Framlong Way, the north head abuts on the Carnary land.

Half an acre of land lying in Peturbornfeld between the land of Mastrihethe on the east part and land of Alice Swayne on the west part, the south head abutting on Mundes Way, the north head abuting on Lamcott paht [*path*].

---

[330] Henry Pope's will was written in February 1535 and proved in May 1537 (SROB, IC 500/2/20/51). This gives a *terminus ante quem* of 1537 to this document.

Three rods of land lying in Lamcott field between the free lands of Andrew Place, chaplain,[331] now of John Heynes[332] on the part of the west and land of the manor on part of the east, the north head abutting on Olds Way, the south head abutting on the land of Mr Bakot.

Half an acre of land lying Bekfield between land called Cottones of the part to the west and land of Mr Poope to the east, the north head abutting on Stokpaht [Stokpath] and the north head abutting on Styepaht. < two lines crossed out> One acre of land lying in Bradynhowfeld between the land of William Pechey on the east and land of the manor of Mildenhall on the west, the north head abutting on Olds Way and the south head abutting on Beke Way.

Half an acre of land lying in Enyngfeld next to the land of Thomas Dow of Isylham on the south part and land of the manor of Aspalys on the north part, the east head abutting the land pertaining to the Lord of York, the west head abutting on land of the manor called Cottons. One and a half acres lying in Lyttely between the land of Mildenhall manor on both sides and the head abutting on Mildenhall common.

One piece of land and meadow lying in Westyndyche between the land of Mildenhall manor on the west and land pertaining to the Carnary on the east part, the north head then abutting Mildenhall marsh, the south head abutting on —.[333]

Memorandum in the handes of Herry Morley for a howse in the fen callyd Hoppers Kot for 12d. a year.

Memorandum John Seman of Schepey have geven a bullock to the use and the profyte of the cherche in recompense <page torn> and stathis be his catell don in the Segefen in a recompense.

[fol.47r]

> £6 19s. 9d.
> £17 10s. 9d.

[fol.47v]
Repositioned between fols 3v and 4r

[fol.48r]
Obligacons delyveryd in the fourth yere of the regin of kynge Edwarde the syxt, 1550.

	Debit
£5	Fyrst an obligacon of 100s. delyveryd to Edwarde Knyght <Item an obligacon of 100s. delyveryd to John Coleke>

---

[331] The quetheword of Andrew Place, chaplain, was received by the churchwardens in 1516. See CWA, fol.14v, which suggests that this gild document must be dated 1516 or later.

[332] John Haynes died in 1519, leaving a small area of land to the charnel in Mildenhall churchyard (TNA, PCC Ayloffe 19). He had acquired a certain amount of free land and also had shops 'in the marketstead'. These three footnotes suggest that, if the documentation is correct and up to date, this folio should be dated between 1516 and 1519.

[333] This sentence is unfinished.

<Item an obligacon of 100s. delyveryd to John Peche the yonger>

£5   Item an obligacyon of 100s. delyvered to Robert Flawner

Receved <£5>   <Item an> oblygacyon of Wylliam Fynche of a 100s. granted <to pay owte of hande 20s. and a nobyll a quarter for the rest>

Item an oblygacyon of a 100s. delyvered to Pawle Lumpkyn

<50s.   Item an oblygacyon of a 100s. delyvered to Walter Daye>

<Item an oblygacyon of a 100s. delyvered to Thomas Man>

<30s.   Item an oblygacyon of a 100s. delyvered to Jamys Alysunder>[334]

<30s.   Item an obygacyon of £3 delyvered to Wylliam Benes>

Receved   20s. £5   Item an oblygacyon of a 100s. delivered to Robert Dyer

<Item an oblygacyon of a 100s. delivered to Edwarde Knyght>

<Item an oblygacyon of a 100s. delivered to John Wochall>

£5   Item an oblygacoyon of a 100s. delivered to Nicholas May 53s. 4d.

50s.   Item an oblygacyon of a £5 delyvered to Thomas Bregman

<£3 40s.> Item an oblygacion of £5 delyvered to Wyllym Gadge

50s.   Item an oblygacion of 50s. dellyverd to Powle Lanne

£5   Item an oblygacyon of £5 delyvered to Robert Clarke alias Webbe

[fol. 48v][335]   **[1550–1551]**

	£	s.	d.
The first quarter			
Item payed to George Bassett		1	8
Item payd to Huberd Thurston		1	0
Item payd to Bontynge			8
Item payd to Stevne Coll for 2 trese for plankes	1	0	0
Item payd for the sawynge of them		18	8
Item for a baddred for 2 of the belles			4
Item for a sorpples mending			2
Item to the bellman for casting of the grat			2
Item payd to Wyllim Clerke		4	4
Item payd to Thomas Poter for his quarter wadges[336]		3	4
Item payd to Necollas Pollyngton for his wadges		1	8
Item payd to Jhon Pollyngton for <buying of a honder of sedge and wode for the same> a honder of thake		4	0

---

[334] See Appendix 2:47 for his will.
[335] This folio is a copy of some of the entries on CWA, fol.43r and is probably dated 1550–51.
[336] From this point Arabic numerals are used. They continue until the last two entries and the sum of the expenditure is reached, when the entries revert to Roman numerals. It is believed that book-keeping by double entry using Arabic numbers was not in common use until the second half of the sixteenth century (R. Morris, *Churches in the Landscape* (1989), p.360). Using several earlier examples, however, Morris suggests that advanced methods of accounting were being used perhaps fifty to seventy-five years before the Reformation.

	£	s.	d.
Item payd for wasshene of the lennen \and/ mending			8
Item payd to Kedde for mending of the stolle			10
Item payd to Mr Poppe for the labourers at the fyere		4	0
Item payd for a honder of thakke		2	4
Item payd to a James Allysander for mendeng of the bybell[337]			6
Item payd for a lode of wodde to melt the led			6
Item payd to the relleffe		15	0
Item payd to to Simon Cadge of Berre for lead	5	10	0
Item payd to Thomas Lanne for helpen of the plomer		1	0
Sum	11	12	4

[fol. 49r][338]

Item 4 messe bokes, 6 anteveners with a verse boke, 4 grayles and a old grayle, 2 halfe legantes and a old legent, 2 sauters and a sauter with ymmes, 5 processyoners, 3 manuelles and a ordnary, 2 pystell bokys and a colet boke

Item a tymber arme gylted

Item a pax off coper and gylte

Item a stafve off coper and gylt longing to the best crosse, a crosse cloth of sylke with keys, 2 baneres clothes of sylke, 4 bellys of laten, a crysmatory, a lawer, a pewter potte, 16 awter clothis, a pese off diaper for 2 auter clothes, 6 ffrontelettes, 3 ffynne towelles off dyaper

Item 8 tuelles of dyaper, a noder off diaper in lenkyth 15 yardes, 3 tuelles of pleyn cloth, 3 ffruntlettes for the warday

Item hangynges for the autere, which with garters, 3 with clowdes, 3 steyned clothis, 3 pektors of Sent Gregory, a clothe of sylke broyderyd with gold for the sacrament

Item 2 clothis of sylke longyng to the sepulcre with a ffrontlet off the same, a ffynne clothe for the sepulcre, a steyned clothe for the sepulcre, 2 tuelles for Good Ffryday, a hangynge off whith crossyd with rede sylke for Lenton, 2 stolys for qwere, a veyle, a leyter cloth off whith with garters, 2 with clowddes, 3 coverlytes, a cloth off clowddes steynyd for the stolys at the auter

Item 5 candelstykkes and a martlage

Item a tabilcloth of dyaper off the gyft of Jane Wode

Item a towel off diaper off the gyfth of Calffe

[fol. 49v]

Orna <damaged> Mildenhall being AD 1508

Item 2 copys off clothe off tyssw with the chesybyls, tunykyls and albys of the same sute for pryste, decon and subdecon

Item an auterclothe with a frontlete off the same

Item a kote for the rode off the same sute

Item 2 copes off white damaske powdirde with chesebill, 2 tunycles and 3 albes of the same sute

---

[337] See Appendix 2:47. In his will James Alexander is described as a painter, but here he appears as a book repairer.

[338] A fragment of a pre-Reformation inventory.

Item 2 copes of clothe off golde and the hole sute of the same for prieste, decon and subdecon

Item a grene cope off motley welvet with the hole sute and a palle clothe of the same

Item 3 copes powdred with garters with the hole sute off the same and 2 westiment off the same with albys

Item a blacke cope off welvet with estriche fethers for messes of requiem and the sute of the same

Item 2 vestimentes of rede sylke for to synge with at duble fests at the lowe awters

Item a nother westimet of rede sylke to synge in a Goode Friday

Item a westymente of red say Item 2 westimentes white for the low awters

Item 2 westiment for werke dayes

Item a westiment that Sir William Place gave for Jesus messe

Item a sute of westiment for the Sonday with a cope of the same beyng off the colour popynggay grene damaskys

Item 2 westments white for to synge with in Lentts

Item 2 copes of blew welvette and a sute of same for priests, decon and subdecon off the same

Item a blew cope of damaske

Item a cope of redde welvet and a cope \of/ redde damaske

Item 2 copes of russet olde

Item a olde grene cope <s>

Item a rede cope with lylyes

Item a crosse of silver and gylte and enamylde, weyying thirty ownces with the staffe of copper gylte belonging to

Item a crosse of silver with a pece of the holy cross therein, parcel gilte, and a fote of copper gylte

Item 4 payer chalices hole and over suspendid \to hanged and putte the best cross

Item a pyxe silver and gilte

Item a senser silver and gilte

Item a sencer silver and parcel gilte

Item a sencer of coper and gilte

Item 2 shippis of silver with 2 sponys of silver for frankencense

Item a crismatory of silver

Item a bason of silver and parcel gilt

Item a green korse girdell harnesshed with silver

Item [*illeg.*] a box of silver and another box of silver and cristall

Item 2 pu\r/cesses sette with perle

Item a purse off gold

Item a nother off motley grene with <> 2 smalle pursys with relykes there in

Item 2 relykes closyd with silver

[*fol. 50r*]

\1 cope blew in/ <*damaged*>

Item pykses off copir and gilte

Item a box full off relykes <*damaged*> relikes

Item box with 2 knoppis off perle and 3 cristall stonys <*illegible and torn*>

Item girdill off Seynte Thomas

Item 2 candillstykes off copir <*damaged*> 2 payer canstikes laten

Item 11 cases w<*illegible*> corperas therein
Item 3 corporas for the <*illegible and torn*> sypres 5 sylke pelows
Item a coper crosse for the worday and the staffe off coper
Item a nother crosse of coper the which is borne to syke folke in the owyr of
  dethe
Item a towell off diapyr 15 yardes length and 3 qwarters brode
Item a towel off red sylke with whyte <in> the endes being off the lengthe 2 ells
  and quarter brode
Item 2 towells off diapir fyne 4 yardes off length a every towell and 3 qwarters in
  bredthe
Item a towel off diaper off 7 yardes longth and halfe yarde brode
Item a pece off diaper in lengthe 7 yardes and 3 halfe yards in bredthe
<Item a towel off diaper of 3 yardes and a halfe in length and half yarde in
  brodthe>
Item a towel off diaper of 6 yardes in length and halfe yarde in breddyth
Item a towel off diaper 3 yardes and a halfe in length and a qwarter and the nayle
  in bredthe
Item a towel off diaper of 5 yardes in length and halfe yarde brode
Item a towel off diaper of 4 yardes longe and halfe yarde brode
Item a diaper towell off 4 yardes \and a half/ longe and a <> qwarter and the
  nayle in bredthe
Item a diaper towell of 3 yardes and 3 qwarters in lengthe and 3 quarters brode
Item a towell off playne clothe off 4 yardes in lengthe and 3 qwarters in bredth
Item a towell off playne clothe of 5 yardes in length and halfe yarde brode
Item a towell <s> of 4 yardes in lengthe and halfe ell brode
Item a towell off 2 yardes <in> and halfe in lengthe and halfe yarde brode
Item a towll off diaper 6 yardes and 3 qwarters in lengthe and halfe yarde brode
Item a towll off diaper off 6 yardes and 3 qwarters in lengthe and halfe elle
  <bode> brode
Item a towel off diaper in length 2 yardes and a halfe in length and a quartere in
  bredthe
Item a towell off playne clothe 2 yards and a halfe in lengthe and a qwarter in
  bredth
Item 2 towells in lengthe a yarde and a halfe and in bredt<*damaged*> halfe a
  yarde
Item a towell<s> of 2 yards in lengthe and a quarte broder
Item 2 awter clothis off fyne diaper in length 3 yards and a yarde in bredthe
Item a <diaper> awter clothe of diaper in length 3 yardes and in bredth/ell
  <longe>
Item a awter clothe off diaper in length 4 yards and in bredthe ell brode
Item a awter clothe of diaper 4 yardes and a halfe in lengthe and in bredthe a yard
  and the half quarter

[*fol. 50v*]
5 *lines are here obscured by paper pasted on to the fragile page to strengthen
  it.* ... and in length 5 yardes and in bredthe yarde and halfe qwarter Item
  a awter clothe off <*damaged*>4 yards and in bredthe a yarde Item a awter
  clothe off lengthe 4 yardes and in bredthe a ell Item a awter clothe off length
  4 yardes and in bredthe a yarde Item a awter clothe in lengthe 3 yardes and
  in bredth ell brode Item a awter clothe off 4 yardes in lengthe and bredthe a

yarde Item a awter clothe in lengthe 3 yardes and 3 qwarters and <*damaged*>
bredthe ell brode Item a awter clothe in lengthe 3 yardes and yarde brode Item
<*damaged*> ter clothethe in length 4 yards and ell brode Item a awter clothe
in lengthe 3 yards and a quarter and ell brode Item a awter clothe in lengthe 4
yardes and yarde brode Item a awter clothe in length 3 yardes and a halfe and
ell brode Item a awter clothe in lengthe 3 yards and a qwarter and yarde brode
Item a awter clothe in length 4 yards and a qwarter and yarde brode Item a
<awter clothe in> koveryng for the awter in length 3 yards and yarde brode
Item 4 koveringys for the awter off lynyg Item a diaper towel in length 4 yards
and halfe ell brode Item a diaper towell in lengthe 6 yards and halfe yarde
brode Item a towel off playne clothe in length 2 yards and a quarter and halfe
ell brode Item 4 masse bokes Item 6 antifeners with a werse boke Item 4
graylys and a olde grayle Item 2 halfe legents and a olde legent Item 2 sawters
Item a sawter with ymnys Item 6 processioners Item 3 manuells
Item a ordinale Item 2 pistill bokes Item a colet boke Item a tymber arm gyltyd
Item a pax off coper and gilte Item a <crosclo> crosse clothe with garters
Item a cross clothe with keys Item a crosse clothe with the kyngs armys Item
a crosse clothe off the Trinite Item 2 baner clothis off sylke with 4 belles off
laton Item a lawer Item a pewter potte Item hangyngs for the awters off whyte
with garters Item hangyngs for the awters with clowdes Item hangynggs for the
awters steynyd
Item 3 pyctours off Seynt Gregory Item a clothe off sylke broyderde with golde
for the Sacrament
Item 2 clothis off sylke longyng to the sepulcre with a frontteletys off the same
Item a fyne clothe for the sepulcre Item a steyned clothe for the sepulcre Item
2 towells for Good Fryday Item a hangyng off <sylke> white crossid with
redde silke for lenton Item 2 stolys for the qwer
Item a wayle Item a lectere clothe off white with garters Item 2 with clowds Item
2 coverletts Item —.

[*fol.51r*]

*A piece of paper, pasted over the top of CWA, fol. 50v and written in an early
twentieth-century hand, reads* On that part of this page which is pasted over,
the following memoranda were made in a somewhat casual fashion.

	£	s.	d.
Memorandum that Thomas Hopper owyt for his ferme		15	0
Item ther is in a pece of <> and other brokyn sylver			
The plate sold to Roger Langham and to Robert			
Suckerman			
The best crosse		14	0
Item the 2 candylstyks			
Item the pyxt			
Item the bigger pax			
Item the best sencer and a shyp			
Item a broken chane			
Item a crysmetory			
Item a lytell crosse			
Item a silver cup			

	£	s.	d.
Sowld for 5s. the unce one with another	6	13	6

Memoradum ther remayneth in plate 85 ounces

No date is given, but the handwriting is the same as that which appears in 38
Henry VIII to Edward VI. Below this entry there are a few scribbled numbers.
The folio continues:

	£	s.	d.
Memorandum receyvyd off the gatheryng for the makyng of the wey at the Mylles		1	8
wher off is payd for the same wey reperyyng first for bere			6
Item for bread and \<sch\> chese for the helpers			◇
Item for ale to the same			◇
Item to John Wylser for his day work with cost to the same			◇
Item to Agnes Harvy for hir quarter			◇
\<illeg.\> \<illeg.\>			

[fol. 51v]

\<illeg.\> ...... off \grene/ damaske
\<Item a clothe and kote for *\<illeg\>* of blew\>
\<illeg.\> lasse hanging in the westry\>
Item hoselyng b◇lle[339]
Item 8 syrplessys
\<damaged\> cloth \<damaged\> yerds in length and a yard in brede
A cope of blu damaske
Item a peyr of chalys
Item a towely in lenthe 6 yerds
Item that Syr Roger Barford hathe gevyn a mes boke be hands of John Dey[340]
Item 3 coveryngs of canvas for the thre auters *\<the piece\>* 3 yerdes and halfe in
    lengthe a pece[341]
Item 4 rochets for the qwere
Item a westemente of blw welvet with all that belonge therto
Item *\<illeg.\>* of chaleys \<\> pax of 31 \<\> uncys parcel geylte
Item 1 fyn auter \clothe/ and 1 fyne towell and 1 redd vestemente
Item a crosse of sylver gylt enamelyd of the gyft of Greneman
Item 1 pyx of sylver with a payr of cheyns to hang abdoght the prestes neke
Item 2 red vestyments of damaske
1 \<ref\> red vestment of saten of Brygys[342]
Item1 cope of whyght brydys, a vestment with 2 tynycles with awbys perteynyng
    to the same of the gyft of Mr Vycar
Item a cope of blake velvet, a vestment, 2 tynycles with awbys perteynyng to the
    same geven by the brothern of Sent Johns gyld

---

[339] The houseling bell rung at the Eucharist.

[340] John Day was executor to the priest, Roger Barford, who died in 1504. See Appendix 2:30 (NRO, NCC Ryxe 27).

[341] There were certainly three altars at St Mary's, but perhaps as many as six side altars for the various gilds for which gild members would have provided vestments and hangings. These therefore would not be included in the parish church inventory.

[342] Satin from Bruges; see also the following entry for white 'brydys'.

Item a pax of sylver <on> parcell gylt
Item a vestment of whyght fustian with red droppys
<Item a sylke clothe of damaske werke popyngaye grene>
Item 1 koveryng of tappystrey to kover the bere
Item 2 clothys stayned with droopys of blood for 2 altars

APPENDICES

Appendix 1
Mildenhall under Queen Mary

Later churchwardens' accounts from the reign of Mary Tudor had survived and extracts were published by Samuel Tymms in *East Anglian Notes and Queries*, I (1864), pp.185, 198. These would have been the choice of the compiler at the time and could not be described as a complete set by any means. Since then the original manuscript containing the accounts has disappeared. The compiler sorted the accounts which he chose to use under separate subject headings. This meant that there was no chronological progression. Here they have been rearranged in chronological order as far as it is possible and, although the entries are sparse, they trace the refurbishment of the church and the gild hall during Queen Mary's reign.

	[1554]		
	£	s.	d.
[Payments for the clock and the bells]			
Item payd to Joones, the carpeneter, for his work in the steple, for makyng of the lattes wyndowe and the 4 light closen, and the mendyng of the weste window and plancheryng of the belsoller and stopping of the well and mending of the soller		7	0
Item payd for thre hundred of bord for to close the lettes windows and the dore in the steple		12	0
Item payde to Syr Thomas for his labor for mendyng of the clock		1	0
Item payde to Syr Thomas for kepyng of the clock at Our Lady day		1	8
Item payd to Planer for a bar of iron and for boults and nayles for the olde clocke house		3	4
IItem payd to Sir Thomas for his labour for mendyng of the clock whan he dwelt at Ely, and for half a quarter for his wages for kepyng of the clock and coming from Eley		1	8
IItem payd to Thomas Buntyng for kepyng of the bells thre quarters at Chrystmas		2	0
Item payd to John Place for a bell rope		1	3
Item payd for two ashin pols for latches for the bells			4
[Payments for liturgical necessities]			
Payd to Robart Planer for a < > cloth and other thyngs that the old Churchdens had in ther tym		3	4
Item payde for a holy water stopp at Bury		5	4
Item payd for the cloth, the vayll and the sorsin of the same		6	2
Item payd for the staynyng of the vayll to sextyn		10	0
Item payd for the Lyne Ryngs, the hookes for the vayll and for mendyng of the fyerpan		1	4
Item payde for a pece of tymber for to hang the Lyne for the vayll and the lace for the Rings			6
Item that we payde for our charge whan we wente to Fornam that we were warned ther to be at the court		1	3

	£	s.	d.

[Payments for external repairs]

Item payde for the makyng of the church style at thewest gate		1	8
Item payde for the tymber for the style			8
Item for nayles for the style and the gate			2

[1555]

[Payments for the clock and the bells]

Item payd to Wyllym Darbe for nayle for the lattys windows and the dore in the steple		4	0
Item payd to Buntyng for his wages for the bells at Eastern			8
Item payd to Buntyng for mendyng of the bawdryck			4
Item payd to John Lane for makyng of the great bell Clapper		6	8
Item payd to Longs for the bars and boults for to hang the clock bell and for spetyng and lead nayles for the plomer		1	5
Item payd to Lansdale for ryngyng of the eyght a clock bell from Mychelmas to Christemes		1	10
Item payd to Robert Cleare for goyng to Hausted for to cause Sparke for to come se the clock			4

[Payments for work on the gild hall]

Item payd to Spyrling of Bury for the tymber and the framyng of the east end of the gyld hall and the fetching home of the tymber from Bury and setting on it up	1	4	0
Item payd for two loggs of iron for the ends of the < > waye of the gyld hall end and for nayles for the loggs		1	8
Item payd for polls for splents and raylbars for the parte wall of the gyld hall and for nayles for the raylbars		2	4
Item for claying of the parte wall of the hall and claying of the walls and mendyng in other places		7	0
Item payd for two lode of claye for the gyld hall and for the cartyng of the claye		1	4
Item for hempe for the splents and for haye for the claye			10
Item payd to Tyd, the mason, for casting and whytyng of the gyld hall walls		3	4
Item payd to Jones, the carpenter, for laying in of a gronsell at the south syde of the gyld hall, and mending of the windows and setting in of the selle and pyllers of the windows		3	4
Item for pynyng of the gronsell and mendyng of the wall, and making cleane of the hall		1	0
Item payd to Nicholas Pollyngton for the gronsell and for the tymber for the pyllers of the windows of the hall		3	0
Item payd to the Goodman Queash for a planch for the said windows of the hall		1	0
Item payd to Robart Coslyn for lyme and ston for the walls of the gyld hall		5	0
Item payd for carryng of lyme, ston and sond to the hall		1	0
Item payd for three hundredth of thach for the gyld hall		8	0
Item payd to John Pollynton for the laying of the three hundredth thach of the hall		5	0

	£	s.	d.
Item payd to Jones the carpenter for making the benche at the gyld hall at the hy table and for nayles for the same			6

[Payments for liturgical requirements]

	£	s.	d.
Item payd to Potter for two candlesticks and for a crymytory cloth of Lawne		4	0
Item payd for a payr of sensors and for a crimitory at Bury		7	0
Item payd for two pounds of wax for the pascall light		1	10
Item payd for the makyng of the light			1
Item payd to Jones, the carpenter, for making of the hers for the sepulter		5	0
Item payd to Thomas Cook for the sepulter and for bordes and tymber for the same			8
Item payd to father Oxford for hanging up of the vayle and settyng up of the sepulter and <takyng> of the sepulter and for the smalle lyne for the vayle		1	8
Item payd for two posts for the sepulter		1	0
Item payd to Oxford and John Pollyngton and Buntyng for takyng of the dows and the oules in the church		1	0
Item payd to the mason for settyng up of the sowth awter and mendyng of the pament		4	0
Item payd for mendyng of the church gates on the northe side and nayls for the gates, and for hewing of the pece of tymber for the Roode lofte and settyng up of the peces, and for the carpenters bord whyle they made the gate and the pece for the Rood lofte, and settyng of the pece up		2	6

[Payment for external repairs]

	£	s.	d.
Item payd to Tyd, the mason, for mendyng of the church wall next the end of the scole house		2	0

[1556]

[Payments for liturgical requirements]

	£	s.	d.
Item paid to the carpenter for makyng and payntyng and settyng of the roode		18	0
Item to Whits wife for the joiners bord whyle he was a framyng of the roode and makyng of the cross and settyng up of the roode and payntyng of the same		2	0
Item payd to Robart for makyng of the barr of iron for to hold fast the Roode and the cross		2	0
Item payd to Nycholas Pollyngton for payntyng of the Dormant that the roode stand on		3	4
Item payd to Thomas Farthing for a day woorke in remouvyg of the Dormant		1	8
Item payd for five boshells of lyme for that same work		1	4

[1557–1558]

**That the thirtieth day of May, in the thyrde and forthe yeares
of King Phyllip and Quene Mary, Anthony Stepney, Thomas**

Cotes, John Smythe and Robert Bloom, churchwardens
of the church of Mildenhall, have made ther accompte
in the presence of the inhabytaunces of the same towne
from the day of ther coming on untyll this present day
above named and so they have been discharged and
have their quiitance.

The new churchwardens elected by the inhabytants of
the township of Myldenhall be these foloyng: Robert
Clark, Jamys Frost, Henry Chylderston and John May
the day and yere above wryttyn, and they received in
mony thyrtene shillings 10d. and one bit of lead weying
< > pounds, and also two sheets of leade lying upon the
vestry. Item they do receive fine [*sic*] obligacions.

	£	s.	d.
[*Payments for the bells*]			
Item for tymber and yernes to mend the frame of Baggott's bell		2	3
Item to Hyll, carpenter, for hanging of the said bell		3	4
Item to Thomas man for a boorde for the sayd bell			8
Item to ringers at the byshopp's visitation			6
Item a plumer for 12 dayes wurke in mendyng the leade and coverryng of Baggott's bell, his boord and wages after 10d. a day		10	0
[*Payments for liturgical necessities*]			
Item payd for a lantern to carry with the sacrament		1	0
First payd for the Rowell		11	8
Item to Pollyngton for payntyng of it		1	8
Item to James Frost for a quarter of wax for the said rowell			3
Item to Luwies for yernes to the said rowell			8
Item to James Frost for 3 pounde of waxe and the of it <*sic*>for the rowell		3	6
Item for pax			2
Item for pictures of Mary and John with the patrons of the church	1	5	0
Item to Hernes, mason, for 4 days worke in laying the altar stone and mendyng the pament in the church and settyng up the ymages		3	4
Item to James Frost for 2 studdes to stande behynde the pictures of Mary and John			3
			[*1558*]
Geven to the newe clerke to bynde hym			4
For Alixander's horse hyer and his expenses bydyng for his brother to be our Clarke			2

Appendix 2

Selected Wills of Parishioners of Mildenhall, 1433–1585

1. Will of John Mason, chaplain, 4 May 1433   NRO, NCC Surflete 147

[*Latin*] To be buried in Mildenhall church;[1] to the high altar of the same church for tithes detained and underpaid 6s. 8d.[2]

To the parish church of Mildenhall a missal with a chalice to serve for ever the chaplain celebrating there in the charnel,[3] whether with the same or other missal and chalice of the church without causing the removal of the others, but if the parishioners do remove them, then the missal and chalice to be in the Charnel permanently, serving for celebration for ever.

To the same church a book commonly called cochour[4] to be laid on a lectern and fixed publicly to the lectern in the same church, to remain in perpetuity on the south side of my tomb there; to the same church a book called a manual.[5]

To Thomas Barker 20s. The residue of my goods to my executors to pay my debts. Executors: John Watts, chaplain, Thomas Barker, clerk and Thomas Bussch, chaplain. Witnesses the same.

Proved at Norwich, 15 July 1434.

2. Will of John Speed, 13 August 1438   NRO, NCC Doke 67

[*Latin*] To be buried in the parish church of Blessed Mary of Mildenhall before the tomb of Richard Bertun; to the high altar of the same church for my tithes forgotten 6s. 8d; to each chaplain present at my obsequies on the day of my death 4d. and the seventh day and the thirtieth day;[6] on the day of my death 20s. to be distributed in alms to the poor.

To each parish chaplain of Mildenhall 12d.; to each parish clerk of the same 4d.

To each of my godsons and goddaughters 12d. If the vicar of Mildenhall will allow mass of requiem to be celebrated on the three days specified, then 3d. to be offered at each mass, but if not only 1d.

To Margaret Red, alias Calfhagh of Oxburgh 6s. 8d; to Agnes, the wife of Robert Adam of Burwell, my cousin, 20s.

The residue of all my goods to Agnes, my wife, William Chapman[7] and John Bryan, chaplain, whom I make executors.

---

1   Burials in church were reserved for clergy, gentry and local patrons who, through their standing in the community, were deemed worthy of church interment.

2   The payment to the high altar was ostensibly a payment towards unpaid tithes, but was, in fact, paid to the priest serving the cure, whether rector, vicar or chaplain. In Mildenhall, where the vicars were pluralists and frequently absent, payment to the high altar would have gone to a parish chaplain.

3   A chalice and a mass book, in manuscript at this date, provided the essentials for celebrating mass in Ralph de Walsham's charnel chapel. This bequest suggests that John Mason had been the chantry priest there.

4   The word 'coucher' referred to the great size rather than the type of book. In 1519 a volume was described as 'less than a boke, and a boke less than a coucher'. Wordsworth and Littlehales, *The Old Service Books of the English Church*, p.64.

5   A manual was a book of occasional offices.

6   These were additional intercessions which closely reflected the funeral liturgy, requested a week and a month later after the interment. That celebrated a month later was known as the 'month's mind'.

7   See Notes on People p.200, for Chapman and Bryan.

137

Witnesses: Thomas Busshe, clerk, Henry Mayner, Thomas Walsokyn of Mildenhall and others.

Proved at Norwich, 10 October 1438 by John Bryan, chaplain. Power reserved to the other executors.

3. Will of Thomas Sigo, dated the octave[8] of the   NRO, NCC Doke 113
Nativity of the Blessed Virgin Mary 1439 at Mildenhall

[*Latin*] To be buried in the church of Blessed Mary of Mildenhall, that is in the middle of the aisle [*passus*] at my father's head; to the high altar for my tithes forgotten 6s. 8d.; to the fabric of the church 10 marks in money; to each chaplain present at my obsequies 4d. and to each parish chaplain 6d. and to each parish clerk 2d; to each boy studying and present there 1d. on my burial day, 7 day and 30 day, to be distributed in alms, single pennies to the poor so that each one craving alms receives a penny on each of those days; after my death weekly to be distributed 13d. per week in alms to thirteen poor people of Mildenhall in greatest need; a suitable chaplain to celebrate for my soul, the souls of my parents and the souls of all the faithful departed for 3 years, taking for his salary 8 marks,[9] but if Robert my son will be the priest the service is to be celebrated just whenever it pleases him.

To each of my godsons and goddaughters 2 bushels of barley.

To John Clark, my shepherd, 10 ewes with lambs; the same John to have 3 roods of land for his lifetime and after his death the 3 roods to remain to Thomas Clark, his son, but if Thomas dies before his mother then the 3 roods to remain to John Clark, the son of the aforementioned John Clark, each to be the other's heir.

To Roger my servant 5 ewes with lambs; to Alice my servant 3 ewes with lambs; to John Clark son of the said John Clark 3 ewes with lambs.

The residue of all my goods to Robert Sygo, my son, and John Gregory whom I make executors.

Witnesses: John Bryan, chaplain, John Sygo, son of the said Thomas Sygo.[10]

Proved at Norwich, 15 January 1439 before Master Thomas Ryngsted, dec.bac., perpetual vicar of the parish church of Mildenhall, legally deputising by executors.

4. Will of John Berton alias Watts,[11] chaplain,   NRO, NCC Doke 164
17 October 1441

[*Latin*] To be ecclesiastically buried in the churchyard of Blessed Mary of Milden-hall.

To the said church for the improvement of divine service, a psalter with a hymn book in it.

To Margery Dobyn a long chair; to Agnes, the daughter of John Dobyn, a little chest; to John Dobyn[12] aforesaid my best gown.

To John Bryon, chaplain, a small psalter with *placebo* and *dirige*.[13]

---

8   16 September.
9   £5 6s. 8d. or 8 marks was a standard annual payment to a priest for short-term prayers.
10   See Notes on People p.109, for the Sygo family.
11   John Berton [Barton] was possibly a local man from Barton Mills. He was executor to John Mason (above, no.1).
12   John Dobyn was described as the parish clerk in the will of William Canvas in 1440 (NRO, NCC Doke 179).
13   The psalter was the most popular and well-known religious text for both clergy and laity, here containing also vespers and matins of the Office of the Dead, in which *placebo*, 'I will please', and *dirige*, 'Direct, O Lord', are, respectively, the first words of antiphons.

Residue of my goods to funeral costs, debts etc, and to executors.

Executors: John Bryan and John Dobyn.

No probate recorded.

5. Will of Henry Mayner' of Mildenhall, 13 October 1443   NRO, NCC Doke 231

[*Latin*] To be buried in the churchyard of Blessed Mary of Mildenhall; to the high altar of the same church for my tithes forgotten 2s.; to the fabric of the same church 20s.

To Richard Machoun, parish chaplain, my confessor, 2d.

To Alice, my sister, a pair of sheets; to Annabel, my sister, a pair of sheets; to Margaret Parmanter, my sister, 3s. 4d.

To Margaret, the daughter of Roger Maynerd, my son, living with me, all my household utensils and bedding, except the two pairs of sheets already bequeathed; to each of the sons and daughters of the said Roger, my son, 3s. 4d.

To Thomas Mayner', my cousin, 3s 4d.

Residue of the goods to Roger Mayner', my son, and Margaret, his daughter, living with me whom I make executors.

Proved at Norwich, 2 November 1443, by Roger Mayner'. Power reserved to the other executor.

6. Will of William Hygne, 2 April 1448   NRO, NCC Aleyn 9

[*Latin*] To be buried in the churchyard of the Blessed Mary of Mildenhall; to the high altar of the same church for my tithes forgotten 20d.

My feoffees to enfeoff Margaret, my wife, of my messuage for her lifetime, including the house called Le Berne; after Margaret's death, the messuage to be sold and divided into 4 parts: 1 part to be disposed for my soul, Margaret's soul and all my benefactors;[14] another part to remain to John, my son, with two almost [*quasi*] black calves and my gown, tunic and cap which are to go to him in recompense for some grain and stipend held by me of his stipend; but if he (still) claims any of the grain or stipend, then he shall have nothing of the above legacy from the messuage or calves etc.; the other two parts to be divided among my 2 younger sons, viz William and Robert. If either of them want and is able to buy the said messuage he to have preference before others at the price others would pay.

Residue of my goods to the said Margaret my wife to pay my debts etc.

Executrix: Margaret my wife.

Supervisor: John Bryan, chaplain.

Proved at Norwich, 4 February 1448 by Margaret, the relict, by Master Thomas Ryngstede, perpetual vicar of Mildenhall parish church.

7. Will of John Frere, 16 May 1448   SROB, IC 500/2/9/144

[*Latin*] To be buried in the churchyard of Blessed Mary of Mildenhall: to the high altar of the same church for my tithes forgotten 2s.; to the fabric of the church 40s.

To Margery my cousin [*cognate*], the daughter of John Playford 40s.; to each of the sons of the said John Playford 6s. 8d. for themselves.

My feoffees to enfeoff Alice, my wife, for term of her life, of all my messuage in le

---

14 Benefactors are persons through or by whom the testator has profited.

Bek,[15] next to the messuage of William Chapman, ½ acre of land in Bekfeld and a close of meadow called Blomesyerd, to the intent that, after her death, the messuage, land and meadow wholly remain to Robert my son and his heirs; if Robert die without heirs, the messuage to remain to my right heirs forever.

My feoffees to enfeoff John Playford and Margaret, my daughter, his wife, of 4 acres of land and meadow at Sedmanesholig, to them and their heirs; if all their heirs die without issue during the lifetime of the said John and Margaret, the 4 acres to be at the disposition of the said Margaret my daughter.

My feoffees to enfeoff Robert, my son, of 3 acres of land at *le Stok*, in 2 pieces, called Glemesfordes and half an acre of land in Lytleye[16] holding them to him and his heirs of the chief lords of the fee for ever.

William Mors to have my messuage in Fornham All Saints on condition he pay me or my executors, at the stated feasts, 24 marks, that is at the feast of the nativity of St John the Baptist next after this date 40s.,[17] and at the feast of All Saints next following 40s. without any delay, and so on, year by year, till the 24 marks have been paid, without any fraud; provided that he produce security for the payment of these amounts, William to enjoy the messuage; but if he do not, my heirs or executors to re-enter and possess the messuage for ever, notwithstanding the sale; out of the money so paid, a suitable chaplain to celebrate in the parish church of Midenhall for my soul, the soul of Margaret lately my wife, and the souls of all my benefactors, and the remainder to be divided equally between Alice, my wife, John Playford, Robert, my son, and Margery and Margaret, the daughters of John Clerk.

My feoffees to enfeoff Robert, my son, of the messuage in which he now lives in the street called le Bek, to him and his heirs. I surrender into the hands of the lord,[18] by William Playford, to the use of Robert my son, all those lands, tenements, meadows, pastures and feedings which I hold of the lord by the rod, by the custom of the manor there, in the town and fields of Mildenhall.

To the said Alice, my [*wife*], a brass pot and the best pan that I have; to the said Alice and her two daughters 60 sheep, that is, all that I have, each of them to have 20 for herself; the same Alice and her 2 daughters to have 9 of my draught animals, that is 3 each.

To the same Alice a cart, 3 stots and 2 mares with harness for the same, and a plough with all the equipment; also to Alice all my grain in my messuage except what is expended in bread and ale for my funeral, 7 day and 30 day,[19] and except 6 quarters of barley, 5 quarters for Thomas Clerk and 1 for John Costyn, and all the firewood in the said messuage.

Also to Alice all my grain of the crop of the lands in Holmereseye with 1½ acres of rye abutting on my messuage in le Bekfield and 6 silver spoons.

To the said Thomas Clerk, my servant, 2 cows; to the aforesaid John Playford 4 of my draught animals of the bovine kind [*genere bovine*][20] and 6 silver spoons; to Robert my son 4 draught animals, 6 silver spoons and a thousand thatch [*thak*]; to the said John Playford and Robert my son the crop of all the lands cropped

---

15 Beck Row.

16 One of the islets out toward the fen. See 'The Parish of Mildenhall' in the Introduction p.xix.

17 The feast of John the Baptist was celebrated on 24 June; that of All Saints on 1 November.

18 This probably refers to the abbot of Bury St Edmunds, the lord of the largest of Mildenhall's three manors.

19 See note 6 above.

20 Oxen.

with grain, to be divided equally between them: to Alice, my wife, the crop of the meadow called Prallys.

To the gild of the Holy Trinity 6s. 8d. to be paid by John Puget; to the gild of St Katherine

6s. 8d. to be paid by Alice, my wife, from her own chattels;[21] to Margaret, the daughter of John Clerk, a brass pot; to Thomas Bown, gentleman, 3s. 4d.; to John Bryan, chaplain, 3s. 4d.

Residue of all my goods, after my funeral has been carried out and debts paid, to John Playford and Robert, my son, executors.

Witnesses: Thomas Bown, gentleman, John Bryan, chaplain, Thomas Chylderston, William Thomson, Roger Chapman and others, given at Mildenhall.

Proved at Fordham [Cambs.], 13 July 1448. Administration to executors.

8. Will of John Staloun,[22] the younger, 6 October 1452   SROB, IC 500/2/9/148

[*Latin*] To be buried in Mildenhall churchyard, on the north side, next to Audrey [*Etheldreda*], late my wife; to the high altar for my tithes forgotten 6s. 8d.; to the fabric of the same church 40s.; to the church of Rome 6s. 8d.; to be delivered to Thomas Martin, clerk,[23] 20s. to be disposed as he advises.

To the fabric of Isleham church [*Cambs.*] 3s. 4d. and another 3s. to be disposed among the poor of the town in greatest need; to the fabric of Multon church 3s. 4d. and among the poor of the town another 3s. 4d. as above; to the fabric of the chapel of St Theobald in Newmarket 20d., and among the poor of the same place 20d. to be distributed as above in both parishes.

To the fabric of the church of Barton Mills [*Berton Togryng*] 20d. and among the poor as above 20d.; to the fabric of the church at Tuddenham 20d. and among the poor there 20d.; to the fabric of the church at Brandonfery[24] 20d. and among the poor 20d.; to the fabric of the chapel of St Lawrence, Eryswell 20d. and among the poor 20d.; to the fabric of Lakenheath church 20d. and among the poor 20d.

A suitable chaplain to celebrate for my soul, Audrey, my wife's and the souls of my parents and benefactors and all faithful departed in Mildenhall parish church for a whole year, taking for his salary 8 marks, and he to assist at divine service there.

To the fraternity of Corpus Christi of the same town 3s. 4d.; to the fraternity of St John the Baptist 20d.; to the fraternity of St Katherine 20d.;[25] for a hundred masses to be celebrated for my soul as soon as possible 40s., that is 4d. for each mass, if my chaplain can have them celebrated on one and the same day:

To be distributed weekly for a whole year among the poor of Mildenhall in most need 6d.; to the convent of Friars Minor of Babwell 3s. 4d. and to Friar William Knyth *alias* Berton 3s. 4d.

To John Staloun of Haverile, barker, 6s. 8d.

Joan, my wife, to have half of all my grain, one part being mine to pay my debts, and the other part wholly hers; also a hundred sheep, that is 60 wethers and 60 ewes, and all my horses with plough, cart and harness, and everything belonging to them.

To John Staloun, the son of John Staloun of Kentford, 20 sheep, that is 10 wethers

---

21 For gilds see the section 'Remembering the Dead' in the Introduction.
22 John Staloun's elder brother, John Stalham, died in 1459 (SROB, IC 500/2/10/107). Staloun may be a corruption of the name or a misreading by the scribe.
23 See below, will 16, NRO, NCC Jekkys 144.
24 A well known crossing point at Brandon on the Little Ouse.
25 See the section on 'Remembering the Dead' in the Introduction, p.xliv.

and 10 ewes: Christian, my daughter, to be supported with my goods, and governed by the advice and counsel of my executors until she is 12 years old; to the same Christian a brass pot and a brass pan; to Isabel, my cousin living with me, a brass pot and a brass pan.

To Thomas Clerke, my executor, for his labour if he is willing to take up administration 13s. 4d., and to Thomas [*Martyn*], clerk 6s.8d.

The residue of all my goods to the said Joan, my wife, and Thomas Clerk of Lakenheath, whom I make executors.

Supervisor: Thomas Martyn, clerk.

Proved before the official of the archdeacon of Sudbury at Mildenhall, 28 February 1452 by executors.

9. Will of John Bryan, chaplain, 3 January 1454   NRO, NCC Aleyn 215

[*Latin*] To be ecclesiastically buried in the churchyard of Blessed Mary the Virgin in Mildenhall on the west side next to my parents; to the high altar for my tithes forgotten 3s. 4d.

To William Place, my cousin, my breviary; to Thomas Martin, clerk, my service book.

To Joan Davy, my cousin, from the money arising from my messuage when it is sold 40s.; to Agnes Aspy, widow, my best cow and 6s. a year for 2 or 3 years after my death [*illeg.*]; to the same Agnes 4 bushels of wheat, 2 quarters of meslin and rye and 3 quarters of malt.

A suitable chaplain to celebrate for my soul and my parents' souls for 2 years.

Thomas Place, my cousin, to have preference in the occupation of my messuage and if he wishes to buy it, to have it 100s. under the price.

To Ralph Jerveys a brass jug: to Agnes, the daughter of the said Agnes Jaspy [*sic*] 2½ quarters of malt.

Residue of my goods to executors.

Executors: Sir Martyn, parish chaplain of Mildenhall,[26] John Dobyn and Thomas Place[27] of the same town.

Witnesses: John Rowlond, chaplain, Robert Sampson, chaplain, John Bakhot, senior, and others.

Proved at Norwich, 21 March 1454 by Thomas Place. Power reserved to executors.

10. Will of Thomas Place, 6 October 1457   SROB, IC 500/2/9/191

[*Latin*] To the high altar of the said church for tithes forgotten 2s.; to the repairing of the same church 2s.

To Audrey, my wife, all my ostilments [*furnishings*] and utensils belonging to my house and 60s. which the executors of John Bryon, chaplain, owe me, as he specified; to John, my son, a cow, a brass laver and a mark in money; to William, my son, a heifer and a mark in money; to Andrew my son a heifer and a mark in money; if Audrey, my wife, be now pregnant and produce a child, that child to have a mark.

A suitable priest to be provided for a year in the said church to celebrate for my soul and the souls of those for whom I am bound.

---

26   This is Thomas Martin, clerk, to whom Bryan bequeathed his service book. Note the title 'sir' for a non-graduate priest.

27   The will of Thomas Place, Bryan's cousin, follows, will 10.

Residue of my goods and chattels, if any remain, to my executors; my wife, Audrey, and William Place, chaplain, my brother.
Seal appended.
Proved in the parish church of Mildenhall, 15 November 1457. Administration to Audrey, wife of the deceased. Power reserved to William Place, chaplain, executor, when he comes.

11. Will of John Taylour *alias* Wyllyamsone, 4 April 1460   SROB, IC 500/2/9/255

[*Latin*] To the high altar of Mildenhall church, for tithes forgotten 12d.; to the fabric of the said church 2s.
To Anne my wife all the utensils belonging to my house.
Anne my wife to have, for term of her life, the part of my tenement in which I live, on the west side, as specified by me, the said John Wyllyamson, that is a parlour with the solar, all the kitchen with the well, half the storeroom and half the yard; if, after all my legacies and debts that I truly owe to anyone, have been fully paid, according to my will, Anne my wife have insufficient to manage with, she to have part of the money from my tenement, as need arises, according to the discretion of my executors, having regard to the respectability and age of my wife.
To be distributed among the poor of Mildenhall in greatest need 5 marks, according to the discretion of my executors.
To Robert Burgeys of Bury 13s. 4d; to Agnes, wife of Robert Burgeys, 3s. 4d.
Residue of all my goods, chattels and debts, wherever they may be, after my debts have been paid, my burial carried out and legacies fulfilled, to executors; Robert Burgeys and John Paynet, to whom for their labour [*omitted*].
Proved at Fornham St Martin, 4 August 1460. Power to executors.

12. Will of William Bakhote,[28] mercer, 11 April 1461   SROB, IC 500/2/9/303

[*Latin*] Dated at Mildenhall. To be buried in the church of St Mary, Mildenhall; to the high altar of the same church, for tithes forgotten. 2s.; to Mildenhall church a silver basin and two silver cruets, of price £3 6s. 8d. to serve the high altar for washing the priests' hands and other holy offices carried out there.
To the fabric of the church of Santon Downham 20d.; to the maintenance of Herringswell church 20d.
Residue of all my goods, debts and chattels, wherever they are, after my debts have been paid, my burial carried out and my legacies fulfilled, wholly to Joan, my wife, executrix.
Proved at Fordham, 22 May 1461. Administration to executrix.

13. Will of Richard Colman, 10 November, 1461   SROB, IC 500/2/9/286

[*Latin*] To the high altar of the parish church of Mildenhall, for my tithes and offerings forgotten 2s.; to the repairing of the parish church of Barton Mills 12d.
To Joan Firmage my daughter my messuage with the adjacent croft in Mildenhall situated between the messuage of John Bakhot called the gildhall of Corpus Christi[29]

---

[28] This is a very brief testament from one of the wealthiest inhabitants of the town. The family were well-respected and appear throughout Mildenhall's documents. Here William makes arrangements for the commemoration of his soul. His possessions and his wealth are left to his wife to administer.

[29] The Corpus Christi gild did not have its own gildhall, but used a building belonging to John Bakhot.

of Mildenhall on the north side and the messuage lately Thomas Scherde's[30] on the south, the west head abutting on the highway and the east head on land of the manor of Mildenhall called Thevyslond; also to the same Joan 1½ acres of land at Lampetts in Mildenhall, as appears in certain deeds made of it, and 1½ acres of meadow in le Westfield, as appears in the deeds made of it; Joan to hold the messuage with the croft and 3 acres of land, for term of her life, of the chief lords of the fees by service etc.

After the decease of the said Joan, the messuage, croft and land to remain to William Firmage, her son and his heirs; if he die without heirs, the messuage to remain to Margaret Holme, wife of John Holme the younger, of Barton, and her heirs; if she die without heirs the messuage etc. to be sold by the executors of the said Margaret Holme for the best price possible, and the whole of the money from the sale faithfully to be disposed by them in pious uses, alms and deeds of charity, according to their discretion, for my soul, the soul of Margaret my wife and the souls of my parents, friends and benefactors, and all the faithful departed as they see most expedient.

To Edmund Colman my son a fen with 5 roods of land lying together in le East-fennys in Mildenhall, as specified in the deeds made of it, to him and his heirs for ever; Edmund also to have my tenement called Sadeleris in Mildenhall for the term of his life, and after his death it to remain to Ed. Firmage and his heirs; if Ed. Firmage die without heirs, the tenement called Sadeleris to be sold by his executors and the money so raised to be disposed in pious uses and deeds of charity as above.

To the same Edmund Colman my son a parcel of land in the field of Mildenhall, one head of which abuts on the gildhall of Corpus Christi to the west and the other on land called Theveslond to the east, for term of his life, he having power to give this parcel of land in exchange when he so wishes, so long as he has land of the same value to hold for term of his life after his death the land to remain to Joan Firmage my daughter for term of her life, and after her decease it to revert to the aforesaid William Firmage and his heirs; if William have no heirs, it to remain to the aforesaid Margaret Holme and her heirs; if she die without heirs the parcel of land to be sold and [the money] disposed by her executors.

Residue of all my goods to John Firmage the elder of Barton, executor.

Proved before Master Robert Spilman, official of the archdeacon of Sudbury, at Fornham, 15 March 1461. Administration to executors.

14. Will of Thomas Tydde, 5 May 1463   SROB, IC 500/2/12/12

[*Latin*] My testament containing my last will: to the high altar of Mildenhall church, for my tithes and offerings forgotten and withheld, in exoneration of my soul 5s: to the reparations of the same church 13s. 4d.

To John Wetewell, my servant 40d.; to Isabel Sabelotte, my servant, a cow price 6s. 8d. or the price.

To the gild of St Mary of Mildenhall 5s.[31]

To Alice Skonyng, the wife of Richard Skonyng, a heifer of 2 years.

I wish a suitable priest to celebrate in Mildenhall church for a whole year for my

---

[30] This is perhaps the same Thomas Sherd whose anniversary was commemorated in St Mary's church, 1527–28. See CWA, fol.17v and also Notes on People, p.209.

[31] See 'Remembering the Dead' in the Introduction, p.xliv.

soul and the soul of Alice, my wife, and for the souls of our parents, friends and all my benefactors and all the faithful departed, taking for his stipend 8 marks.

The residue of all my goods and chattels, whatever and wherever they be, after my debts have been paid and my burial done and my legacies fulfilled, I leave to my faithful executors to dispose of it for our souls in deeds of charity according to their discretion as they see most expedient, and to keep and support all my children which I have put in the care and control of my executors until they come of legal age.

Executors: William Chylderston and John Halstede, to each of whom I leave 5s. for their faithful labour in this matter.

Proved at Fornham St Martin, 16 May 1463. Administration to executors. Seal of official appended.

15. Will of John Bakhot, 20 December 1464   SROB, IC 500/2/10/379

[*Latin*] To be buried in *le south ele* of St Mary's church of Mildenhall, next to my parents; to the high altar of the said church a noble; to the said church 40s. together with my best silver girdle, to the honour of the Trinity[32] and SS Ed' [*sic*] and Nicholas in the following manner: one of the parish clerks of Mildenhall to have the girdle on the vigils of the said Saints Ed' and Nicholas[33] each year, by the advice and discretion of the wardens of the said church for the time being, to the praise and honour of those saints.

To the great gild of the Trinity of Bishop's Lynn a noble; and a noble to the gild of Corpus Christi; and 40d. to the gild of St John of Mildenhall.

A suitable chaplain to be chosen by the discretion of my executors to celebrate for my soul and the souls of my father and mother and all my parents, children and benefactors, for 4 years after my death.

To each of my godsons and goddaughters, a ewe.

To Richard Busshe, my nephew, and to each of the sons and daughters of John Bakhot, my son, a ewe and a hogget. To Margaret Knygth, my kinswoman, my green silver girdle.

Richard, my son, to have the arrears of rent and service belonging to me, in whosoever's or whatsoever hands they be, together with all my rents and services as they are more clearly entered in the rent-rolls and other evidences made of them; to the same Richard, my son, a bowl with a gilt [?]rim; my household to be kept together with my goods up to the feast of St Michael, the archangel[34] next, inclusively.

To John Bakhot, my son, my best striped gown.

To Margaret, my wife, all the utensils and bedding belonging to my house except what belongs to my body, together with my own 3 horses; to the said Margaret half of all my growing grain at the harvest next after my death, and half my bovine animals and half of the 2 flocks pasturing and lying in Herringswell and in Mildenhall after the feast of St Michael next after my death, the ewes previously bequeathed being first extracted, and except the oxen and cows, and all the ewes and wethers neces-

---

[32] The Trinity was especially favoured in England as Thomas Becket had chosen the first Sunday after Whitsun to be regarded as Trinity Sunday for observance by the churches in his province. Bakhot's will is prefaced by an invocation to the Trinity.

[33] St Edmund, king and martyr, was the patron saint of East Anglia, his feast day being celebrated on 20 November. St Nicholas, a fourth-century bishop of Myra, was patron saint of children, sailors, merchants and pawnbrokers. His feast day was celebrated on 6 December.

[34] 29 September was St Michael's day, which marked the culmination of the harvest season. It was also a quarter day on which rents and payments were due.

sary and sufficient for the upkeep of my house up to the feast of St Michael next, out of the 2 flocks.

Any obscurities, doubts, difficulties contradictions [etc.] in this my testament and last will to be clarified, amended and expounded by Richard, my son, as seems necessary to him to prevent it causing disputes.

The residue of all my goods to the discretion and disposition of Margaret, my wife, and Richard, my son, executors, providing always that my debts have been paid to my creditors out of my goods and debts.

Proved at Fornham [St] Martin before the official, 4 March 1464/65. Administration to Richard Bakhot executor. Power reserved to Margaret, the wife of the deceased, when she comes.

16. Will of Thomas Martyn,[35] **chaplain, 2 June 1469   NRO, NCC Jekkys 144**

[*Latin*] My body to Christian burial; to the high altar of Mildenhall 3s. 4d.; to the reparation of the vestments and ornaments of Mildenhall parish church 20s.

To the reparation of the way called Slystrelane 6s. 8d.

To Isabel Rycheman 6s. 8d.; to Katherine Sokyrman 3s. 4d.; to Stephen Martyn, my brother 40s, and to his wife 6s. 8d.; to Thomas Martyn and Margaret Martyn, the children of the said John [*sic*] Martyn 6s. 8d.

To the house of the abbey of Marham 20s.,[36] out of which I wish each sister to have 4d.; to the prioress of the said abbey 5s.; to the poor of the town of Marham 6s. 8d.; to the reparation of the churches of Holy Trinity and St Andrew 13s. 4d.

To Agnes Sherewyn 40s. and a silver spoon, a basin and a laver; to my sister 20s. and a silver spoon. To Thomas Gardner 40d.; to Henry Pope 40d.

To the gilds of St John the Baptist and Thomas the Martyr 6s. 8d.

To each of my godsons and goddaughters 12d.

I wish to have a priest to celebrate for my soul and for the souls of my parents and friends for 2 years, taking for his salary for the 2 years 16 marks in money.

To Thomas Martyn, the son of John Martyn, my brother, my portesse if he shall be a priest.

The residue of all goods I commit to the discretion of Master Richard Bakhott of Mildenhall, Thomas Barkere of the same, chaplain, and Robert Morys of the same, whom I make executors and to each of whom I leave 6s. 8d. for their labour.

Proved at Norwich before the official of the bishop of Norwich's consistory, 21 July 1469.

17. John Smyth, shoemaker, 27 December 1472   SROB, IC 500/2/11/23

[*Latin*] My body to Christian burial; to the fabric of Mildenhall church 40s.; a suitable priest to celebrate in Mildenhall church for my soul and the souls of my wives and all the faithful departed for 2 whole years.[37]

---

35 Thomas Martin was a chaplain in Mildenhall for twenty years and, during this time, frequently mentioned in parishioners' testaments. For priests and parochial personnel, see Table 2, above.

36 Marham was a house of Cistercian nuns in Norfolk, a small establishment with seldom more than thirteen nuns. The inclusion of Marham's churches of Holy Trinity and St Andrew (now destroyed) and the poor in the town suggests that Martin had originated from this area.

37 This document shows clearly how, in the mind of some testators, the division between artefacts and property was still separate. Here, the first section of the document represents the testament, written in Latin and dealing only with gifts of personal effects or moveable property. The second section in English represents the last will where immoveable property, such as land and buildings, could be apportioned and documented but, due to feudal tenurial restraints, could not be devised

To John Martyn of Drenkeston 20s.; to Thomas Martyn of the same 20s.

To the reparation of the church of Newton in Suffolk 40s.

To Joan, my wife, all my utensils belonging to my house and all my goods in my house: the residue of all my goods and chattels, after my debts are paid and legacies fulfilled, to my executors.

Executors: Joan, my wife, principal executor, John Blythe and John Halse of Mildenhall.[38]

[*English*] In dystrybuan of all my lands and tenements, meadows, pastures with the appurtenances lying in the fields and towns of Mildenhall, Worlington and Barton-by-Mildenhall. Joan, my wife, to have for term of her life, all my place with the appurtenances in the which I dwell, within the town of Mildenhall, as well free as copy;[39] and all the appurtenances therto longing called Curles within the town and field of Mildenhall and 6½ acres of arable land within the town and fields of Mildenhall wherof 3 acres lie in a piece in Cottonfeld between 2 meers next the land of William Pope on the west part and the north head abutteth upon a water-meer, 1½ acres of Peterburghes next the land of Harry Wentworth, esquire, sometime Shardelowes on the east part, the south head abutteth upon Tremewey; 2 acres lie in the same field next the land of the manor called Prattyswong on the east part, the south head abutting upon Tremowey and the north head abutteth upon Mundyswey. After the decease of the said Joan, if she be with child at this time as I trust to God she is, be it man child or woman child, then all the said mese, meadow enclosed, 6½ acres of arable land to remain to that said child and his heirs for evermore, under such condition as I shall declare in this my last will. If the said child decease ere it be married or else having no issue, then the mese, meadow, 6½ acres of arable land to be sold and the money disposed by my executors to the churches of Mildenhall, Worlington, Barton and other places next adjoining to the pleasure of God and my soul to profit.

My meadow enclosed and all my arable land therto adjoining called the Qwygh-dysh, containing 9 acres, as the metes and bounds appear in the fields of Worlington and Barton, to be sold and the money disposed by my executors, and to pay thereof 16 marks to the priest that shall pray for my soul and the remnant of the money to be disposed in other deeds of charity and mercy whereas it shall be thought most profitable for my soul and for the soul and the souls of Alice, Margery and Joan, my wives. If my wife or child that shall be my heir in time to come make any challenge or claim in that the said meadow and land or any parcel therof called the Qwhyt-dyche, then my wife and child shall lose and never have possession nor enjoy the said meadow enclosed called Curles, 6½ acres of arable land which I have assigned my wife for life and after her decease to the child being at this time in her womb which I trust to God shall be my heir in time to come under this condition and also that my said wife and child never have possession of my said mese, meadow called Curles [*etc.*] nor no parcel thereof till such time as my said wife and also my child

---

by will. Yet it was necessary to write down the testator's wishes for his or her property after death and, for convenience sake, the instructions of the last will were attached to the testament. From the mid-fifteenth century the two separate documents become one, to be known as the last will and testament.

38 John Smyth was married three times and here he names his wives as Alice, Margery and his present wife, Joan. No children appear to have survived from these unions. The will is written in the hope that Joan has conceived, but the will is not proved for another eighteen months. No further reference to Smith, the shoemaker, has been found.

39 Freehold as well as copyhold.

have released and disclaimed all their right, title and claim that they have or shall have in the said meadow enclosed and land called Qwhygthdyche. Furthermore it is my will that he which so purchase the said meadow and land called the Wihtdiche of my executors and be put from his possession [*etc.*] then he or they that be so vexed, troubled and put from their possession to have, enjoy [*etc.*] the said meadow called Curlis, 6½ acres of land arable, to them and their heirs for evermore with sufficient lawful estate made to them that have purchased the said meadow and called the Qwhitdiche without any contradiction of my wife and child.

Witnesses: J Grene, priest, John Brygthwell, Henry Hamond and Thomas Cullyng of Mildenhall.

Proved at Fornham, 18 April 1474.

18. Will of Denise (Dionesia) Constabill, 4 August 1473   SROB, IC500/2/11/4

[*Latin*] To be given Christian burial in the churchyard of the church in Mildenhall; to the high altar of the same church of Blessed Mary of Mildenhall for my tithes and oblations forgotten and withheld and in exoneration of my soul 20d.; to the reparation of the same church 3s. 4d.

To the house of nuns in Thetford 3s.

To Agnes, my servant, a white cover, a pair of sheets, a candlestick, a posnet, 3 dishes, 2 pewter saucers.

To Denise, my goddaughter, the daughter of Simon Marioth, a pair of sheets, a blanket and a candlestick.

To John Chadenhale 4 yards of woollen cloth.

To the old house of friars of Thetford 5s. to celebrate half a trental.

To Thomas Cullyng 40d. and a silver spoon. To John Smyth 3 yards of blanket.

To Richard Hygne 6 yards of blanket.

The residue of all my goods and chattels to Joan, my daughter, she to keep my anniversary[40] each year for 12 years, disposing each year in bread, ale and cheese the value of 6s. 8d. for

my soul and for the souls of Richard Cunstable [*and*] Robert Hynge,[41] my husbands, and all my benefactors. My children to be executors, Joan, my daughter, and Thomas Cullyng.

Proved at Mildenhall at the ordinary visitation, 18 August 1473 by the executors.

19. Will of Richard Bakhott, 7 June 1474   TNA, PCC Wattys 19

[*Latin*] To be buried in the church of Blessed Mary of Mildenhall; to the high altar of Mildenhall church for tithes underpaid 10s.; to the reparation of the vestments and other ornaments, books and other things in the care of the sexton 40s.

To the gild of Corpus Christi 6s. 8d.; to the gild of John the Baptist 3s. 4d.; to the gild of St Thomas 3s. 4d.

To Marion Begott [*Bakhott, Baggott*] 10 coombs of Barley; to Isabel Woodrise

---

[40] An anniversary was known by many names such as twelvemonth day, year-day, year's mind, or obit. These were all re-enactments of the burial rite with a draped herse and the Office of the Dead recited on the eve and a requiem mass celebrated on the day of the anniversary. The cost of the service was perhaps as little as 3s. 4d., but the commemorative feasting, as above, would cost more.

[41] Denise Constabill's celebration took the form of an annual mass on the anniversary of her death, the refreshment to follow costing 6s. 8d. See Middleton-Stewart, *Inward Purity*, pp.137–40. Denise was probably the daughter-in-law of William Hygne, will 6, p.139. Her allegiance appears to have been to Thetford, leaving money to both nuns and friars there.

5 coombs of barley; to Robert Bywold 5 coombs of barley; to John Woodrise 10 coombs of barley.

To Nicholas Bakhott, my brother, three ewes at Michaelmas next; to the same Nicholas five horses with an iron-shod cart at the discretion of my executors; to the same Nicholas all the ostilments of my house; to the same Nicholas twelve silver spoons, the best bell of my mother with a pair of beads of silver with a crucifix and other things attached; another belt of my mother of his choice and another pair of beads of his choice on condition that he keeps them and gives them to his wife so that they might be a better reminder of the soul of my mother.

To the same Nicholas 40 coombs of rye, 10 coombs of wheat: to the same Nicholas a new mazer[42] which I lately bought at London; to the same Nicholas another small mazer on condition that it be not sold; to the same Nicholas 20 sheep pasturing in this town.

To Richard Bussh two cows and two calves; to the same Richard four brass pots, four pewter dishes and four pewter platters and a saucer for salt: to the same Richard 30 ewes and the messuage in which John Halse now lives, to him and his heirs. If he should die without issue it to be sold by my executors and the money disposed for my soul and all the souls of my parents and of Thomas Martyn, chaplain.[43]

To the same Richard Busshe 4 silver spoons and a bowl which is with Isabel Stone and two beds, on condition he does not sell the spoon and bowl; to the same Richard and Joan, his sister, to have £10 from my goods and my father's and if they make any claim or worry my executors then they shall have nothing. Six well-disposed priests for a year, that is, three in Cambridge and the other three in Mildenhall church.

To each of my godsons and goddaughters an ewe.

To Nicholas, my brother aforesaid, five roods of arable land at Lampetts.

To John Austyn, the younger, a pound.

The residue of all my goods to the disposition of my executors whom I make Master Paul Geyton, perpetual vicar of Mildenhall parish church, Simon Burgoyn, doctor of laws, William Dak, *dec. bach.*, Nicholas Bakhote, my brother and John Brightwell of Mildenhall, the elder, to dispose.

Witnesses: John Corbett, parish chaplain of Mildenhall, John Austyn of the same, the elder, and others.

Proved at Lambeth, 20 October 1474 in the year above stated by Paul Geyton and Simon Burgoyne, clerk, and Nicholas Backhote and John Brigthwell, the elder, in the person of William Dak, their proctor and executor.

20. Will of John Langham, 17 February 1476   SROB, IC 500/2/11/65

[*Latin*] My body to Christian burial; to the high altar of Mildenhall church for my tithes forgotten 2s.

To John Langham, my son, all the tools of my craft, lomys, chetylys [*shuttles*], redys and slayes[44] with their appurtenances, but I wish the *Le slayes* to be sold by my executors and the money used for the maintenance of my wife until the said

---

42   A drinking cup fashioned from the wood of the maple tree.
43   Thomas Martyn, the chaplain, had appointed Master Richard Bakhott as one of his executors.
44   These two terms are synonymous and were 'grill-like objects which kept the warp evenly spaced and the weft straight' (P. Walton, 'Textiles', in *English Medieval Industries*, ed. J. Blair and N. Ramsay (1991), p.328).

John becomes expert in the craft of weaving and then new slayes to be bought and given to the said John.

To John Langham of Lakenheath, my brother, a gown of Rosett to John Langham, my cousin of Bury St Edmunds living in Rysby Gate strete, a doublet; to Robert Langham of Bury, my brother, a le hoseclothe[45] of kersey;[46] to Thomas Langham of Bury St Edmunds, living in Rysby Gate strete, my brother, another le hoseclothe of kersey; to the wives of the said men, to each of them ½ yard of kersey: to Thomas Ive of Lavenham 1½ yards of kersey for himself and his wife, my sister.

To Joan, my wife, my messuage to her and her heirs.

The residue of all my goods to Joan, my wife, she to provide for my children and dispose [etc].

Executors: Joan, my wife, principal executor, and Thomas Langham of Bury St Edmunds, my brother, with her.

Proved before the official of the archdeacon of Sudbury at Fornham St Martin, 10 March 1476 by executors.

21. Will of Alice Morley, 5 September 1480　　　　　SROB, IC 500/2/11/201

[*Latin*] To be buried in the churchyard of Mildenhall parish church; to the high altar of the said church for my tithes and offerings forgotten 16d.; to the reparation of the said church 2s.; to the gild of the Blessed Virgin Mary 12d.

To the Friars Preachers of Babwell, a comb of barley; to the house of friars of Thetford, called Le Oldehows, a coomb of barley.[47]

To John Morley, my son, a cauldron; to Henry Morley, my son, the best brass pot; to the said John, my son, the next pot, and so on for the others, Henry to have first choice; to the said John another pot called le metepotte; to the said Henry a basin; to John a pan; to the same John the largest platter; to the said Henry 2 platters; to the same a new pan; to the said John a le chetyll and another pan called le chyldes panne; to the same John a candlestick and a salt-cellar.

To the same Henry the best iron-shod cart and another cart called le wayne cart; to the said John another iron-shod cart with the cart called le tumberell; to the said Henry a horse called le forehors; to the said John another horse called le kobe; to the same John le bodyhors; to the said Henry another horse called le Brekke. To Thomas Place a horse foal.

To Edward Holme a coomb of barley; to William Tydde, a coomb of barley; to each of my godsons and goddaughters a modium of barley; to Robert Holme, my brother, a coomb of barley.

To Thomas Tydde, my son, 3s. 4d.

To Agnes Place, my daughter, my tabard and furred tunic.

To the said John my furred gown; to Henry, my son, another gown and my under-tunic.

The residue of all my goods and chattels I leave to my faithful executors, they to dispose for my soul and for the souls of all friends as seems to them best to please God and profit the heath of [*my*] soul.

Executors: the said John Morley and Henry Morley, my sons, of whom I beg my

---

45　Cloth suitable for hosiery.
46　A coarse woollen cloth.
47　The Franciscan friars had countered opposition from the abbey officials when they first settled in Bury but in 1263 they were granted a site outside the north gate at Babwell. This friary at Thetford was Dominican.

beloved [*damaged*] Thomas Tydde to be supervisor and helper, so that any deficiencies in them may be made up.

Proved before the official of the archdeacon of Sudbury at Fornham, 30 November 1480.

22. Will of Agnes Sygo, lately the wife of Robert Sygo of Mildenhall in Suffolk, widow, 20 April 1484
SROB, IC 500/2/11/302

[*Latin*] My body in Christian burial in Mildenhall churchyard; to the high altar for tithes forgotten 12d.; to the reparation of the same church 2s.

To John Sygo, my cousin, a cow.

I wish a suitable priest to celebrate for my soul and for the said Robert, my husband's soul and all my friends' and benefactors' for a whole year if my goods are sufficient for it.

To Joan [?John] I give a cow and if he wishes to buy my table, best bedcover and laver, he to have them before all others.

I wish all my other goods to be sold by my executors and all the money from them to be disposed in good and charitable deeds for my soul and the souls of Robert Sygo and all my friends and benefactors according to the discretion of my executors. Executors: Thomas Baron, priest of Mildenhall church and John Sygo, my kinsman.

Proved before the official of Sudbury, 2 July 1484. Administration to executors. And because the testator's goods were insufficient to meet the legacies and other costs, the executors were acquitted from exhibiting further accounts.

23. Will of Matilda Curteys, 7 June 1485
SROB, IC 500/2/11/337

[*Latin*] My body to Christian burial in the churchyard of Mildenhall church; revoking all wills made before this 7 June; all my debts to be fully paid by my executors if any they be that can be reasonably proved by my executors; to the high altar of the same church 2s.; to the fabric and upkeep of the said church 4s.

To John Sigo, my son, a half acre of land in Holmeresey [*Holmsey*].

To Richard Sigo, my son, a chest called le sprewse huche, 2 tables, one standing in the hall and the other in the chamber and the best brass pot, a lead vessel, a small brass pot holding a pottle of latten, 3 candlesticks of latten, 5 pieces of pewter, a cover called le qwylte, a pair of sheets, 2 silver spoons, a green girdle of silk, harnessed, a pair of jet beads, 2 silver necklaces, a chair, a long cloth, a towel, a sword with the buckles; also to the said Richard a horse called le grey and another called le dune and all the others except one called Koke and an iron-shod cart.

To Alice, the wife of the said Richard, the best tabard, a furred tunic and the best girdle bar one.

To Isabel, my daughter, a brass pot, a large pan, a trivet, a pewter basin, a small pan, 5 pieces of pewter, 2 silver spoons, a blue girdle of silk, harnessed, a pair of jet beads of the best, the best chair, a table, a chest, a tablecloth, a towel, a blue furred gown, a cover called le qwylte and also a tabard, but my will is that if after my decease Isabel trouble my executors about half an acre of land upon which Thomas Tyde of Holywell entered after the decease of William Curteys, my late husband, or for its value, then I wish the said Isabel to have nothing of the aforesaid goods bequeathed to her.

To the said Alice, wife of Richard Sigo, my son, my best hood; to Robert Sigo, my son, a pan holding a gallon, a candlestick of latten, a brass pot holding a gallon; to Joan, the wife of Robert Sigo, my son, a pair of amber beads; to Robert Sygoo, the younger, a heifer and a black chest and 4 bushels of barley: to Richard Sygoo, my godson, a heifer.

To Margery, my servant, a calf; to Margery, my servant, a hood and a pair of sheets.

To Isabel Sygoo, the daughter of Richard Sygoo, a calf.

To John Cole a calf of the age of 1 year; to Isabel Cole my best under-tunic.

To John Halse the best calf; to the wife of the said John Halse another under-tunic and a green girdle: to each of my godsons a modium of barley if they come when summoned or soon afterwards.

The residue of all my goods, chattels and debts I leave to my executors to dispose for my soul and for the souls of my father and mother and for the souls of all my friends [as] seems most to please God and best to profit the health of my soul.

Executors: John Halse, the elder, and Richard Sygoo, my son, faithfully to execute as they answer before God, the great judge, on the last day of judgement.

Supervisor: William Pope.

Witnesses: Richard Webbe, Robert Day, John Curteys, Robert Reve, John Fulborne, John Bulwer and William Docking.

Proved before the official of the archdeacon of Sudbury at Fornham, 13 February 1485.

24. Will of Robert Pachett, 20 February 1488   SROB, IC 500/2/11/410

[*Latin*] My testament containing my last will.

To be buried in the churchyard of Mildenhall; to the high altar of the said church for my tithes and offerings forgotten 20d.; to the house of friars of Babwell, for a trental to be celebrated for my soul 10s.

To the reparation and emendation of the common way between my gate and the stone cross 16d.; to the making of a new sepulchre in Mildenhall church 20d.

To John Pachett, son of John Pachett, a le grey.

To John Pachett, my son, a brass pot called le maylpott.

To Robert Pachett, son of the said John, a foal of the age of one year.

To Margaret, my wife, my whole messuage in which I live for term of her life on condition that she keep herself sole and a widow. If she should remarry, then I wish William, my son, to enter the messuage as soon as she is married. After Margaret's death, if she remains a widow, I wish the messuage, with its appurtenances, to remain to the said William, my son, to hold to him and his heirs. If William should die without issue, then I wish the messuage with the appurtenances be sold and all the money from it be disposed in the celebration of masses and other deeds of charity for my soul and all my friends and benefactors. If John, my son, wishes to buy the messuage, then I wish him to have it before all others within the price for which it could be sold to others by 13s 4d.

To the said Margaret, my wife, and William, my son, all the utensils and ostilments belonging to my house except the pre-excepted.

The residue of my goods and chattels I leave to my executors to dispose for my soul and for the souls of all my parents and friends as seems to them [*best*] to please God and profit my soul.

Executors: Margaret, my wife, the principal executrix and William Patchett, my son, and I beg John Pachett, my son, to be supervisor and aid.

Witnesses: John Makeworth, Richard Halsted, John Foxe, John Bukke and others.

Proved before William Duffeld, in Dec. Lic., official of the archdeacon of Sudbury, at Newmarket, 12 June 1488.

25. Will of William Elys, 5 September 1493   **SROB, IC 500/2/13/16**

[*Latin*] To be buried in the churchyard of Mildenhall; to the high altar of the said church for my tithes underpaid 20d.; to the reparation of Mildenhall church 6s. 8d.; to the reparation of the common way by my gate 40d. and 3 loads of sand.

To Alice, my wife, my whole messuage in which I live and 3 acres of land for the term of her life and after her death I wish the messuage and 2 acres of land to be sold and the money from them to be disposed for my soul and for the souls of all my friends.

To Alice, my wife, all my utensils and the ostilments belonging to my house.

To each of my godsons a ewe amd a measure of barley.

To the gild of Blessed Mary, after the death of my wife, 1 acre of land lying by the gate of Master Pope.[48]

I wish to have a suitable chaplain to celebrate in Mildenhall for a whole year after the death of my wife, taking 8 marks for his labour out of the said messuage and 2 acres of land.

To the reparation of the common way at Petyrborowe, 3 loads of sand.

I wish to have a cross made at my head.

To each of the poor living in Westrowe, ½ a measure of barley or malt.

The residue of all my goods and chattels I leave to my wife whom I make my sole executrix with Sir Thomas Baren supervisor.

No probate recorded.

26. Will of William Charnoke, 4 August 1500   **NRO, NCC Popy 571**

[*English*] To be buried in the churchyard of Mildenhall; to the high altar of the same church 20d.; to the reparation of the same church 3s. 4d.

To John, my son, 8 marks; to Joan, my daughter, a sheep.

To the gild of Our Lady a coomb[49] of barley; to the gild of St Anne a coomb of barley.

To the 4 orders of friars a coomb of barley, to each house.

To a priest 10s. to sing a trental[50] for my soul and all Christian souls.

To the gild of the Trinity of Lakenheath 5s.

The residue of all my other goods to Margaret, my wife, and Thomas Houghton whom I make executors; to Thomas Houghton 3s. 4d.

Witnesses: Sir William Bambour, parish priest, William Bray and Thomas Chiston and more.

Proved at Norwich, 23 October 1504 by Margaret, the executrix. Power reserved to the other executor when he comes.

27. Will of William Bray, 10 August 1503   **SROB, IC 500/2/12/128**

[*English*] To be buried in the churchyard of Mildenhall; to the high altar 20d.; to the reparation of the said church 6s. 8d.

To the church of Gaysley a vestment, price 13s. 4d.; to the church of Cavenham a vestment, price 13s. 4d.; to the reparation of the church of Worlington 2s.[51]

---

48 William Elys was probably a member of St Mary's gild. The sale of the messuage and two acres of land would have provided sufficient income for a service for one year; Master Pope lived near West Row where there is still a property called Popes.

49 A dry measure equivalent to four bushels.

50 A trental consisted of thirty masses.

51 Perhaps Bray was a native of Gazely or Cavenham, both within a few miles of Mildenhall. Worlington was just across the river Lark from Mildenhall.

To the gild of Corpus Christi a coomb of barley; to the gild of Our Lady a coomb of barley.

I will that a priest shall sing in the church of Myldenhall by the space of half a year.

To Joan, my wife, my shop in the market and 8 acres of land in Heynyng between the Heath and Bryons Welows towards Halywell [*Holywell Row*].

To Joan Bray, my daughter, my place that I dwell in with my meadow and 6 acres of land lying between Monnys Wey and Charnok Wey, to enter the said place with the meadow and lands at the day of her marriage.

If it be so that Joan, my wife, be with child, then I will that it have 6 acres of land lying between the old way and Monnys Wey and a house lying in the Westrow after [*the*] decease of William Jakatyn and Margaret, his wife; to Joan, my wife, my carthorse and a cart and plough, harrow and barugh and all my corn so that she pay the farm and the rent of the lands.

To Joan, my wife, and to Joan, my daughter, all my shops in Myldenhale to part between them; to Joan, my wife, a grey mare and 2 black bullocks and a young heifer; to Joan, my daughter, a garled bullock.

To William Jakatyn a heifer and 2 calves and a mare colt.

To Joan, my wife, and Joan, my daughter, all my household except my featherbed and the best pot and a spruce hutch which I will that Joan, my daughter, shall have.

To John Bray, my brother, 6s. 8d.; to each of his children 3s. 4d.

To Thomas Rumbylow of Higham, my best gown and my best doublet.

To the charnel of Ralph Walsham 5 roods of land lying by Swath Cross on condition that the priest remembers my soul in his bederoll.[52]

To John Cosyn of Berton [*Barton*] all my copy lands and meadows in Cavenham and if it be so my wife be not with child or that the child decease ere it be married and also if Joan, . my daughter, decease ere she be married, then I will that the lands with the meadow bequeathed to them remain to Joan, my wife, for the term of 20 years and after the said term of 20 years I will that the said lands with the meadow and the houses be sold by my executors and be disposed after their good discretion in deeds of mercy for the weal of my soul; provided always that Joan, my wife, sufficiently repair and sustain all my said tenements as long as she shall occupy and also until Joan, my daughter, shall have possession.

I will that Joan, my wife, keep my erthetyde[53] or obituary as long as she liveth.

To each of my godchildren a bushel of barley.

The residue of all my other goods, my debts paid and my funeral costs fulfilled, I [*leave*] to my executors, that they dispose them for the weal of my soul as they shall think most best to the pleasure of God and profit of my soul.

Executors: Thomas Howton and William Pypere of Cavenham and John Cosyn of Berton and I bequeath each of them for their labour in executing this testament 13s. 4d.

Suipervisor: Master Herry Pope, to whom for his labour 20s.

I require all my co-feoffees to deliver their estate which they have of and in all my lands and tenements aforesaid as soon and whensoever they be required by my executors according to this testament.

---

52 The charnel chapel received a small area of land from this bequest, sufficient for Bray's name to be mentioned in the reading of the bede-roll, encouraging the congregation to say prayers for his soul.

53 Time of my burial.

Proved in Fornham St Martin parish church, 20 September 1503 before John Orly, Dr. Dec., official of the archdeacon of Sudbury. Administration to executors.

28. Will of John Chyldyrston, the elder, 6 March 1504   SROB, IC 500/2/13/156

[*English*] To be buried in the churchyard of Myldynhale; to the high altar of Myldynhale for my tithes forgotten 20d.; to the reparation of the said church 3s. 4d.

To John my son a mare and a calf when time cometh that he is of age of 21 and an acre of arable land lying in the Bekkefelde of Myldynhale, the north head therof abbutteth on a meadow plot of mine and the south head abbutteth on the Flokpath, to him and his heirs. If he die without issue then I will it remain to my wife or her assigns; to Thomas my son a mare and a calf when time cometh that he is of age 21 and a plot of meadow ground lying in the Bekke of Myldynhale, the north head therof abbutteth on the king's highway, to him and his heirs. If he die without issue then I will it remain to my wife or her assigns; to Anne my daughter a calf; to Alice my daughter a calf; to Anne Taylor a coomb of barley; to William Taylor a colt of a year age.

The residue of all my goods, my debts paid and my funeral costs fulfilled I bequeath to Margaret my wife whom I make my executrix and faithful attorney as she will answer before God at the day of Judgement to perform this will and Thomas Cook be helper to my wife and I will have he has for his labours 3s. 4d.

Witnesses: George Gatynby, clerk, Thomas Cole, John Fullere and many others.

Proved before the official of the archdeacon of Sudbury at Fornham St Martin, 31 March 1505.

29. Will of Sir George Gatynbe, priest, 13 March 1504   NRO, NCC Ryxe 146

[*English*] To be buried in Mildenhall church; to the high altar of the said church 10s.; to the reparation of the said church 6s. 8d.; to the gild of St George 3s. 4d.

A priest to sing for half a year in Mildenhall church to pray for my soul, my father's and my mother's and for Sir Edward Kirby's soul and all Christian souls, taking for his stipend £2 6s. 8d.; a priest to say once within the said period the trental of St Gregory with dirige and commendation that belong to the said trental.

To Master Paul Garton, a porteous in print that was Sir Edward's.

To Margaret Motte a counter; to John Motte, my godson 3s. 4d. To each of my other godsons 12d.

To Sir William Reve a festyvall, a rochet and a pair of beads next the best.

To Sir Roger a surplice and the poke and a book called *Vita Christi* in English.

To Sir John of Barton a pair of amber beads of fifty [*of L*].

A demi-gown to Agnes Myddleton; to Margaret Segoo a short gown and a pair of sheets.

To Edward Gardyner a quarter of barley and a gown.

To William Britewell 20d.; to John Williamson a pair of hose.

To each of my brethren 6s. 8d.

To Gregory Bladwell a pair of hose. To my three sisters a yard of linen cloth each. The church of Rymond Hereham [?] to have a pair of chalices, price 5 marks.

To George Grene a pair of blankets; to Thomas Gardener's wife a pair of sheets; to Fuller's wife a pair of sheets that were Sir Edward's; to each of Motte's maidens a sheet; to George Bladwell a pair of sheets and a pillow. To Master John Connyeres a sarsenet tippet with a black hat and a tache.

Residue of my goods to the disposition of my executors.

Executors: Master John Conyers of St Nicholas Hostel of Cambridge, Sir William Bewe [Rewe?] and Gregory Bladwell.
Proved at Norwich, 7 April 1505 by Sir George [sic] Bladwell, one of the executors. Also appearing for the other executors Master Paul Geyton, vicar of Mildenhall.

30. Will of Roger Barforth, priest, 6 November 1504   NRO, NCC Ryxe 27

[*English*] To be buried in Mildenhall church; to the high altar of the said church for my tithes forgotten and not well paid 10s.; to the reparation of the said church 10s.; to the reparation of Chippenham church 3s. 4d.; a lawful priest to sing in Mildenhall church for half a year to pray for my soul and the souls of Sir William Day, my fathers and my mothers souls and all Christian souls, having 4 marks for his stipend; the same priest to say thrice St Gregory's trental[54] and every day to say dirige and commendation when he say mass of the trental; 13d. to be given to 13 poor men or women of the town of Mildenhall, every Friday, for half a year, they to say Our Ladys sawte for my soul and Sir William Day's soul, my father's and my mother's souls; to the gild of Corpus Christi 3s. 4d.

To Denise Barforth a messuage in Chippenham with a croft and a car[55] and half an acre of land lying over Pudemans Hill; the said Denise to have a customary house in Chippenham in a street called Green End with the lands belonging; to the said Denise a featherbed, a green coverlet, a blue hanging, a transom, a pair of sheets, a pair of blankets; if the said Denise die before marriage all the above bequests to go to Margaret her sister; to Katherine Goodehike a mattress of the best, a white coverlet, a still pan with feet and a posnet; to Margaret Barforth a posnet, a pot with a stell; to Alice Mayor a great pan, a pair of sheets, a heifer aged 2 years.

To Agnes Brythewell 4 ewes; to Joan Spenser my god-daughter to have 20 comb of barley for 20s that I received of Thomas Makeforth for her and a pair of sheets; to Elizabeth Pope my god-daughter a mass book and 6s. 8d.; to each of my godchildren besides 12d.; to the youngest daughter of Wattesons of Burgtwe a brass pot; to Thomas Goodyke a pair of sheets, a heifer 2 years old.

My executors to keep my year day yearly and spend 11s. 8d. on it; the residue of my goods to my executors.

Executors: John Bury and John Day, supervisor Master Herry Pope 10s. each.
Witnesses: Sir George Gatenby, parish priest, Master Herry Pope, John Bury, John Day, Geoffrey Brewett and others.
Proved at Norwich, 4 December 1504 by executors.

31. Will of William Dey, 6 August 1506   NRO, NCC Garnon 106

[*English*] To be buried in Mildenhall churchyard; to the high altar of the same church 40d.; to St John's gild 12d.; to St Thomas' gild 12d.

Everyone of my <god>[56] children both sons and daughters to have 20s. from my executors when my house is sold; my wife to have half my moveable goods; my wife to have her dwelling in my place for her lifetime. To Margery Motte a basin; to Margery Howhton an almery; to Mildenhall church a vestment.

The residue of my goods to Amy my wife and Thomas Howhton whom I make executors.

---

54 St Gregory's trental consisted of thirty masses, three to be said at each of the principal feasts in the year.
55 A bog or a fen.
56 Here *god* has been crossed out.

Thomas Howhton to have my best table for his labours.
Witnesses: Sir Thomas Law and many others.
Proved at Mildenhall, 7 August 1506 by the executors.

32. Will of John Lynge, 28 February 1509   SROB, IC 500/2/15/121

[*English*] To be buried in the churchyard of Mildenhale; to the high altar of the same church for tithes forgotten 8d.

To Margaret Wall my daughter 6s. 8d.; to Christian Constable my daughter 6s. 8d.; to Matilda my daughter my house in Halywell, lying in Slye Street Lane, and to her heirs. If she die without issue, I will that it be sold and done for me, my wife and my benefactors.

The residue of my goods I bequeath to Matilda Banham whom I make executrix.

Witnesses: John Egyll and John Dockyng and others.

Proved before the official of the archdeacon of Sudbury in Kentford parish church, 15 May 1521.

33. Will of Margery Howton, widow, 1515   NRO, NCC 28 Brigges

[*English*] To be buried beside my husband in Mildenhall church; to the high altar of the same 6s. 8d.; to the reparation of the same church 20s.; towards the making of a tabernacle of St John the Evangelist on the south side of the high altar in the chancel £6 13s. 4.; towards the gilding of St Christopher 6s. 8d.; to the mending of the broken bell in Worlington if the parish do amend it 6s. 8d.; a priest to sing for me, my husband and all our friends souls in Mildenhall parish church for 2 years, he to have 8 marks a year for his wages; to the reparation of either of the chaunters [*chantries*] in Mildenhall 6s. 8d.

To the four orders of friars, a coomb of barley each; to the nuns of Susham 2s.; to the nuns of Theford 2s.

To Isabel Dunham a pair of jet beads gaudied with silver and a silver ring; to my god-daughter Margery Dey a pair of beads gaudied with (casteltin); to my godson John Mote a coomb of barley; to each of my other godchildren 2 bushells of barley. Thomas Hull to have my close in Eriswell with all the lands belonging to it for £10 and to fulfil my will with it as far as it will extend, and to enter into it immediately after my decease.

To Richard my brother 6s. 8d. and the 5 coombs of malt that I owe him; to Andrew my brother 6s. 8d.; to Simon my brother 6s. 8d.; to Robert my brother 6s. 8d.; to Margery my god-daughter my blue gown and 6s. 8d in money; to John Hull the son of Thomas Hull an acre of land in Peterborowes between 2 meres to him and his heirs. If he decease before coming to lawful age, his next brother to have it and so descending.

The 2 roods of this side Wammell, 2 acres over the way, an acre in Old Wey, half an acre in same field and 5 roods in Peterborow and an acre at Brykes Hyll to be sold or kept by my executors and the money disposed as follows: to keep a year day[57] yearly for me, my husband and our friends and to dispose after as the rent will extend.

My place called Pongs with the land belonging to be sold by my executors towards the performance of my will and Thomas Hull, if he will buy it, to have it within the price of everyman.

---

[57] Here Margery requests an anniversary to be kept for her and her late husband as long as the money lasts.

To my godmother Smythe and her husband for their lifetimes and the longer liver, their dwelling in my house next Herry Taylour, paying the rent and finding reparations.

To Thomas my servant my best colt and 6s. 8d. in money; the house that I dwell in to be let to farm as long as my executors please, and afterwards to be sold by them and the money disposed according to their discretion for the health of my soul.

To Mildenhall church a pax of silver of 18 ounces and my name to be written on it; to the reparation of Our Lady's chapel 6s 8d.; to the reparation of the bell ropes of the following churches, each of them a stone of hemp, i.e. Isleham, Kennett, Herringswell, Tuddenham, Cavenham, Icklingham [*All Saints*?] and Icklingham, [*St James*?], Barton, Eriswell a stone between them, Lakenheath [*sic*]. To Kentford half a stone.

40 eln[58] of my coarse cloth in the shop to be given to poor folks.

To the high altar of Mildenhall church my best diaper cloth; to Our Lady of Grace in Ipswich my best beads.

To Sir Robert Dow my little feather bed.

To John Hull my daughter [*sic*] my best gown, my best kirtle, my best girdle, a silver piece, my beads next the best, my great table and table cloth; to my said daughter my close in the East fen.

My feoffees enfeoffed in my lands to deliver estate to my executors whensoever required and also to Thomas Hull of the house that he dwells in and other that I have given him.

A trental to be said for me and my husband in the Friars of Thetford.

The residue of all my goods to the disposition of my executors whom I make Thomas Hull, my son-in-law, and Thomas Geson 6s. 8d.

Witnesses: Master Vicar, Sir John Puwke, Sir William Reve, Sir John Lee, Master Nichoas Bagot, Herry Tailor, Thomas Symonds, Sir William Nevell, Margery Mote, Beatrice Bell and Isabel Dunham with others.

To Alice my servant a coffer which stands with books and 6s. 8d. in money.

To the high altar my finest sheet.

Proved at Hoxne, 18 June 1517 by executors.

34. Will of Sir Simon Etton, 11 July 1516   NRO, NCC Brigges 26

[*English*] To be buried in the churchyard of Mildenhall against the porch of the charnel;[59] to the church of Mildenhall 6s. 8d.; to the high altar for tithes forgotten 1s. 8d.

To the Trinity gild 3s. 4d.

To each of my godchildren 4d.

To Nicholas Etton, a basin and 2 of the great plates save one and the laver longing to the basin and a hanging laver and the laver brazen pot and the chafer; John Etton to have 2 platters and a kettle, the oldest of the two; to Robert Etton 2 platters and a kettle.

To my goddaughter Atwell a platter, one of the biggest platters, and 2 salers and 2 small platters and a saler: Margaret Betteman to have a platter and a saler; William Betteman to have 3s 4d.; Isabel Sokerman to have 2 salers and a frying pan.

---

58   This word is difficult to read. If it is 'ell', an ell in England measured 45 inches.

59   Simon Etton was probably the chantry priest of the charnel. His requests suggest that he had a special affection for the place. 'Upon the charnel' suggests that the trental of masses would be celebrated in the upper chapel.

To Master Vicar my best amber beads.

My bullocks, 12 coombs of malt and my sheep to be sold to the best value and disposed among the poor people within the town of Mildenhall to the value of 30s. The poor people of Freckenham to have disposed among them 10s.

An honest priest to sing in the charnel of Mildenhall a quarter of a year; a trental of masses to be sung for my soul upon the charnel in Mildenhall.

The residue of all my goods to the disposition of my executor, James Etton, my brother.

Supervisor: Master Vicar of Mildenhall.

Witnesses: John Jerves, Robert Sygo, Thomas Escall with many more.

No probate recorded.

35. Will of John Haynes, 8 July 1519   TNA, PCC 19 Ayloffe

[*English*] To be buried in the parish church of Mildenhall by my wife Agnes.

To the high altar of the same church for my tithes and oblations negligently forgotten in discharge of my soul and conscience 20s.; to the reparation of the same church 40s.

To the charnel of Mildenhall half an acre of free land lying at Cestins Wong to pray for my

soul, my wife's soul, my father's and mother's souls and for all Christian souls;[60] to an honest priest to sing for my soul and Agnes my wife's soul 2 years, £10 13s. 4d. in Mildenhall church.

To Simon Heynes, my eldest son, scholar in Cambridge 40s *per annum* until the time he be beneficed, which money to be raised of all such lands as I have in the towns and fields of Mildenhall so that when he is beneficed he shall have no more the said yearly stipend.[61]

To Thomas, my son, my house against the vicarage joined and annexed to the house which I bought of Heynes, my brother, which house, also, I will he have; the same Thomas to have all such lands, tenements [*etc*] within the bounds and precincts of Mildenhall which were Simon Heynes, my father's, of which lands partly he gave me by will and partly came to me because he died intestate inasmuch as I was the next heir, as it is plain after the law of the land; to the same Thomas a hundred wethers, 2 hundred ewes and 20 bullocks, the youngest a year old, and the best bed upon the Lord's chamber with the sparver yellow and crimson complete with the covering of imagery, a pair of sheets and a pair of blankets and half a garnish of pewter vessel; to the same Thomas 4 acres of land in Holmesey and if Thomas should die under 20, it to be divided equally between Henry and William my sons, but if he live, he to have it to give and to sell all the lands.

To Henry, my son, the place in the Mill Strete which John Dobson doth dwell in at this time, and also the house which is annexed to the same that I bought of Robert Calf, and 10 acres of free land which I bought of Sir Andrew Place, priest, and the

---

[60] The addition of another half acre to the landholding of the charnel would provide 'permanent cover' for the souls of Heynes and his immediate family, the land constituting capital which would perpetuate soul prayers. The following bequest to Mildenhall church is paid at the going rate of £5 6s. 8d. a year from income. This was a service chantry, running for a stated number of years, which was a common way to obtain 'temporary cover'.

[61] The 40s. a year paid for the education of Simon, the eldest son, at Cambridge has to be balanced against the bequests to Thomas, Henry and William, his brothers, who inherit from their father the wherewithal to obtain a living for themselves.

meadow at Wylde Street containing 19 acres, and also the other of meadow that is joined and annexed to it containing 2 acres which I had of Master Pope by permutation; to the same Henry a hundred ewes, 20 bullocks, the youngest of a year old: to the same Henry my owne bed that that I do lie in with a sparver of dornix[62] and a covering with imagery, a pair of sheets and a pair of blankets and half a garnishe of pewter. Should Henry die under 20, the lands bequeathed to him to be divided equally between Thomas and William, my sons, and if he live to 20 years he to make will upon it and to give and to sell as Thomas shall do.

To William, my son, the house that was Agnes Gelhams and 10 acres of land belonging for which I agreed with Thomas Beyngfeld, knight; to the same William an acre of land in Holnessey [*Holmsey*] which was given to Agnes, my wife, by the last will of Sir William Tydde, priest: to the same William a meadow which I bought of Master Colder of London and Horne of Snaylwell, lying at Slistrete Lane; and also a featherbed in the parlour with the white hanging, a blue coverlet with white roses and red, a pair of sheets, a pair of blankets, half a garnish of pewter; to the same William a hundred wethers, a hundred ewes and 20 bullocks, the youngest a year old. If William should die under 20, the land to be divided equally between Thomas and Henry, but if he live to 20, he to give or sell or otherwise dispose it as the other two.

To Katherine my daughter £10, a featherbed, a bolster, a covering, a pair of sheets and a pair of blankets, a great hutch with imagery painted and her mother's best gown purfiled with gray, her best girdle, a pair of coral beads with all that pertaineth to them.

To Elizabeth my daughter £10, a featherbed with the bolster, a coverlet, a pair of sheets, a pair of blankets, a spruce hutch and her mother's gown purfiled with otter, her girdle next the best, a pair of beads of amber with all that belongs to them; if Katherine die under 18, Elizabeth to have all her bequests, but if she live, she able to give or sell similarly for Elizabeth.

If my moveable goods will not pay my debts and fulfil my will, the shops in the marketstead of mine and the meadow at Wilde Strete which was Thomas Tydds and all my free land unbequeathed to be sold by my executors. But if my moveables will pay my debts and fulfil my will then the shops, meadow and free land to be divided equally among Thomas, Henry and William, my sons.

To Reynold Dale, my brother, a bay mare and after his decease it to remain to John Wright, the son of Ellen, the wife of the same Reynold; to my sister Alice Browne 2 acres of grass in Hardiche and a calf; to Simon Heynes, my brother, a cow of 2 years of age; to Agnes Sokerman,[63] my sister, a cow of 2 years; to William and Robert, the sons of Robert Clerke, a bullock each; to every son of John Dale, my brother, a mare; to John Morley, the son of Henry Morley, a cow of two years; to every servant that I have by the year hired a calf; to John Mott, my godson, an ewe and a lamb; to every godson that I have besides, a lamb.

If all my children, both sons and daughters, die before the stated age, then the land

---

62 Dornix was the name of a Flemish town, the material originally from there being described as silk, worsted, woollen or partly woollen, made for hangings, carpets and even vestments. See *COED*, p.468.

63 Agnes, Heynes' sister, had married into the Sokerman [Suckerman] family of Mildenhall. The family played a part in the late sixteenth-century history of Mildenhall. See Craig, *Reformation, Politics and Polemics*, pp.53, 57–59.

bequeathed to my sons to be divided among Robert Heynes, my brother, and his children.

The residue of all my goods to the disposition of my executors whom I make Simon Heynes my son, Master in Arts and Fellow of the Queens College in Cambridge and Thomas Heynes, my son.

Supervisor: Thomas Rolf of Reach, my father-in-law.

Witnesses: Sir John Ripley, parish priest, Robert Clerke, John Gardiner, John Dale, Reynold Dale and many others.

If two of the sons die, the third to have all their bequests. If all die under age, all their bequests to be divided between Katherine and Elizabeth my daughters.

Proved at Lambeth, 13 July 1519 by Simon Heynes and Thomas Heynes, executors.

36. Will of Thomas Hall [*Hull*],[64] 10 January 1524   TNA, PCC Porch 19

[*English*] To be buried within the north porch before the image of Our Lady;[65] to the high altar for tithes negligently withholden 6s. 8d.; to Christ Church,[66] Norwich 12d.; to the reparation of Mildenhall church 13s. 4d.

To the hutch that standeth at the high altar in St John's church, Beverley, 6s. 8d.; to the reparation of the books of the said St John that be enclosed in silver which the deacon and subdeacon beareth on festival days 20s.; to St John's shrine there a gold ring with a ruby therein and to two other shrines there every of them a gold ring and all the same legacies to be carried and delivered incontinently after my decease to the said church.

To Robert Coraunt, sometime my fellow 6s. 8d.

To every of my children a gold ring.

To John Hall, my son, all my lands and tenements called Norkes in Wickhambrook according to the last will of Thomas Houghton;[67] to Henry, my son, all my lands and tenements in Wickham and Barmysfeld, late Batemans, to him and his heirs; to Miles,[68] my son, all my lands and tenements in Mildenhall to him and his heirs. If the said John should decease without issue, then I will all his lands and tenements equally to be divided between Henry and Miles; if Henry should decease without issue then I will his lands and tenements be divided amongst John and Miles; if Miles should die without issue then I will John and Henry have his lands and tenements in Mildenhall equally divided among them so that every of them shall inherit the others part; I will that all the above lands and tenements bequeathed to my three sons remain in the hands of Joan my wife during her life, to keep my said children and reparation therof without strip or waste.

---

64 Thomas Hall [Hull] was the son-in-law of Margery Howton: see above, will 33. His surname was Hull, but the correct spelling has suffered in the will's transcription. The opening bequests to St John's church, Beverley, leave no doubt as to his origins. His name also appears in the survey of 1524.

65 The image of Our Lady was set above the north door in the alcove, which is now void. Hull would have been buried under the porch paving, a favourite place for burials as worshippers would have been reminded of those interred on the way in by an inscription on the gravestone, a plaque attached to it or affixed to the adjacent wall.

66 This is a payment to Norwich cathedral, the mother-church of the diocese.

67 Unfortunately Thomas Howton's will has not survived. He is mentioned in the churchwardens' accounts, CWA fols 2v and 3r. On CWA, fol.11r, Howton's quetheword of 16s. 4d. is entered, *c.*1513–1514.

68 Miles Hull was elected churchwarden on 6 November 1553. See CWA, fol.45v.

I will that every of my said children have a portion of my household stuff when they come to lawful age by the discretion of my wife, their mother.

To Elizabeth, my sister, the wife of John Feryng in Chemisford 13s. 4d.; I will that all such bills of debts or obligations that the same John and his heirs stand bound in which may hereafter come to my executors' hands, the same bills and obligations to be cancelled and made void for ever.

I will that an honest priest do sing for me and all my benefactors' and friends' souls in the church of Mildenhall by the space of half a year.

To Margery my maid 6s. 8d.

To the buying of a vestment to be for the church of Mildenhall 26s. 8d., for a priest to sing in it the time of my service and after to remain to the said church for ever.

I will that all such feoffees that now are enfeoffed in all my lands and tenements and other premises whatsoever they be and wheresoever they be, the same to be enfeoffed and seized to the use of this will and testament: the residue of all my goods and chattels I commit and put into the hands of my executors whom I make Joan, my wife, and Nicholas Palton, they to dispose for the weal of my soul as they will discharge their conscience.

Master John Wylkenson, vicar of Mildenhall, and Miles Crosby to be supervisors, and each of them to have for his labour 10s.

Wiltnesses: Thomas Busshe, John Maryott, Thomas Hoberstye, William Scott and others.

Proved in the cathedral church of St Paul, 28 May 1527.

37. Will of Thomas Hopper, 10 August 1524   SROB, IC 500/2/14/91–92

[*English*] To be buried within the church of Mildenhall within the north aisle; for tithes and oblations negligently forgotten 10s.

To the reparation of the church of Salle [*Sawyl*] in Norfolk 3s. 4d.;[69] to the reparation of the parish church of Troyce [*Trowce Newton*] besides Norwich 3s. 4d.; to the parish church of St Laurence, Norwich, to the reparation therof 3s. 4d.; to the church of Austin Friars of Norwich for a trental to be sung there 10s.

To Margery my wife my tenement called Harham with an acre of land lying at Munys and a 5 roods [*of*] lands with a pightle in East Fenes, to her and her heirs for ever; I will that Margery have all my utensils and moveables, wholly as they been, to her and her assigns for ever.

To the buying of a pair of chalices for the church of Mildenhall £6; to the mother church of Norwich 20d.

I will that the house[70] and 2 acres of land which I dwell in and the pond yard over against it be sold by my executors and the money thereof coming to bring me to the earth and pay my legacies and debts.

The residue of my goods and chattels I put and remit to the distributing of my executors whom I make Margery my wife and Nicholas Palton and the same Nicholas to receive for his labour 10s.

Master John Wilkynson to be supervisor.

Witnesses: Master Vicar, Nicholas Palton, William Breton and others.

---

69 The bequests for the upkeep of these four Norfolk churches, two in the city and two within the county, suggest that Hopper was not a native of Mildenhall.

70 Hopper was not a local surname. Thomas and Margery do not seem to have had children and so he is quite easily identified in the accounts. His house, Hopper's Cot, was down in the fen and both he and his wife attended to the church washing. He was churchwarden 1509–10, CWA, fols 7r–9r.

I will that after my decease there be a priest found for me to sing and pray for me, my father's and mother's and all my benefactors and friend's souls in Mildenhall church as long as £4 will extend and amount to.[71]

Proved before the official of the archdeacon of Sudbury in Mildenhall parish church, 23 September 1524.

38. Will of Humfreye Duffeld, 28 May 1530   NRO, NCC Attmere 120

[*English*] To be buried in Mildenhall church; to the high altar of the said church for my tithes forgotten 10s.; to the same church my best coverlet and a black vestment for the priest to sing in and my best diaper cloth for an altar cloth; to the reparations of the said church 20s.; a priest to sing for a year in Mildenhall church for my soul, my wife's soul, Master Paul Gayton's [*Gacon's*] soul and all Christian souls and have for his stipend £5 6s. 8d.[72]

To Joan my wife £20.

To the reparations of St Peter's church in Eriswell 16d. and to the church of St Lawrence[73] 16d.; to the church of Barton 20d.; to the church of Tuddenham 20d.; to the church of Freckenham 20d.; to the church of Isleham 20d.; to the church of Worlington 20d.

To Paul my son all such lands and tenements as lie in Spalding and Pinchbeck in Lincolnshire that his mother has right to, that all the money coming of the said lands and tenements be put wholly to the keeping and bringing up of my four youngest children, William, Cicely [*Cysleye*], Bess and Alice for 6 years; to the said Paul my son 20s. and my little mazer.

To Thomas my son £4.

To Joan my wife 1 acre of land in the West Field of Mildenhall, sometime John Blyth's and if my wife die, my son William to have it.

To the elder Robert my son £4; to Cecily, Bess, Agnes and Alice my daughters £12 to be equally divided amongst them; to Thomas my son my house in the East End which I bought of Peter Shomaker which was sometime John Latts.

To Paul, my son, my 2 shops in Newmarket.

To Sir John Pykavell, my kinsman, 6s. 8d: to William, my son, £4: to Margery, my daughter, £6 and 10s. *per annum* coming out of a piece of land in Spalding called Dedmonds Lane.

To Cecily, Margery, Bess, Agnes and Alice my daughters each a pair of fine sheets; to my cousin Agnes Cheke 12d. and every one of her children 12d.; to every one of my godchildren 2 bushels of barley.

To Mother Gardiner 20d.; to Thomas Man 3s. 4d.; to William Langham 3s. 4d.

If Joan my wife will have the money and stuff that I bequeathed to her daughters Cecily and Elizabeth until they come to 20 years old, she to have it on this condition, that she be bound by obligation to save them harmless and discharge my executors for their legacies. If she will not, the legacies to remain in the hands of the executors. If any of my children die before 20 years, then that part to be divided between those living; if all children die before that age, all the legacies to be disposed for my soul etc.

The house that I dwell in to be sold to fulfil my legacies, but my executors to let

---

[71] £4 would have provided prayers for roughly nine months.

[72] This was the going rate at the time. It was increased by statute *c.*1530.

[73] In Eriswell 'near the Hall on the north side of the parish, was a chapel dedicated to St Lawrence, the remains of which is now a dove-cote' (White, *Suffolk 1844*, p.588).

my house to support my year day for 6 years next following my death, for my soul, my wife's soul, Master Paul Gayton's soul,[74] spending 10s. each year on the year days and out of it, 3s. 4d. to the poor people where most need is and to the priests and for wax and ringing 6s. 8d.

If Joan my wife will buy my house, she to have it £4 below the price; if not, my executors sell it for the best price. The residue of my goods to be priced by 2 men at 20d. each.

To be buried with solemn dirige and 3 masses, one of Our Lady, another of the Holy Ghost and the third of requiem and every priest of Mildenhall to have 6d.[75] Executors at my burying to bestow £3, and similarly, with solemn dirige and 3 masses and £3 at my month day.

Goods having been priced to be shared equally, half amongst my children and the other half by the discretion of my executors for my soul; to each of my executors 10s. besides their costs.

If Joan my wife will not be content with the legacies I have assigned her, the legacies to be void and remain to the executors, and she to have the third part of my moveables, she to see my debts paid and legacies given.

Executors: Paul [*Powle*] my son and William Langham.

Supervisors: my wife and Thomas my son.

To my wife for her labours 3 of the best silver spoons. To Thomas my son 3s. 4d.

Witenesses: Sir William Reve, Sir James Mygelaye and others.

Proved at Hoxne, 25 June 1530 by Paul Duffelde, the other executor renouncing.

39. Will of Henry Nowce, otherwise Tourner,[76]   SROB, IC 500/2/19/219
2 May 1535

[*English*] My body to ecclesiastical sepulture; to the high altar of Myldnall for my tithes and oblations negligently forgotten and not paid 20d.; to the reparation of the church of Myldnall 6s. 8d. and a rope to make a bellrope.

To Alice my wife my tenement or messuage with the appurtenances which I now dwell in for the term of her life, so that she keep it in good and sufficient reparations. If it fortune the said messuage or tenement to decay and not be kept in good and sufficient reparations, then I will that immediately upon such decay of the said messuage Margaret, my daughter, enter the said messuage, notwithstanding my gift before mentioned.

After the decease of Alice I will the said messuage or tenement with the appurtenances remain wholly to Margaret my daughter for the term of her life and, after her decease, I will it remain to the issue of Margaret. For lack of issue male, I will it remain to the issue female of the said Margaret. If it fortune Margaret to decease without issue then I will the messuage or tenement be sold by my executrix and the money therof coming disposed as follows: First I will that £4 be bestowed in and about the reparation of the highway in a certain street in Myldnall called Fridaye Streate and I will it be railed and posted; I will that 5 marks of money be given to the church of Myldnall.

To Margaret my daughter my messuage or tenement with the appurtenances in the

---

74 Paul Gayton had been vicar of Mildenhall for forty-one years, 1471–1512.

75 These entries show the choice that existed for testators who could afford to choose from multiple commemorative practices.

76 This is an instance of an occupational description becoming a surname. From his will, it is revealed that Henry Nowce was a turner or a worker in wood.

High Town of Myldnall which I lately bought of Katherine Broughton and Thomas her son, on condition that Margaret pay the purchase of the said messuage which is behind and not paid; to the said Margaret a howed bullock with a flaxen mane; to the said Margaret a grey mare and a doon mare which I lately bought of Thomas Sigoo; to the said Margaret a sorrel mare which I bought at Lakingheth: the residue of my mares I give to Alice my wife [*also*] to Margaret a gelding, being brown bay; to Alice my wife 12 milch bullocks; to the said Alice my carts with the harness to them belonging, with all my other geldings and mares, not before bequeathed.

I will that Alice my wife have my boat with the tackle to it belonging, to keep her markets, utter[77] my ware and fetch home my timber from Well[78] and other places and I will that Robert Ballard my servant help her to keep her markets, carry home my timber from Well and other places and work it for my wife by the space of a whole year next after my decease, taking of my said wife such wages as he taketh of me and at the end of the said year next after my decease, I will the said Robert Ballard, my servant, have the said boat with all the tackle and other things to it belonging.

To the said Robert Ballard, my servant, my tools in the shop and all my other shop-gear; to the said Robert my best riding coat and my jerkin of leather; I will the said Robert work my timber for my wife with my tools and shop-gear, and if he refuse to help my wife and do as before assigned, then I will that he have no parcel of the legacy before bequeathed.

To Alice Fuller my kinswoman a heifer [*hecke fare*] of 2 years old and a weanling.

To Thomas Langham a heiffer of 2 years old; to John Langham a weanling; to William Langham a weanling; I will the said heiffers and weanlings be delivered to the said Thomas, John and William when they come to 16 years of age.

To Henry Burrell a calf of one year old, to be delivered on this side my thirty day.[79]

To John Newce my brother a heifer of 3 years old.

To Alice Egle a heifer of 2 years old and to Henry her son a weanling.

To every one of my grandchildren a bushel of barley.

To Robert Tyrrell 6s. 8d. which Robert Man of Stowe Lanton [*Stowlangtoft*] doth owe me.

I will that 4 marks be bestowed by my executrix in deeds of charity amongst poor people at my burial day and 30 day.

I will an obit or year day be yearly kept by my executrix or her executors for my soul and my friends' souls by the space of 20 years next after my decease, and that she or they yearly at about the said obit or yearday bestow 10s. as follows: amongst priests and clerks 3s. 4d.; the residue amongst poor people.

The residue of all my goods and chattels I give to my executrix whom I make Alice my wife, she to pay my debts and legacies and dispose them in deeds of charity for my soul and my friends' souls as to her discretion seemeth most expedient to the pleasure of God and profit of my soul.

Supervisor: John Lane, praying him to aid, assist and help my wife in and about the administration and execution of this last will and testament, and I give him for his pain taking in this behalf 20s.

---

77 To put forth goods upon the market or to issue for sale.
78 Henry Nowce had a boat in which he carried timber from the town of Wells-next-the-Sea, Norfolk. A charter had been granted to Ramsey abbey in 1202 to expand Wells to accommodate the abbey's export of grain (Pevsner and Wilson, *Norfolk 1. Norwich and North-East* (1997), p.711) and Wells became a major port in eastern England.
79 Within the month.

Witnesses: John Frost, Henry Moreley, Margaret Man, Thomas Larke and others.
Proved before Thomas Bigg, in Dec. Bac., commissary of Bishop Richard of Norwich and official of the archdeacon of Sudbury in the archdeaconry of Sudbury, by royal authority at Myldnall [blank], September 1535. Adminstration to executrix. Seal of official appended.

40. Will of John Halsted of Westrowe, 8 January 1537   SROB, IC 500/2/20/23

[*English*] To be buried in the churchyard of Mydenhale; to the high altar of the same church for tithes and oblations not fully paid 5s.; to the reparation of the church of Myldenhale 10s.

I will there be bestowed at my burying day and at my 30 day 4 marks, equally to be divided, i.e. at every of the said 2 days 26s. 8d., among priests, clerks and poor people.

I will that at every of the said days there be killed and disposed in deeds of charity a young bullock or steer over and besides the said 4 marks toward the relief of the poor people.

To the Friars Augustine in Theford and to the Grey Friars in Babwell, every of them to have 5s to sing and pray a whole trental for my soul and all my benefactors' and friends' souls within a whole year next after my death.

I will that Rose my wife have, for the term of her life, my parlour and my chamber within it, with free going and coming thereto all times; also the same Rose to have of Richard Halsted, my son, meat and drink and firing sufficient during her life; to Rose, my wife, 3 milch good bullocks, one ballyd[80] horse, a young bay mare and 4 ewes, yearly to be kept at the charges of the said Richard my son; to Rose my wife a pan, a pot of brass which Rose brought to me, a stelyd posnet and a little kettle 6 parcel of pewter, one with another of all sorts, 2 candlesticks; to Rose my wife a coomb of malt yearly, to be paid by my executors during the life of the said Rose.

To every of my godchildren 4d.

To the mending of the streets in Westrowe a coomb of malt.

To Alice Rolfe my daughter 6s. 8d.; to Thomas Rolfe her son a calf: to Margaret Rolfe and Grace Rolfe, every of them, a ewe.

The residue of all my goods and chattels I remit and put it to the distribution and disposing of my executor whom I make the said Richard Halsted, my son, my sole executor, he to pay my debts and legacies and dispose in deeds of charity for me and all my benefactor' and friends' souls to the pleasing of God, relieving of my soul and discharging his conscience.

John Rolfe to be supervisor, he to have for his labour in performing the same will 6s. 8d.

Witnesses: Nicholas Palton, Thomas Bakhoott, Thomas Pollyngton, Lewis Bovell with others.

Proved before Thomas Bygges, commissary, at Bury St Edmunds [no date].

41. Will of Richard Treupeny, labourer,   SROB, IC 500/2/19/576
17 August 1537   SROB, IC 500/2/20/193

[*English*] To be buried in St Mary churchyard of Mildenhall; to the high altar of Mildenhall for my tithes negligently forgotten 12d.

---

80 An uncastrated horse.

I will that Margaret my wife shall have after my departing all that I have, my son Robert paying my debts.

This is the sum of my debts: First I owe to Mr Thomas Pope 18s.; I owe to William Patchet 2s., Robert Blome and Robert Cole 20d., Thomas Fisher of Aiswell [*Eriswell*] 8s. 4d. The sum is 30s.

The residue of my goods I will my wife Margaret shall have all, whom I make my executor, and I will William Clement shall be supervisor.

Witnesses: Harry Olever, my ghostly father,[81] William Clement and John Browne.

Administration granted 13 March 1537 at Fornham. Paid 8d.

On verso of will: West Row

Item I owe Thomas Hart of Myldynhale 12d. and to Nicholas May of Myldynhale 12d.

Item to Thomas Donyng of Eiswell 12d.

Item to Caritor of Lakynhythe 12d.

Item to Alice Broune 20 groats.

Item to William Egyll of Lakynhithe 12d.

42. Will of William Peche of Wyldestrete,   SROB IC 500/2/19/557
Mildenhall, 12 July 1538

[*English*] To be buried within the churchyard of Mildenhall; to the high altar of the church of Mildenhall for tithes and oblations negligently forgotten and not paid 3s. 4d.; to the reparation of the said church 10s.; to Christ Church in Norwich 6d.

Whosoever hereafter fortune to enjoy and have my meadow lying in Wyldestrete, both free and copy, after my decease, I will that the same person shall pay to Joan, my daughter, £4.

I will William Peche, the son of William Peche, my son, have in money paid to him by William Peche, my son, when he, William Peche the younger, come to lawful age, £10 going out of such lands and tenements, meadows and pastures and other premises with the appurtenances, lately purchased of the alderman and brethren of the gild of the Blessed Trinity in Mildenhall.[82] If it fortune the said William Peche, the younger, to die ere the £10 be paid as above, then I will the £10 be distributed and disposed in deeds of charity by my executors for the wealth of my soul, my wives' souls and all our benefactors' and friends' souls.

Margaret, my wife, have to her and her assigns for term of [*her*] life 3 acres of meadow lying in Breche in Mildenhall, and after her decease I will the 3 acres with the appurtenances wholly to remain to William, my son, and his heirs forever; to Margaret, my wife, 6 milch bullocks of the best sort and 4 horses or 4 mares or geldings of such as I have and as she will choose and elect, and 10 coombs of barley malt and all my utensils and household stuff, except one brass pot which was bought of Skarrer, which I will the said Joan, my daughter, have; to Joan, my daughter, my feather bed that I lie in with all things to the same bed belonging, as I have used it in my life.

I will there be disposed at my burial day, among priests, clerks, and other deeds of charity £1 6s. 8d.; and also to dispose for me and my benefactors and friends souls' at my 30 day in deeds of charity 40s. by the hands of my executors. I will that my executors shall yearly dispose and distribute in Mildenhall, in deeds of charity at

---

81   A confessor, one that would hear confession.
82   See 'Gild of the Holy Trinity' in the Introduction, p.xlvii.

an obit or anniversary, yearly to be holden there by the space of 5 years, every year 20s. to pray for me and all my benefactors' and friends' souls.

To the reparation of the street in Wyldstr[*te*] 20d. and to the reparation of Beckstrete 20d. and it to be paid in 5 years at common days within the said streets.

To Agnes my servant a bullock of 3 years of age; to John Bayle my servant a heifer of 2 years of age.

The residue of all my goods and chattels I put and remit it to the disposition and distribution of my executors whom I make William Peche, my son, and John Peche, my brother, they to pay my debts and dispose for me to the honour and pleasure of God, comforting my soul and my benefactors' souls and to the discharging of their conscience; to the said John Peche, my brother, for his pains herein taking 6s. 8d.

Witness: Nicholas Palton.

Proved at Fornham St Martin, 15 March 1545.

43. Will of Nicholas Meye, warrener, 26 March 1540   SROB, IC 500/2/19/279

[*English*] To be buried in the church or churchyard of Mildenhall;[83] to the high altar in Mildenhall for tithes and offerings negligently forgotten 20d.; to the reparation of the church in Mildenahll 20d.

To Katherine my wife my tenement free that is in the Bekke in Mildenhall called Flegges, with all the appurtenances for the term of her life and after her decease I will that the tenement remain to Nicholas my eldest son to him and his heirs forever. If Nicholas die without issue then I will the tenement remain to John my son and his heirs for ever. If John die without issue then I will it be sold by my executrix and the money to be evenly divided amongst my daughters, every of them in like portion; to Katherine my wife my tenement free, that is in the market stead, next unto two tenements of Michael Howes of Cambridge for term of her life, and after her decease I will that the said tenement remain to John my son and his heirs forever; if John die without issue or ere he be of age of 21, then the said tenement to be at the disposition of the said Katherine as she shall think most best; to Katherine, my wife, my tenement late Gosses which abutteth on Greene hill with all the appurtenances to her and

her assigns for ever; to Katherine, my wife, my tenement copy in the Market steade next to my free tenement, freely to give and sell, with 2½ acres of copy land which lieth in the field called Eastefeld and also my copy of the warren.

All these copies before rehearsed, I, the said Nicholas, have made surrender into the hands of Richard Polington to the use of the said Katherine my wife and her assigns for ever; to Katherine my wife all my moveable goods and chattels that I have, the said Katherine to receive my debts and pay my debts. I put it to the disposition of the said Katherine if so be that God do send for me, to bring me honestly to my burial and to do deeds of charity for my soul and all Christian souls as shall think most meritorious for my soul, which Katherine I make my chief executrix.

Richard Polyngton to be supervisor to help and further my wife unto the performance of this my last will and testament and the said Richard to have for his labour 6s. 8d.

Witnesses: Thomas Hart, John Oxford, John Feltwell with others.

---

83 An unusual entry in that burial in church would involve extra payment and yet the amount is not stipulated here. The contents of the will suggest that Nicholas Meye was well able to afford internal interment.

Proved at Newmarket before Sir John Burye, official etc., 25 May 1540. Administration to executor.

44. Will of William Reve, charnel priest, 4 January 1545[84]

SROB, IC/500/1/10/81

[*English*] I commend my soul [to] almighty God my saviour and redeemer trusting only in him and in his merits to have the inheritance where unto he have purchased me by the effusion of his precious blood. To be buried in the choir of Myldenhale before the parish priest's stall; to the high altar for the discharge of my conscience in that I have negligently forgotten anything due to God either in tithes or oblations 3s. 4d.; to the reparations of the said church 6s 8d.

My executors shall find one lawful priest that can preach and help in the choir to serve God, shall sing for me and for all those that I am bound to pray for and for all Christian souls, one quarter of a year immediately after my death in the parish church of Myldenhale; and the said priest to make a sermon openly in the church of Myldenhale when they think most people in the said church be present.

To my sister, Margery, 40s. and my chamber whole as it is at this present, as my bed complete, cupboard, sheets, coverlets, blankets or other whatsoever it be; and if the said Margery chance to die then I will that her daughter of the same Margery whose name is Agnes Largent, shall have the foresaid chamber with the appurtenances there belonging.

To my brother Harry 20s. and my brystow gown: to Thomas Reve, the son of John Reve,

13s. 4d.; to William Reve, my godson, the debt that he owe me.

Towards the charges of my funeral at my burying day 20s.; on my church day and year day to be bestowed 40s.

I make my disposers and executors of this my last will and testament John Mason and Thomas Cottes, they to have for their labour each of them 6s. 8d.

The residue of my goods not bequeathed or that be left, my debts with legacies paid, to be disposed by the hands of my executors in deeds of charity; for a more surety that these things may be done according to this my will, I will and put my singular trust in Thomas Skott, vicar of Myldenhale, to be my supervisor so that my executors shall call at all times the said Thomas Skott see them bestowed according to my will or in deeds of charity or other needful things as they three shall think of their consciences or by their discretion as God help them and all souls, he to have for his labour 6s. 8d.

Item I give to Thomas Skott, vicar, my best surplice.

Witnesses: Thomas Hooke, John Geste, cowper.

Probate, 30 March 1545.

45. Will of Robert Merchall, 10 April 1546

SROB, IC 500/2/21/219

[*English*] To be buried in the churchyard of Mildenhall, for my tithes and offerings negligently forgotten and too little paid 4d.; to the reparation of the church 20d.

My goods and chattels, both great and small, of what kind soever they be, with all my stuff of household and all utensils that to me belongeth and be mine at the day of

---

[84] See the will of Sir George Gatynbe, priest (above, will 29), dated 13 March 1504, in which William Reve, a chaplain, was bequeathed a festival, a rochet and some beads. If this is the same William Reve, he must have been well over sixty when he died.

my decease, immediately after [*be*] viewed and divided in three parts by the discretion of the honest men such as shall view, pryse and make the inventory of all the foresaid goods and chattels and Christian, my wife, to have the first part and John, my son, to have the second part, and Edmund, my son, the third part. Furthermore the said John and Edmund to have the custody of the part that doth belong to Christian, my wife, to the intent that the said John and Edmund, betwixt them both, to see and to maintain and keep the said Christian, their mother, for the term of her life.

If the said my sons, or any of them, will not give to the said Christian, their mother, competent living according to the words before spoken, then I will the said Christian shall recover and take, by virtue of this my last will and bequest, the third part of all such goods as be mine as is before named at the day of my decease.

Should any of my two sons, John or Edmund, decease and be not married, then I will the other have the third part belonging to the deceased, to the intent to maintain and keep the said Christian: if it fortune they both decease, then Christian to have the third part of the substance or value thereof to the maintenance and furtherance of her living.

To Edmund Holby a bullock of three years of age and a comb of malt and three geese.

To Christian, my wife, my ambling[85] mare to ride upon the holy day to church and home again.

To everyone of my godchildren 4d.

John and Edmund, my sons, to bring me honestly to earth after the custom of the Church and to dispose for me in deeds of charity to the pleasure of God and health of my soul and discharging their conscience.

Supervisor: my well-beloved in Christ, John Polington, to whom, for his labour, 2s.
Witnesses: James Alexander, Edmund Holbye with other.
No probate recorded.

46. Will of Richard Cole, tanner, 25 December 1547   TNA, PCC Populwell 7

[*English*] All other wills renounced; to be buried in the churchyard of Mildenhall; to the high altar there for my tithes and offerings negligently forgotten and too little paid in the discharge of my conscience 3s. 4d.; to the reparation of the church there 40s.

My tenement which I now dwell in, with all my bark that I have bought and is not reserved at this present day and all the tan vats and vessels as longeth to the same occupation and other instruments as belong to the said occupation, shall remain within the said tenement, the said tenement being in Mildenhall in the street called the Myll Street both free and copy next unto the tenement of Thomas Cotes and the parte est and the copy of John Basset on the part west with all the said premises immediately after my decease.

To James Norman, my servant, a feather bed, a bolster, a pair of sheets and a covering and a cupboard that standeth in the hall.

All my household stuff to be divided betwixt my executors and Isabel my wife, except the apparel that belongeth unto my body my executors to have; and the womens' apparel that belongeth unto her she shall have, my executors to array my said wife Isabel in clothing good and honest sufficiently unto her body, new bought and made immediately after my decease; the table in the hall beneath and form with

---

85 Moving at an amble. *COED*, p.44.

the stained cloths to remain in the hall to the use of the same hall at the disposition of my executors.

To Isabel, my wife, my tenement called Sadlers for her lifetime and after it to remain to the disposition of my executors as my will shall assign; to the said Isabel £40 in money to be paid within one year next immediately after my decease; to the same Isabel 2 milch bullocks and a young horse, the best that I have in the fen to choose amongst 6 which I have there at this present time to be delivered by my executors immediately after my decease.

My executors to have the use of my shops which I have in Newmarket that I hold by copy of Sir Giles Alyngton, kt. to the use and performance of my will, the said executors to keep them in sufficient reparation and to pay the rent to the lord; my executors to have the use of 27 acres of land arable in Mildenhall Fields and 4 acres of meadow to the performing of my will; my executors to have the use of my tenement in the West Rowe next unto the tenement of John Rolfe on the south and the tenement of Harry Wright on the north to the performance of my will during the term hereafter assigned, and also my barn with 3 roods of land in Derebowht called the Stone berne, in like condition as aforesaid: all the foresaid lands, meadows and tenements which I have assigned to the use of my executors to be sold by them before the term of 10 years be expired.

Executors and attorneys: Stephen Cole of Chippenham, yeoman, and Robert Thurston of Mildenhall, tanner.

To my 4 prentices, that is William Butler, Simon and Robert [blank] and Robert Felde, every of them 20s. to be paid by my executors immediately within one year after my decease.

To 5 of my godsons, that is Thomas Rolffe 6s. 8d., Roger Rolffe 6s. 8d., John Fynch 6s. 8d., Thomas Cotes 6s. 8d., Miles Hull 6s. 8d.; the residue of my godsons and goddaughters, 12d. each to be delivered every of them within one year after my decease.

To Robert Feld, my prentice, £4 in money so that he doth keep and serve out his years at the assignment of my executors, or else not; to Katherine Felde 10s. to be paid as aforesaid.

To the poor people of Mildenhall parish, £10 in money, to be distributed 10 years immediately after my decease, that is every year 20s. to be distributed and dealt at 2 several times in the year, that is at Christmas 10s. and Our Lady day the Annunciation, the other 19s. and so from year to year.

The residue of my lands, tenements [etc.] goods and chattels [etc.] with all other utensils wholly to the hands of my executors to dispose [etc.].

Supervisor: John Holte of Cockfield, gent.

Every of them [that is executors and supervisor] to have £3 in money for their pains, they to bring me honestly unto my burial according to the use of the church.

Witnesses: Thomas Cottes, Edmund Wright and Thomas Venal, Thomas Man and John Oxford with many others.

To Thomas Cole, clerk, and to George Cole, my brethren 40s. each. To William Fynch 40s.

Proved before the archbishop of Canterbury, 5 April 1548 by executors.

47. Will of Margaret Jerold, widow, late the wife   SROB, IC 500/2/21/157 of John Jerold,[86] 21 September 1549

[*English*] My body to be buried in the churchyard of Mildenhall aforesaid; to the reparation of the church of Mildenhall 6s. 8d.[87]

Unto the reparation of the way betwixt the Mill bridge and the bridge next unto Barton staithe 10s., to be done by the hands of my executors immediately within the space of one year after my death; unto the reparation and a mendings of the way in the Mill street 10s., to be done by my executors in like wise.

My executors shall bring me honestly unto my burial according to the use and custom of the church and for the discharge thereof and for the poor people I will that there be done for me then 20s. at my month's day < > to be done likewise in other 20s.

To the leading of the market cross 6s. 8d.

To Thomas Clarke alias Webb, the son of Thomas Webb, my black mare that is bald and my young garlyd bullock and one pair of sheets and one brass pot; to Mark Webb one brown bullock that brings forth <*illeg.*> and one brass pot and three pewter plates; to Margaret Webb, the daughter of Robert Webb, three pewter dishes and one candlestick and one brass pot; to John Webb, the son of the same Robert, one brass pot; to Agnes Webb, my goddaughter, the daughter of John Webb, two pewter dishes and one candlestick and one latten basin; to Luke Webb, one pewter platter and one chafing dish; to Margaret Webb, the daughter of John Webb, one pewter platter and one candlestick; to Edmund Webb, the son of the same John, one yearling cow calf and one silver spoon; to Margaret Webb, the daughter of Thomas Webb, the senior, one promised voyder of pewter and one pewter platter and one table cloth and two pillow beares.[88]

To Margaret Costyn, that is married unto Burrye, one brass pan with two urns and one pewter platter.

To Agnes Clark, the daughter of Joan Coole, a voyder and a platter of pewter and one candlestick; to Thomas Clarke, the son of the same Jane, one pewter platter and 12d.; to Margaret Clarke, the daughter of the foresaid Joan, one pewter platter and one candlestick.

To Margaret Peerson, my servant, one bullock, the which Luke Russell has in ferme and my best douge and a yellow covering and a pair of sheets and a bolster and three pewter platters and a brass pot and a tablecloth and a candlestick and two kerchiefs.

To Margaret Coots, my goddaughter, a brass pot and a latten skomer, a spit and a towel; to Isabel Coots a pewter platter; to Mary Coots a pewter platter and a candlestick.

To John Geson, the son of Margaret Geson, one douge and a coverlet.

To Margaret Qwasch, the wife of Thomas Qwasch, two silver spoons.

To all the children of John Chapman of Ereswell that be unmarried 12d.

To John Webb, the son of Thomas Webb 20s., and that I will he shall have a part of the money the which does remain in the hands of the said John Webb, that is to say £14 for a certain tenement the which is in the street called the West End in Mildenahll for the which tenement the said John Webb does owe unto me at the day

---

86   John Jerold was a dyer and left his son two boiling 'ledys', used in dyeing cloth, with one press of lead and two pairs of shears (IC 500/1/7/75).

87   Money is here left for the repair of the church, but bequests to the high altar are not included. In the next section, money is left for the poor.

88   Pillow-cases. *COED*, p.1342.

of the making of this, my last will, the < > foresaid £14 to be paid £3 by year unto the sum of the said £14 be paid and I will that my executors shall dispose every year £3 unto the poor people for the space of four years next after my decease, and at the last year of the paymets, that is to say the fifth year, to the poor people 20s., part of the 40s. the which he must pay in the fifth year for his legacy as is above said.

To Thomas Jerold, the son of John Jerold, late my husband, my tenement or messuage that I do now dwell in with all and singular the appurtenances after my decease unto him and his assigns freely for ever; to the same Thomas Jerold my copy meadow called Wrong meadow that lies next unto the foresaid tenement freely to him amd his assigns, for ever paying the lord all rents and service.

I have given surrender of the said copy meadow into the hands of Thomas Venall and Thomas Qwasch, tenants unto the right honourable lady, my Lady Mary's grace.[89]

I will and desire my feoffees to deliver estate to the said Thomas Jerold of and in the same tenement or messuage after my decease according unto this my present last will.

The residue of my goods, movables and immovables, stuff of household with all utensils thereto belonging, corn and cattle of what kind soever they be, my will and legacies to be discharged and fulfilled I give freely unto the said Thomas Jerold after my decease, whom I ordeyn and make my faithful executor; and Thomas Quasch my other executor, and the said Thomas Quasch to have for his pains and labour for the performance to see then my present last will and testament fulfilled, 10s unto this.

Witnesses: John Geste, John Oxford, Thomas Webb with others.
Proved at Mildenhall, 23 September 1550.

48. Will of Thomas Rolff, the elder, of Mildenhall   SROB, IC 500/2/13/96
Westrowe, yeoman, 28 October 1551

[*English*] To be buried in Christian burial. To Elizabeth, my wife, my messuage which I dwell as it lies butting upon the south and west of the highway and towards the north upon <the> Thomas Pope, gentleman, and towards the east upon < > my son, John Rolff, to have and to hold until Thomas, my second son, of that name come to the age of twenty years if the said Elizabeth, my wife, do keep herself sole and unmarried And if the said Elizabeth, my wife, do marry before the said Thomas, my son, come to the age of twenty years then I will <that the said> that at the day marrying of Elizabeth, my wife, the said Thomas, my son, shall have my said messuage with the appurtenances, to have and to hold to the said Thomas, his heirs and assigns in fee simple. Provided that if the said Elizabeth, my widow, do keep herself sole and that unmarried after that the said Thomas, my son, shall come to the age of twenty years, then I will that the said Elizabeth, my wife, shall have the dwelling in the new chamber during the time of her widowed [*sic*] and her life natural, with free ingress and egress into and from the said chamber with the easement of the well and other things < > and convenient for her not < > being hindrance to the said Thomas.

To the said Thomas Rolff, my second son aforesaid, one hutch barred with iron, one cupboard, a pair of querns, one table, one form; to the foresaid Thomas, my

---

[89] D. Loades, *Mary Tudor: The Tragical History of the First Queen of England* (2006), p.35. After the birth of Elizabeth, her half-sister, Henry VIII's elder daughter, Mary Tudor, later Queen Mary, was known as 'the Lady Mary, the King's daughter'.

son, three platters of pewter, the best candlestick, a saltcellar; to the said Thomas, my son, a bullock, two geldings, two mares, a cart and a plough with the harness and plough gear belonging thereto to be delivered to him at the <age> of sixteen years; to Thomas, my son, all my copy lands and < > pasture lying in the town of Mildenhall.

To Francis Rolff, my son, three acres of free land lying at Mundesfield to have and to hold to him, his heirs and assigns: to the said Francis, my son, one bullock, two dishes and one lawer of pewter, one candlestick to be delivered to him at the age of sixteen years \ten combs thereof to be delivered at the feast of the purification of the Our Lady next after my death/.

To Roger, my son, twenty combs of barley and the other ten combs to be delivered at such day twelve month after; to Thomas and Rolff, my nephew and godson 12d.; to Robert Rolff, my godson 12d.; to Agnes Gest, my goddaughter 12d.

To Elizabeth, my wife, all my sheep that be in Mildenhall saving one ewe and one lamb which I do give to Thomas Rolff, my youngest son.

To Thomas, my youngest son, five marks of good and lawful money of England and one bullock all with legacies I will shall be delivered to him at the age of sixteen years; <to Thomas Rolff, my second son, one yard called the Field yard> provided always that if Elizabeth, my wife, do marry before that Thomas, my second son, Francis, my son and Thomas, my youngest son, or any of them come to the age of sixteen years then I will that the said Elizabeth, my wife, shall, before she be married unto any man, <other delyd> be bound with sufficient sureties to John Rolff, my eldest son, supervisor of this my testament to deliver <the said legacies> to the said Thomas, Francis and Thomas, my sons beforesaid, at the age of sixteen years all the legacies aforesaid with all [*illeg.*] and profits that therof shall arise and come of them after the day of her marriage; or else I will that the said Elizabeth, my wife, deliver out of her hands to the said Thomas, my second son, Francis and Thomas, my youngest son, all the legacies before that she be married and that the one shall be others heir of them for the receiving of every part and parcel of < > the said legacies in case any of them depart or die before the said age of sixteen years .

My beasts of bullocks and calves <be> any kind of that kind \not before bequeathed/ of beasts shall equally and evenly be divided between Elizabeth, my wife, and Roger, my son, immediately after my decease.

To John Rolff, my eldest son, my gown furred with black lamb; to Thomas Rolff, my second son, <wone> whole bed with all things therto belonging apt and fit for a man to lie in; to Roger, my son, one pair of sheets, two dishes of pewter.

Residue of all my goods and chattels, movables and not movable not before bequeathed with all my implements utensils and stuff of household and all my debts to me due and to be due I wholly and freely give them to Elizabeth, my wife, whom I ordain and and make my sole executrix of \this my testament and last will/, and I ordain the said John Rolff, my eldest son, of this my testament and last will my supervisor.

\To the relief of the poor people of this town 40d./

Also I have \made a/ < > of my said copylands in to the hands of John Rolff, my eldest son, to the use of Thomas, my second son, in the presence of William Bugge, the elder.

Witness John Rolff aforesaid, Robert Whytney, priest, William Rought, William Bugge, the elder, Thomas Rowght, notary with others.

Witnesses of this <bequest> Thomas Skott, vicar, John Rolff, the elder, James <Alexander>

Proved 26 September 1553.

49. Will of James Alysander, painter, 3 January 1553   SROB, IC 500/1/16/119
[*Latin*] In the name of God Amen.
[*English*] My body to be buried in the sanctuary where it shall please God to take this my present life.
Item I give to Joan, my wife, the house and the land belonging thereto for the term of her life and the surrender of the same is in the hands of Robert Dobson to the use of this will. Item I give unto the said Joan, my wife, all my cattle, household stuff and all my other moveables, whatsoever they be, to the intent that she shall pay all my debts here among my neighbours.
I will the said Joan, my wife, to pay unto my brother in law George Manuell £3.
I will that my house and the land thereto belonging be sold after the decease of my wife by the hands of mine executors: and of the same money I will that mine executors shall pay unto William Alexander, my son, 53s. 4d.
I give unto my executors whom I choose and ordain William Alexander and George Alexander, my sons, for their labour each one of them 26s. 8d. I will that the residue of the money which shall remain of the sale of my house shall be equally divided at every pay unto my children that shall remain [*on lyve*] at every such paye.
Item I will that if George, my son, will buy my house that he shall have it 20s under the price that other men will give.
Thus I do finish my last will the day and year above specified.
Witnesses: Thomas Scott, vicar of Mildenhall, and Thomas Potter.
No note of proof.

50. Will of Robert Halstede, the elder, weaver,   SROB, IC 500/1/15/56
22 October 1553
[*English*] My body to be buried when and where it shall please almighty [*God*] to call me out of this present life; to the reparation of the church of Mildenhall 12d.
To Robert, my son, eight pieces of pewter and two pots of brass, two steel pans, one frying pan, one chaffing dish of latten, two trivets, one latten ladle, three candlesticks, one gridiron, one pair andirons with one spit, one pair pot hangers, one pair pot hooks, one pan, one kettle, three chairs, one table, one stool, four bedsteads, one cupboard and four coffers. Also <four> one great stained cloth with two flock beds, one covering for a bed, two quart pots of pewter, one pint pot, three saltcellars of pewter, one transom for a bed with eight pieces of linen whereof are six sheets and two table cloths; to the same Robert, my son, ten combs of barley; to the said Robert, my son, all my looms with all that belong to the said looms.
To Isabel, my wife, all such goods as she had or brought to me as well cattle, corn and stuff of household and all other utensils of household of what kind soever they be of, she to have them, to give and sell them forever; to the said Isabel, my wife, all my crop of corn as barley and rye straw and chaff except the forsaid ten combs before given to Robert, my son, and the straw and chaff of the said ten combs which I will he have immediately after my departing; being excepted out of the foresaid crop of corn nineteen combs of barley and two bushels which is due debt unto John Oxford.
The residue of my goods not before given nor bequeathed [*illeg.*] my debts and legacies fulfilled and paid, I honestly to be buried, I put them into hands and dispossion of Robert Halstede, my said son \whom I do make my sole executor/ he to do for

me three deeds of charity and other good works of mercy that it may be to the great laud and praise of God will and profit of my soul.

Witnesses: John Lane, William Fynche and Thomas Rolffe with many others.

Proved 3 December 1555.

51. Will of Robert Mason, organ player and clerk, 31 January 1558   SROB, IC 500/2/28/224

[*English*] To be buried at the discretion of my executors.

As touching my worldly goods I will they shall be distributed after this sort: to Elizabeth, my wife, my house at Hadnam-on-the-Hyll [*Haddenham*], to be her own and proper, to give and sell at her pleasure.

To John Mason, my son, £40 in money at his age of twenty; to Joan, my daughter, £10 in money at the day of her marriage.

If my son depart before the receipt of the money then I will that half his portion will be divided immediately between my brother-in-law, John Austeyn, my own brother, Thomas Mason and Elizabeth Kyd, my sister, in equal portions; the other portion to my wife and £10 to be distributed to the poor.

If my daughter dies before before the day of her marriage then I will her portion be distributed thus: my wife to have 40s., and 40s. to be given to the poor; the residue of it to be divided immediately by equal portions between John Austen, Thomas Mason and Elizabeth Kydd as before.

I will that 10s. be distributed to the poor at the day of my burying.

The residue of my goods I commit them to Elizabeth, my wife, whom I make sole executrix, to dispose for my soul and all Christian [*souls*] as she shall think good.

John Austeyn to be overseer and he to have for his labour 20s. and all his ordinary charges.

To Agnes Austen, my sister, 20s.

Witnesses: Robert Wallett, Thomas Pytrell, Robert Daynes, Thomas Currye and Richard Borowgh, the writer.

Executrix granted administration at Bury St Edmunds before the official of the archdeaconry of Sudbury, 7 August 1559.

52. Will of John Polyngton, thatcher, 8 April 1559   SROB, IC 500/2/28/293

[*English*] To be buried in the churchyard when it shall [*please*] God to take from me this present life; to the high altar of Mildenhall aforesaid for my tithes and oblations at any time neglected, forgotten or not paid 12d.; to the reparation of the church of Mildenhall aforesaid 6s 8d.; to the poor people which shall be present at my burial day 10s., and at the same day twelve month after, other 10s. as is aforesaid.

To John, my son, and his assigns my house with the land and the appurtenances thereto belonging to remain unto the said John and his assigns for ever; and if it fortune the wife of the said John, my son, named Alice, being now his lawful wife, to survive the said John, her husband, then I will that she shall have the said house with the lands and appurtenances there belonging during the term of her natural life; to John, my son, my shodde carte with all my cart goods, my ploughs and my plough gears, my harrows and rowll with all such things as belong to husbandry being at this time in my occupying; to the same John, my son, three acres of rye ready sown in the fields and two milch bullocks, the best that he can choose, and a brown mare with her colt that suckles on her, and a young stonyd horse and all the timber that is about my my [*sic*] ground whatsoever it be; to the said John my featherbed that I lie on with the covering and a folte [*folding*] table with the form and lanncetyll as they stand in the hall and an almery and shelf as they stand bare in the buttery.

The said John and Julyan, my daughter, shall part all my fuel equally and rather that Julyan have the better part. All my brass, pewter and latten be equally divided by my executors in three parts and Julyan to choose first, John, my son, next and Robert, my son, last, and in like sort I will that all my coffers and bedsides to be parted and divided: to the said Julyan, one of my coverings of my beds.

I will that Hugh Kynsley and Juliane, my daughter, or other of them shall have their dwelling freely in the house that they dwell now in for one year; I will Julyan, my daughter, to have my cupboard that stands in the hall; to the said Robert, my son, my cupboard that standeth in the parlour.

I give to the said Robert, my house that he now dwells in with the appurtenances as the said Robert have it now in occupying for the term of his natural life, and if it shall fortune that Katere, the wife of the foresaid Robert to survive her husband that then she to have and enjoythe said house with the appurtenances as the foresaid Robert have now in occupying for the term of her natural life. After the decease of the said Robert and Katere, I give the said house with the appurtenances thereunto belonging even as the said Robert have it in occupying, unto William Polyngton, my godson and his assigns, and I will that the said William shall pay of his assigns unto Nicholas Polyngton, his brother and my godson, 40s. of lawful money of England. But if it fortune the said William to depart this present life without lawful issue, then I will and give the said house with the appurtenances as is aforesaid to Nicholas, my godson, and his assigns: but if it shall fortune the said Nicholas to depart without issue of his body lawful then I give the said household appurtenances even as the said Robert have it now in occupying unto the said Robert and his assigns for ever; to the said Robert. my son, my grey gelding that I bought of him, and a red garlyd cow, my bare [?] cart, two combs of malt and two combs of rye; to William Polyngton, my godson, a silver spoon.

To Juliane, my daughter, my house that is called Langhams to remain unto the said Juliane and her heirs for ever, and if the said Julyane shall depart this world without heirs of her body lawful, then I will and give the said house as it is before given to Juliane so to remain to Richard Capp of Wangford and unto his assigns for ever.

To John Costen, my godson, my house in Halewell that is called Costynes with the appurtenances thereto belonging and to remain to the said John Coyten and his assigns for ever on condition that the said John or his assigns shall pay or cause to be paid unto Robert, his brother, Joan and Helen, his sisters, each one of these to be paid when they and every of them shall come to the age of thirty years.

To Isabel Lonnen, my sister, her dwelling in the said [sic] so long as she keep her sole and unmarried.

To the said John one milch cow called Mother Costyn and five combs of barley with all the tools of my occupation; to Juliane, my daughter, one milch cow called Mad Crowne.

To John Kynsley, <my daughter> my godson, one silver spoon.

To Hugh Kynsley, my son in law, one acre of rye, ready sown in the field and five combs of barley and one of the best pigs and the [illeg.] that stands in the house where he dwells and my querne.

John, my son, and Robert, my son, and Juliane, my daughter, shall part all my fowls equally between them: to the said Juliane my gown and my cloak; to Hugh Kinsey before named my blue coat, my fustian doublet and all my hose and my jacket; to

John Costyn my black coat: to Robert, my son, my bufe leather jerkin; to John. my son, worsted jerkin and one silver spoon.

To Agnes Fuller that was my servant two combs of barley; to Thomas Langham, my tenant, his dwelling freely in the house he now dwells in for the space of one quarter of a year after my decease and after the quarter I will the said Thomas shall pay his yearly rent unto Hugh Kinsley.

To John, my son, my grey mare that I did buy of him; to Hugh Kinsley my bay mare. To Margaret Marshall. my kinswoman, one bullock called Young Mother and five combs of barley and my silver ring.

To every one of my god children 4d.; to Isabel, my sister, 12d.; to Joan Wall, my sister, two combs of barley; to Joan Cappes, my goddaughter, a silver spoon; to every one of William Cappe's children one ewe and a lamb to be delivered to the said children at midsummer next after my decease of the sheep that I have going at Wangford if there be so many, or else unto every one of the said children one or more indifferent so far as they will extend. The residue of all my sheep unbequeathed I give them to John, my son, and the quarter harness which is in the constable's custody.

To Hugh Kinsley my watching staff.

To every one of William Cappe's children a bushel of barley; to Joan Cappe, my daughter in law, two keychne cloths, the price 2s. To Helen Kinsley, my daughter's daughter a black howed calf and five combs barley; to Margaret Marchall my little table and my middlemost spit.

The residue of all goods, chattels or movables of whatever kind or sort so ever they I put them to the disposition of John, my son, and William Cappe of Wangford, my son in law, whom I ordain and make ministers and executors of this my proper will and last testament to the intent my debts be paid, my legacies delivered, I honestly brought to the earth and that and it shall be left to divide among my children according to their discretion and I give to the said William Cappe for his pains beside his ordinary charges ten combs of barley and my well-beloved Henry Wall to be supervisor and he to have for his pains 3s. 4d.

Witnesses: Robert Daynes, John Mychell and William Cater with divers others.
Proved 9 October 1559.

53. Will of Katherine Childerston, widow, 16 November 1568   SROB, IC 500/1/2/82

[*English*] To be buried in the parish churchyard of Mildenhall.

To Henry Chapman 6s. 8d. of lawful English money, a form and a chair to be delivered unto him at his full age of eighteen by my executors hereafter named. To Margerie, my daughter, the wife of John < >, my silk thromed hat to be delivered immediately after my decease.

To Joan, my daughter, the wife of Edward Goold, < > platter to be delivered unto her immediately after my decease. To Margery Goold, Margaret Goold and Mary Goold the < > and daughters of the said Edmund Goold, to every of them a bushel of barley or, instead of the same, 12d. a piece of lawful money of England to be delivered by my said executor unto their said father, Edmund Goold, to their uses < > after my death.

To Emme, my daughter, the wife of Thomas Rogers of Stanton, a bere towel to be delivered unto her immediately after my decease. To Margery, my daughter, the wife of Sampson Alderton of Wecheham, my halldaye kercher, a tearing apron, a working

178

day rail, my best cap, a working day kercher to be delivered unto her immediately after my decease.

I will that my executors hereunder named shall bestow about my burying in bringing my body honestly to the ground as it shall seem to them best, 10 shillings of lawful money of England; and the residue of all my goods and chattels, moveable and moveable of what kind or sort soever there be my debts, my legacies discharged, my funeral expenses performed, and wholly put them to the disposition of my said son-in-law, Robert Chapman, whom I ordain and make my executor of this, my last will and testament, to see the same fulfilled as my trust is in him, these being witnesses William Childerston, John Yonge, Humfreye Johnson and Christopher Dalleson as written hereof and others.

54. Will of George Alysander, weaver, 2 May 1575   SROB, IC 500/2/37/125
[*English*] To be buried in the churchyard of Mildenhall.

To Thomas, my son, one loom standing next the street and seven slays <of the best> to the same for the which I will that the said Thomas shall bring up or cause to well and honestly up Elizabeth, my daughter.

To Margaret, my wife, all my whole right and title and interest which I have in my now mansion house with all the appurtenances thereto belonging in Mildenhall and to her heirs for ever if the said Margaret, my wife, shall herself bring up or cause to be well and honestly brought up three of my children, that is to say Simon, my son, Lucy and Katherine, my daughters, to the full years of eighteen; but if it fortune the said Margaret, my wife, to decease before my said three children come to the years of sixteen I will that the said house shall be sold to the most price and furtherance that can be and the same to be equally divided among my said three children, Simon, Lucy and Katherine, towards their bringing up.

The rest of my goods unbequeathed I give unto Margaret, my wife, whom I make my sole executrix, to pay my debts and to take my debts and to see my body brought to the ground.

Witnesses: Alexander Stephenson, minister, John Bawicke and William Stone.
Proved 12 December 1575.

55. Will of Katherine Tirrell,[90] 4 June 1585   NRO, NCC Janigo 208
Although sick and disquieted in body, yet of whole mind and perfect remembrance, praise be to God, do make and ordain this my last will and testament.

First before all things I most humbly commend my soul unto the hands of Almighty God, my maker and redeemer, and my body I will to be buried in holy sepulture whereto my executors hereunder named shall thought meet and convenient.

Towards the reparation of the parish church of Mildenhall aforesaid 2s.; and to the poor man's box of the same town 2s.

To Henry Tirrell, my brother, the feather bed, the covering and the trendle bedstead[91] which my kinsman John Fulsye gave me by his will.

To my brother, John Tirrell, and Richard Tirrell, my brethren, to each of them 20s. apiece of lawful English money.

To Joan Foxe my oldest gown to be delivered unto her immediately after my decease; and 10s. of lawful English money to be paid to her within one year after my decease.

---
90 See CWA, fol.31v.
91 A low bed on wheels or castors, stowed under the main bed; usually for children or servants.

To the widow Cator, late the wife of William Cator, deceased, 2s. 6d.

And the residue of all my other movable goods and cattles, corn, cattle, portions, utensils of household stuff of what kind, name, nature, quality of condition [*illeg.*] the same be of known or called by, my debts paid, my legacies herein contained discharged, my body honestly brought to the earth, I wholly give and refer them to the use of Agnes, my sister, whom I ordain and make sole executrix of this my [*illeg.*] last will and testament, she to pay my debts and to perform this my last will and testament as I hope she will do.

Witnesses: Christopher Dalloson and Robert Suckerman.

Proved 22 February 1586.

Appendix 3

Extracts from William Lyndwood's *Provinciale,*
from the translation made in 1534

'That the parishioners of all churches of our province of Canterbury may be certain of all our defaults that appertain to their charges, lest betwixt them and their parsons any doubt should rise in succession of time, we will and command that hereafter they find all these things hereunder specified:

a legend, an antiphonary, a grail, a psalter, a book of sequences, an ordinal, a mass book, a manual, a chalice, a principal vestment with its chasuble and alb, a cope for the choir with all its appurtenances, a pall for the high altar with three towels, three surplices, a rochet, a cross for procession and another to serve for the dead, a censer, a lantern and a little bell to go before the Body of Christ in the visiting of the sick, an honest pyx for the said body, a veil for the Lent season, banners for Rogation, dayes bells with their cords, a bier for the dead, a vessel for holy water, a pax, a candlestick for the Paschal, a font with his lock, images in the church, the principal image in the chancel, the closing of the churchyard, the repairing of the body of the church both within and without, as well as images in glass windows, the repairing of books and vestments whensoever it happen them to need.

As for all other things that be not here expressed, as well concerning the reparation of the chancel as other things they must be repaired throughout by the parsons or vicars or other to whom it appertaineth after the diversity of approbated custom of the places.'

From *Lyndwood's Provinciale: the text of the canons therein contained, reprinted from the translation made in 1534*, edited by J.V. Bullard and H. Chalmer Bell (1929), pp.105–6.

William Lyndwood (1375?–1446), bishop of St David's, was the principal authority for English canon law, completing his *Constitutiones Provinciales Ecclesie Anglica[n]e* in 1443. Bullard and Bell state that the 1534 translation was made at the insistence of Henry VIII in the early years of the Reformation.

FEASTS AND FESTIVALS

Advent Sunday: the beginning of the ecclesiastical year celebrated on the fourth Sunday
before Christmas.

All Saints Day: 1 November, also known as All Hallows.

Annunciation or Lady Day: 25 March, one of the major Marian feasts in the pre-Reformation
church and an important date for half-yearly rents to be paid and financial matters to be
settled. Its counterpart in the autumn was 29 September, Michaelmas.

Ascension: one of the most important feasts in the Christian year celebrated on the fifth
Thursday or the fortieth day after Easter.

Assumption: a late feast, the story of the Virgin Mary's assumption into heaven coming from
the thirteenth-century *Golden Legend*.

Candlemas, Candilmesse, Candelmes, Candylmasse: 2 February. The combined celebration
of the Purification of the Virgin and the Presentation of Christ in the Temple.

Church Holy Day: 29 November, an alternative title for Dedication Day.

Corpus Christi: the first Thursday after Trinity Sunday. Promulgated in 1264, this feast
became one of the most important in the late medieval Church. Its widespread influence
touched not only the beliefs and practices of the western Church, but also art and architecture within church buildings.

Crouchmas, Crouchmass, Crowchemese, Crwchmesse: see Holy Cross Day.

Crysmas, Chrystmes: Christmas Day, 25 December.

Dedication Day: because of its position in Mildenhall's liturgical calendar, it is likely that
this was St Andrew's Day (30 November). Mildenhall church is sometimes accorded
two patron saints, St Mary and St Andrew, but there is no mention of the latter in its
pre-Reformation records. It has been suggested that St Andrew was a late addition to the
dedication, possibly even in the Victorian era.

Epiphany: 6 January, commemorating the baptism of Christ but, in the western Church, the
feast also celebrated the coming of the kings or the three magi from the east.

Hallomas, Hallowmass, Hallowmesse: mass celebrated at All Hallows (1 November), also
known as All Saints.

Hester: Easter.

Holy Cross Day: 3 May commemorated the finding of the true cross by St Helena in the
fourth century.

Lammas, Lamesse [*Loaf mass*]: the custom was to consecrate bread made from the first ripe
corn at mass on 1 August. Lammas is still celebrated in some rural parishes in Suffolk.

Low Sunday: first Sunday after Easter.

Mihelmes, Myhelmes, Myschellmas: Michaelmas: 29 September. This was one of the great
feasts of the Christian church, but also an important day in the agricultural year, when
rents were paid, half-yearly accounts settled and tenancies taken up or quitted. Michaelmas signified the end of the growing season and the onset of winter. Its counterpart in
the spring was Lady Day. See Annunciation.

Nativity of Christ: 25 December.

Nativity of the Virgin Mary: 8 September.

Octave: eight days after a feast.

Palm Sunday: the sixth Sunday in Lent commemorating the entry of Christ into Jerusalem.

Passion Sunday: the fifth Sunday in Lent.

Pentecost: also known as Whit Sunday. The feast celebrating the descent of the Holy Ghost
on the Apostles on the fiftieth day after Easter; and, after Easter, the second most important festival in the western Church.

Presentation of Christ: see Candlemas.

Purification: see Candlemas.

Quadragesima: the forty days of Lent.

Quinquagesima: the fiftieth day before Easter, beginning on the Sunday before Ash Wednesday.

Relic Sunday: the first Sunday after 7 July.

Rogationtide: Monday, Tuesday and Wednesday before Ascension, kept as a period of fast and supplication, especially for the coming harvest.

St Andrew: 30 November.

St Christopher: 25 July.

St David: 1 March.

St Edmund: 20 November. King, martyr and patron saint of East Anglia.

St George: 23 April. Patron saint of England from the mid-fourteenth century when Edward III founded the Order of the Garter under his patronage.

St James the Great of Compostela: 25 July.

St John the Baptist: 24 June.

St Michael: see Michaelmas.

St Nicholas: 6 December.

St Peter in Chains: 1 August. Also Lammas Day, see above.

St Philip and St James the Less: 1 May.

St Stephen: 26 December.

St Theodore: 11 November.

St Thomas Becket Day: 29 December, commemorating his murder in Canterbury cathedral in 1170.

Septuagesima: the third Sunday before Lent and the seventieth day before Easter.

Sexagesima: the second Sunday before Lent and the sixtieth day before Easter.

Trinity Sunday: a feast in honour of the Holy Trinity, which became particularly popular in England. St Thomas Becket was consecrated bishop on Trinity Sunday in 1162.

Vigil: a nocturnal service of prayer, or the eve of a festival, often kept as a fast.

Whit Sunday: the seventh Sunday after Easter commemorating the day of Pentecost when the converts in the primitive Church wore white robes.

GLOSSARY

abdoght: about.

agen: again.

albe, albeys, albys, aubre: alb-s, full length white linen garment over which a chasuble, dalmatic or tunic would be worn by a priest.

ale, all: see **churchale**.

almery, aumbry: a small cupboard or niche in the chancel wall in which vessels were kept containing wine and water for the mass.

almes, alms: charitable payments made to orphans, widows, the elderly poor and sick.

altar, altor, auter, autere, awter: the pre-Reformation stone table at which mass was celebrated.

ambling: a riding horse, moving at an amble.

amice, amys: a piece of linen worn by a priest at the neck to prevent soiling of the outer vestments.

anniversary: a re-enactment of the funeral service on the anniversary of death, also known as twelvemonth day, year-day, yeremynde, or obit.

antyfener, antiphoner, antevener: a large book containing music which accompanied the mass, often in two parts: *antiphonale sanctorum* (for the immoveable feasts of the saints) and *antiphonale temporalis* (for the moveable liturgical feasts). The antiphoner also contained scriptural passages sung before and after the psalms. See Lasko and Morgan, *Medieval Art in East Anglia*, p.46 and illus.69.

appurtenance: that which pertains as an accessory.

arme: arm or relic. See CWA, fol.50v.

armys: arms.

ashin, asschen: ashen, from the ash tree.

asperys, aspys: hasps.

at genst: against.

aube: see **albe**.

aubres, awbys: orphreys, embroidered panels of fabric applied to priests' garments.

aumbry: see **almery**.

awter: altar.

bbaddradd, baddred, badryk, baudrick, baudryk, bawderek, bawderyk, bawdre, bawdryc, bawdryce, bawdrye, bawdryke, bawdrykk, bawdrykyd: baldrick, here a leather strap with which a bell clapper was attached to a bell.

barker: a tanner.

barrys: bars of a window.

baudrick: see **bbaddradd**.

bawderek: see **bbaddradd**.

bede-roll: a list of the dead publicly prayed for at mass.

bedsydes: besides.

beguinage: a dwelling for Beguines, a semi-religious sisterhood founded in the Netherlands in the twelfth century.

bellys: bells.

beloss, belowe: bellow-s.

belsoller: bell chamber.

beqweth: bequeath, bequest.

bere: bier.

beretowel: bier cloth.

blake: black.

bokerham, bokerum: buckram, an open-weave fabric of linen; in early continental and English use, buckram was regarded as a linen fabric of fine quality.

bokyll, bookyl: buckle.

boord-s, bord, bourd, bowrds, bowrdes, burd: board or plank; or as in board and lodging.

borud: borrowed.

boshell, bosschell: bushel, a dry measure of eight gallons. See above, p.lxxiii.

boss: a stud or raised ornament.

boult-s: bolt-s.

bourd: see **boord**.

bourdeyns: metal bosses placed in the middle and near the corners of leather covered boards.

bovate: the area of land which a single oxen could till in one year.

bowrds: see **boord**.

breddyth, brede, bredthe, brodthe: breadth.

breviary: book containing daily prayers in the pre-Reformation church.

brode: broad.

brodthe: breadth.

browder, broyder-de: to embroider, to ornament with needlework. Browder may have become an occupational surname for one who sewed or mended cloth, as is suggested on CWA, fol.3r.

Brydys, Brygys: Bruges.

bryge-s, brygge: bridge-s.

bufe: from buffle (French), buffalo; strong oxhide leather dressed with oil.

burd: see **boord**.

burnet: burnt.

byndes: also known as binding threads, used for attaching thatch to the rafters beneath. See also **swayes**.

cace: case.

Candelmes, Candilmes, Candylmesse, Candyllmesse: see above, Feasts and Festivals.

candykkes, candylstykes, canstykys: candlesticks.

capon: castrated cock.

careng, careynge, carying: carrying.

carnary: see **charnel house**.

carryas: carriers.

carucate: 120 acres of land based on the area a team of oxen could plough in one year.

cassyk: cassock, a long sleeved garment buttoned at shoulder and waist.

castyn: casting or plastering.

celebrate: to perform the mass with proper rites and ceremonies.

censer, senser, sensere: the metal container for burning incense, a **thurible**.

certeyn: in East Suffolk a service chanted for the souls of the departed, ensuring that the inclusion of the donor's name would be read from the bede-roll and read in prayers from the pulpit; in West Suffolk this was known as a **sangrede**.

chalder, chaldes: a measure of capacity holding 32 bushels at this period.

chaleys, challes, challys: chalice. A pair of chalices represents a chalice with its paten, the small plate that covers the cup and bears the host: using 'a pair' in this sense is similar to a pair of scissors or spectacles, two parts making one whole, thus a pair of chalices does not mean two chalices just as a pair of organs does not mean two organs.

chamlet: a fine cloth made from the long hair of the angora goat.

chane-s, cheyn-s: chain-s.

charke: chalk.

charnel, carnary, charnel house: a building for bones disturbed by new burials or new building.

chasuble, chesebill, chesyble, chesybyl: the embroidered garment worn by the priest over the alb, originally a circular garment with an opening for the head.

chaunterys: chantries, an endowment set up for prayers to be said for nominated souls of the dead.

cheffe: chief.

cherche ale: see **churchale**.

chesebill, chesyble, chesybyl: see **chasuble**.

chetyl: kettle.

chetylys: shuttles.

cheyn-s: chain-s.

chrismatory, chrysmetory, cressmatory, cressmetore, crismatory, crysmetory: the vessel or box holding the three holy oils for (a) baptism, confirmation and ordination; (b) for the sick; (c) for exorcism.

churchale, cherche ale, chyrch all, chyrchall: a fund-raising occasion to profit the church.

Church Holy Day: see above, Feasts and Festivals, p.183.

churchreves, chyrcherevis: churchwardens.

chylde: child.

chymnes: chimneys.

chyrch all, chyrchall: see **churchale**.

chyrcherevis: see **churchreves**.

claper, clappetts, clapyr: clapper within a bell.

claspys: clasps.

classewrygtte: glasswright.

cleyying: plastering.

coap-ys: see **cope**.

cob: see **kobe**.

colerd: coloured.

colet, collect: a short prayer often containing one main petition.

colet boke, collect book, collet book: a book containing the collects.

coll: charcoal.

collect: see **colet**.

colme, collme: soot or coal dust.

comb, coomb: a dry measure equal to four bushels.

comesseneres: commissioners.

commun: communion.

confessor: one who hears confessions.

contyd: counted.

coomb: see **comb**.

cooper, cowper: a maker of barrels, buckets and tubs.

coote: cottage, cot or shed.

cope, coap-ys, copys: the semi-circular cloak of rich material worn by priests over their vestments.

coper, copir, copyr: copper.

coppell, copyll: couple.

Corperys Christi: see **Corpus Christi**.

corporas: the small cloth on which the chalice and paten, containing the body and blood of Christ, were placed.

corporas case: a bag of material, often embroidered or painted, in which the **corporas** was kept.

Corpus Christi: see above, Feasts and Festivals.

cotting: cutting.

coucher: a very large service book used in the medieval church, often supplied with its book stand.

cower, kower: cover.

cowncell: counsel.

187

cowper: see **cooper**.

credyll: cradle for hoisting builders or building materials.

cressmatory, cressmetore: see **chrismatory**.

crismatory: see **chrismatory**.

crost: cross.

crosse-cloth: a banner hanging from a cross.

crotchet: a metal hook.

crouchmasse, crwchmesse: see above, Feasts and Festivals, p.183.

crucifer: the server carrying the cross.

cruets (cruttes), crwttes: the flasks for holding wine and water, usually kept in the **aumbry**.

crwchmesse: see **crouchmasse**.

crysmetory, crymytory: see **chrismatory**.

dabebynge: daubing. See CWA, n.333.

dalmatic: an over tunic worn by the deacon over an **alb**.

deacon, decon: a minister immediately below the priest, able to baptise but not to celebrate the Eucharist.

Dec. Lic.: *in decretis licentiatus*, a licentiate in canon law.

Dedicacion, Dedycacacion, Dellykacyonn, Dydycacon Day: see above, Feasts and Festivals, p.183.

dext: desk.

diaper, diaperwork, diapir, diapre: cloth patterned by the interweaving of threads, extensively used for altar cloths.

dirige: the opening word of the antiphon in the Office of the Dead. The English word *dirge* is derived from this.

dirtryngs, distryngs, dysstryngs: a writ directing the sheriff to distrain; to seize goods, especially goods for debt.

dore, dower: door.

dormant, dormantte: a joist; a large beam lying across a room.

dornyxe: a coarse damask used for curtains and carpets from Doornijk, in modern Belgium.

double feast: in the Roman missal and breviary, these were the more important feasts on which the antiphons were sung in their entirety, before and after the psalms.

dow-s: dove-s.

dower: see **dore**.

drayng', drenyn: draining, referring to draining the **paschal candle** after it was extinguished. It was used again the following Easter.

drenyn: see **drayng'**.

droopys: drops.

dune: dun.

Dydycacon Day: see **Dedicacion Day**.

dysstryngs: see **dirtryngs**.

earnest, ernest: a pledge or instalment.

Easter sepulchre: a purpose built structure in wood or stone, or a tomb of a patron of the church, on or in which the host was placed during the last days of Lent from Maundy Thursday to Easter morning. A tomb standing to the left of the high altar was often utilized, thus making it a prime position in the church.

ell, eln: a cloth measure equal to 1¼ yards (45 inches) and originally a measure of length taken from the arm.

enfeoff: to grant out as a feoff or estate.

eren: iron.

ernest: see **earnest**.

erthetyde: time on earth, a life time.

estriche: ostrich.

estriche board: timber from the Baltic.

fader: father.

fagett: faggot.

fauttes: faults.

fearme, ferme, fferme: rent.

fellapis, Feluppys: pertaining to St Philip.

feoffee: trustee.

ferme: see **fearme**.

fere: fire.

feyng: to fay or fey, to cleanse of mud and filth.

feyrspott: fair ground.

ffedyng: feeding.

fferme: see **fearme**.

ffrontlet-s, ffrontelette-s: frontal.

foder, fodder, fother, fothyer: lead weighing between 19 cwt and one ton sufficient to cover 160 square feet: when supplied in sheets or webs it was more expensive than if it were purchased as raw material. See Salzman, *Building in England*, pp.263–64.

foldage: the practice of feeding sheep in movable folds.

forehors: the foremost horse in a team, the leader.

fote: many crosses stood in a cross-foot which enabled them to be free-standing: the base of the cross was often threaded to receive a staff in order that the cross might be used as a processional cross.

fother, fothyer: see **foder**.

fount: font.

friars minor: the order of Franciscans or Greyfriars.

fustian: a coarse cloth made of cotton and flax; or fustian of Naples, a cloth similar to cotton velvet.

fyn: fine.

gardelys, gerdelles, gyrdyllys: girdles used for tying **albs** or other loose liturgical garments.

garled, garlyd: spotted or speckled.

garnish: a set of vessels for table use, especially of pewter.

garters: a decoration often embroidered on or woven into fabric.

gathering: collection.

gaudied: ornamented.

gemewys: a hinge consisting of an identical pin-plate and hanging-plate with no strap. See Salzman, *Building in England*, pp.298–99.

ger, gere, geyr: gear or general stuff. 'To wash the church gere' was to launder the small items of linen.

gerdelles: see **gardelys**.

gere, geyr: see **ger**.

gild: a brotherhood, confraternity or association formed for the mutual aid and protection of its members: there were also female gilds, although these were not so common.

glacewryeth: see **glasewryth**.

glaser, glasery-s, glasser-s, glasyars, glaysair: glazier-s.

glasewryth, glaswreyt, glacewryeth: glasswright, glazier.

glasser-s, glasyars: see **glaser**.

glaysair: see **glaser**.

gluyeng: glueing.

grat, greate: grating, framework of bars or laths fixed in an opening, often to deter animals entering the churchyard. Also 'a greate': of work done at a fixed price. (See CWA, fol.21v for both meanings.)

grayle, grail, grayleys: the gradual, a service book or books containing music for the mass, two often being sufficient, one on either side of the choir.

greate: see **grat**.

grete, grett: great.

gronsell, grounsell: ground sill, the bottom plate of timber into which upright members are tenoned.

gryndall: a narrow ditch or drain.

gyfth: gift.

gylld: gild.

gynne: a pulley with a rope fixed above the position to which a load was to be moved. The rope had a hook at one end, the other end passing round an axle rotated by a wheel.

gyrdylls, gyrdyllys: see **gardelys**.

Halamesse, Halowmasse, Hallowmesse: see above, Feasts and Festivals, p.183.

hallday: holiday.

hallowater stoppe, halywater stoppe: holy water stoup.

Hallowmesse: see **Halamesse**.

halowyng: hallowing, blessing.

halywater stoppe: see **hallowater stoppe**.

hempe: hemp or *cannabis sativa* grown for processing as canvas, rope etc.

hers, herse: hearse or Easter sepulchre, a wooden housing to the north of the chancel on or in which the bread representing Christ's body was kept from Maundy Thursday until Easter Day. A funeral herse was a wooden frame covered by a pall.

hester: Easter.

hew, hewyng: to cut away, cutting away.

heyd: horse hide. This was constantly in demand for covering **baudricks** (see **bbaddradd**).

heyer, heyre: haircloth.

high altar: the principal altar which stood in the chancel at the east end of the church. Gifts to the high altar were customary payments willed to the parish priest in lieu of tithes forgotten, and therefore they were not entered in churchwardens' accounts.

hoche, huche, hutche, hutgche: a chest or cupboard.

hoggett: a yearling sheep.

holy rood: the crucifix on the rood-beam.

honder, hunderde: hundred.

horgans, horganes, horganys: organs.

hosecloth: cloth for a variety of hosiery and stockings.

hoselyng, houseling: the houseling cloth was held below the mouth of the recipient at mass to catch any crumbs that might fall during the administration.

host: the bread or wafer representing the body of Christ which was offered to communicants.

housel: from OE *húsel*, sacrifice, meaning the consecrated bread at mass.

houseling: see **hoselyng**.

hownssis: ounces (oz.).

huche, hutche, hutgche: see **hoche**.

hunderde: see **honder**.

hyllmony: see **ill money**.

hyryng: hiring.

hyusse: hoist.

ierne, iyern, iyerne-s, iynr, iyren: iron-s; see **yeorn** for further spellings.

ill money, illmony, hyllmony: coin with no monetary value.

indulgence: see **pardon**.

inkyll: linen tape.

iyern, iyerne-s, iynr, iyren: see **ierne**.

kersey: coarse woollen cloth.

kerver: carver.

kewynges, kivering, koveryng: covering.

kivering: see **kewynges**.

klapers: clappers.

knopp-is, knoppy-s: a bud, loop or tuft.
kobe, cob: a short legged, stout variety of horse.
koveryng: see **kewynges**.
kower: see **cower**.
kykeyng: keeping.

laberar-s, labborous: labourer-s.
laces: used to fasten clerical garments.
lach-es: latch-es.
Lammas, Lammesse: see above, Feasts and Festivals, p.183.
lancicle, lanncetyll: long settle.
lanter, lanthorne: lantern.
lasse: lace.
laten, laton, latent, latten: a copper alloy which could be buffed to a high polish: it was often used for church plate which was then silvered or gilded.
lates, lattes, lettes: lattice, often fitted in tower windows.
lathis: laths as in lath and plaster.
laton: see **laten**.
laver, lawer: a vessel or basin for washing.
lawn: linen.
lectere, lectorne, lectron, letorne, leyter, leytorn: lectern.
leder, Leeder, lethyr: leather.
legend, legent: the lesson book, containing lessons read at matins, etc.
lekyll: little.
lenton, lentun: lenten, pertaining to Lent, the forty-day season of abstinence from Ash Wednesday to Easter eve.
lenthyn: lengthening.
lethyr: see **leder**.
letorne: see **lectere**.
lettes: see **lates**.
leyter, leytorn: see **lectere**.
lip glue: see **mouth or lip glue**.
lode: load or an artificial water course.
lomys: looms.
lyne: line or cord.
lynen, lynyg, lynnynge, lynyn, lynynge: linen.

mandorla: an almond-shaped panel or decorative space from the Italian for almond.
manual, manuell: the book containing occasional offices such as baptism, marriage, etc.
marcyment, marsement, mercyment: amercement or penalty.
mark: unit of money worth 13s. 4d., half a mark being 6s. 8d.
marsement: see **marcyment**.
martiloge, martlage, martloge: martyrology, a list or register of martyred saints.
maygame: a play performed on May Day.
medyng: mending.
meer, mere: a boundary, pool or a lake.
mensa: altar table or altar slab.
mercer: a dealer in textile fabrics.
mercyment: see **marcyment**.
mere: see **meer**.
mese: a mead, field or pasture.
meslin: mixed grain, usually wheat and rye.
messe boke: the mass book containing everything necessary for the celebration of mass.
messe-s: masse-s, the service of holy eucharist, the chief service of the medieval church.
messuage: a dwelling and offices with the adjoining lands appropriated to the household.

191

mett: meat.

Michel quarter: Michaelmas quarter which started on 29 September, St Michael's Day.

Mihelmes, Mihilmes, Myhellmasse, Myhellmesse, Myhylmas, Myschelmas: Michaelmas: see above, Feasts and Festivals, p.183.

missal: see **messe boke**.

miunny, mony: money.

modium: a measure of capacity, dry and liquid, of varying size, commonly rendered by bushel. See above, p.lxxiii.

mony: see **miunny**.

mouth or lip glue: a compound made by boiling glue and sugar, used for joining paper. It was moistened with the tongue.

mukd: mould.

Myhellmasse, Myhellmesse, Myhylmas: see **Mihelmes**.

mylle-s: mill-s.

Myschelmas: see **Mihelmes**.

napre, napry: napery, linen.

navykyll: incense boat or ship.

nayeles, nayels: nails.

net: neat or cattle.

net heurd: cow herd.

noble: unit of money worth 6s. 8d. or half a mark, a mark being worth 13s. 4d.

norse, norys: nurse.

obligacon, oblygacon: a contract or agreement to secure repayment of money which has been lent.

obsequies: funeral rites and solemnities.

obulus: a halfpenny, usually abbreviated to *ob.*

obyte: obit, see **anniversary**.

on to: unto.

opus anglicanum: literally 'English work', the much prized English embroidery worked on linen in split long-and-short stitch and underside-couching.

ordinal, ordnory: ordinal, a manual indicting variations to the holy office during the year.

ordles: organs.

organce, orgin-s, orgony-s: organ-s.

orphreys: elaborately embroidered borders of cloth, applied to priests' garments or other hangings in the church.

ostilments: furnishings.

overwhyt, owereyht: overweight.

ow, owt: owe.

ower: our or over.

owereyht: see **overwhyt**.

owght: out.

owyr: hour.

owyt: owe.

pakthred: a particularly strong twine or thread used in book binding.

pall, palle, paule, pawle: a cloth covering for a coffin or, in a funeral procession, cloth thrown over a **herse** covering the body which was then carried on a bier.

pament, pammen, pammets, payment, paymet: tile-s made from East Anglian clays.

pamenting: paving.

parafraces: paraphrases of Erasmus, a commentary on the Gospels by Erasmus which Edward VI ordered to be placed in every church in 1547.

pardon or **indulgence**: a pardon or indulgence involved an exchange of money for the promise of salvation.

pareschecherke: parish clerk.

pascal, pascale, paschal, paskall, passkall: pertaining to Easter. When used alone (CWA, fol.2v) it refers to the paschal candle.

paten: the small plate on top of the chalice which bore the host.

paule, pawle: see **pall**.

pax: a small plate of precious metal or gilded base metal engraved or painted with the Crucifixion. It was kissed by the priest and the congregation at mass.

payment, paymet: pavement; see **pament**.

pece, pese-s: piece-s.

pecenge, pesenge: piecing.

peckookes: peacocks.

pentyse: pentice, a lean-to building with a single slope roof.

pese-s: see **pece**.

pesenge: see **pecenge**.

peynes: pains.

peyxte-s, pykse-s, pyxe-s: the box which housed the host: the outer shell was often made from ordinary material such as wood or copper; but the lining which would come in contact with the host, Christ's body, was made from the most expensive material that could be afforded such as gold, silver, enamel or ivory.

piscina: a niche, usually to the south of an altar, in which the priest washed the chalice and paten after mass, now invaluable for identifying sites of earlier masses.

pistill, pystell book: an epistle book.

placebo: from the Latin, I shall be pleasing, the opening word from vespers in the Office of the Dead.

planch: plank.

planchering: inserting a wooden floor.

pleynt: a complaint.

pond, pownd, pund: pound.

porteferium, portiforium, **portesse, porteous**: a breviary or book of daily prayers.

posnet: a small metal vessel having a spout and three feet.

powdered, powdirde, powdred: scattered with embroidered emblems.

pownd: see **pond**.

ppeyr: pair.

predella: the uppermost step or platform on which the priest stands to celebrate the mass.

preste-s: priest-s.

processioners, processyoners, prosecenary, prosessenary, processionary: the illustrated office-book containing music for anthems and for the responses sung in processions at mass, both at Rogationtide and on feast days, the illustrations showing the position taken by the clergy during procession. See Williamson, 'Liturgical music in the late medieval parish church', pp.203–6; Wordsworth and Littlehales, *The Old Service Books of the English Church*, pl. opposite p.166. In the Great Hospital processional from Norwich (BL, Add. MS 57,534), the coloured illustrations show, by means of an artistic shorthand, the positions of the priests, thurifer, crucifer etc.

prysed: priced.

pund: see **pond**.

purcesses, purssis, pursys: purses.

purfile: a wrought or decorated border, an embroidered edge to a garment.

purssis, pursys: see **purcesses**.

pycter: picture.

pykse-s: see **peyxte-s**.

pynnys: pins.

pystyll bokys: epistle books.

pyxe-s: see **peyxte-s**.

quadragesima, xl: see above, Feasts and Festivals, p.184.

quarter, qwarter: either three months, a quarter of a year, sometimes referred to as **term**, or a fourth.

quarterage: a quarterly payment.

quere, qwer, qwyer: choir.

quetheword, quethod, quethowrde, queword, quheod, qwe, qwethe, qwetheworde, qwethwurd, qwhetod: a customary bequest made to the parish church by a testator: in wills this is invariably entered immediately below the gifts to the high altar and paid into church funds through the churchwardens' accounts.

queyres: quires.

quinquagesima, l: the fifty days preceding Easter and the Sunday preceding Ash Wednesday.

quytest, quytus: quittance.

qwarter: see **quarter**.

qwer: choir.

rail, rayle: a garment of fine linen formerly worn by women around the neck.

rasse, rassyng: erasing.

raylbar: horizontal member of a timber-framed wall.

rayle: see **rail**.

reband, rebon: ribbon.

receayte, reseytes: receipts.

redys: grill-like objects keeping the warp evenly spaced and the weft straight.

relikes, relykes, relyks: relics.

rengars: bell ringers.

reparyng, reperyyng: repairing, reparation.

resaytes, reseytes: see **receayte**.

reve: either a high official, bailiff or steward; or to pull or tear.

reysthys: rushes.

rochet, rochetys: sleeveless surplice or surplices particularly suitable for use by the clergy at baptisms.

rod, rode, rood: either a measurement of 5½ yards; or the cross which stood on the rood beam or hung above it at the junction of the chancel and nave.

rode lofte: the gallery supported on the rood beam, situated between the chancel and nave.

roffe, roufe: roof.

Romescot, Romeschot, Rumscote, Rumskot, Rumskote: an annual payment made to St Peter's, Rome, sometimes called Peter's Pence.

rood: see **rod**.

rop, roop, roopys, ropeis, ropis, roppis, ropys: rope-s.

rosett, russet: a coarse homespun woollen cloth.

rowell, ruell: the light or lights which hung before the rood, also called the common light. The rowell was sometimes circular and supported several candles.

rowll: a small sharp pointed wheel on the end of a spur to prick a horse into action.

russet: see **rosett**.

sacre bell, sacry: the sacring bell rung three times at the elevation of the host.

saler: a salt-celler.

salter, saulter, sawlter, sawte, sawter: the psalter, a book containing the psalms and canticles.

sangerd, sanggered, sangrede: possibly from OE *sang-read*, 'sing-read', another name for **anniversary**, a commemorative service in which the souls of the dead were remembered. In West Suffolk a sangrede was a perpetual service, cheaper than a chantry, financed perhaps by a gift of property, the rental from which paid priest. The name of the dead person would be included in the bede-roll, the prayers being said from the pulpit.

sanntes bell: sanctus bell, rung immediately before the mass.

saulter: see **salter**.

saunde: sand.

194

sawdde, sodder, soder, sodre, sondyng, sowd, sowde, sowder, sowderyng, sowdyg, sowdyng, sowdyr, sowed, sowyd: solder.

sawlter, sawte, sawter: see **salter**.

say: fine textured cloth resembling serge for clothes and furnishing, sometimes containing silk thread.

sayvype: no interpretation has been found for this word on CWA, fol.44r.

scheche, scherche, sheche, sherche: church.

schelynges: shillings.

schepe, shepe-s, shippe, shippis, shyp, shypp: a vessel called a ship or **navykyll**, containing incense.

scherche: see **scheche**.

schet: sheet.

schoryng, skoryng, skowryng, skuyng, sqworyng: scouring or cleaning.

schotyng: melting and moulding or sheeting (of lead).

schrewyng, schryvys: shriving.

schryfft: shrift, shrive.

schryvyng pue: see **shryvy, schryvyng pue**.

schryvys: see **schrewyng**.

schyn, skennys: skin-s.

sedge: coarse rushes and grasses, used when ridging a thatched roof.

sedilia: the seats in the south wall of the chancel for the celebrating cleric, deacon and subdeacon.

selyng: ceiling.

sencere-s, sensere, sensyr: censer-s.

sentens boke: a reference to the Great Sentence, not a book but the form of excommunication read in church four times a year 'when the people is most plenary in church'. See Wordswoth and Littlehales, *Old Service Books of the English Church*, pp.270–72.

septuagesima, lxx: see above, Feasts and Festivals, p.184.

sepulker, sepulcker, sepukyr, sepulter, sepulture: a tomb.

servardes: servants.

seventh and thirtieth day: referring to prayers celebrated one week and one month after a death.

sexagesima, lx: see above, Feasts and Festivals, p.184.

sextyn: sexton. See Introduction, n.138.

shepe-s: see **schepe**.

sheche, sherche: see **scheche**.

shippe, shippis: see **schepe**.

shottyng: melting metal.

shoyng: shoeing.

shryvy, schryvyng pue: shriving stools or pews where the penitent was absolved by the priest. See Nichols, *Seeable Signs*, pp. 222–41, pl.54; Duffy, *Stripping of the Altars*, pp.54–68.

shyp, shypp: see **schepe**.

skains: skeins.

skennys: see **schyn**.

skomer, skummer: a shallow ladle.

skoryng, skowryng: see **schoryng**.

skribis: scribes.

skummer: see **skomer**.

skuyng: see **schoryng**.

slay-e: a tool used to separate the threads of the warp and in 'beating up' weft.

smyht, smythe: smith.

sodder, soder, sodre: see **sawdde**.

solar, soler, soller: an upper storey. With reference to the holy rood it refers to the painted canopy above the crucifix.

sond, sonde: sand.

sondyng: see **sawdde**.

soper: supper.

sorplese, sorplyse, sorpples, surpleces, surples, surplyces, surplysse, surplysse, swrpe-lyse, swrplyse, syrples, syrplesse, syrplessys: surplice-s, a white linen over-garment with wide sleeves worn by choristers and assistants other than priests.

sowd, sowde, sowder, sowderyng, sowdyg, sowdyng, sowdyr, sowed: see **sawdde**.

sowht: sought.

sowyd: see **sawdde**.

sparver: a canopy for a bed or cradle.

spiking: see **spyken**.

splent-s: lath-s used in walls and tied in with string.

sponys: spoons.

spowte-s: spout-s, often made of lead, supported by iron stirrups. See Salzman, *Building in England*, p.266.

spyken, spiking: a headless sharp nail. See Salzman, *Building in England*, p.304.

sqworyng: see **schoryng**.

stafve-s: stave.

staunch: a lock to raise or lower the level of water. This was all that was needed to keep water levels right and the traffic moving.

stawys: stays.

stell: a stand, especially for a barrel.

stepple, stepull: a steeple, which in connection with Suffolk churches means a tower.

steyned, steynyng: stained, staining or painting.

stock, stopp, stoup: a basin for holy water.

stolle-s, stolys: stall or stool.

stonyd: uncastrated (of a horse).

stonys: stones.

stopp: see **stock**.

stopys: stoppers.

storopes: stirrups.

stott: castrated ox or a draught horse, probably castrated.

stoup: see **stock**.

strakys: wooden spars.

subdeacon: a religious order above the acolyte but below the deacon.

surpleces, surples, surplyces, surplysse, surplysse: see **sorplese**.

sustentation: support or maintenance.

sute (of vestments): a full suit comprised the clothing and apparels for priest, deacon and subdeacon, which might run to over thirty articles.

swayes, wayes: properly known as sways, alternatively spars, they were customarily made of hazel and used for pinning down thatch, frequently being used along the ridge to make an attractive pattern.

swepyng: sweeping.

swrpelyse, swrplyse: see **sorplese**.

sypres: Cyprus, relating to cypress wood.

syrples, syrplesse, syrplessys: see **sorplese**.

tabard: a short coat, sleeveless or with short sleeves or shoulder pieces, common menswear.

tabernacle: a stone or wooden canopied structure not unlike sentry boxes in shape, but often beautifully carved and highly coloured containing a painted or carved image. Many were hacked down during the Reformation. See Dymond and Paine, *Spoil of Melford*, p.1 n.3.

tabourer: one who plays the tabor, a small drum usually played with one stick.

taklyng: tackling.

taske: tax, task.

tear: fine, delicate.

tentyr hokys: sharp, hooked nails on a frame for stretching cloth.

term, terme: a limited period of time, for example a quarter of a year.

thache, thake, thakke, thatche, thathe: a generic term for many types of roofing including wheat straw, rye straw and reed. It was commonly used for roofing in the fen districts. See Salzman, *Building in England*, pp.225–26.

thachyng, thakeng: thatching.

thake, thakke: see **thache**, also **thachyng**.

thands: the hands.

thatche, thathe: see **thache**.

therde: thread.

thevis: thieves.

throme-ed: fringed.

throw: through.

thrums: a row or fringe of threads.

thurible: see **censer**.

thurifer: the server carrying the **censer**.

tithe: a tenth part of the produce of land or stock, allotted for the maintenance of the clergy and other church purposes.

trivet: a three-footed stand.

tong: tongue.

too: two.

towll, tuell-s, tuelle-s: towel-s.

troper: the service book containing embellishments to the text of the mass or of the breviary office, sung by the choir.

trosyng, truss, trussing, trusyng: to tighten a bell up on its stock after it has worked loose.

tryyng: to sift, strain, separate or purify.

tuell-s, tuelle-s: see **towll**.

tuinyng: tuning.

tumberell: a cart with two wheels.

tunicle-s, tunycle, tunyky, tunykyl-s, tynycle-s: the outer liturgical garment worn by the subdeacon over the alb.

twylly, twill: a cloth with a raised diagonal pattern running across it, made by the weft passing under one and over two threads of the warp.

twyn: twin, twain.

tym, tymys: time-s.

tynycle-s: see **tunicle-s**.

tyssew, tyssw: tissue.

unce-s, uncys, unnces, unsis: ounce-s (oz.).

vages: wages.

vayll: veil.

vellum, velym: a superior writing surface made from calf, kid or lamb skins.

vesitacion, vicytation, vysytacon: visitation referring either to the meeting of the Virgin Mary and Elizabeth in the New Testament; or to the annual visitation of the archdeacon or other official to approve the churchwardens' inventories.

veyle: veil.

vicary: vicar.

vicytation: see **vesitacion**.

vigil: a nocturnal service of prayer, or the eve of a festival, often kept as a fast.

voyder: a tray, basket or other vessel into which dirty receptacles are placed during a meal.

vysytacon: see **vesitacion**.

wadges, wagis, wagus, wagys: wages.

warke, wok: work.

warkemansche, workmachip: workmanship.
wayes: see **swayes**.
wayle: veil.
wayne cart: wagon.
webbys: webs or rolls of lead used for roofing or for coffins.
weche: week.
weker: vicar.
wele, wely-s, weyll, whell, whelle: wheel-s.
werday, worday: workday.
werse: verse.
wether: a ram, especially one that has been castrated.
wetlether: white leather.
wey: way as in road or weigh as in weighing.
weyeffys: wives.
weyht: weight.
weyle, weyll: veil.
weyr: wire.
whell, whelle: see **wele**.
whith, whyght, wyght, wyht, wy, wytte: white.
whytyng: whitewashing.
wok: see **warke**.
wong: part of an open field or meadow.
woole: either wool or woole, an archaic word from Kent meaning to twist a chain around the neck of a horse, Halliwell, *Dictionary of Archaic Words*, II, p.938. Its use on CWA, fol.32v probably meant attaching staging to the steeple with tackling.
worday: see **werday**.
workmachip: see **warkemansche**.
wryghtyng: writing.
wryth: wright.
wy, wyght, wyht: see **whith**.
wythys: willows.
wytte: see **whith**.

year-day: see **anniversary**.
yeard-s, yerde-s: yard-s.
yeorn, yerne-s, yerren, yoron, yryn, yron, yrone, yyern: iron-s; see **ierne** for further spellings.
yerde-s: see **yeard-s**.
yerne-s, yerren: see **yeorn**.
yerss: wires.
yerys: years.
yngom: income.
ynkyll: linen tape used for string, garters etc.
yoron, yryn, yron, yrone, yyern: see **yeorn**.

NOTES ON PEOPLE

ALEN, John, churchwarden *c.*1511–14. See further Breen 2008, p.70

ALEXANDER, ALEXANDRE, ALEXAUNDER, ALYSANDER, ALYSSANDER

George, weaver, 1575 (SROB 500/1/34/68). For his will see Appendix 2:54.

James, painter, 1553 (SROB, IC 500/1/16/119). Paid £1 in part payment of an obligation. Was paid for mending the bible on two occasions and for noting the processionary in 1541–42 and 1551–52. For his will see Appendix 2:49.

John, *c.*1542. Mended the veil cloth and also Backhotte's bell. Paid for keeping the bells and for mending the great organs.

ANNABBLE, of Bury. In 1551–52 paid the churchwardens £3 2s. for the lectern which weighed 209 lb. Acquired 8 lb of copper for 3s. 4d. See CWA, fol.42v.

AUSTEN, AUSTEYN, HAUSTEYN

John, chaplain. Paid 6s. 8d. to the churchwardens in 1503–04, presumably for a quetheword from a former parishioner. See further Breen 2008, p.75.

Robert, citizen and salter of London and a native of Mildenhall. Paid 6s. 8d. to bury his mother in the church. CWA, fol.3v.

BAGOT, BAGGOTT, BAKHOT, BAKHOTE

John, 1464 (SROB, IC 500/2/10/397). See Appendix 2:15 for his will in which he left his silver girdle to the honour of the Trinity and Saints Edmund and Nicholas to be worn by one of the parish clerks of Mildenhall on the vigils of both these saints. His name appears with that of John Chylderston at the top of Coll. fol.9r in 1449, directly above the names of the three incoming wardens.

Nicholas. Richard's brother, his co-executor with others.

Nicholas, Master. Stands surety for a debt *c.*1505–14. CWA, fol.47r. See further Breen 2008, pp.58 and 68.

Master. Supplies board for a door in 1505.

Richard, 1472 (TNA, PCC Wattys 19). See Appendix 2:19 for his will.

Simon, chaplain. A member of the wealthy Mildenhall family of mercers. Appears in Richard Bakhot's will as executor in 1434 (NRO, NCC Surflete 181) and as executor for Thomas Brynkele in 1439 (NRO, NCC Doke 87). Later appointed rector of Worlington, the parish on Mildenhall's southern boundary.

William. Died 1461 (SROB, IC 500/2/9/303, 1461). See Appendix 2:12 for his will.

BAKER, John [*recte* Barker]. His wife sold thatch to the churchwardens for 1s. 2d. in 1447.

BAKHOT, BAKHOTE. See BAGOT.

BALLIS, William. Elected churchwarden for the year 1505. See further Breen 2008, pp.31, 63 and 86.

BARFORD, BARFORTH, Roger, priest. Parish chaplain, dying sometime between 6 November and 4 December 1504 (NRO, NCC 27 Ryxe 27). See Appendix 2:30 for his will. Bequeathed 10s. to the reparation of Mildenhall church. In 1514, the mass book which he had given was bound and, in the same year, a further 4 marks was paid for his quetheword. Left 4 marks for a priest to sing for the souls of himself, his parents and Sir William Day, a fellow chaplain. John Dey, who paid Barforth's quetheword, was churchwarden at the time of Barforth's death and also was one of Barforth's executors. The entry in the 1514 accounts is a good example of how long an interval there could be between death and the payment of a bequest. See further Breen 2008, p.74.

BASSETT, George, churchwarden c.1550. Resigned the following year. Was paid 6s. for 'a boke of the new order', CWA, fol.38v, and a further 1s. 8d. c.1559, CWA, fol.48r.

BERTON, alias WATTS, John. 1441 (NRO, NCC Doke 164). See Appendix 2:4. Executor to John Mason, the chaplain.

BRADLEY, John. Elected churchwarden in 1514.

BRAY, William, 1503 (SROB, IC 500/2/12/128). See Appendix 2:27 for his will, in which he referred to his shop in the market. He left a widow, Joan, and a daughter of the same name. See further Breen 2008, pp.52 and 66.

BREON, BRION, BRYON, BYRON, Robert, *fl.*1507–17. Carpenter hired to make a door and 'the crown of Our Lady'. Repaired the 'credyll', the shriving pew and the herse.

BREWER, BRUER, John, woodcarver. Mended the paschal head, carved angels for the paschal head and also repaired the lectern in 1507–08.

BRYAN, John, parish chaplain, 1452 (NRO, NCC Aleyn 215). See Appendix 2:9 for his will. Elected churchwarden in 1449, having inherited property in Mildenhall from his father, John (NRO, NCC Surflete 172). Executor to John Speed, 1438 (NRO, NCC Doke 67). Co-executor to Robert Sopere's will at Barton Mills, 1439 (SROB, IC 500/2/9/7). Executor to Thomas Brynkele of Mildenhall (NRO, NCC Doke 87). Supervisor for the estate of William Curteys, the elder, of Mildenhall, 1443 (SROB, IC 500/2/9/40) and the estate of Isabel Fysch of Worlington, 1448 (SROB, IC 500/2/9/63). Gave a stone called The Coyne for the cistern to the church (CWA, fol.12v). Churchwarden from 1449–52. He died in 1454.

BYRON. See BREON.

CADGE, Simon, of Bury. Supplier of lead c.1552–1553, when windows were repaired and the vestry re-roofed. CWA, fols 43r, 44v and 48r.

CANNAS, John, 1473 (SROB, IC 500/2/11/15). Son of William Cannas (NRO, NCC Doke 179, 1440) inheriting land and tenements with liberty of fold. William Gylbyn and Cannas paid to the churchwardens 24s. raised at the 'Halywell' churchale in 1453.

CHAPMAN

John, of Cakestrete. Churchwardens received 6s. 8d. for his soul in 1452.

John, carpenter. See **FLEWMAN** below.

William. Between the fourth Sunday of Lent and Trinity Sunday in 1446 he made ten payments of 3s. 4d., recorded in the Collections. Neighbour of John Frere in Beck Row.

William, the testator of SROB, IC 500/2/10/379, may not be the same person.

CHARNOCKE, CHARNOKE, William. Died in 1500 (NRO, NCC Popy 571). See Appendix 2:26 for his will and see further Breen 2008, pp.32 and 86.

CHESTON, CHISTON, CHYSTAN, CHYSTON

John, of West Row. In 1528 resigned as churchwarden.

Robert, c.1546, left 3s. 4d. to Mildenhall church.

Thomas, of West Row. In 1528–29 he donated 3s. 4d. to the church. Died in the following year, the churchwardens receiving 1s. 8d. towards the reparation of the Lady chapel. In 1524, he was worth £20. See Hervey 1910, p.230.

CHILDERSTON, CHYLDERSTON, CHYLDERSTONE, CHYLDRISTON.

This is a surname that appeared frequently in the Mildenhall accounts. In 1844 there were still seven Childerstones (Edward, Francis, Henry, Isaac, James, Jonathan and Thomas) living in Holywell Row and Wilde Street. By 1885 there were three, living in Beck Row and Holywell Row, see White, *History of Suffolk 1844* (repr.1970) p.597 and White, *History of Suffolk 1885*, p.503.

John, 1455 (SROB, IC 500/2/9/179. Bequeathed ewes, lambs and a pair of fuller's shears. Left to his wife, Margaret, a messuage in 'Le' Halywell and property in Mildenhall market place (to be sold for soul prayers) and beehives to provide tapers for the light of Blessed Mary in Mildenhall church. Margaret and John Sly, vicar of Soham, were his executors.

John, the elder, 1504 (SROB, IC 500/2/13/156). See Appendix 2:28 for his will. See further Breen 2008, pp.35 and 39.

Katherine, 1568 widow (SROB, W1/2/82). See Appendix 2:53 for her will.

Simon, 1454 (SROB, IC 500/2/9/230). Brother of John and William. Paid 3s. 4d. for prayers to be said for his daughter, Isabelle Bryghtwell. Bequeathed 100s. towards buying a bell or a vestment and left money to the gilds of Corpus Christi and St Katherine. Christian, his wife, and her son, John Bryghwelle, were executors.

Thomas. In 1452 the sum of 3s. 4d. was received by the churchwardens for the soul of Margaret, his daughter, and three weeks later 2s. was received for the soul of William, son of Thomas Chylderstone. See further Breen 2008, pp.32 and 86.

William. Elected churchwarden 1551 and retired the following year.

CLARKE, CLERKE

Simon. Retired as churchwarden 1553–54.

William. Elected churchwarden in 1546. In 1548 the churchwardens' accounts showed a further £23 10s. had been received from the sale of church plate.

CLEMENT, John. Churchwarden *c*.1511–14. See further Breen 2008, pp.20 and 62.

CLERKE. See CLARKE.

CLYFTE, Richard. Elected churchwarden in 1543.

COLE, COLLES

Goodwife. Supplied board and lodging for visiting workmen in 1550 and later that year supplied refreshment for the glaziers when the glass was removed. See CWA, fols 41r and 43v.

Richard, tanner, 1547 (TNA, PCC Populwell 7). See Appendix 2:46 for his will.

Thomas. Bought the sepulchre and part of the organ fittings for 17s. 2d. in 1551. CWA, fol.42v. Thomas Hart bought some of the timber from the sepulchre.

CONSTABE, CONSTABILL, CONSTABOLE

Denise. Died in 1473 (SROB, IC 500/2/11/4). See Appendix 2:18 for his will.

Richard. Churchwardens received 3s. 4d. for a processionary sold to Constable in 1447 and a further 3s. 4d. for the sale of another book in 1449. See Coll. fols 4v, 5v.

COOK, Stephen. Elected churchwarden 6 November 1553.

COOLE

Richard, timber merchant 1540–1541, referred to as Coole the carpenter.

Robert. In 1540–41 made the church gate, and later made the bier, a window in the school house and the tower ladder. He also worked on the new bell frame.

COOTES, Thomas, tailor. Paid for making the poor child's coat. CWA, fol.36r.

COSTYN, COSTYNG

Robert, *fl*.1505–07. Owed 6s. 8d. for his mother's quetheword which was paid two years later.

William, churchwarden *c.*1511–14. Was paid 1s. for washing the church gear after Thomas Hopper retired.

COTTES, Thomas. Retired as churchwarden in 1553–54.

CURREY, Humphrey. Elected churchwarden in 1551.

CURTEYS, Matilda, 1485 (SROB, IC 500/2/11/337). See Appendix 2:23 for her will.

DEY

John. Mentioned frequently in the accounts and in wills, certainly from the beginning of the sixteenth century. See further Breen 2008, pp.47 and 90.

William, 1506 (NRO, NCC Garnon 106). See Appendix 2:31 for his will; also Breen 2008, p.70.

DOBYN, John. Described as parish clerk in the will of William Cannas, 1440 (NRO, NCC Doke 179). Executor to John Berton, chaplain (1441), to John Bryan, chaplain (1454), and to Emma Curteys (1455). Paid the churchwardens an unspecified 10s. in 1449. See Coll. fol.7v.

DOCKYNG.

John. In 1548 he paid for sways for thatching.

Thomas. Churchwarden in 1543.

DOMINYK, Simon, vicar of Mildenhall, 1375–1408. Was at Newmarket on 14 June 1383 with other rebels and arrested on the charge of having insulted Ralph Attwyk the Cambridgeshire escheator at his house in Newmarket. Threatened to behead Attwyk unless he gave up the daughter of Ralph de Walsham, of Mildenhall, who had lately been carried off. A second rebel group from Bury caught the prior of Bury and took him to Newmarket. On 15 June the prior was taken to Mildenhall Heath and executed. Domynyk was implicated in this, but there was no evidence. He did pay for a pardon, however, his name being entered on the Pardon Rolls.

DONNOME, John. Paid 6s. 8d. for the quetheword of Isabel Glover. 3s. 4d. was received for his quetheword in 1515.

DUFFIELD, DUFFELD, DUFFYLD

Humfrey, Umfrey, 1530 (NRO, NCC Attmere 120). See Appendix 2:38 for his will. Elected churchwarden in 1516. In 1528–30 paid 9s. 6d. rent to the wardens for land with which Thomas Sherd's obit had been endowed. In 1524 worth £20. See Hervey 1910, p.218.

Paul, son of Humphrey above. Elected churchwarden in 1538.

ETTON, Simon, priest, 1516 (NRO, NCC Brigges 26). See Appendix 2:34 for his will. Parish chaplain and churchwarden in 1505. Requested burial against the porch of the charnel chapel, one of the Mildenhall chantry chapels, suggesting that he had been the chantry priest there.

FENALL, VENAL, Thomas. Churchwarden in 1543.

FLEWMAN, John, [*recte* Newman] carpenter. In the early 1540s, Newman's rate of pay was 8d. per day as opposed to that of the local carpenter, Robert Coole, who received 6d., both working on the new bell frame, CWA, fol.32r. Newman may have been brought in with John Chapman for this specialist job, the timber being supplied by Richard Coole and John Garard. Newman was paid a further 6s. 8d. and, in the third and fourth quarter, Newman and Chapman together were paid £2 13s. 4d. with a final payment of £1 6s. 8d. paid to Newmand [*sic*] and Chapman.

FRENDE, Thomas. Received a casual payment in 1449. Coll. fol.8r.

FRERE, John, 1448 (SROB, IC 500/2/9/144). See Appendix 2:7 for his will. Frere's widow paid 6s. 8d. for his soul, the money going towards the bell tower.

FULLER, FULLERE
Christopher. Paid 2d. for daubing the schoolhouse in 1549.

John. A debtor of Isabel Gallyon. In 1450 he paid 6s. 8d. towards the bells and in 1453 he paid a further 6s. 8d. in two instalments.

GALYON, Dame Isabel. In 1447 paid 1s. towards the reparation of bells, plus a further 6d. donation. See Coll. fol.4r. Witnessed John Childriston's will in 1455 (see also **FULLER, John** above). For further details see Northeast, *Wills of the Archdeaconry of Sudbury*, I, no.489, n.13.

GARDENER, John, smith and keeper of the clock. Supplied hinges, hooks and staples to the vestry door and made a censer. Repaired the clock in 1505–1506 and took over its keep from John Screvenere who had been paid at a rate of 10d. a quarter. Gardener's wage was increased to 1s. 3d. Perhaps he was also the church-warden in 1507. His will is dated 15 August 1519 but it is damaged and has no probate (SROB, IC 500/2/12/26). He left 40s. 'for stone and carriage to mend high-ways', repairs such as this always being considered as charitable works. He left a detailed list of smiths' tools to his son, Harry. See further Breen 2008, p.57.

GATYNBE, GEYTONBY, Sir George. Described as parish priest in 1503. In 1504 6s. 8d. was received for his quetheword. Died in 1504 (NRO, NCC Ryxe 146). See Appendix 2:29 for his will.

GESYE, GESYN
Thomas. Elected churchwarden for the year 1505.

William. Elected churchwarden in 1507. See further Breen 2008, pp.61 and 78.

GEYTON, Paul, vicar. Fellow of All Souls, Oxford, vicar of Mildenhall 1471–1512, canon of St Mary in the Fields, Norwich, and prebendary of the Chapter Mass, 1476–92; also vicar of Exning, but had vacated the living by 1500. In 1505–06 he paid 8s. for the painting of the solar above the rood, CWA, fol.1v, and gave 6s. 8d. to the painting of Our Lady, CWA, fol.3v, which was paid through the accounts CWA, fol.4v. Executor to Richard Bakhott (TNA, PCC Wattys 19) in 1474.

GEYTONBY. See **GATYNBE**.

GREGORY
John, churchwarden 1446–49. Executor to Thomas Sigo in 1439. Was he also the brother of William Gregory, Lord Mayor of London, who died in 1466?

William, 1465 (TNA, PCC Godyn 16). Lord Mayor of London. Bequeathed to Master Thomas Sygo, his cousin, 13s. 4d. to pray for his soul. Left 13s. 4d. to Robert Mildenhall, his son-in-law, and 5 marks to Cecily Mildenhall, his daughter. Requested an obit to be kept for him in Mildenhall church, 40s. to be spent on priests, clerks, wax, ringing of bells, bread, cheese and a distribution to the poor.

GYLBYN, William. With John Cannas he paid the churchwardens 24s. which had been raised at the 'Halywell' churchale in 1453.

HALL (for Hall read Hull), Thomas. Son-in-law of Margery Howton. See her will in Appendix 2:33 where he is named as Thomas Hull, married to Joan, her daughter. In his will (Appendix 2:36), throughout which the name Hall is substituted for Hull, he refers to 'John Hall, my son, all my lands and tenements called Norkes in Wick-hambrook according to the last will of Thomas Houghton: to Miles, my son, all my lands and tenements in Mildenhall to him and his heirs'. Miles Hull (see below) occurs in the churchwardens accounts during the reign of Mary Tudor. Thomas's will shows that he had a particular affection for St John of Beverley and the name Hull may have been a locative surname. Described in the 1524 subsidy as a yeoman. Appointed to be the high collector of the subsidy within Lackford hundred. At that time he was worth £30 in goods and died the same year. See Hervey 1910, p.218.

HALSTEDE, HALSTEAD, HAWLSTED

George. 1s. 8d. was received for his quetheword in 1515.

John of Westrowe, 1537 (SROB, IC 500/2/20/23). See Appendix 2:40 for his will. In 1524 he was worth £18 in moveables. See Hervey 1910, p.230 and Breen 2008, p.21.

Mawte, In 1515 her quetheword of 3s. 4d. was received by the churchwardens.

Richard, son of John Halsted of West Row (see above). Executor to his father's will. Provided two bellstocks costing 8d. and undertook unspecified work and carriage with Nicholas Palton, John Oxford, a man and a horse which cost the churchwardens 3s. 2d.

Robert (SROB, IC 500/2/24/226). Paid 10s. for renting the gild hall in 1547. In the following year a further 8s. was received by the wardens. In 1551–52 Robert paid 8d. for half a year due at Michaelmas, and the next year the churchwardens received 16s. in rent from Robert for 'the town house', the church house under its post-Reformation name. A Robert Halsted had been the alderman of the gild of St Thomas *c*.1516, perhaps the father of Robert above and mentioned in Breen 2008, p.48. CWA, fol.46r.

Simon. Owed 3s. 8d. for the quetheword of his father *c*.1553. Was this the Robert Halstead named above? See further Breen 2008, pp.23 and 84.

HAYNES, HEYNES, John, Churchwarden, resigning in1504. died in 1519 (TNA, PCC Ayloffe 19). See Appendix 2:35 for his will.

HOPPER

Margery, wife of Thomas. Was paid 2s. for washing the church cloths.

Thomas appears in the accounts *c*.1505–1524. Died in 1524 (SROB IC 500/1/16/119). See Appendix 2:37 for her will. Paid £1 1s. annual rent to the churchwardens at Michaelmas in 1504 and 1505. In 1506 he paid two half-year rents of 8s. at Michaelmas and Lady Day. Paid for washing the church linen, for which he charged 2s. per half-year. Churchwarden in 1509. See further Breen 2008, p.15.

HOWTON, HOWTTON

Margery, 1515 (NRO, NCC Brigges 28). See Appendix 2:33 for her will. Her quetheword of £1 was received by the churchwardens *c*.1516. Mother-in-law of Thomas Hall (Hull), above.

Thomas, husband of Margery. Made the rowell and supplied wax for it, and also supplied board and nails. Died in 1513 when 16s. 8d. was paid for his quetheword. See further Breen 2008, p.58.

HULL

Miles. Grandson of Margery and Thomas Howton above and the third son of Thomas Hall (Hull), inheriting land in Mildenhall in his father's will. Elected churchwarden, 6 November 1553.

Thomas. See **HALL**.

HYGNE, William, 1448 (NRO, NCC Aleyn 9). See Appendix 2:6 for his will.

HYND. Only his surname is known. Paid for mending the clock and for board and wages 13s. 4d. in CWA, fol.39r. Received 5s. in 1551 for taking down the roodloft, CWA, fol.39v. The payment for his board suggests that he was not a resident of Mildenhall and had come from outside the parish.

JACOBE, Thomas. Elected churchwarden in 1546.

JEROLD

John, dyer. Left to Thomas, his son, two boiling leads 'the which longeth unto the occupation of dying of cloth with one press of lead and two pairs of shears'. Churchwarden in 1543.

Margaret, 1549 (SROB, IC 500/1/9/111). See Appendix 2:47 for her will. Widow and second wife of John Jerold, churchwarden. Bequeathed to the reparation of Mildenhall church 6s. 8d. and to the reparation of the way between the Mill bridge and the bridge next to Barton staithe 10s.

KIDD, KYD. Only his surname is known. Mended the shriving pew c.1543. In 1551 mended the organ seat for 8d. and the next year mended stools in the church.

LANE

John. In 1528 supplied nails, made the pentice, and fashioned a door for the lantern on top of the tower. In 1540 the churchwardens received rent of 4s. from him for the common plot and this was repeated in 1541, but this may have been his son, also named John. In 1541 a John Lane made a clapper for Bagot's bell and was paid for work on the 'great steeple' (i.e., the tower) and the great bell. In 1548 he provided a lock and two keys for the poor hutch and the hutch for the register, and later in 1550–51 the churchwardens received £5 5s. from Lane on Lady Day. The following year he paid £2 9s. 4d. for iron at the general dismemberment of the church goods. Retired as churchwarden in 1553, but no will has survived.

Thomas. Bequeathed £4 to church reparation c.1514. See further Breen 2008, p.59.

LANGHAM

John, 1476 (SROB, IC 500/2/11/65). See Appendix 2:20 for his will.

Roger. In 1548 he and Robert Suckerman sold the church plate for £72 15s.

LOVENESS, William. Supplied iron and nails for the refurbishing of the windows 1540–41, and for hanging the bells and mending the clock.

LYNGE, John, 1509 (SROB, IC 500/2/15/121). See Appendix 2:32 for his will.

MACHOUN, Richard, parish chaplain. In 1443 he appears in several wills as a witness. In Henry Mayner's will (Appendix 2:5) Machoun was described as 'my confessor' and was bequeathed 2d. Executor to Margery Goch in 1443.

MAN

John. In 1546 his legacy of 1s. was received by the churchwardens.

Thomas. In 1546 Thomas paid a debt of £2 for Martin Sidley, gentleman. Man paid a further £1 for Master Sidley, followed by another £2. In 1550 the wardens received 13s. 4d. for Sidley's debt. Man paid 10s. once more, but whether on Sidley's account is not stated.

MANDALL, John, of Thurston. In 1510 he made the bell wheel. CWA, fol.8r.

MAREYNER, Nicholas. In 1449, 2s. was received for his soul. See Coll. fol.4v.

MARTYN, Thomas, chaplain, 1469 (NRO, NCC Jekkys 144). See Appendix 2:16 for his will. Executor to John Bryan: see Appendix 2:9.

MASON

John, chaplain, 1433 (NRO, NCC Surflete 147). See Appendix 2:1 for his will.

Robert, organ player, 1558 (SROB, IC 500/2/28/224). See Appendix 2:51 for his will.

MAY, MEY, MEYE

John, the younger of the Beck. Received 18s. 4d. for supplying thatch for the town house, and John Pollyngton was paid 13s. 4d. for thatching it.

Nicholas, warrener. See Appendix 2:43 for his will.

Nicholas. Received 1s. 2d. for timber c.1528–30. In 1551 his obligation to the churchwardens and the town is noted in the accounts.

Thomas. Churchwarden resigning in 1504. His wife owed the churchwardens £1. In 1505 £1 was received for his quetheword. See further Breen 2008, pp.35 and 88.

MAYNER', Henry, 1443 (NRO, NCC Doke 231). See Appendix 2:5 for his will.

MERCHALL, Robert, 1546. For his will see Appendix 2:45.

MEY, MEYE. See **MAY**.

MEYER, Dom Robert. In 1449 paid 5s. in the accounts and sold the church-wardens two wainscots for 2s.

MORLE, MORLEY

Alice, 1480 (SROB, IC 500/2/11/201). See Appendix 2:21 for her will.

Henry. Paid rent for Hopper's cottage c.1528.

Henry. 5d. was received for his soul in the Coll. fol.4r.

MORS, Henry. The churchwardens received 6s. 8d. for his soul in 1450. See Coll. fol.10v.

NOWCE, Henry, otherwise Tourner, 1535 (SROB, IC 500/2/19/219). See Appendix 2:39 for his will.

OLDBURY, Thomas. Educated at Merton College, Oxford. M.A. and B.Th. by 1449. Rector of Ewelme 1453–55. Granted a papal dispensation to hold an incompatible benefice in addition to Ewelme, March 1453. Vicar of Mildenhall April 1453. Oldbury was supervisor to Emma Curteys' will (SROB, IC 500/2/9/224). He died before October 1471.

PACHET, PATCHATT, PATCHET

John, *fl.*1505, carpenter. Repaired doors and made the sepulchre, hung the little bell and mended its wheel several times. See further Breen 2008, p.58.

Robert, 1488 (SROB, IC 500/2/11/410). See Appendix 2:24 for his will. Left money to repair the road 'between my gate and the stone cross' but did not say where he lived in the parish.

Robert, chantry chaplain. Witness to Simon Heynes' will in 1524, and to Alice Bateman's will in 1527. In the *Valor Ecclesiasticus* of 1535, Patchett was named as the chaplain of Edmund de Mildenhall's chantry.

William. Son of John above. Churchwarden in 1514. Mended the bells and was possibly the same Pachet who in 1536–37 was named with Polyngton to 'keep' the bells for which he received 8d. Pachet later received 4d. for carpentry work 'among' the bells and provided a stay for the first bell. See further Breen 2008, p.59.

PAGE, Robert. Elected churchwarden in 1507.

PALMER. He may have been the bell founder from Bury involved in the taking down and re-hanging of the bells in 1540–41.

PALTON, Nicholas. Elected churchwarden in 1528. Rented foldage of sheep from Edmund de Mildenhall's chantry (see Robert Pachet, chantry chaplain above).

PARKER, Thomas. Educated Trinity College, Cambridge. B.A. 1535, M.A. 1541, B.D. 1548. One of the original fellows of Trinity, 1546. Vicar of Mildenhall from 1556 until accession of Elizabeth when he left England. Last heard of living in Milan in 1581. See Venn 1924, p.308.

PATCHATT, PATCHET. See **PACHET**.

PAYNET, John, smith. Churchwarden, elected in 1449. Received £12 10s. 9d. for church funds between 1449 and 1452. In 1454 he was sold two ropes for 11d. by the churchwardens.

PECHE, PECHEY, PETCHEY

John, of Beck Row. Elected churchwarden in 1528. Paid 6d. for the rood-loft hutch at the beginning of the disbursement of church goods under Edward VI. CWA, fol.34v.

Peter. Elected churchwarden 6 November 1553.

Robert. Churchwarden c.1511–1514.

Robert, the younger. Elected churchwarden 1538.

William. 6s. 8d. received by churchwardens 'of the last will', no date given.

William of Wilde Street. Resigned as churchwarden in 1528. See Appendix 2:42.

PETCHEY. See **PECHE.**

PLACE. The Place family appear frequently in the Collections, Churchwardens' Accounts and wills.

Andrew, priest. In 1516 the churchwardens received £2 'of the last will' of Andrew. See further Breen 2008, p.70.

John. Elected churchwarden in 1507. In 1524, John Place, perhaps his son, was worth £10 in moveables. See Hervey 1910, p.230. A donation of 8d. was made to Our Lady's chapel in 1528 by John Place. See further Breen 2008, p.62.

Richard. The churchwardens received 5s. 'of the last will', *c.*1516.

Simon. 6s. 8d. was received for his quetheword, 1505–06. See further Breen 2008, p.27.

Thomas, 1457 (SROB, IC 500/2/9/191, 1457). Cousin of John Bryan, chaplain, and one of his executors. See Appendix 2:10 for his will.

William, chaplain. Executor to Thomas Place, his father, in 1457.

William. Living at Lynn and paid the churchwardens 15s. after the death of his wife.

PLAYFORD, PLAYFORDE, an important Mildenhall family in the fifteenth century. See further Breen 2008, pp.58 and 67.

George. Paid an unspecified 6s. 8d. to the churchwardens in 1449. Executor to John Playford, his uncle, and to John, the elder, his father (see both below). He had a wife, Margaret, and sons called John and Thomas.

John, 1468 (SROB, IC 500/2/10/404). Churchwarden between 1446 and 1449. Possibly the son-in-law of John Frere. Brother to John Playford II (known as John, the elder, see below). Father to John and Robert Playford. Lived at Beck Row and requested burial in Mildenhall church.

John, the elder, brother to John. See above. Lived in West Row street and was to be buried in Mildenhall church.

Thomas. In 1436 co-executor of the will of Walter Pratt of Mildenhall (NRO, NCC Doke 11) where he was described as 'my attorney'. Bought straw worth 8d. from the churchwardens in 1446. See Coll. fol.1v. Brother of John, the elder, see above.

POLINGTON, POLLINGTON, POLLYNGTON. A Mildenhall family whose members feature frequently in the sixteenth-century accounts. John, Richard and Thomas appear on CWA, fol.35v.

John, thatcher. Received 13s. 4d. for thatching the town house and 6d. for carrying timber from the Feyrspott. Was paid 1s. 1d. for boards for the bier and 4s. for sedge, wood and thatch *c.*1552. Died in 1559 (SROB, W1/22/234). See Appendix 2:52 for his will.

Nicholas. In 1551–52 succeeded his father as clock-keeper at 1s. 3d. per quarter. In 1552 was paid for mending the bellows of the great organ and his wage for keeping the clock was increased to 1s. 8d. a quarter. Paid 1s. for a hutch.

Richard. In 1528 was paid 2d. for mending the bellow of the great organ. For keeping the clock in the Easter term he received 1s. 3d. for the quarter. Paid 1s. 3d. in 1538, 1541, 1542 and 1543 for keeping the clock and 4d. in 1543 for mending the organs. In 1543–44 he paid the churchwardens 8s. which he had received for the sale of the vicar's gravestone. Attended the court day for the fen with John Oxford for 10s. 3d., and in 1546, 1548 and 1550 received 1s. 3d. a quarter for keeping the clock.

Thomas. Was paid 7s. for thatching.

POPE. The Pope family contributed greatly to the parish, overseeing all types of activities and expenses. There is still a Popes farm lying out in the fields towards West Row (see Map 1).

Henry. Paid 3s. 4d. for 5 rods of Lampland at 20d. a year for two years. See CWA, fol.20r. In 1505–06 he conveyed £6 14s. to the wardens which the vicar, Paul Geyton, had given towards the painting of the solar of the holy rood. Featured frequently in the accounts and in local wills. In the 1524 subsidy returns, he, or perhaps his son, was described as a gentleman worth £40 in moveables and was one of the commissioners for the Lackford Hundred and the half-Hundred of Exning (Hervey 1910, p.230). In his will dated 1535 he left £3 10s. to the making of the great bell (SROB, IC 500/2/20/51). See further Breen 2008, pp.21 and 79.

Pope, Master, possibly son of Henry above. In the churchwardens accounts 'paid to Richard Polyngton and John Oxford at the command of Mr Pope at the court day of the fen' (CWA, fol.28r). Stood surety for a debt of £4 (CWA, fol.47v). Was paid £2 for labourers at the fire (CWA, fol.43r).

Thomas, 1559 (SROB IC 500/1/28/19). He was the son of Henry above.

POTTER, Thomas. In 1548 elected churchwarden. Received 3s. 4d. per quarter for caring for the organs, CWA, fols 33v, 34r, 35r, 35v, 41r and 48r. Potter, Edmund Wright and John Frost received 10¾ oz. of broken silver during Edward VI's reign and he was paid 6d. for a lock on the poor man's hutch.

POULE, the plumber, his other name unknown. Active *c*.1528, when he was employed on making the lantern.

PUNGE [*recte* PINGE], Matilda, widow of John Wryghte and John Pinge. Paid 6s. 8d. for their souls to the churchwardens in 1454. The previous year 10s. had been paid in two instalments for the soul of John Pimge.

QUASSHE, Thomas. His name appears at the top of the 1528 accounts on CWA, fol.17r, but it has been scratched out. A Thomas Quasshe was elected churchwarden in 1546, CWA, fol.33r, but this may be Thomas junior. The wardens received 12s. from Quasshe for cloths in 1548, CWA, fol.35r. Owed the wardens 3s. 4d., CWA, fol.40r, and £5 remained in his hands at the annual church meeting, 1551–52, CWA, fol.42r.

REVE, William, chantry priest. In *Valor Ecclesiasticus* of 1535 he was named as the chaplain of Ralph de Walsham's chantry, valued at £6 12s. 7½d. *per annum*, which was founded by licence in mortmain by Ralph de Walsham on 26 July 1386. See above, Introduction, 'Remembering the Dead': 'Chantries' and see *LP 10 Richard II*, part I, m.38. Died in 1545 (SROB/ IC 500/1/10/81). See Appendix 2:44 for his will.

ROLFF, ROLLF
Thomas. Elected churchwarden in 1514. See further Breen 2008, p.24.

Thomas, yeoman (SROB, IC/500/1/13). See Appendix 2:48 for his will.

RYNGSTEDE, Thomas, Bachelor of Canon Law (Cantab.) by 1417. Dean of St Mary's in the Fields, Norwich, 1426–44. Perpetual vicar of Mildenhall from 1432 to 1453. Obtained a papal indult to farm the vicarage of Mildenhall. Canon of Lincoln and prebendary of Brampton from 1440–51 and prebendary of Caistor (Lincs.) 1451–54. The Mildenhall churchwardens received two £1 payments from him in 1446, one by the hand of Richard Machoun, the chaplain, and in 1447 a further 8d. was received. See Coll. fols 1r, 1v, 4r. Supervisor for the will of Thomas Goche (NRO, NCC Doke 60) in 1438 and proved William Hygne's will in 1448 (NRO, NCC Aleyn 9).

SADYLER, John. Made the baldricks in 1505–07 and paid a quetheword of 6s. 8d. for a John Sadyler in 1505–06.

SCHERD, SHERD

Ralph. 9s. 6d. was received by the churchwardens from land rented by him. CWA, fol.20r.

Thomas. There is little information about Thomas or his obit (sangrede), and what is documented is confusing. In 1527–28 a sangrede had been overpaid by 4s. and the churchwardens' accounts, CWA, fol.17v, indicate that money was paid back, presumably to Sherd's trustees. On the same folio, but at a later date, priests and clerks were paid 4s. 8d. for an obit for Sherd and his wives. The next celebration (CWA, fol.18r) cost 4s. and was paid to the vicar. During the following quarter (CWA, fol.18r), 'prystes, clerkes and poore pepyll' received 4s. for Sherd's commemoration and that of his wives, Anabyll and Alys. The payment had increased to 5s. within a few months, CWA, fol.19r, and a further 4s. was paid to the vicar and a deed drawn up for Sherd's land. In 1528 there is an entry for 9s. 8d. received from the land of Ralph [*sic*] Sherd; and in 1530 another from the land of Thomas Sherd of which Humphrey Duffield was then the tenant, CWA, fol.20r. These entries are the only ones that have survived in the accounts showing a run of income or expenditure for commemorative purposes, but they are not supported by ancillary documentation. The accounts for the next five years are missing and by the time they resume many obits, anniversaries and chantries had been abandoned as the Reformation took hold.

SCHENE, John. Retired as churchwarden, 1553–54.

SCREVENERE, John. Keeper of the clock in 1505 at 10d. a quarter. Received 6d. for mending the books in 1516–17.

SHERD. See **SCHERD**.

SIDLEY. See **SYDLEY**.

SIGO, SYGO, SYGOO

Agnes, 1484 (SROB, IC 500/2/11/302). See Appendix 2:22. The widow of Robert. Buried in Mildenhall churchyard and requested soul prayers for Robert and herself for one year, but her goods were insufficient to meet legacies and other costs.

John (NRO, NCC A.Caston 173, 1482). To be buried in Mildenhall church next to Thomas, his father (see below). His wife, Isabel, was his executrix and her son, Thomas Tyd, was co-administrator. The church fabric received 40s. from John who requested prayers for his soul for two years. The messuage in Halywell, once his father's, was to be sold to provide soul masses. Andrew Place, chaplain, was a witness to his will with Sir Thomas Barowne, 'my confessor'.

Margery. The churchwardens received 3s. for her soul in 1452.

Robert, son of Thomas (see below) and his executor. Churchwarden 1446–49.

Robert (Master Robert Sygo). His dates are unknown but he left land in Mildenhall to Cambridge University pertaining in 1559 to the Master and Fellows of Trinity College. See will of Thomas Pope, esquire, SROB IC 500/1/28/19.

Thomas, 1439 (NRO, NCC Doke 113). See Appendix 2:3 for his will. He was the father of Robert (see above) and John.

SKOTT, Thomas. He was churchwarden in 1538, when the wardens received 19s. 9d. on their election. Thomas Skott was also entered as Lord of Misrule at the Christmas celebrations in 1528.

SMITH, SMYTH

John, shoemaker, 1472 (SROB, IC 500/2/11/23). See Appendix 2:17 for his will.

John. Mended three antiphoners and supplied leather. Mended a processionary in 1507 and the epistle book in 1511. CWA, fols 6v, 7v, 8r and 9r. See further Breen 2008, pp.58 and 62.

SOKERMAN, SUCKERMAN

Robert. In 1548 Suckerman and Roger Langham sold the church plate for £72 15s. Allowed £1 5s. on 12 August 1548 'for that they lacked weight of certain plate' from the sale. They received 14s. for the best cross and a further £6 13s. 6d. for church goods including the silver cup at 5s. the ounce. See CWA, fol.50v. In 1551–52 he was paid 5s. for 'that he laid out at the camp'. See CWA, fol.41r. In 1568 his goods were valued at £5. He was an important community leader and had sons Simon (see below), Robert, Andrew and William.

Simon. His signature appears twice on CWA, fol.45v.

SPARHAWKE, John. Elected churchwarden on 6 November 1553.

SPEED, John, 1438 (NRO, NCC Doke 67). The churchwardens received four donations for his soul (Coll. fols 2r, 4r, 18r, 20v), paid by William Thomson, tailor, or by John Dobyn in the name of William Taylor, a total of £1 13s. 4d. See Appendix 2:2 for his will.

STALHAM, otherwise STALONN, STALOUN. The surnames Stalonn and Staloun seem to have been a misreading of Stalham by the clerk.

John Stalham the elder wrote his will on 10 April 1459 and it was proved two years later in 1461 (SROB, IC 500/2/10, 341). In this he refers to his niece, Christian Stalham, 'daughter of the late John Stalham my brother of Mildenhall'.

John, 1452 (SROB, IC 500/2/9/148). See Appendix 2:8 for his will, in which he refers to his daughter, Christian. Brother of John above. Churchwarden 1446–49. In 1453 the wardens received £2 for his soul.

STON, Robert, goldsmith *c.*1541.

SUCKERMAN. See **SOKERMAN**.

SUTTON

Richard. 1451 (SROB, IC 500/2/9/107). Brother of William Sutton, the glover. A member of Sir Thomas Tuddenham's household at Oxborough. Asked to be buried at Mildenhall and bequeathed 6s. 8d. to the church fabric.

William, glover. Brother of Richard above. Elected churchwarden 1449. In 1452 paid 6s. 8d. for the soul of his brother, Richard.

SYDLEY, SIDLEY, Martin, gentleman. Churchwardens received £1 from Richard Cole and Mr Sidley in 1540–41. In 1546 Thomas Mann paid £2 for the debt of Martin Sidley, gentleman, and a further £1 in 1547. CWA, fol.37v shows a further £2 being paid by Thomas Man in two instalments and Man's last payment for Sidley came to 13s. 4d. paid in 1550–51.

SYGO, SYGOO. See **SIGO**.

TAYLOR, John, *alias* Wyllyamson. See Appendix 2:11 for his will dated 1460.

THOMAS, Sir. Surname unknown, but he was employed in making new books for the 'new' services during the Reformation.

THOMSON, William, tailor. Made four payments for the soul of John Speed (see Coll. fols 2r, 4r, 18r and 20v) which totalled £1 13s. 4d. The entry on fol.20v refers not to William Thomson, tailor, but to William Taylor, perhaps an example of an occupation becoming a surname. Thomson also appears as a witness to the will of John Frere. See Appendix 2:7.

THURSTON

Hubert. Paid 11d. CWA, fol.48r.

Robert. Elected churchwarden on 13 October 1550 and retired on 15 November 1551. Received an unspecified 1s. from the churchwardens, noted in the accounts.

TIRRELL, TYRRELL

John. In 1510–11 the churchwardens received 1s. for Tyrrell's quetheword. See further Breen 2008, p.90.

Katherine. Paid 10s. by the churchwardens for providing meat and drink for the carriers and those who helped transport the ring of bells from Bury St Edmunds, CWA, fol.31v. Provided board and lodging for the carpenter and other helpers when they made the bellframe. The will of a Katherine Tirrell (NRO, NCC Janigo 218) is dated 4 June 1585. See Appendix 2:55. This is unlikely to be the same Katherine as above, but is, perhaps a daughter-in-law.

William. In 1549 as cow herd in charge of the Eriswell bullocks, received 1s. 8d.

TREUPENY, Richard, labourer, 1537 (SROB, IC 500/2/19/576 and IC 500/2/20/193). See Appendix 2:41 for his will.

TURNER, John. Supplied bread to the camp at Bury in 1549 during 'the camping time'. See CWA, fol.39r, n.287.

TYD, TYDDE

John. The churchwardens received £1 for his soul in 1454.

John. Received a payment of 2d. from the churchwardens in 1543–44.

Robert, 1452 (SROB, IC 500/2/9/128). The churchwardens received 3s. 4d. for his soul in 1453. The executor was John Halstede.

Thomas, 1463 (SROB, IC 500/2/12/12). See Appendix 2:14 for his will.

TYLNEY, Mother. Paid 18s. 6d. for housing the masons and the glaziers in 1548–49.

TYRRELL. See **TIRRELL**.

TYSON, John. Parish clerk in 1524, worth £1 in wages (Hervey 1910, p.218).

VENAL. See **FENALL**.

WALSHAM, Ralph de. Highest tax-payer in Mildenhall in 1381, holding the position of *Sergeant de Pays*. He was not necessarily a rebel but, during the East Anglia uprising, his daughter had been abducted. Walsham's name was linked with Simon Dominyk, vicar of Mildenhall, arrested on the charge of insulting the Cambridge escheator at Newmarket, threatening violence unless Walsham's daughter was released (see Dominyk above).

WEDERES, WODERYS

John. Wardens received 4s. on 21 April 1448 for his soul. See Coll. fol.4v.

Thomas. Elected churchwarden in 1528.

WENGE, WYNGE

Francis. Supplied thatch for the town house c.1550.

John. Requested his son, Thomas, to celebrate a year's masses for his soul (NCC, NRO Neve 33, 1456). See further Breen 2008, p.49.

Thomas, priest. Buried at Mildenhall in 1500 (NRO, NCC Cage 135).

WILLES, Nicholas. Elected churchwarden in 1514.

WODERYS. See **WEDERES**.

WYLKYNSON, Master John, vicar of Mildenhall, 1512–41. An entry on CWA, fol.25r suggests that Wylkyson had died owing lead (or its worth in money) which was church property. On fol.26r his gravestone had been distrained and on fol.27r Richard Pollington sold the gravestone for eight shillings, presumably to cover Wilkynson's debts, the stone having been valued by the 'four honest men' who bought it.

WYNGE. See **WENGE**.

BIBLIOGRAPHY

MANUSCRIPT SOURCES

Bury St Edmunds, Suffolk Record Office
IC 500/2/9–37: Archdeaconry Court of Sudbury, Will Registers 1439–1575
E18/400/1:3: Bunbury papers
EL 110/5/1: The Collections of St Mary's Church, Mildenhall, 1446–1454
EL 110/5/3: The Churchwardens' Accounts of St Mary's Church, Mildenhall, 1503–1553

Kew, The National Archives
Prerogative Court of Canterbury, Will Registers 1383–1549

London, British Library
Add. MS 19077–19113: D.E. Davey, 'Collections for the History of Suffolk by Hundreds and Parishes'

Norwich, Norfolk Record Office
Norfolk Consistory Court Will Registers 1383–1585, proved in the Consistory Court of the Bishop of Norwich

PRINTED PRIMARY SOURCES

Botelho, L.A., ed., *Churchwardens' Accounts of Cratfield 1640–1660*, SRS, 42 (1999)
Breen, Anthony, *The Mildenhall Rentals 1501*, Suffolk Family History Society (2008)
Brewer, J.S., *et al.*, eds, *Letters and Papers Foreign and Domestic of the reign of Henry VIII*, 21 volumes (London, 1880–1965)
Bullard, J.V., and Chalmer Bell, H., eds, *Lyndwood's Provinciale: the text of the canons therein contained, reprinted from the translation made in 1534* (London, 1929)
Butler, H.E., ed., *The Chronicle of Jocelin of Brakelond concerning the Acts of Samson, Abbot of the Monastery of St Edmund* (London, 1949)
Dymond, D., ed., *The Churchwardens' Book of Bassingbourn, Cambridgeshire, 1496–c.1540*, Cambridgeshire Records Society, 17 (2004)
Dymond, D., ed., *The Register of Thetford Priory 1482–1517*, 2 volumes, NRS, 59 (1995)
Dymond, D., and Paine, C., eds, *The Spoil of Melford Church: The Reformation in a Suffolk Parish* (Ipswich, 1989)
Foster, J.E., ed., *Churchwardens Accounts of St Mary the Great, Cambridge, from 1504 to 1635*, Cambridge Antiquarian Society (1905)
Harper-Bill, C., ed., *The Register of John Morton, Archbishop of Canterbury 1486–1500*, III, *Norwich Sede Vacante*, Canterbury and York Society (2000)
Hervey, S.H.A., ed., *Suffolk in 1524: being a return for a subsidy granted in 1523*, Suffolk Green Books, 10 (1910)
Lewis, R.W.M., ed., *Walberswick Churchwardens' Accounts, AD 1450–1499* (London, 1947)
Northeast, P., ed., *Boxford Churchwardens' Accounts 1530–1561*, SRS, 23 (1982)
Northeast, P., ed., *Wills of the Archdeaconry of Sudbury, part I, 1439–1461*, SRS, 44 (2001)
Northeast, P., and Falvey, H., eds, *Wills of the Archdeaconry of Sudbury, part II, 1461–1474*, SRS, 53 (2010)

Redstone, V.B., ed., 'II. Chantry Certificates, No. 45', *PSIA*, 12 (1906), pp.30–69

Tymms, S., ed., *The East Anglian; or notes and queries on subjects connected with the counties of Suffolk, Cambridge, Essex and Norfolk*, I (1864)

Tymms, S., ed., 'John Baret of Bury, 1463', in *Wills and Inventories from the Registers of the Commissary of Bury St Edmund's and the Archdeacon of Sudbury*, Camden Society, Old Series, 49 (1850)

Watkin, A., ed., *Archdeaconry of Norwich: Inventory of Church Goods temp. Edward III*, 2 volumes, NRS, 19 (1947–1948)

Williams, C.H., ed., *English Historical Documents, 1485–1558* (London, 1967)

SECONDARY SOURCES

Atchley, E.G.C.F., 'Medieval parish-clerks in Bristol', *Transactions of the St Paul's Ecclesiological Society*, 5 (1905), pp.106–107

Bailey, M., *Medieval Suffolk: an Economic and Social History 1200–1500* (Woodbridge, 2007)

Baldwin, F.E., *Sumptuary Legislation and Personal Regulation in England* (Baltimore, 1926)

Barnwell, P.S., Cross, C. and Rycraft, A., eds, *Mass and Parish in Late Medieval England: The Use of York* (Reading, 2005)

Barton, A., 'The ornaments of the altar and ministers in late medieval England', in Barnwell, Cross and Rycraft (2005)

Bebb, R., *Welsh Furniture 1250–1950: a Cultural History of Craftsmanship and Design*, I (Kidwelly, 2007), pp.158–9

Beeson, C.F.C., *English Church Clocks 1280–1850: History and Classification* (London, 1971)

Blair, C., and Blair, J., 'Bell founding', in *English Medieval Industries: Craftsmen, Techniques, Products*, edited by J. Blair and N. Ramsay (London, 1991)

Bony, J., *The English Decorated Style: Gothic Architecture Transformed 1250–1350* (Oxford, 1979)

Brown, M.P., ed., *The Luttrell Psalter: a facsimile* (London, 2006)

Bryant, G.F., and Hunter, V.M., eds, *'How Thow Schalt Thy Paresche Preche': John Myrc's Instructions for Parish Priests*, part 1, *Introduction and Text*, Barton-upon-Humber WEA (1999)

Burgess, C., 'A service for the dead: the form and function of the anniversary in late medieval Bristol', *Transactions of the Bristol and Gloucester Archaeological Society*, 105 (1987), pp.181–211

Campbell, J., *The Anglo-Saxons* (London, 1991)

Cautley, H.M., *Suffolk Churches and their Treasures*, 4th edition (Ipswich, 1975)

Cheetham, F., *Alabaster Images of Medieval England* (Oxford, 2003)

Cheney, C.R., ed., *Handbook of Dates for Students of English History*, Royal Historical Society (1981)

Coles, J., and Hall, D., *Changing Landscapes: The Ancient Fenland* (Cambridge, 1998)

Craig, J.S., 'Co-operation and initiatives: Elizabethan churchwardens and the parish accounts of Mildenhall', *Social History*, 18, no.3 (1993), pp.357–80

Craig, J.S., *Reformation, Politics and Polemics: The Growth of Protestantism in East Anglian Market Towns, 1500–1610* (Aldershot, 2001)

Cross, F.L., ed., *The Oxford Dictionary of the Christian Church* (Oxford, 1957)

Cuthbert, E.G., and Atchley, F., 'Jesus Mass and Anthem', *Transactions of the St Paul's Ecclesiological Society*, 5 (1905), pp.163–169

Darby, H.C., *The Medieval Fenland* (Newton Abbot, 1974)

Drew, C., *Early Parochial Organisation in England: The Origins of the Office of Churchwarden*, St Anthony's Hall Publications, 7, Borthwick Institute of Historical Research (1954)

Duffy, E., *The Stripping of the Altars: Traditional Religion in England, 1400–1580* (London, 1992)

Duffy, E., *The Voices of Morebath: Reformation and Rebellion in an English Village* (London, 2001)

Duggan, A., *Thomas Becket* (London, 2004)

Dyer, C., *Everyday Life in Medieval England* (London, 2000)

Dymond, D., and Martin, E., *An Historical Atlas of Suffolk*, 2nd edition (Ipswich, 1999)

Easton, T., and Bicknell, S., 'Two pre-Reformation organ soundboards: towards an understanding of the form of early organs and their position in some Suffolk churches', *PSIAH*, 38, part 3 (1995)

Emden, A.B., *A Biographical Register of the University of Oxford to AD 1500*, 3 volumes (Oxford, 1957–1959)

French, K.L., 'Parochial fund raising in late medieval Somerset', in *The Parish in English Life 1400–1600*, edited by K.L. French, G.G. Gibbs and B.A. Kümin (Manchester, 1997)

French, K.L., *The People of the Parish: Community Life in a Late Medieval English Diocese* (Philadelphia, 2001)

Galloway, D., and Wasson, J., 'Records of plays and players in Norfolk and Suffolk 1330–1642', *Malone Society*, 11 (1980–1981)

Gelling, M., *Place-names in the Landscape* (London, 1984)

Gilchrist, J., *Anglican Church Plate* (London, 1967)

Guy, J., *Tudor England* (Oxford, 1988, paperback 1990)

Halliwell, J.O., *A Dictionary of Archaic and Provincial Words, Obsolete Phrases. Proverbs and Ancient Customs from the Fourteenth Century*, 2 volumes, 4th edition (London, 1860)

Haward, B., *Suffolk Medieval Church Arcades, 1150–1550: a measured drawing survey with notes and analysis*, SIAH (1993)

Hoppitt, R., '29. Rabbit warrens', in Dymond and Martin (1999)

Hughes, A., *Medieval Manuscripts for Mass and Office: a Guide to their Organization and Terminology* (Toronto, 1995)

Hutton, R., *The Rise and Fall of Merry England: The Ritual Year 1400–1700* (Oxford, 1994)

Kümin, B.A., *The Shaping of a Community: The Rise and Reformation of the English Parish c.1400–1560* (Aldershot, 1996)

Lasko, P., and Morgan, N., *Medieval Art in East Anglia 1300–1520* (Norwich, 1974)

Loades, D., *Mary Tudor: The Tragical History of the First Queen of England*, TNA (2006)

MacCulloch, D.J., 'A reformation in the balance: power struggles in the diocese of Norwich, 1533–1553', in *Counties and Communities: Essays on East Anglian History presented to A. Hassell Smith*, edited by C. Rawcliffe, R. Virgoe and R. Wilson (Norwich, 1996)

MacCulloch, D.N.J., *Suffolk and the Tudors* (Oxford, 1986)

Mâle, E., *The Gothic Image: Religious Art in France of the Thirteenth Century*, translated by D. Nussey (1972)

Marks, R., and Williamson, P., eds, *Gothic: Art for England 1400–1547* (London, 2003)

Marshall, P., *The Catholic Priesthood and the Reformation* (Oxford, 1994)

Martin, E., '13. The Neolithic: 14. The Bronze Age: 15. The Iron Age', in Dymond and Martin (1999)

Middleton-Stewart, J., *Inward Purity and Outward Splendour: Death and Remembrance in the Deanery of Dunwich, Suffolk, 1370–1547* (Woodbridge, 2001)

Middleton-Stewart, J., 'Parochial activity in late medieval Fenland: accounts and wills from Tilney All Saints and St Mary's, Mildenhall, 1443–1520', in *The Parish in Late Medieval England*, edited by C. Burgess and E. Duffy, Harlaxton Medieval Studies, 14 (2006)

Morris, R., *Churches in the Landscape* (London, 1989)

Mortlock, D.P., *The Popular Guide to Suffolk Churches*, I (Cambridge, 1988)

Nichols, A.E., *Seeable Signs: The Iconography of the Seven Sacraments 1350–1544* (Woodbridge, 1994)

Northeast, P., 'Parish gilds', in Dymond and Martin (1999)

Northeast, P., 'Suffolk churches in the later middle ages', in *East Anglian History: Studies in honour of Norman Scarfe*, edited by C. Harper-Bill, C. Rawcliffe and R.G. Wilson (Woodbridge, 2002)

Oman, C., *English Church Plate 597–1830* (London, 1957)

Owst, G.R., *Preaching in Medieval England: an Introduction to Sermon Manuscripts of the Period c.1350–1450* (London, 1965)

Peacock, E., ed., *English Church Furniture, Ornaments and Decorations at the period of the Reformation: as Exhibited in a List of Goods destroyed in certain Lincolnshire Churches AD 1566* (London, 1866)

Pevsner, N., and Radcliffe, E., *The Buildings of England: Suffolk* (Harmondsworth, 1974)

Pevsner, N. and Wilson, B., *The Buildings of England: Norfolk 2: North-west and South* (Harmondsworth, 2002)

Pfaff, R., 'The English devotion of St Gregory's trental', *Speculum*, 49 (1974), pp.75–90

Potter, T.W., *Roman Britain* (Manchester, 1997)

Pounds, N.J.G., *A History of the English Parish: The Culture of Religion from Augustine to Victoria* (Cambridge, 2000)

Randall, G., *Church Furnishings and Decoration in England and Wales* (London, 1980)

Raven, J.J., *The Church Bells of Suffolk* (London, 1890)

Rees, H.G. St M., *An Illustrated History of Mildenhall, Suffolk, and its Parish Church of the Blessed Virgin Mary* (Gloucester, 1961)

Rubin, M., *Corpus Christi: The Eucharist in Late Medieval Culture* (Cambridge, 1991)

Salzman, L.F., *Building in England down to 1540: a Documentary History* (Oxford, 1952, reissued 1992)

Salzman, L.F., *English Medieval Industries of the Middle Ages* (Oxford, 1923)

Sandler, L.R., *Gothic Manuscripts 1285–1385: a Survey of Manuscripts Illuminated in the British Isles*, I (London, 1986)

Scarfe, N., *A Shell Guide to Suffolk*, 2nd edition (London, 1965)

Scarisbrick, J.J., *The Reformation and the English People* (Oxford, 1984)

Scholes, P.A., *The Oxford Companion to Music* (Oxford, 1988)

Scott, K.L., *Later Gothic Manuscripts 1390–1490* (London, 1996)

Sear, J., 'Trade and Commerce in Mildenhall c.1350–c.1500', Master of Studies Degree in Local and Regional History (Cambridge, 2007)

Sherlock, D., *Suffolk Church Chests*, SIAH (2008)

Simpson, J.A., and Weiner, E.C., *The Compact Oxford English Dictionary* (Oxford, 1991)

Skeat, W.W., *The Place-Names of Suffolk*, Cambridge Antiquarian Society (1913)

Steward, A.V., *A Suffolk Bibliography*, SRS, 20 (1974)

Swanson, R.N., *Indulgences in Late Medieval England: Passports to Paradise?* (Cambridge, 2007)

Toulmin-Smith, J., *The Parish, its Obligations and Powers: Its Officers and their Duties* (London, 1853)

Venn, J., and J.A., *Alumni Cantabrigiensis*, Part I (Cambridge, 1924)

Walcott, M.E.C., *Sacred Archaeology: a Popular Dictionary of Ecclesiastical Institutions* (London, 1868)

Walton, P., 'Textiles', in *English Medieval Industries*, edited by J. Blair and N. Ramsay (London, 1991)

Westlake, H.F., *The Parish Gilds of Medieval England* (London, 1919)

White, W., *History, Gazetteer and Directory of Suffolk 1844* (Sheffield, 1970)

Williamson, M., 'Liturgical music in the late medieval parish church: organs and voices, ways and means', in *The Parish in Late Medieval England*, edited by C. Burgess and E. Duffy, Harlaxton Medieval Studies, 14 (2006)

Wood, A., *The 1549 Rebellions and the Making of Early Modern England* (Cambridge, 2007)

Wood-Legh, K.L., *A Small Household of the XVth Century, being the account book of Munden's chantry, Bridport* (Manchester, 1956)

Wood-Legh, K.L., *Perpetual Chantries in Britain* (Cambridge, 1965)

Wordsworth, C., and Littlehales, H., *The Old Service Books of the English Church* (London, 1904)

INDEX OF PEOPLE AND PLACES

Roman numerals refer to pages of the introduction. An asterisk * after the reference indicates that the name occurs more than once on that page. An 'n' following the reference indicates that the subject is to be found in a footnote on that page.

Modern forms of Christian names have been used but the original spelling of surnames has been retained and chief variants given. References may relate to two or more individuals bearing the same name. Where no Christian name appears in the originals, [*unnamed*] appears in the index. Where a Christian name is given in square brackets, e.g. [Richard], the name does not appear on that page but has been deduced from the context.

Only the names of the testators of the wills in Appendix 2 have been indexed; these are indicated by the page number followed by the will number in the appendix.

Major place-names have been capitalized and given their modern form. For places not in Suffolk, counties have been indicated, apart from well-known cities.

Alen, John, lxviii, 59, 199
Alexander, *see* Alysander
Aleyn, Simon, xlviin
Algat, Robert, xli
Algood, William, 36
Alysander (Alexaunder, Alexzander, Alixander, Alysunder), George, weaver, 179 (will 54), 199
    James, painter, xxxiii, xliii, 93, 101, 102, 104, 115, 116, 123, 124, 124n, 175 (will 49), 199
    John, 199
    [*unnamed*], 81, 136
Anion, Thomas, xlii
Annabble, [*unnamed*], of Bury, 114, 115, 199
Austen (Austin, Austyn, Hausteyn), John, chaplain, xli, li, 43, 43n, 199
    Robert, lii, 49*, 49n*, 199
    [*unnamed*], mother of Robert, 49*, 49n

B[*damaged*], Thomas, churchwarden, 43
BABWELL, house of Franciscan friars, liii
Bachote, *see* Bagot
Bacun, Master, 54
Bagot (Bachote, Bakhot(e), Bak(k)ot), family, xxxviii, liv, 14n, 45n
    John, xlvin, xlviiin, xlix, 14, 14n, 145 (will 15), 199
    Master, 45, 122, 199
    Mistress, 117
    Nicholas, 120*, 199; Master, 50, 199
    Richard, xxxviiin, xlvin, xlviiin, 148 (will 19), 199
    Simon, rector of Worlington, xxxviii, 199
    William, mercer, xxxvii, xxxviin, 143 (will 12), 199
Baker, Jone (Joan or John), 50
    Robert, 61, 77*

Bakhot, *see* Bagot
Balles, William 76
Ballis, William, lx, lxviii, 44, 199
Bambour, William, xli
Bansty, [*unnamed*], 45
Barber, Alice, 115
Baret, John, lv
Barforth, (Barford), Roger, Sir, priest, xxxii, xxxiin, xli, xlviin, xlixn, liiin, 49, 50, 50n, 62, 62n, 63, 63n, 128, 128n, 156 (will 30), 199
Barker(e), Alice, 105
    John, wife of, 8
    Thomas, xli
Baron (Barowne, Barun), Robert, xlviiin
    Thomas, xli, xlin
BARTON MILLS, xix
    inhabitants of, xxxviii
    river bank of, 120
Barton, Henry, Sir, lord mayor of London, xxix, lxiii
Barun, *see* Baron
Basset(t), George, xxxiii, lxx, 109, 112, 114, 115, 123, 200
    John, 67
    [*unnamed*], miller, 91
BASSINGBOURN (Cambs), parish church, vestments of, xxxv
Bateman, Alice, xxviiin, xlviin
    John, 43
BECCLES, parish church, rebuilding of, lxiii
Becket, Thomas, archbishop of Canterbury, xxxiii, xxxiiin, xlvi
    erasure of name, lxvii, 85, 85n
    plays about, lvii–lviii, lxvii
Benes, William, 123
Beneth, William, 50
Berton *alias* Watts, John, chaplain, xxxiin, 138 (will 4), 200

Bery, Edward, 43, 43n
Billis, Richard, 43
BISHOP'S (KING'S) LYNN (Norfolk), church
    of St Nicholas, xxv
  expenses travelling to, 95
  pageants and plays at, lvii
  play about St Thomas the martyr at, lviii
  warehouse of Hanse traders at, 95n
  water route to, 30n, 95n
Blake, Thomas, 49*, 49n
  [unnamed], wife of Thomas, 49*
Blome (Bloom), Robert, 120, 136
Blythis, Henry (Herry), 44
Bodye, Mr, 102
Boltton, Mother, 65
Bowne, Katherine, liiin
Bowthe, Thomas, 112
BOXFORD, churchwardens of, 102n
Bradley, John, lxviii, 63, 63n, 200
BRAMLEY (Hants), churchwardens' accounts
    of, 46
BRANDON (BRANDON FERRY), 30, 30n, 63,
    63n
Bray, William, xlvin, xlviin, l, li, 43, 43n, 153
    (will 27), 20
Brayser, Richard, liv
Brede, William, 117
Bregman, Thomas, 123
Breon, see Bryon
Brewer (Bruer), John, 51, 53, 59, 200
BRIDPORT (Dorset), Munden's chantry in, xlixn
Brion, see Bryon
Browech, Margaret, 43
Broweht, Simon, 67
Browet(t), John, 86
  [unnamed], 79
Bruer, see Brewer
Bryan, family, lx
  John, chaplain, xxxiin, xxxviii, xxxviiiin, xl, lx,
      lxiii, lxiv, 8, 14, 20, 26, 142 (will 9), 200;
      father of parish chaplain, xxxviiiin
  see also Bryon
Bryghtwell, Isabel, 25, 25n
Brygman, Thomas, 115
Brynkele, Thomas, xxxviii, xxxviiiin, xlixn
Bryon (Breon, Brion) John, 44, 44n*
  Robert, 53*, 55, 69, 200
  [unnamed], 57
BUNGAY, chapel of St Thomas, in churchyard,
    lviii
  church of St Mary, lviii
  pageants and plays at, lvii
  service of Thomas Becket at, lviii
Bunting (Buntyng(e), Bountynge, Bontyng),
    Thomas, 133
  [Thomas], 134*
  [unnamed], 115, 117, 118, 123, 135
Burgayne, Emma, 65
BURY ST EDMUNDS, xxxvii, 30, 30n
  abbey (convent) of, xx, xxi, xxxix, lix
  abbot of, xxi, lix, 80n

dissolution of, 91n
monk of, liii
bells taken to, 88, 88n, 90, 98
camp at (1549 rebellion), 109*, 109n, 112,
    112n
carriage, of lead from, 117
  of timber from, 134
  of timber to, 57
charnel house, ln
church, St Mary's, ln
  John Baret's clock in, lv
commissioners at, 119
costs incurred at, 89*, 108
court at, 89*
hire of horse to, 117
inhabitants of, xxxixn, 51, 114, 116, 118, 124,
    134
items purchased at, 64, 133, 135
Norman gate, ln
pageants and plays at, lvii
sermon at, 39n
silver pax made at, 92n
silver pyx mended at, 72
visitation at, 80, 80n
  of commissioners at, 102, 102n
workmen from, 60n, 98
Bury (Bure), John, 49*, 50*, 50n
Busch, Thomas, 91
  [unnamed], 53
Bygge, John, xlvin

Cadge, Simon, 116, 118, 124, 200
Cage, William, 100
Cake, Thomas, xxxv, xxxvn
Calfe, Robert, 58
CAMBRIDGE, church, St Mary the Great,
    churchwardens' accounts of, xxxn, lxn
  parish, almshouse in, lxn
  porch, lxn
  rood-loft, 46n
  vestry, lxn
  creator of vaulting from, xxx
  inhabitants of, 84
Canvas (Cannas), John, 31, 31n, 200
Chadenhalk (Schadynhalk), M, 50
  Mother, 50; father of, 50
  Robert, liii
Chapman, John, 28, 58, 89, 90*, 91, 200
  William, xlvin, liv, 2, 3, 4, 200
Charnell, Richard, Sir, lviii
Charnok(e), Margaret, 86
  William, xlviin, xlviiin, 153 (will 26), 200
Cheston, see Chiston
Chevington, Joan de, xlix
Childerston (Childyrston, Chylderston,
    Chyldyrstone), Edmund, xlvin
  family, lx, lxviii, 14n, 28n, 200
  Henry, 136
  John, xxviiin, 14, 14n, 44, 44n, 201; the elder,
      44n, 155 (will 28), 201
  Katherine, widow, 178 (will 53), 201

Margaret, 28
Thomas, xxvn, 28*, 28n, 201
Simon, xlvin, xlviin, 25, 25n
William, xlix, lxx, 28, 112, 114, 201
Chiston(e) (Cheston, Chyston, Chystyn), John,
    xlviin, 44n, 76*, 100, 200
Robert, 100, 100n, 200
Thomas, lii, 49, 77, 78, 200
William, 50
[unnamed], 78
Chylderston, see Childerston
Chyllwhaytt, [unnamed], 91
CLARE, inhabitants of, 28
Clark(e), see Clerk(e)
Clars, Margaret, 28
Cleare, Robert, 134
Clement (Clemend), Joan, 105
John, lxviii, 59, 67, 201
William, 105
Clerk(e) (Clark(e)), John, 114
Robert, 93, 100, 136
Simon, lxx, 119, 120, 201
Thomas, 49, 54
William, lxix, 100*, 102, 102n, 105, 115, 123,
    201
Clerke alias Webbe, John, 55n
Robert, 123
Clyff (Clyfte), Richard, lxix, 94*
Coke, Agnes, 78
John, xli
Cole (Coll(e), Colles), Goodwife, 117, 201
Richard, tanner, 115, 170 (will 46), 201
Thomas, xxxiv, xlviii, 44, 44n, 115, 115n, 201
Stephen, 115*, 123
William, xlvii
Coleke, John, 122
Colman, Richard, xlvin, 143 (will 13)
Constable (Constabill, Cunstable), Dionesia
    (Denise), lii, 148 (will 18), 201
Joan (née), lii
Richard, lii, 8, 9, 9n, 201
Conyers, Margery, 105
Cook, Stephen, lxx, 120, 201
Thomas, 135
Coole (Coolle), Richard, li, 86, 89, 201
Robert, 86, 87, 89*, 201
[unnamed], wife of [unnamed], 112, 112n, 113
Cootes, Thomas, tailor, 105, 201
William, xxviiin
Coper, [unnamed], 100
Corbett, John, xli
Coslyn, Robert, 134
Costyn(e) (Costyng, Costen), Hubert, 113
Katherine, 54, 54n
Robert, 49, 201
William, lxviii, 59, 63*, 63n, 65, 66*, 69, 69n,
    201
[unnamed], mother of Robert, 49
Cosyng, Robert, 118
Cot(t)es, Robert, 54
Thomas, lxviii, lxx, 71, 76, 119, 120, 136, 202

Cotter, William, 27
Couper, Robert, 86
Cunstable, see Constable
Curles, way leading to, 12
Curr(e)y (Curren), Humphrey, lxx, 112, 112n,
    114, 202
Thomas, 112n
Curtes (Curteys), Emma, xxixn
John, 50, 50n
Matilda, 151 (will 23), 202
William, xxixn, xxxviii, xlvii, xlviin
[unnamed], wife of John, 50

Darbe, William, 134
Day(e) (Dey(e)), John, xlviin, xlviiin, liiin, lx,
    lxviii, 44, 50*, 50n, 62, 128, 128n, 202; of
    Worlington, 86
Robert, 50
Walter, 115, 123
William, xlvin, xlviiin, 156 (will 31), 202
Deynis, William, liiin
Dob(e)son, Joan, 95, 95n
John, lxvii, 78
Dobyn, George, 45
John, Dom., 4n, 13, 29, 34, 202
Docking (Do(c)kyng), John, lxviii, 67, 67n, 104,
    202
Thomas, lxix*, 77, 77n, 94*, 202
[unnamed], 121
Domynyk, Simon, l, 201
Don(n)om(e), John, 49, 58, 202
[unnamed], 65
Dow, Thomas, 122
Drax, John, 121
Duff(i)eld, (Duffyld, Dofeld), family, lx
Humphrey, xxxvi, xxxvin, lxviii, 59, 66, 66n*,
    78, 163 (will 38), 202
Paul, lxix, 83, 202
DUNMOW (Essex), inhabitants of, 85
DUNSTABLE (Beds), priory, clock of, ivn
Dyer, Mother, 99
Robert, 49, 123

EAST HARLING (Norfolk), church, tower of,
    xxx
Edward VI, xl, 102n, 108n, 109n, 114n, 118n
Edward the Confessor, xxi
Egyll, John, 86
ELY, xx, 107
cathedral, Prior Crauden's chapel window, xxii
common, 69, 69n, 77
    The Sheld, 77
inhabitants of, 28n, 133
renting pasture to, 65, 65n
Elys, William, xlviin, 153 (will 25)
Emson, Agnes, 65
ERISWELL, xix
bridge going to, making of, 48, 48n
herd of, 108, 108n
inhabitants of, 77

Et(t)on, Simon, Sir, xxxviii, xxxixn, xlii, xlviin, l, lx, lxviii, 44, 44n, 158 (will 34), 202
Everard (Evrod), Alice, 121
  Henry (Herry), 89, 89n

Farthing, Thomas, 135
Fayerwar, John, 44
Federyk, Robert, 28
Fenall, *see* Venall
Ferneley, Richard, xlii
Ffrynge, Thomas, 50
Flanner (Flawner), Hubert, 113*
  Robert, 114, 123
  William, 67
FORDHAM (Cambs), inhabitants of, 11
FORNHAM ST MARTIN, court at, 133
  property in, 17
Frende, Thomas, 13, 202
Frere, Alice, 17, 17n, 34, 34n
  John, xlviin, 17, 17n, 34n, 139 (will 7), 202
  Margaret, 17n
  Robert, 34
Frost(e), James, 136*
  John, xxxvii, lxix, 103*, 107
Fryer, Robert, 43
Fuller(e), Christopher, 107, 202
  John, lxii, 17, 32, 33, 54, 202
  Richard, 44
Fynche, William, 115, 123
Fynne, John, 49
Fysch, Isabel, xxxviii, xxxviiin

Ga(d)ge, William, 115, 123
Gal(l)yon (Gallion, Gallyon), Isabel, Dame, xxx, liv, lxii, 7, 7n, 17, 32, 33, 203
  William, 7n
Garard, John, 89
Gard(e)ner(e), (Garner, Gard(i)nyr, Gerner), family, lx
  Joanna, 78, 78n
  John, xxviiin, xliii, lxviii, 45, 45n, 46, 47, 51*, 52, 53*, 54*, 55*, 56*, 57*, 58*, 59*, 60*, 61, 62*, 63, 64, 65, 66*, 68*, 69*, 70, 70n, 78n, 203
  Jone, 67
  Simon, 65
  Thomas, lxviii, 55, 61, 65, 65n
  William, 100
Gatynbe (Geytonbe), George, Sir, xxxiin, xli, xlviiin, 43, 43n, 44n, 155 (will 29), 203
Gaussaydr, Robert, 44
Gayton, *see* Geyton
Gerold, *see* Jerold
Geson (Gesum, Gesyn, Gyson), Thomas, lii, 45, 49, 76*, 76n
  William, lxviii, 49, 50, 51, 65, 203
Gesye, Thomas, lx, lxviii, 44, 203
Geyton (Gayton), Paul, vicar of Mildenhall, xxv, xxxix, xli, 44, 44n, 45, 48, 61, 61n, 203
Geytonbye, *see* Gatynbe

Gille, Robert, de Schaftesbury, chaplain, xxx, xxxin
Glover, Isabel, 49, 54
Godynge, [*unnamed*], xli
Goodale, Agnes, 30
  Thomas, 30
Goodeall, Mawte, 43
Goodrise, Simon, xlviiin
Gosse, Mother, 115
Grauntt, John, xli
Gre(e)ne, John, xli
  Roger, 35
Gregory, John, lxiii, 13, 121, 203
  William, lord mayor of London, xxix, xxixn, 203
Greneman, [*unnamed*], 128
Guthlac, St., xix, xixn
Gylbyn, William, 31, 203

Hadn(h)am, John, 67
  [*unnamed*], 95
Hall, Robert, 7
  see also Hull
Halsted(e) (Halstead, Hawlsted, Haustede), George, 66, 203
  John, liiin, 121, 166 (will 40), 204
  Mawte, 65, 204
  Richard, 86, 89, 204
  Robert, weaver, 102, 107*, 107n, 111, 114, 115*, 120, 121, 175 (will 50)
  Simon, 50, 204; father of, 50
Harngham, Robert, 121
Hart(e) (Hert), John, xlviiin
  Thomas, 86, 90, 91, 93, 102, 115
Harvy, Agnes, 128
HAUGHLEY, inhabitant of, 84, 84n
Hausteyn, *see* Austen
HAWSTEAD, journey to, about clock, 134
Hay(e), Agnes, 85
  Mother, 103
  [*unnamed*], husband of Agnes, 85
Haynes (Heynes), John, li, lx, lxviii, 43, 122, 122n, 159 (will 35), 204
Helgey, Margaret, lxiii, 16
Hendy, William, 43, 43n
Hennys, John, 46
Henry V, heraldic emblems of, xxix
Henry VII, lxx
Henry VIII, lxx, 57n, 62n, 85n*, 86n, 102n, 103n
Hernes, [*unnamed*], mason, 136
Hert, *see* Hart
Heynes, *see* Haynes
Holme, Agnes, 28
  Maud, 66
  Richard, lxviii, 55
  Thomas, 78
HOLM (Norfolk), abbey of St Benet of, abbot of, 80
Holt, Master, 89, 113
Hop(p)er, Margery, 57, 59, 59n, 61n, 204
  Thomas, xxxvii, xxxviiin, lii, lxvii, lxviii, 43,

43n, 51, 52, 53, 53n, 54*, 55, 55n, 57*, 58*, 61*, 64, 65*, 66, 67*, 68, 68n, 75n, 78n, 120, 127, 162 (will 37), 204
Howt(t)on (Houghton), Margery, xxvn, xxxvi, l, lii, 67, 157 (will 33), 204
   Thomas, lii, 45, 47, 61, 61n, 120, 204
Hull(e) (Hall), Miles, lxx, 120, 120n, 204
   Thomas, xxxvi, 120n, 161 (will 36), 203
Hygham, Mr, 108
Hygne, William, 139 (will 6), 204
Hyll, [unnamed], carpenter, 136
Hynd, [unnamed], xliii, 109, 110
Hynge, Robert, lii

Innes, William, 99, 104*
IPSWICH, craft/trade gild, barbers, lviii
   wax chandlers, lviii
   Corpus Christi procession at, lviii
   pageants and plays at, lvii
   of St Thomas, lviii
   religious gild in, xlvii
ISLEHAM (Cambs), inhabitant of, 122
IXWORTH, journey to, 86

Jacob(e), Thomas, lxix, 100, 104, 204
Jaketyne, Catherine, 50
   William, 50
Jerold (Gerold), John, lxix, 94, 204
   Margaret, widow, 172 (will 47), 204
Jhonsin, Humphrey, 102
Johnson, John, 102
Jones, [unnamed], carpenter, 134, 135*

Katherine of Aragon, 62
Kerver, Richard, 47
Kny(g)ht (Knyte), Edward, 122, 123
   Jeffrey, 85
   [unnamed], 118
Kyd(e) (Kedde), [unnamed], 96, 96n, 100*, 113, 115, 116, 124, 205
Kyng, Thomas, 89
Kynght, Edward, 114

LAKENHEATH, xix
   gilds of, xlviiin
   inhabitants of, xxin
Lan(n)e (Layne), Joan, 67
   John, lxix, lxx, 67, 73*, 73n, 74*, 79, 83, 86*, 90*, 91, 92, 94, 95, 100*, 102, 103*, 104, 110, 112, 115*, 116, 118*, 119, 120, 134, 205
   Paul, 123
   Robert, xli
   Thomas, 50, 51, 124, 205
   William, li
   [unnamed], wife of Thomas, 50
Langham, Humphrey, 66n
   John, 149 (will 20), 205
   Roger, xxxvii, 103*, 113n, 127, 205
   William, lxviii, 66, 66n*
Lanne, see Lane

Lansdale, [unnamed], 134
Lany, Thomas, 65
Lark (river), xix, xxi, 105n
   sluice on, 105n
LAVENHAM, church, rebuilding of, lxiii
Lawe, Thomas, xli
Lee, John, xli, xlii
Lestlathe, Isabel, 31
   Thomas, 31
LEVERTON (Lincs), churchwardens' accounts of, 46n
LIÈGE (Belgium), beguinage in, xlvii
LONDON, city of, arms of, xxix
   lord mayor of, xxix*, lxiii
   Salters' Company, member of, lii, 49n
LONG MELFORD, church, Jesus aisle, 97n
   organ, xxxiv
   rebuilding of, lxiii
   rood-loft, xxxiv
Longs, [unnamed], 134
Lov(e)nesse (Lonnes, Lonesse), William 87*, 88, 90*, 91*, 92, 93, 114, 115, 205
Loth, Mr, 119
LOWESTOFT, church of St Margaret, xxvn
Lupkynne (Lumpkyn), Paul, 114, 123
Luwies, [unnamed], 136
Lynge, John, 157 (will 32), 205
Lynnde, John, 65
Lynne, Dom John, liii
Lytyll John (?Littlejohn), [unnamed], wife of [unnamed], 100*, 101

M[damaged], Thomas, churchwarden, 43
Machoun, Richard, parish chaplain, 2, 205
Makworth (Makwurthe), Elizabeth, 65
   Thomas, 50, 121*
Man(n)(e), John, 100, 205
   Thomas, 99, 102, 107*, 112, 114, 123, 136, 205
Mandall, John, of Thurston, liv, 57, 205
Mansell, John, 67
Mareyner, Nicholas, 8, 205
Marshall, John, 115*
Martyn (Martin), Thomas, chaplain, xxxiin, xl, xli, xlvin, xlviiin, xlix, 146 (will 16), 205
Mary I (Mary Tudor), xliv, 81n, 118n, 133
Mason, John, xxxiin, 101; chaplain, 137 (will 1), 205
   Robert, organ player and clerk, 176 (will 51), 205
   [unnamed], wife of [unnamed], 100
Massage, John, Reverend, of Thaxted (Essex), 7
Matthew, William, xli
Maw, Agnes, 46
May, see Mey
Mayner', Henry, 139 (will 5), 205
Melmay, John, 27
Merchall, Robert, 169 (will 45), 205
Mey(e) (May), John, 89, 90, 136, 205; the younger, 11

Nicholas, warrener, xxin, 75, 114, 123, 168
   (will 43), 205
Robert, 50
Thomas, lx, lxviii, 43, 50, 205; wife of, 49
Meyer, Alice (Halys), 44
   Robert, Dom., 13, 206
Meyrer, Reginald, 95
Midelton, Robert, xlii
Mildenhall, Edmund de, xlix
   chantry of, xlix
   family of, xlix
   see also Myldenhale
MILDENHALL, xix, *passim*
   amercement of, 85, 85n
   Beck (Bek(e)) Row, xx, xxn, lvi, lvii, 2n
      churchwardens of, lix, 94
      churchale at, 8, 10, 27, 35
      collections from, lxii, lxv, 2, 3, 4, 5, 6, 7, 9,
         10, 11, 12, 13, 14, 15, 16, 17, 18, 19, 20,
         21–31, 32, 33–39
      inhabitants of, liv, lxii, lxix, 13n, 71, 77,
         100, 110
      May ale at, 54, 54n
   bridge, going to Eriswell, 48, 48n
   buildings in, almshouse, 45, 54n, 118*, 119
      church house, 49, 54*, 68, 70*, 84, 93n
         rent for, 49, 61
      cottage, Hopper's Cot ('kot') (Hopperys
         cotte), lxvii, 53n, 75, 78, 122
         Le Fysch Cote lately Hoppers, lxvii, 78,
            78n
         Old Coote in the Fen, lxvii, 86
      gild hall, xlvii, 102, 112, 112n, 134, 135
         of Corpus Christi gild, 143, 143n
         of Holy Trinity gild, 93n
         of St John's gild, 116*, 116n
      school house, xliii, 80, 80n, 84, 85, 85n, 87,
         88, 96*, 104, 107, 108, 135
      townhouse, 93n, 107*, 110*, 115*
         yard of, 93
      Warren Lodge, xxi, plate 1
   Cake Street (Cakestrete), xx, xxn, xxin, liv, 3n
      churchale at, 8, 10, 35
      collections from, lxii, lxv, 3, 4, 5, 7, 9, 10,
         17, 18, 19, 20, 21-31
      green, xlvii
      inhabitants of, lxii, 28, 65
   chantry certificate of, xlix
   charnel chapel ('the Carnary'), in churchyard,
      l-li, 122n
      land of (in fields), 121, 122
   church, of St Mary, xxii–xxxi
      land of (in fields), 74, 74n, 121
      property owned by, 53n
      rebuilding of, lxiii
      see also Subject Index *sub* church
         (building), plate, vestments, etc.
      vicar of, xxii, xxxix–xl
   common, lxvii, 69, 69n, 77, 86, 94, 94n, 122
      bridges on, 86
      Ely common, lxvii

      house in, 75
   common water, amercement for, 87
   cross, in marketplace, new, 83
      stone cross, 121
      Swath Cross, 1
      Swaye Cross, xlviin
   fair, xxi
      fair ground (ffeyr spott), 86, 87
   fen, xix, 30, 30n, 86, 96
      cottage in, 86
      East Fen, 120
      Hurst Fen, xix
      pasture in, 65
      Sedge fen ('Segefen'), lxvii, 77, 122
   fire in, xlvii
   Halywell(e), *see* Holywell
   High Town (the Town), xix, xx, lvi, lvii, 2n
      churchale at, 7, 16, 26, 27, 29, 32
      churchwardens of, lix, 66, 94
      collections from, lxii, lxv, 2, 3, 4, 5, 6, 7, 9,
         10, 11, 12, 13, 14, 15, 16, 17, 18, 19, 20,
         21–31, 32, 33-39, 79
      inhabitants of, lxii
      May ale at, 54, 54n
   Holywell (Halywell, Halywelle) Row, xx, xxn,
      xxin, lvi, lvii, 2n
      churchale at, 3, 31, 38, 67
      collections from, lxii, lxv, 2, 3, 4, 5, 6, 7, 9,
         10, 11, 12, 13, 14, 15, 16, 17, 18, 19, 20,
         21–31, 32, 33–39
      inhabitants of, lxii, 49
      land in, 28n
      May ale at, 54, 54n
      messuage in, xlviin
   lake in, lxvii
      draining of, 69, 69n
   lands in, lxvii, 74n, 75, 77
      Almyscroft, 121
      Almyscroft fields, 121
      Bekfield, 122
      Chelmys (messuage), xlvii
      Cottones, 122
      Enyngfeld, 122
      hall, land of (in fields), 121
      Lamcott field, 122
      Lampland, lxvii, 78*
      Landdysdale, 54
      Mildenhall field, 1
      Millfield, 121
      open fields, xlvin
      Peturbornfeld, 121
      Twamell fields, 121
      le Welmer, 1
      Wyndesmyllafeld, 121
   manor, of Aspalys, land of, 122
      of Cottons, land of, 122
      of Mildenhall, xxi
         land of, 121*, 122*
         manor house, xxviii
   market, xxi
      market cross, xxi, 83

market place ('marketstead'), xxviii, 72n
    shops in, xxi, 122
    shambles, xxi
marsh, 122
Mastrihethe, 121
mill, 105n
parish of, xix–xxi
    whole, collection from, 77*, 78*
places in, Cestin's Wong, li
    Corpus Christi yard, xlvii
    Forkes Fen crouch, 121
    Hall Yard, lxvii, 44, 44n
    Holmsey Green, xx, xxn
    Kenny Hill, xx, xxn
    Littley, xx, xxn, 122
    Thistley Green, xx, xxn
place-name derivation, xix
roads, paths, ways in, Beke Way, 122
    Charnock Way, 121
    common way, 121*
    Curles, way leading to, 12
    Framlong Way, 121
    Halywell street, xlviin
    High Street, xxii, l, 113, 113n
    king's highway, 120
    Lamcott path, 121
    mills, way at, 93
        gathering for, 128
        repair of, 128
    Mundes Way, 121
    Old Way, 121, 122*
    Stokpath ('Stokpaht'), 122
    Styepath ('Styepaht'), 122
    Styway, 121
Rows, churchwardens for, 67, 67n
Town, the, see High Town
treasure, xix
West End (West Row), amercement of, 108
West Row (Westrowe), xix, xx, lvi, lvii, 2n
    churchale at, 7, 27, 33, 38, 67n
    churchwardens of, lix, 94
    collections from, lxii, lxv, 2, 3, 4, 5, 6, 7, 9,
        10, 11, 12, 13, 14, 15, 16, 17, 18, 19, 20,
        21–31, 32, 33-39, 78
    inhabitants of, lxii, lxix, 76, 78*, 78n, 166
        (will 40), 173 (will 48)
    May ale at, 54, 54n, 58
Wilde Street (Wyldestrete), xix, lvi, 10n, 26n
    churchale at, 10, 35
    collections from, lxii, lxv
    inhabitants of, lxii, 76, 167 (will 42)
    land in, 28n
    'young men and women' (as a group),
        churchale of, 4, 4n
        collections from, lvi, lxv
Morby, Henry, lxix, 100
MOREBATH (Devon), purchase of Bible at, 99n
Morle(y), Alice, xlviin, 150 (wil 21), 206
    Henry, 7, 7n, 75, 122, 206
    John, 49, 58, 65
    Richard, xlviin

Robert, 49*, 49n*
Mors, Henry, 16, 206
Mortlock, family, lxviii
Mort(y)mer, Robert, 86n
    Rose, 86, 86n
Mot, Margery, 49
    [unnamed], mother of Margery, 49
Mygel(a)y, James, xlii
Myldenhale, John, of Bury St Edmunds, carver,
    xxixn

Newman, John, 89*, 90*, 91
Nores (Norrys), Richard, 64, 77
Northeast, Peter (historian), lxiii
NORWICH, bell-founder from, liv
    bishop of, 80, 80n
    carnery chapel, ln
    cathedral close, ln
    dean of, 46
    diocese of, xxxix
        charitable payment to, 46, 46n, 47, 47n, 53,
            56, 57, 60, 63, 64*, 68, 69, 70, 71, 73
        mason from, xxv
NOTTINGHAM, alabaster from, 46n
Nowce, Henry, turner, xxixn, 164 (will 39), 206

Oger, Roger, xli
Oldbury, Thomas, xxxix, xli, 206
Olever, Harry, xlii
Ouse, (river), xxi, 30n
OXBOROUGH (Norfolk), inhabitants of, 29n
Oxf(f)ord, Father, 135
    John, 89, 96, 101, 101n
    [unnamed], 135

Pachet(t) (Pacheth), family, lx, 45n
    George, 54*
    John, 45, 45n, 46*, 47, 51*, 51n, 52, 53, 59*,
        206
    Robert, 152 (will 24), 206; chantry chaplain,
        xl, xlii, xlix, 206
    William, lxviii, 45*, 45n, 47, 49, 54, 63*, 206
    [unnamed] 79, 81
Page (Pege), Robert, lxviii, 51, 206
Palmer, [unnamed] 89*, 206
Palton (Paltun), Nicholas, lxviii, 71, 76, 89, 206
Pantelle, [unnamed], wife of [unnamed], 105
Pare, Mother, 115
Parker, Thomas, vicar, xxxix, 206
Patchett, see Pachet
Payn, John, lv
Paynet, John, lxiv, 14, 26, 38, 38n, 206
    Ralph, xlviiin
Pe(a)che(y) (Pe(t)chey), Christian, xlviin
    family, lx, lxviii, 102n
    John, xxxvii, lxviii, 71, 76, 102, 102n, 206;
        the younger, 114, 123
    Peter, lxx, 120, 206
    Robert, lxviii, 59, 86, 206; the younger, lxix,
        83, 206

William, xlvii, lxix, 50, 67, 76, 107, 122, 167 (will 42), 206
Pege, *see* Page
Petche, *see* Pe(a)che(y)
Pey, Robert, 44
Place (Plase), Andrew, xli, 67, 122, 122n, 207
George, xlviin, lxviii, 67, 67n, 107
John, lxviii, 51, 77*, 77n, 133, 207
Richard, 67, 67n, 207
Rose, xlviin
Simon, 50, 207
Thomas, xxxviii, 142 (will 10), 207
William, Sir, chaplain, xxxviii, 125, 207; of Lynn, 49, 207
[*unnamed*], wife of William of Lynn, 49
Planer, Robert, 133
[*unnamed*], 133
Playford(e), family, 3n, 13n, 207
George, 13, 207
Katherine, l*
John, xlvin, xlviin, lxiii, 13, 13n, 120, 207
Thomas, xlvin, xlviiin, lxiii, 3, 13n, 207
Plummer, John, 44
Pol(l)yngton, (Po(u)llington(n), Pollytun, Polyng), John, thatcher, 79, 87*, 104, 109, 116, 123, 134, 135, 177 (will 52), 207
Nicholas, xxxvii, xliv, 102, 109, 110, 112, 113*, 116, 117*, 118*, 119*, 123, 134, 135, 207
Richard, xxxvin, xliii, xliv, 75, 84*, 85*, 87, 88*, 93*, 94, 94n, 95*, 96*, 97, 98, 99, 107, 108*, 109
[Richard] 91, 96, 100, 101*, 103, 104*, 207
Thomas, 104, 207
[*unnamed*], 71, 72, 79, 136
Po(o)pe, Henry, liv, lxvii, 45, 78, 78n, 121*, 121n, 208
Master, Mr, 50, 96, 116, 122, 124, 208
Pope (Bishop of Rome), xxxiii, lxvii, 85, 85n
Porye, Peter, 114
Potter, Thomas, xxxiv, xxxvii, xliii, lxix, 101n, 103, 104, 107, 112, 116, 123
[Thomas], 101*, 102, 104, 112, 113*, 116, 118*, 119*, 208
[*unnamed*], 135
Poule, [*unnamed*], plumber, 73n*, 74*, 75, 90, 208
Powle, Jone (?John), 49
Prat(te), John, 100
Robert, 121
Punge, John, 32, 32n, 38, 207
Matilda, 32n, 38, 207
Purdy, [*unnamed*], 104
Puttock, Thomas, liii
Puwke, John, xli
Pynhorne, Katherine, 54

Quasshe, Thomas, lxix, 71n, 100, 114, 208
[Thomas], 71, 103, 111
Queash, Goodman, 134

RANWORTH (Norfolk), antiphoner of, xxxiin
Rawling, William, 67
Re(e)ve, Alice, 58
John, abbot of Bury, 80n
Robert, 43, 43n, 58
William, charnel priest, xxxiin, xl, xli, xlii, li, 76*, 76n, 169 (will 44), 208
Ripley, John, xlii
Robb, Agnes, of Fordham (Cambs), 11
Rolf(f), family, lxviii
Thomas, yeoman, lxviii, 63, 173 (will 48), 208
Rugg, William, bishop of Norwich, 80n
Ryngstede, Thomas, xxxix, 2, 2n, 3, 8, 208

Saddeler, William, 120
Sadyler, John, liv, 45, 45n, 46*, 50, 208
SALISBURY (Wilts), parish of St Edmund, churchwardens' accounts, lxviin
Salste, Robert, 94
Salter, James, 78, 78n
John, lxvii
Samson, abbot of Bury St Edmunds, xxi
Sarnyd, John, 51
Savage, John, 120
Savernak, William, xlixn
Sawer, Richard, l
Schadynhalk, *see* Chadenhalk
Schene, *see* Shene
Scherd, *see* Sherd
Schrevener, *see* Screvyner
Scott (Skott), Agnes, 78n
Thomas, lxix, 78, 78n, 83, 209; vicar, xxxix, xlii, xliin, 92n, 109*
Screvyner (Sc(h)revener(e)), John, xxxii, xliii, 45, 45n, 46*, 47*, 66, 209
Sedley, *see* Siddley
Seman, John, 122
Seyman, [*unnamed*], 77
SHELFANGER (Norfolk), dramatic production at, lviii
Shene, (Schene), John, lxx, 119, 120, 209
Sherd (Scherd), Alice, 73, 74, 75, 209
Annabel, 73, 74, 75, 209
Ralph, 77, 209
Thomas, lii, 72, 73, 74*, 74n, 75*, 78, 209
SHIPPEA HILL (S(c)hephey, Sheep Isle) (Cambs), inhabitant of, 77, 77n, 122
Shyrloke, Richard, 108*
Siddley (Sydley(e), Sedley), Martin, Mr, gentleman, 99, 102, 102n, 107*, 112, 210
see also Sydle
Sigo, *see* Sygo(o)
Skynner, Isabel, 16
Sly, John, 120, 121
Smith (Smyt(h)(e)), John, xxxii, 50*, 55, 55n, 56, 57, 58*, 82, 136, 209; shoemaker, 146 (will 17)
Robert, 46
Sokerman, *see* Suckerman
Sopere, Elizabeth, of Barton Mills, xxxviii
Robert, of Barton Mills, xxxviii, xxxviiin

SOUTHWOLD, church, pulpit in, 69n
  inhabitant of, lv
Sparhawke (Sparhauk(e), Sperhawke), John, lxx,
  50, 102, 114, 120, 210
  Richard, 49
Sparke, [unnamed], clockmaker from Hawstead,
  134
Speed, John, xxxviiin, 4, 4n, 7, 29, 34, 137 (will
  2), 210
Spyrling, [unnamed], of Bury, 134
Stalham, John, xlviiin, xlviiiin, 13n, 210
Staloun, John, the younger, xlvin, xlviin, xlviiin,
  lxiin, lxiii, 13, 32, 32n, 141 (will 8), 210
Step(p)ney, Anthony, 112, 135
Ston, Robert, 91, 210
STUNTNEY (Cambs), inhabitants of, 94, 94n
Style, Richard, 50
Suckerman, (Sokerman, Suk(k)erman), Robert,
  xxxvii, 103*, 112, 112n, 113n, 127, 210
  Simon, xlviin, 120*, 210
Sutton, Richard, 14n, 29, 29n, 210
  William, lxiv, 14, 14n, 26n, 29, 29n, 210
SWAFFHAM (Norfolk), churchwardens'
  accounts, lxviin
Swayn(e), Alice, 121
  William, 49
Sydle, Mr, 86
  see also Siddley
Sygo(o) (Sigo), Agnes, widow, xlin, 151 (will
  22), 209
  family, 13n, 28n
  John, 209
  Margery, 28, 209
  Matilda, 13n
  Robert, lxiii, 13, 13n, 28n, 209; Master, 209
  Thomas, xxxiin, xlixn, 138 (will 3), 209
  William, 13n
Symond(e) (Symund), George, 65
  Thomas, liiin, 67
Symonds, Ralph, 121
  Robert, 65, 65n

Tabard, Richard, 86
Tawmage, Master, 66
Taylor, Margery, 31
  Thomas, 44
  William, 34 [recte Thomson, tailor]
Taylour alias Wyllyamsone, John, 143 (will 11),
  210
Terrell, see Tirrell
THAXTED (Essex), inhabitant of, 7
Thetford, Mother, 97
THETFORD, lviii
  Clunaic house, lviii
  house of Austin friars ('the New House'), liii
  house of Dominican friars ('the Old House'),
    liii
  items transported to, 89
  priory, 62n
  road to, 57n
  roper from, 100

St Mary's chapel in Bailey End, 7n
Thomson, William, 4, 4n, 7, 8, 29, 210
  see also Taylor, William
Thurston (Thurstann), Hubert, 123, 210
  Robert, lxx, 112, 114, 115, 210
THURSTON, inhabitant of, liv, 57
Tirrell (Terrell, Tyr(r)el(l)), John, 58, 211
  Katherine, 89, 89n, 90*, 179 (will 55), 211
  Robert, xlvii
  Thomas, li
  William, 108, 108n, 211
Treupeny, Richard, labourer, 166 (will 41), 211
Tuddenham, Sir Thomas, of Oxborough, 29n
Tuppyng, Thomas, xli
Turner, John, 109, 109n, 211
Tyd(d)(e), John, 36, 36n, 95, 211
  Richard, 65
  Robert, lxiin, 35, 35n, 211
  Thomas, xlviin, 8, 121, 144 (will 14), 211
  [unnamed], mason, 134, 135
Tyler, William, 52
Tylney, Mother, 103, 211
Tyr(r)ell, see Tirrell
Tyson, John, xliiin, 211

Umfrey, [unnamed; or forename], 75
Undley Common, xix

Vekery, see Weker(y)
Venall (Fenall), Thomas, lxix, 94*, 202, 211
Vouster, [unnamed], 118, 118n

Wakman, [unnamed], 52
WALBERSWICK, church, St Andrew's, clock, lv
    flint tower of, liii
  parish, gathering for glass window, lxn
    clerk of, xlii
Walsham Ralph de, l, 211
WALSINGHAM (Nfk), Our Lady of, 62n
Warburton, Edmund, xlii
Warde, William, 67
Wareyn, family, 28n
  Isabel, (née), 28, 28n
  John, 28, 28n*
  William, 28n
Warren, Robert, 65
Watts, see Berton alias Watts
Wayneman, Henry, li
Waysett, see Wyset
Webb(e), Alice, xxvn, xlviiin
  Edward, lxviii, 55
  Robert, 114*
  Thomas, 99
  see also Clerke alias Webbe
Wederes (Wederys), see Wo(o)derys
Weker(y) (Vekery, Vikery), Master [the vicar],
    48*, 61*, 66, 71, 74, 75, 86, 93, 128
Weng(g)e, Francis, 110, 211
  John, xxxixn, 211
  Richard, carpenter, xxixn
  Thomas, xxixn; Sir, xxxix, 211

see also Wynge
WESTHALL, parish church, screen in, xxviiin
WESTMINSTER, abbey, chantry chapel of
   Henry V in, xxix
Weynge, William, 58
Whit, [*unnamed*], wife of [*unnamed*], 135
Wichforde, Richard de, vicar of Mildenhall, xxii
Willes, Nicholas, lxviii, 63, 63n, 211
Wilson, Geoffrey, xlii
   John, 89*
Witwell, Thomas, xlviin
Wochall, John, 123
Wode, Jone [Joan], 43
Wodehirst, Robert, mason, from Norwich, xxv
Wo(o)derys (Wederes, Wederys), family, 32n
   John, xlviin, 8, 211
   Robert, 32, 211
   Thomas, lxviii, 71, 77, 76, 211
WOLLATON (Notts), antiphoner of, xxxiin
Woodrise, Richard, xlviin
Worde, Mother, 105
WORLINGTON, xix, 105n
   inhabitants of, xxxviii, 86
   rector of, xxxviii [Simon Bagot]
Wotton (Wotun), John, 89, 90, 96*, 100, 101
Wright(e) (Wryght(e)), Edmund, xxxvii, lxix,
   103, 107
   John, xlii, 32n, 38
   Margaret, of Lakenheath, xxin
   Matilda, 38
   Roger, xxxix

Wryt(t)e, Harry, 105
   Margery, 105*
Wrytle, [*unnamed*], 8
Wylde, William, xlvin
Wyl(l)kynson (Wilkinson), John, vicar, xxxiv,
   xxxix, xli-xlii, 50, 61n, 92n, 94, 94n, 211
Wyllyamsone, *see* Taylour *alias* Wyllyamsone
Wylser, John, 128
Wylson, *see* Wilson
Wyng(e), John, 49
   Thomas, xli, xlin, xlixn, 211
   [*unnamed*], father of John, 49
   see also Wenge
Wyset (Wayset), Robert, 121*

Yorewly, Anthony, of Cambridge, 84
York, Lord of, 122

[*unnamed*], Bess, great, 105
[*unnamed*], boy [*unnamed*], [*supported by
   parish*], 100*, 100n, 101*, 102*, 103
[*unnamed*], James, tailor, 90
[*unnamed*], Margaret, Mistress, 67
[*unnamed*], Richard, Sir, priest, xxxiii, 92
[*unnamed*], Robert, 135; of Bury, 51; of Lincoln,
   100
[*unnamed*], Simon, Sir, priest, 53
[*unnamed*], Thomas, Sir, of Ely, 133, 210
[*unnamed*], William, barber, 86
[*unnamed soul*], 28

INDEX OF SUBJECTS

Roman numerals refer to pages of the introduction. An asterisk * after the reference indicates that the subject occurs more than once on that page. An 'n' following the reference indicates that the subject is to be found in a footnote on that page.

The items in the wills in Appendix 2 have not been indexed. The nine wills that are in the 'Baldwyne' Register (reference SROB, IC 500/2/9 and 500/2/10) have been indexed in Northeast and Falvey, *Index of Wills of the Archdeaconry of Sudbury, 1439–1474* (SRS, 2010).

agreement, *see* obligation
ale, for flashing, 81
  see also food and drink
almshouse, lxn, 45, 45n
  chimney of, 45
    mending of, 118
  crotchets for, 118
  rafters ('rafte') for, 118
  thatching of, 119
altars, 128n*
  aumbry of, mending of, xxv, 60
  desk, mending of, 83
  high, xxv, xxxv, xxxvi, 69, 69n
    bequest to, 78n, 86n, 100n
    lamp of, lxx
  Jesus altar, xxxv, 97n
    cross on, xxxv, 97
  in Lady Chapel, xxxv
  low, 125*
  of stone, destruction of, lxvii, 110, 110n
    survival of, 118n
  St John's altar, xxxv, 69n
  St Margaret's altar, xxxv, xlviii, 112
  side altar, xliv, 69n, 128n
  south altar, setting up of, 135
  stone, laying of, 136
  vestry altar, xxxv, 69n, 72, 72n
amercement, 85, 85n, 87, 98, 98n, 107, 108
animals, bullocks, 108
    for use of church, 122
    pasturing of, 65, 65n, 86
  cattle, 122
    driving of, 94, 94n, 119
  horse, 56, 89
    hire of, 117, 136
  see also birds
anniversary, *see* church services
arm, *see* relic

bargain, regarding carpenter's day rates, 90
bedding, coverlet, xxxvi
bede-roll, l, lii, 49n
beehive, xxviiin

bells (general), xxxi, liii–liv, lxii, lxiv, 7n, 47, 62, 119
  baldrick, liii, liv, 45, 46*, 47, 48*, 64, 104, 115, 123
    mending (making) of, 54, 58, 64, 69, 70*, 72, 75, 134
    white leather for, 69
  buckles for, 69
  carpentry for, 81
  clapper, liii, liv, 46, 51*, 64
    carriage of, 51
    making (mending) of, 51, 54, 55, 57, 60, 63, 64, 69, 72, 90
  exchange of, 86
  forelocks for, 80
  frame (new) for, xxx, liii, 89, 89n, 90
    ironwork for, 90
  hallowing of, 58, 58n
  hanging of, 89, 90
  income from, 86
  ironwork for, 46
  keeping, 79, 80, 102, 133, 134
  latches for, 72, 108, 133
  'lytell' (handheld?), 111*
  of latten (handheld?), 124, 127
  overweight of, 86
  recasting of, liv
  removal of, to Bury, 88, 88n
  repairs to (mending), 7, 46, 54, 69, 80
  ringing, 79
    at 8 o'clock, 134
    for royalty, 57, 70
  rope, liv, lxix, 13, 46, 47*, 48, 51*, 52*, 53*, 54, 55, 58*, 59, 60*, 62, 64, 66, 68*, 69, 72, 80, 88, 89, 90, 95*, 96, 97, 98, 100, 102n, 110, 119*, 133
    joists ('dormanttes') for, 92
    locks for, 100
    making (mending), 52, 63, 66, 70
    piecing of, 119
  running costs of, liv
  seen at Bury, 98
  standard, lxv, 13

227

stock, liii, liv, lxiv, 13, 62, 86*, 89
  nails for, 79
trussing of, 48, 60, 66, 68*
wainscots, for bell (chamber), 13
weighing of, at Bury, 88, 88n, 89
wheel, liii, liv, lxiv, 13, 47, 89
  mending (making) of, 62, 66, 68, 71, 95, 97
  nails for, 97
  piecing of, 119
  small nails for, 80
  white leather for, 69
bells (specific), 'Bagot's', liv-lv, 59, 136
  baldrick for, 91
  boards for, 136
  clapper for, making, 91
  frame, mending of, 82, 136
  hanging of, 136
  line for, 104
  mending of, 96, 101
  ropes, 72, 88, 93
  timber for, 82
  trussing, 75
  wheel, mending of, 59, 96
first, stay for, 80
  wheel, mending of, 82
'fore bell', 72
  mending wheel of, 80
fourth, lv
great, liv
  baldrick for, 79
    mending of, 110
  bequest to, 78
  buckle tongue for, 79
  clapper for, 66
    making of, 108, 134
  'gynnes' for, 73, 73n
  iron bolt for, 75
  latch for, 73
  mending of, 73, 79
  moving of, 73n
  ringing, 79
  rope, 72, 80
    ending of, 73
  taken to Bury, 89
  wheel, 79
  wood for, 79
housling, 128, 128n
number 7, xxx
number 8, xxx
sacring, hanging of, 48
  line for, 87
sanctus, xxv, lv
  rope for, 53
  wheel, mending of, 73
second (little), xxx, liv, lxv, 46, 46n
  baldrick, making (mending) of, 74, 74n, 92
  clapper, making (mending) of, 63, 92
  hanging of, 46
  making of, 13
  reparation of, 63
  rests for, 46

rope for, 48, 70, 101
stocking of, 63
taken to Bury, 90
trussing, 62
tuning of, 63
wheel, mending of, 51, 53, 57, 63, 87
third, liv, 57, 72
  rope, 75*, 80
    mending of, 97
  trussing, 74
  wheel, making of, 75
  new, 57
bell-ringer, liii, 46, 57, 136
bell-ringing, accident, liii
bequests to church (terminology), bequest/
  bequeathed, 50, 67, 76, 77*, 78*, 95*
  donation, 77*, 78*
  gift, 63, 65, 77, 115, 124*, 128*
  goods, 97
  last will, 67*
  legacy, 85*, 86, 100*
  quetheword, xliv, xlivn, lxii, lxiv, 4n, 43*,
    44*, 49*, 50*, 51, 54*, 58*, 61*, 62, 65*,
    66*, 67*, 86*, 86n, 122n
  testament, 107
  will, 65*, 67
  [not specified], 43, 49, 50, 54
bier, boards for, 87
  iron and nails for, 87
  making of, 87
  tapestry covering for, 129
bills, writing of, 52
birds, capons, 105
  chickens, 105
  doves, 135
  pigeons, 105
  owls, 135
  see also animals
board (board and lodging), for visiting chaplain,
  53, 53n
  for workman, 36, 48, 54, 56*, 57, 58, 59, 60,
    64*, 68, 74, 75, 81, 81n, 82*, 84, 88, 88n,
    89, 90*, 91*, 92*, 93*, 95, 98*, 99, 102,
    103, 107, 108*, 109*, 110*, 112*, 112n,
    113, 116, 117, 135*, 136
  on holy day, 117
  (beer), 79
  (breakfast), 79
  (drink), 73
  (meat), 72, 81, 83*, 118
  (meat and drink), 66, 87, 88, 117
  (supper), 79, 89
boards, see materials
bond, see obligation
bookbinding materials, 81n
  boards, 81
  buckles, leather, 81
  burden, 82
  clasps, 36, 71, 71n
  'dowes' (dowels?), 36
  flour, 82

glue, 36
'mouth', 82
ink, 82
red, 82
lining, leather, 81
skin, 82
packthread, 36
parchment, 36, 71, 82*
silk, 36
skin, 57, 70, 81
skin, calf, 82
red leather, 81, 82*
thread, blue, 82*
great, 82
red, 82*
white, 82*
vellum, 82
box, full of relics, 125
with crystals and knops of pearl, 125
boy [unnamed], 100*, 100n, 101*, 102*
see also poor
bread and wine, for communicants, 118, 118n, 119*
see also food and drink
bridge, 86
making of, 48, 48n
building materials, see materials
burial in the church(yard), 49*
making good after, 83n
payment due, 49*
butts, archery for, amercement for, 85, 98, 98n

camp, (rebel), at Bury, bread to, 109, 109n
expenses at, 112, 112n
money to, 109, 109n
candles (for lighting) (not religious), 104, 104n
candles (lights) (general), lxvii, 47n, 59n, 72
wax for, xxxvii
see also materials
Paschal candle, 47, 47n, 51, 51n, 55n, 59n, 61, 66, 91n, 95, 97
candlestick for, 51n
draining of, 52
head, angels for, 53
mending of, 71
line or cord for, 51, 83
making of, 55, 55n, 57, 57n, 63, 70*, 73, 74, 75, 83, 88, 91, 99, 101, 101n, 135
rope for, 66
wax for, 51, 53, 59, 63*, 64, 70, 73, 75, 83, 88, 91, 135
see also lamp; lights
candlesticks, xxxvii, 100, 107, 124, 127, 135
copper-gilt, 71
polishing and burnishing, 76
copper, 125
latten, 71, 125
polishing and burnishing, 76
scouring, 72
soldering, 71, 76
scouring, 51, 59, 71, 91, 95

silver, mending of, 98
canopy, xxxv, xxxvn
carriage, 51, 57*, 64, 89
by water, 30n
of bells, 88, 89*, 90, 119
of bible, 99
of charcoal, 79
of clay, 56, 134
of hutch (chest), 104
of lead, 68, 116*, 117*
of lime, 74, 103, 116, 118, 134
of sand, 56, 64, 74, 113, 117, 134
of stone, 88, 96, 134
of tiles, 95
of timber, 87, 116, 134
overland, 30n
censer, see plate
chalice, see plate
chantry, xxxv, xlviii–li
certificates, xl
see also parish records
chapel, bell, li
chaplain, xlviii
stipend of, xlviii
foundation of, xxxv
perpetual, xl*
property to fund, xlviii
charitable expenses (diocesan) (Norwich alms), 46, 46n, 47, 47n, 53, 56, 57, 60, 63, 64*, 68, 69, 70, 71, 73, 74
charnel chapel ('the Carnary'), l–li, 122n
chest (coffer, hutch), xxii, xxx, xxxiii, xxxvii*, 45*, 102, 102n, 107*
carriage of, 104
for the poor, 103, 103n
lock for, 104
for the register, 103, 103n
in vestry, broken by thieves, 87, 87n
mending lock of, 91
ironwork for, 83
key for, xxxiii, 80, 83, 84, 84n
lock for, 52, 52n, 53, 53n, 75, 85
mending, 99
on rood-loft, 102
choir, xxxii, 92n
rochets for, 128
choir master (rector chores), xxxii, xlii, lxv, 87, 87n
choristers, 92n
chrismatory, see plate
church (building), xxii–xxxi
aisle, xxv, liii, lxiii
north, roof of, xxix
paving of, 80
south, 69n
roof of, xxix
windows, xxv
arcades, xxv
battlements, fixing stones of, 80
bell chamber (solar), liii, 57
inserting wooden floor in, 133

229

mending, 133
  sweeping of, 63, 69, 69n
bequest to reparation of, 43n, 44n, 45, 49n, 50,
  58, 63n, 67n, 77*, 77n, 78n*, 95n, 100n
burial within, request for, lxvii
chancel, xxii, xxv, 69n
  arch, xxv
  door, key for, 53, 60, 60n
    lock for, 52n
  lectern in, 87
  roof, xxiin
  window, xxii, xxiin, plates 3 and 4
chapel, cleaning, 118
  door, lock for, 99
  Lady Chapel, xxviii, xxix, xxxiv, 55, 55n,
    112n
    bequest to, 77*, 78
  in north chancel, 72n
  of St John the Baptist, xxv, xlviii, 112n,
    116n
  of St Margaret, xxv
  of St Michael, xxviii
chimney, 60
choir (stalls), cloths for, mending of, 57, 73
  curtains for, mending of, 73
  hooks, 57
  ironwork for, 57, 113
  line and nails for, 98
  mending of, 116
  removal of, 112, 112n
  setting up, 113
choir, chair, mending of, 81
cleaning/sweeping, 62, 110
clerestory, xxv, lxiii
  window in, mending of, 97
door, bars for, 60
  key for, 96
  lock for, 52, 52n, 75
  main, 43, 43n
  making of, 55
doorways, xxviii
funeral slab of Richard de Wichforde in, xxii
grave, in church, mending of, 71
gutters, scouring of, 46
lantern, 75
  door for, 73
  leading of, 73, 73n
nave, xxv, plate 4, liii, lxiii
  roof, xxv, plate 4
    angel roof, xxix
nether storeys, glazier's work on, 80
paving ('pamenting', 'pathyn'), 47, 51, 59, 62,
  81, 83, 83n, 85
  floor tiles (pament), 48
  in a grate, 73
  laying, 85
  lime for, 73
  mending of, 56, 68, 70, 87, 96, 99, 135, 136
  repairing floor, 110, 110n
  stone for, sawing of, 109
  tiles, 95

pentice, boards for, 73
phases of, xxi
pinnacle, 56
porch, chapel door over, 91
  Galilee porch, xxx
    vaulted roof, xxx
  mending of paving in, 87
  north, xxviii, plate 6
  paving, mending of, 87
roof, leading of, 47n, 64
  mending lead of, 97
staircase to sanctus bell-tower, 92n
steeple (tower), xxx, liii, liv, lv, 17, 56
  beer drunk in, 79
  bell frame (new), constructed in, 89, 89n
  building of, liii, lxiv
    collections for, xxx
  clay for, 91
  door, boards for, 133
    key for, 113
    lock and keys for, 90
    mending, 90
    mending lock for, 71, 72, 118
    nails for, 79*, 134
    staple for, 118
  inspected by carpenter, 84, 85
  ladder for, 87
  leads, pulled down, 119
    'reved' (removed), 90*, 90n
  making clean, 63, 80, 118, 119
  middle solar of, mending of, 91
    nails for, 91*
    repair of, 90*
  roof, laths for, 92
  soldering on spire, 81
  stage (scaffolding) of, 90, 93
    line for attaching, 90
  timber for, 90
    burnt, removed, 119
  well of, 133
  windows, laths for, 70
    lattice, 133
      nails for, 134
    mending of, 87, 108, 118
    work on, 72, 72n, 133
vanes (on pinnacle), 56*, 56n
vestry, xxii, plate 2, 69n, 72n, 136
  almery in, key for, 96
  chest (hutch) in, 83, 87, 87n, 91
  cleaning, 89
  door, 45, 90
    hinges ('gemewys') for, 55
    key for, 92
    lining, 60
    lock for, 89, 90
      mending of, 59, 87, 88
      removal of, 91
    making of, 52
  repairs to, 87n
  roof, laying lead, 118, 117n
    lead for, 117

setting up (wooden frame), 117, 117n
taking down, 115, 115n
solar door, key for, 92, 92n
wall, making of, 90
over door, making of, 88
stone for, 90
windows, glass, repairing of, 88
hewing of, 88
iron for, 88
walls, flashing, 80
mending of, 83, 135
whitewashing, xxviii, 103, 103n, 104
see also chuchyard wall
window, 117, 117n
glass, 83, 88*, 93, 103, 103n, 109, 109n, 116
coloured, 98n, 99, 109n
mending of, 88, 118
mending iron bars for, 93
replacing, 103n
sweeping of, 63
glazing of, 68, 72, 98n
mending of, 87
west, 133
mending of, 82
church box (for money), 52, 54, 84
niche for, 52
church goods, delivered to Bury, 119, 119n
church house, 49
bed for, 54
board for, 70
mending (repairing) of, 54, 68
thatching, 70, 84
church services, anniversary, lii-liii, 74, 74n, 75
commemorative masses, xliv
mass of Jesus (Holy Name of Jesus), 97n
cope for, 125
obit, 73
Requiem Mass, cope, black, for, 125
sangred, lii, 59, 59n, 66, 66n, 71, 72, 74, 75
Sunday procession, xxxvi
trental, lii-liii
St Gergory's trental, lii
churchale, see parish activities
churchwardens, 13, 14, 26, 48, 50, 51, 59, 63, 66, 71, 76, 83, 84*, 91, 94, 97, 99, 102n, 103, 105, 113n, 114
appointment of, lix, 2n
churchreeves, 43, 63
expenses, at visitation, 102, 102n
names of, lx, 13, 14, 26, 43, 44, 51, 55, 59, 63, 66, 67, 71, 76, 83, 94, 100, 102n, 107, 112, 114, 119, 120, 135, 136
number of, lix
old (before sale of church goods), 133
priest as, xxxviii*
status of, lix-lx
term of office, lix
churchyard, 1
chalk for, 63
charnel in, xxxix, 122

cistern [location unknown], lxiii, 20, 20n
cleaning of, 63
gate, boards for, 87
bolt for, 118
iron for, 91, 113
ironwork for, 81, 86
lock for, 48, 62, 68, 75, 91, 95, 96, 119
market, mending of, 72, 72n
mending (making), 47, 52, 57, 66, 68*, 80, 82, 85, 86, 91, 92, 95, 96, 99, 113*, 113n, 119
nails for, 91
on north side, mending of, 135
staple for, 48, 75
west, 134
mending of, 72, 72n
timber for, 97
grate, cleaning of, 62, 62n, 79, 97, 99, 101
paving of, 73
removing earth in, 93
stile, making (repairing) of, 53, 134
timber for, 134
wall, 48
bank against, 91
lengthening of, 64
reparation of, 63
roughcasting of, 48
see also church
clergy (parish), chaplain (unspecified), xxx, xxxviii*, xl-xlii, lxiii, lxiv, 2, 8, 14, 20, 26, 44n*, 53, 122, 137 (will 1), 138 (will 4), 142 (will 9), 146 (will 16)
annual rate of pay of, xxx, xl
chantry chaplain, xl, 62n
chantry priest, xxix, 158 (will 34)
income of, lxvii
charnel chaplain, li*, 76, 169 (will 44)
curate, xl
deacon, xxv, xxxv
suit of vestments for, 124, 125*
gild chaplain, xl
parish chaplains, xxviii, xli, lx
priest, xxv, xxxiii, xxxv, xxxvi, xxxviii-xlii, 155 (will 29), 156 (will 30)
payment to, 73, 74, 75
suit of vestments for, 124, 125*
rector, xxxviii
subdeacon, xxv, xxxv
suit of vestments for, 124, 125*
vicar, xxii, xxv, xxxiv, xxxix-xl, xli, 2n, 4, 44, 44n, 45, 48, 48n, 50, 61*, 61n*, 66, 74, 75, 86, 92, 92n, 94, 94n, 128
clock, xxx, xliii, lv*, 46*, 47*, 95
bell of, hanging of, 134
chimes, lv
clock house, 133
making of, 119
dial, lv
fetching man to see to, 134
iron work for, 96
keeping, see winding

knot of, making of, 82, 82n
ladder for, 109
ladder piece for, 87
nails for, 110
repairs to, lv, 47*, 48, 54, 56, 57, 61, 71, 72,
    73, 90, 93, 97, 99, 104, 109, 114, 119, 133*
ropes for, 48, 59, 95
    mending, 72
teeth for, 102
wheel, mending of, 73*, 87, 101
winding of (keeping), lv, 45, 45n, 47, 51*,
    52*, 53*, 54, 55*, 56, 57*, 58*, 59*, 60*,
    61, 62*, 63*, 64, 65, 66*, 68*, 69*, 70*,
    71, 72*, 73, 74*, 75, 79, 80, 81*, 82, 83*,
    84*, 85*, 87, 88*, 91, 93, 94, 95, 96*, 97*,
    98, 99, 100, 101*, 103, 107, 108*, 109*,
    110*, 112, 113, 118, 133*
wire for, 57, 83, 92, 93, 113
cloths (liturgical), xxxi, 103, 128, 133*
    donated to church, 78
    for altar stalls ('stolys at the auter', or
        stoles), 124
    for choir stalls ('stolys for qwere', or
        stoles), 124, 127
    for lectern, white, with garters, 124, 127
    for the sacrament, silk, embroidered with
        gold, 124, 127
    for the sepulchre, fine, 124, 127
        stained, 124, 127
        with frontlet, 124, 127
    mending of, 70
    plaincloth, 111*
    ribbon, 111
    silk, of damask work 'popyngaye grene',
        129
    stained, of the Resurrection, 111
    see also washing
altar cloth, xxxv, xxxvi, 51, 69, 72, 111*,
    124*, 126*, 127*
    fine, 128
    mending of, 51, 55
    of diaper, 106*, 126*
        fine, 126
    of plaincloth, 106*, 126*
    staining of, 88
        with drops of blood, 129
    with clouds on, 124
    with garters, 124
altar covering ('koveryng'), 127*, 128
altar frontal (frontlet), xxxv, xxxvi, 124*
altar hanging, 103n, 124*
    stained, 124, 127
    white, with garters, 124, 127
    with clouds on, 124, 127
    with pictures of St Gregory, 124, 127
banner cloths, 100, 100n
    silk, 124, 127
corporas case, 111*, 126*
    with pictures on, 111
corporas cloth, 111*, 126*
coverlet, 124, 127

    with lions on, 111
    covering, tapestry, for the bier, 129
cross cloth, of the Trinity, 127
    with garters, 127
    with keys, 124, 127
    with king's arms, 127
curtains, for choir, 73
hair cloth, xxxvi
hanging, xxxv, lxviii
    Lenten, white, with red silk cross, 124, 127
    painted, xxxvi
    white, crossed with red silk, xxxvi
Lenten veil, see veil (Lenten)
pall cloth, xxxv, 47, 49, 125
    mending of, 71
tablecloth, 124
towel, xxxvi, 111*, 124*, 126*, 127*, 128
    diaper, 106*, 126*, 127*
        fine diaper, 126
    fine, 124, 128
    for Good Friday, 124, 127
    plaincloth, 106*, 126*, 127
    red silk with white ends, 126
veil (Lenten), 51, 51n, 73, 73n, 81n, 108n,
    124, 127, 133, 135
    hooks for, 133
    laces for, 133
    line for, 51, 64, 73, 133*, 135
    mending of, 81
    pulleys for, 48, 48n
    rings for, 133
    staining of, 133
    see also textiles
clothing, jacket, 89
coffer, see chest (hutch)
coffin, making of, 59
collection (gathering) (replacing pardon), xxx,
    xliii, liii, 76, 76n, 77*, 78*, 79*, 84*, 84n,
    86*, 94*, 94n, 95, 100*
    box for, 54
    for making way at the mills, 128
        repairing way, 127
    of Our Lady, 54
common land ('comyn'), receipts from, 51
    rent for, 86, 102, 115
    overstocking of, 77
common day work, bread for, 112
communicants, bread and wine for, 118, 118n,
    119*
communion table, purchase of, lxviii, 118, 118n
complaint, against old vicar, 92
counsel, asking for, 108
court, at Bury, costs of, 89*
    at Fornham, 133
    day, 96
    manor, 121
    of Augmentations, li
cross, see plate

debt, for occupying church house, 49
    of lead (or, payment for), 49*, 61

to gild of Thomas Becket, 99
to parish, 49*, 99*, 112
to private individual, 17
declaration for vicar's gravestone, recording of, 93
decoration, emblems, heraldic, of Henry V, xxix
   scenes from life of Christ and Our Lady, xxix
   St George, xxix
deed (of land), making/writing of, 75
diet ('dete'), of elderly parishioner, 99 (*or* debt)
distraint of goods, 92, 93
drama, *see* parish activities
drinking, *see* parish activities

earnest, *see* pledge
Easter sepulchre, xxv, xxxiv, xxxivn, 59n, 88n, 115, 115n
   cloths for, 124, 127
   erecting (new), 47
   iron clasp for, 95
   making (new), 46, 46n, 135
   posts for, 135
   setting up, 66, 70, 71, 73, 74, 75, 81, 83, 95, 97, 99, 101, 135
   taking down, 66, 70, 71, 74, 75, 81, 83, 95, 97, 101, 135
   timber gear of, 115

fair ('fyre', 'fyere'), bread and drink at, 119
   labourers at, 116, 124
   spot ('ffeyr spott'), 86, 87, 87n
feasts and festivals, pardon day, lxvii
   Blessed Virgin, Annunciation of, 86
      Purification of, 50, 66, 67, 77, 78, 94
   Candlemas, lxvii, 43*, 43n, 45, 50, 53, 54, 57, 58*, 61*, 65, 67*, 84, 86, 86n, 94, 95
   Corpus Christi, lxvii, 13, 43, 43n, 44, 50, 51, 54*, 58*, 61*, 65*, 67*, 76n, 77*, 78, 84*, 86, 94*
   Dedication Day (church holy day), lxvii, 43, 43n, 44, 50, 51, 54*, 57*, 61*, 65*, 67*, 77*
   May day, 86, 94*, 100
   Michaelmas, lxvii, 43, 43n, 44, 50, 51, 54*, 58*, 61*, 65*, 67*, 77*, 84, 86, 94, 95, 100
   St Philip and St James, lxvii, 12n, 13, 43, 44, 50, 51, 54*, 58*, 61*, 65, 66, 67*, 76, 76n, 77, 78
feasts and festivals, used as payment date, lxiii, 183–4
   Ascension day, Sunday after, 101
   Blessed Virgin, Annunciation of, 51, 55, 61, 62*, 65, 66, 77, 78*, 101, 104, 112, 113*, 133
      Purification of, 72
   Candlemas, 100, 100n, 101, 104
   Christmas, 45, 53, 57*, 72, 79,100, 103, 113*, 133, 134
   Crouchmas, 104
   Easter, 45, 47, 66, 71*, 72*, 73, 134
   May day, 101

Hallowmas, 102, 112, 112n
Holy Rood day, Sunday before, 101
Lammas, 104
Lent, first Sunday in, 101
Michaelmas, 44, 46, 46n, 48, 52, 57, 58*, 59, 61, 63, 65*, 72, 75, 78*, 101, 102, 112, 113*, 114, 134
Midsummer, 58, 59, 71, 72, 101, 104, 113
New Year's day, 100
Palm Sunday, 101
feasts and festivals, used in dating, 183–4
   All Saints, 112
   All Souls, 94
   Blessed Virgin, Annunciation of, 62
      Assumption of, 107
      Purification of, lii
   Candlemas, 80*, 83, 84, 85*, 86, 91, 98
   Crouchmas, 85, 91, 92
   Hallowmas, 79, 80, 82, 84, 85, 86, 93, 98
   Lammas, 79, 81, 82, 84*, 92, 93
   May day, 80, 81, 83* 84
   St David, lxiii, 13
   St George, 74, 76
   St James, 86
   St Luke the evangelist, 121
   St Peter *ad vincula*, 84, 84n
   St Theodore the martyr, lxiii, 13, 26
   St Thomas (29 December), 44
   Trinity Sunday, lxiv
feasts and holy days, liturgical, 183–4
   vestments for double feasts, 125
   Ascension day, 59n
   Corpus Christi, feast of, origins of, xlvi–xlvii
      procession, lviii
   Easter, xxxivn, 46n, 57n, 59n, 63, 88, 88n
      eve, 51n
      vigil of, 47n
   Finding of the Holy Cross, 76, 76n
   Good Friday, towels for, 124, 127
      vestments for, 125
   Holy Name, 97n
   Holy Week, Saturday of, 59n
   Lent, xxxvi, 64n, 73n
      hanging for, 124, 127
      white vestments for, 125
   Maundy Thursday, 46n, 59n
   May day, 79n
   Nativity of the Lord (Christmas), Lord of Misrule at, 78, 78n
   Palm Sunday, lxii, 73
   Relic Sunday, 20n, 38n
   St John, 82
   Whit Sunday, 71, 71n
fire pan (pan for fire), 47, 47n, 53, 63, 63n
   mending of, 80, 133
fixings and fittings, bar, 60, 133, 134, 135
   bolt, 75*, 118, 133, 134
   clasp, 95
   cleat, 108
   crotchet, 118
   hasp, 60

hinges, 45

hooks, 45, 57, 133

key, 52, 52n, 53, 54, 55, 60, 60n, 80, 83, 84, 90, 91, 92*, 95, 96*, 103, 113*

laces, 57, 60, 62, 72

    for rings, 133

latch, 108

line, 51*, 64, 73, 83, 85, 87, 90, 98, 104, 133, 135

lock, 52*, 52n, 53, 54*, 55*, 56, 59, 60*, 62, 66, 68, 70, 71, 72, 74, 75*, 80, 85, 87, 88, 89, 90*, 91*, 93, 95*, 95n, 96*, 99, 100, 103, 104, 118, 119, 134

nails, 13, 45*, 45n, 46*, 47, 53, 54, 56*, 59, 60, 62, 70, 72, 73, 74, 75, 79, 83, 87, 88, 90*, 91*, 92*, 92*, 93, 97, 98*, 99, 100, 108*, 109*, 110, 112, 113, 116*, 117*, 119, 133, 134*, 135*

    great, 82, 116

    (for) lead, 64, 73, 74*, 91, 92*, 116, 118, 134

    pin-nails, 85, 85n

    small, 80, 82

    'spyken', 79

pin, iron, 108

rafters ('rafte'), 118

rings, 133

rope (not bellrope), 38, 51, 52

    for clock, 48, 59, 95

    for paschal candle, 66

staple, 45, 48, 51, 75, 90, 118

    great, 79

tenterhooks, 59

font, xxix, xxxi, 95n

    lock for, 95, 95n

        mending of, 93

    mending (reparation) of, 63, 104

    soldering, 88

    water, hallowed, in, 95n

food and drink, ale, 127

    beer, 79, 112, 127

    bread, for common day work, 112

        sent to camp at Bury, 109

    bread and cheese, 127

    bread and drink, 116

        at the fair ('fyre'), 119

    bread, cheese and ale, distributed at anniversary, lii

    drink, 112, 117

    malt, 112

    meat and drink, 117

funeral, coffin, 88n

    hearse at, candles on, 88n

furniture, bed, 54

    bench, 135

    table, 102

gathering, *see* collection

gift, to parish church, 49, 50

gild (craft/trade), barbers', lviii

    wax chandlers', lviii

gild (religious), xxv, xxviii, xxxv, xl*, xliv, xlvi–xlviii

    aldermen, xlvi

    altar, xliv

    bequests of land to, xlvi

    members, xxxv

    membership of, xliv

    of the Blessed Cross, xlvin

    of Corpus Christi, dedication of, xl, xlvi

    of the Holy Trinity, dedication of, xl, xlvii, xlviiin

    of St Anne, xlviii

    of St George, xlviii

    of St James, xlviii

    of St John the Baptist, xlviii

        vestments given by, 128

    of St Katherine, xlvii

    of St Mary, xl, xlvii

    of St Thomas, xl, xliv, lxx

        aldermen of, 120*, 121

        brothers of, 120*, 121

        lands of (details), lxx, 120*, 121*

    side altar, xxxv

    torches, xlviiin

gild hall, xlvii, 102, 112

    bench for, 135

    chimney, mending of, 112, 112n

    claying of walls, 134

    cleaning, 134

    framing of, 134

    groundsill for, 134

    high table, 135

    of Corpus Christi gild, 143, 143n

    of Holy Trinity gild, 93n

    of St John's gild, 116*, 116n

    thatching of, 134

    walls, (rough)casting, 134

        mending, 134

        'part wall' (?partition), 134

        railbars for, 134

        splints for, 134

    whiting, 134

    windows, mending, 134

        sills and pillars for, 134

girdle of St Thomas, 125

grate (at church gate), bricks for, 80

    casting of, 123

    cleaning (feying) of, 54, 62, 62n, 93, 97, 99

        by bellman, 101

    hole of, 79

    lime for, 80

    paving around, 73

    work by mason and men on, 80

gravestone, 93, 93n, 94, 94n

    declaration for, 93

great ('a greate') (fixed price for work), 80*

gryndyll (ditch, drain), keeping of, 108*

harness (unspecified), scouring of, 68, 68n

hearse, 51, 53*, 115, 115n

    making (new) of, 135

mending of, 53
setting up, 55, 57, 57n, 59, 61, 63, 64, 88,
    88n, 91
taking down, 53, 55, 57, 59, 59n, 61, 63, 64,
    88, 91
household goods, napery, xxxvi

images (general), setting up of, 136
of St Christopher, xxvn, 102, 102n
of St John the Evangelist, xxv
of St Leonard of Noblac, xxvn
of Virgin Mary, xxv
    crown for, 53, 53n
    in church, xxv
    in doorway, xxviii
    mending of, 55
incense boat, see plate: ship
injunctions, of Henry VIII, 84, 84n, 102n

jewels, crystal, 125
crystal stones, 125
pearls, 125
stone (precious), 92

key, see fixings and fittings
king's arms, on a cross cloth, 127
    see also royalty

laces, see fixings and fittings
ladder, see tools and equipment
lamp, lxx, 73
basin, scouring of, 72
oil for, 73
    see also candles; lights
land, gift of, 74n, 75, 78
land and property, fen, 120, 122
field, 120, 121*
free land, 122, 122n
house, 122
land, 121*, 122*
marsh, 120
meadow, 121, 122
messuage, 120*, 121*
pasture, 120
pertinences, 121*
pightle, 121
rents for (specified), 120*, 121*
shops, 122n
lantern, to carry with sacrament, 136
    see also tools and equipment
law suit, breach of contract, liv
leather, see textiles
lectern, xxxiii, 64, 114, 114n
at altar end, mending of, 87
case for, 63
for Bible, 87, 87n
in chancel, scouring of, 87
leather 'closer' of, mending of, 87
mending of, 57, 59, 73
lights, common light (rowell), 47n, 59, 136
    irons for, 136

making of, 52, 55, 57, 58, 60, 62*, 64,
    69*, 71, 72, 74, 82, 136
painting of, 136
wax for, 47, 47n, 48, 53, 57, 63, 66*, 69*,
    71, 72, 82, 136*
of Virgin Mary, xxviiin
lime, see materials
line, see fixings and fittings
liturgical books (general), xxxi, xxxiin, lxvii,
    lxviii, 9, 107, 109, 109n, 114, 114n
binding of, 81
erasing Thomas Becket from, 85, 85n , 99,
    99n
mending of, 55, 55n, 56, 62, 66, 70, 70n,
    71, 75, 81*, 82
antiphoner, xxxi, xxxiin, xxxii, 124, 127
    mending of, 57
Bible, xxxiii, 87n
    bossing of, 99
    mending of, 116, 124
    purchase of, 99, 99n
    removal of, 104
book of service (Book of Common Prayer),
    xxxiii, 109, 109n, 114n, 118, 118n
collect book, 124, 127
epistle book, xxxii, 124, 127
    mending of, 58
gradual (grail), xxxi, 124, 127
    old, 124, 127
lesson book (legend), xxxi, 124, 127
    old, 124, 127
manual, xxxi, xxxii, 124, 127
martyrology ('martlage'), 124
Mass of St John, 3 quires of, 82
missal (mass book), xxxi, xxxii, 55, 62, 124,
    127, 128
    new, binding of, 6
ordinal, 124, 127
processional (processionary), xxxi, xxxii,
    xxxiii, 86, 97, 97n, 124, 127
    binding of, 92
    mending (making) of, 58, 60
    noting, 93
    sale of, 8
psalter, xxxi, xxxiii, 109, 113, 119, 124, 127
    with hymns, 124, 127
troper, xxxi
verse book, 124, 127
locks, see fixings and fittings
lodge (temporary shelter), 118, 118n

mass, see church services
materials (building and other), alabaster, 46, 46n
boards, 45*, 46*, 59, 60, 64, 70*, 73, 87*,
    100, 108, 115, 116, 133, 135, 136
    ceiling, 100
    sawing of, 70, 88
bricks, 45, 80
chalk, 63
charcoal, 58, 79
clay, 56, 85*, 85n, 91, 107n, 117, 134

coal dust (or, soot: 'collme'), 81, 81n, 119
'dowes' (dowels?), 36
earth, 93
firing (?firewood), 69
glass, 83, 88*, 93, 103, 103n, 109, 109n, 116
  coloured, 98n, 99, 109n
glue, 82
grass, 8, 8n
gravel, 93, 115
hair, 107n
hay, 134
hemp, 52, 56, 60, 74, 134
joists ('geyste'), pairs of, 117
laths, 53, 70*, 92
lime, 52, 60, 66, 74, 80, 83, 85, 88*, 92, 93,
  95, 102, 103, 107, 109, 110, 113, 116, 117*,
  118*, 119, 134, 135
  dead, 118
lye, 119
'menor' (rubbish or dirt), 110, 110n
oil, 56
  for lamp, 73
  for ropes, 60*
packthread (twine), 36
planks, 57, 108, 134
  trees for, 115, 123
plates, 116
poles, 134
posts, 115, 135
railbars, 134
reeds, 116
resin ('rosen', 'rosson'), 56, 116
rods, 104, 116
sand, 56, 59, 64, 66, 73, 74*, 80, 85, 87, 103,
  110, 113, 116*, 117*, 119, 134
sedge, 118, 123
solder, 46, 46n, 52, 56*, 58, 60, 69*, 71, 81,
  82, 84, 88, 92, 93*, 98*, 102, 103, 110,
  116*, 118
'spetyng' (for plumber), 134
splints, 134
stone, lv, lxn, lxiii, 20, 80, 88, 89, 96, 109,
  110, 134
  quoin, 20, 20n
straw, lxiii, 3
  rye, 45
stud (upright post), 136
tallow, 56*
thatch, 8, 8n, 45, 70, 84, 104*, 104n, 110*,
  114, 116*, 123, 124, 134
tiles, paving, 58, 95*, 95n
timber, 4, 57*, 70, 72, 75, 82, 87*, 89*, 90,
  93, 97, 100, 108, 116, 117, 119, 133, 134*,
  135*, 136
  burnt, 119
  price per foot, 89*
wax, xxxvii, 47, 51, 53*, 57, 59, 63*, 64, 65,
  66*, 69*, 70*, 71, 72, 73, 74, 75, 82, 83,
  88, 91, 135, 136
wire, 51, 53, 57, 71, 83, 92, 93*, 113
withies, 104

wood, 56*, 60, 64, 79, 116, 123, 124
  ash poles, 91, 133
  faggot of, 92
  firewood, 56, 73, 74*, 80, 92*, 93*
  spars (strakys), 64
  see also fixings and fittings; jewels; textiles;
  tools and equipment; writing
May ale, May games, *see* parish activities
measurement, unit of, lxxii–lxiii
  acre (land), 78, 120, 121*, 122*
  barrel (beer), 112
  bushel ('collme'), 119
    (lime), 81, 83, 85, 92, 95, 102, 107, 109,
    118, 135
  chalder (lime), 103, 117
  comb (charcoal), 79
    ('colme'), 81
    (lime), 80
  ell (cloth), 106*, 127*
    (diaper cloth), 126*
  faggot (wood), 92
  foot (board), 88
    (glass), 93
    (glass, coloured), 98n, 99
    (timber), 89*
  fother (lead), 47, 64
  gallon (ale), 81
  hide (leather), 96
  horse hide (leather), 54, 70, 74
  hundred (sedge), 118, 123
    (thatch), 45, 104, 110*, 114, 116*, 123,
    124, 134
    (wood), 123
  hundred (weight?) (lead), 64, 68, 98
  load (clay), 56, 91, 117, 134
    (gravel), 93
    (lime), 116
    (lime, dead), 118
    (sand), 56, 59, 64, 73, 74, 85, 103, 113,
    116*, 119
    (wood), 64, 116, 124
  noble (money), 123
  ob' worth (nails), 45
  ounce (lace), 98, 99
    (parcel gilt), 128
    (plate), 103, 128
      price per ounce, 103
    (ribbon silk), 72
    (silver), 64, 64n, 84, 103, 107, 125, 128
      price per ounce, 128
  pound (brass), 114, 114n
    (copper), 114n, 115
    (iron), 84, 86, 115
      price per pound, 86, 91
    (latten), 84,107
    (lead), 49, 50, 68, 73, 86, 87, 91, 93, 117,
    136
    (sand), 74
    (solder), 69, 81, 82, 84, 87, 93, 98*, 110,
    116
    (thread, fine), 98

(wax), 47, 59, 63, 68, 69, 70*, 71, 72, 73, 75, 82, 83, 91, 135, 136
   price per pound, 73
(wire), 83
quarter (malt), 112
rod (land), 78*, 121*, 122
sheet (lead), 75
skein (thread), 98
skin (leather), 81, 82*
   calf-skin (leather), 82
stone (hemp), 56
web (lead), 73, 74
yard (buckram), 70, 98
   (canvas), 98, 128
   (cloth), 70, 106*, 111*, 127*, 128
   (diaper), 124, 126*
   (haircloth), 69
   (plaincloth), 126*
   'and the nayle' (diaper), 126*
mensa, xxv
metal (including precious), base, 113n
  brass, 102*, 114n
    overweight of, 86
  copper, xxxvii, livn, 53, 72, 76, 87, 91, 107, 107n, 114n, 125, 126
    copper gilt (copper and gilt), xxxvi, 71, 76, 124*, 125*, 127
  iron, lv, 52, 72, 75*, 86, 87, 88, 90, 91*, 95, 100*, 108, 115, 134, 136
    bar of, 133, 135
    cost per pound, 86, 91
    ironwork, lxn, 51, 53, 54, 57, 72, 79, 81, 83, 86, 88, 89, 96*, 108, 113*, 117
    log of, 134
    old, 84, 88
      workmanship of, rate for, 88
    plate of, 48, 79*
  latten, xxxvii, 53, 53n, 71, 72, 76*, 107, 107n, 124, 125, 127
    old, 84
  lead, lv, 30, 49*, 50*, 54, 61, 64*, 68, 73, 73n, 76*, 80, 81n, 86*, 87*, 92*, 93*, 97, 98, 103, 116*, 117*, 118*, 124*, 136*
    ashes, 64, 64n
    sheeting, 47, 75, 76, 136
    webs (rolls), 73, 74, 76
  parcel gilt, xxxvi, 125, 128, 129
  pewter, 124, 127
  silver, xxxvii, 64, 72, 84, 92, 98, 103, 105, 125*, 127, 128
    broken, xxxvii, 103, 107, 127
    silver gilt (silver and gilt), 125*, 128
    silver and parcel gilt, xxxvi, xxxvii, 125*, 129
  tin, livn
Misrule, Lord of, *see* parish activities
monasteries, dissolution of, xliii
money, 'brok', 91
  church, 63
  ill (coins of no value), 52, 64
  loan, 106, 106n

odd, 86
mould, lengthening of, 64
  making of, 56, 56n, 116
music, church, xlii

nails, *see* fixings and fittings

obit, *see* church services
obligation (agreement, bond), 79, 102, 103, 114, 114n, 120, 122*, 123*, 136
  payment of, 29, 115*
occupation, 'alabaster man', xxv, 46
  barber, 86
  barker, liii
  bellfounder, liv, 79*
    reward to, 79
  bellman ('belman', 'bellsman'), 101, 102, 110, 115, 118, 123
  blacksmith, *see* smith
  book repairer, 124n
  bookbinder, xxxii*, lxv, 36, 75, 81, 81n, 82*
  butcher, xxvn
  carpenter, xxixn, xxxiv, lxn, lxvii, 8, 45, 45n, 51n, 72, 72n, 73n, 75, 81, 82, 84*, 85, 89*, 90*, 108*, 109*, 110, 112, 113, 117, 119, 133, 134, 135*, 136
    master, 89n
    wage rate of, 89*, 89n, 90
  carpenter's mate, 90*
  carrier, 89
  carver, xxixn, 47, 47n, 51
  clerk (not religious), 64, 102, 119
  clock-keeper, 70n
  clockmaker (clocksmith), xliii*, lv, 47, 48*, 119
  cope-maker, 98n
  drover, 86
  embroiderer ('browder', 'broiderer'), xxxv, 48, 48n, 64, 99
  fishermen ('fysshers'), 100
  glazier ('glass-wright'), xxviii, 46n, 47, 52, 55, 61, 75, 80, 82, 87*, 93*, 97*, 98, 98n, 103, 103n, 109, 116*, 117
  glazier's man/servant, 82, 93*
  glover, lxiv, 14, 14n, 29n
  goldsmith, 64, 74, 84, 91
  helper, 89, 92*
  joiner, 135
  labourer, lxn, 81, 116*, 117*, 119, 166 (will 41)
    at the fair, 124
  leather worker, 45n
  lumber merchant, 115n
  mason, xxv, xxxiii, lxn, 60, 66, 70, 74, 80, 82, 83, 85, 88, 95, 96, 103, 103n, 109, 110, 112, 117, 119, 134, 135*, 136
    chief, 116
      'fermer' of, 117
      man of, 117
    'roughmason', 86n

mason's man/servant, 66, 80*, 83, 109, 112, 119
mercer, 14n, 143 (will 12)
messenger, 89
miller, 91
neatherd, 108
nurse, 101*, 102*, 103, 104*
organmaker, lxv, 113
painter, xxxiii, xxxiiin, 47, 124n, 175 (will 49)
players, travelling, lviii, 56, 56n
plumber, 46, 46n, 52, 55, 56*, 58, 59, 60, 61, 64*, 69*, 71, 73, 73n, 74*, 81, 84, 90, 91*, 92*, 93, 97, 98*, 102, 105, 107, 110, 116*, 118*, 124, 134, 136
    daily rate of pay, 97n
plumber's man/servant, 56, 60, 64*, 81, 84, 91, 92*, 93, 98, 102
porter, 89
roper, 100
saddler, livn, 45n
schoolmaster, xliii
scribe, 108, 109
    visitor's, 102
servant, 89
shoemaker, 146 (will 17)
smith, xliii*, liv, lv, lxiv, 14, 38n, 45, 54, 64, 66, 70n, 75, 78n, 102, 104, 108, 109
tabourer (drummer), lvii, 56, 56n
tailor, 4, 7, 29, 90
tanner, lii, 170 (will 46)
thatcher, 176 (will 52)
turner, xxixn
vestment making, lxv
warrener, xxin, 168 (will 43)
weaver, 175 (will 50), 179 (will 54)
woodcarver, xxviii
wood-worker, xxixn*
see also clergy; parish officers; status
occupational surname, liv, 45n, 47n, 48n
offertory box, 43, 43n
organ(s), xxxiii, xxxiv, xxxivn, 54, 61, 113, 113n, 119
    bellows of, xxxiii
        mending of, 52
    great, bellows of, mending of, 71, 98
        glueing of, 80
        mending, 83, 104
    keeping, 53, 54, 60, 63, 66, 68, 69*, 70*, 71, 74, 75*, 87
    key for, 113
    linen cloth for, 97
    mending of, 95, 97
    playing of, 45n, 52, 52, 57, 58, 61, 69, 79
    removal of, 112, 112n, 113n
    suit of, 115, 115n
organist (organ player), xxxiii, xxxiv, xlii, xliii, 176 (will 51)
    wages of, 52, 58, 72, 79, 80, 82, 83
    see also parish clerk
Our Lady, painting of (?image), 51, 51n
overweight, of bells, 86

of brass, 86

painting, of solar over rood-loft, 44, 44n
    of statue of Virgin Mary on rood-beam, 48, 48n
paper, see writing: materials
Paraphrases of Erasmus (on wall), xxxiii, 108, 108n
    setting up of, 108
pardon (indulgence), granted by Pope (Bishop of Rome), xxxiii, lxvii, 85, 85n
    erasing from the wall, 85, 85n
pardon day, lxvii, 12n, 43*, 44*, 45, 50*, 51, 53, 54*, 57, 58*, 61*, 65*, 66*, 67*, 77, 85n, 94n
parish activities, churchale (drinking; potation), lv–lviii, lxii*, lxiv, lxv, 3, 4, 7*, 8, 10, 26, 27*, 29, 31, 32, 33, 35, 38*, 51, 61, 56n, 65, 67, 67n, 86*, 90, 94*, 97
    charges concerning, 99
    pots for, 90
    drama, lv–lviii,
        play, lvii, 56n, 86
        play of St Thomas, lvi, lvii, lxvii, 44, 44n
    May ale, lvi, lvii, 54*, 54n, 56, 56n, 58*
    May games, lvi, lvii, 79, 79n
    Misrule, Lord of, lvii, 78, 78n
    pageants, lvii
    processions, lvii
        Corpus Christi, lviii
parish clerk, xxxiii, xxxiv, xlii–xliii, 2, 66, 68, 109n, 176 (will 51)
    as organ player, 52, 52n, 57, 58, 61, 62*, 66, 68, 69, 70, 71, 73*, 74, 80, 81, 84*, 101n
    for ('keeping') the organs, 53, 54, 54n, 60, 61, 63, 66, 66n, 68, 69*, 70*, 74, 75*, 85*, 87, 88, 90, 91, 92, 93*, 95, 96, 97*, 98, 99, 101*
    new, 136
    payment to, 73, 74, 75, 83, 136
    wages of, xlii–xliii, 45*, 45n*, 46*, 47*, 48*, 51*, 52*, 53, 54*, 56, 57*, 58, 59*, 60*, 61, 62, 63*, 64, 65, 68*, 71, 71n, 72, 73*, 73n, 74*, 75*, 80, 81*, 82, 84, 85*, 88, 95, 96*, 107, 108*, 109*, 110*, 133
parish records, bishop's inventory, 118
    book (of church goods), 102
    book for the town (parish), 109
    book-keeping methods, 123n
    certificate of church goods, liv
    chantry certificates, xl
    churchwardens' accounts, contents of, lix, 102n
        physical description of, lxv, plate 8
        presentation of, 2n
    collections, contents of, lix-lxv
        physical description of, lx, plate 8
    inventories of church goods, xxxi, xxxiii, xxxvi, lxvii, 48n, 53, 100n, 102, 102*, 108, 108n, 109n, 109*, 111, 111n
        making (writing) of, 108, 108n, 109*

pre-Reformation, 124, 124n
parish register, xxxiii
register of christenings and burials, 85, 85n,
103n
hutch (chest) for, 103, 103n
sacrist rolls, 52n
parishioners, annual meeting of, lix
see also status
pasturing of animals, income from, 65
Peter's Pence, see taxes
pew, mending of, 95
pictures, of Mary and John, studs (posts) for, 136
with the patrons of the church, 136
of St Gregory, on altar hanging, 124, 127
piscina, xxv*, xxviii
pillows, 126
plate (general), xxxi, xxxvi–xxxvii, lxviii, 103
sale of, xxxvii, lxvii, 102n, 103, 103n,
105n, 127
basin, silver, xxxvii
and parcel gilt, 125
bond for, 102
box, silver, 125
and crystal, 125
censer, 47n
best, 127
copper and gilt, 125
damage to, 52n
gilding of, 74
latten, 53
bottoming of, 71, 76
mending of, 53
polishing and burnishing, 71, 76
wire for, 53
with a ship, 71
making (repair) of, 45n, 46, 52, 52n, 64,
70, 74, 98
pair of, 135
silver, new, 64, 64n
and gilt, 125
and parcel gilt, 125
chain, 127
chalice, xxxvii*
mending of, 69, 88
pair of, 63, 88, 113, 125, 128*
hallowing, 63
soldering, 88
chrismatory, 124, 127, 135
cloth for, 135
copper, 91
silver, 125
stoppers for, 92
towels for, mending of, 88
communion cup, 113n
communion plate, 107
cross, best, 127
boards of, 116
cloth for, 124
copper, 53, 76, 126
carried to the sick in the hour of death,
126

polishing and burnishing, 76
scouring, 53
copper-gilt foot for, xxxvi, 125
gilding of, 74
latten, polishing and burnishing, 71
Lenten, 64
mending of, 88
little, 127
mending of, 74, 75, 97
parcel-gilt, xxxvi
piece of Christ's cross in, xxxvi, 125
sanding of, 75
silver, 125
silver-gilt, enamelled, 125, 128
stave (staff) for, copper, 126
and gilt, xxxvi, 124, 125
wooden, red, xxxvi, 64n
cruets, pair of, xxxvii, 68, 68n
cup, silver, 127
holy water stoop, 117, 133
hanging of (for?), 59
lining of, 81, 81n
making of, 81
laver, 124, 127
mending of, 73
paten, xxxvii
pax, 91, 128, 136
'best', making of, 92
bigger, 127
copper and gilt, 124, 127
silver, 92, 92n
parcel gilt, 129
stone set in, 92, 92n
pyx, 67, 127
copper and gilt, 125
making (mending) of, 55, 68
silver and gilt, 125
mending of, 72
with chains to hang round priest's neck,
128
ship (incense boat), 127
gilding of, 74
latten, polishing and burnishing, 76
mending (making) of, 52*, 52n, 74, 98
silver, 125
spoon, silver, for frankincense, 125
vessels, silver, 105
and parcel gilt, xxxvi
pledge (earnest, guarantor, surety), 49, 50*, 55,
55n, 79, 102n
for bargain, 90
poor, xxxvii
accommodation for, 45
see also almshouse
attendance at funerals, xliv
boy, 105
see also boy
child, making of coat for, 105
payments for, 105
shoes for, 105
deserving, 45

dole at funerals to, xliv
hutch (chest) for alms for, 103, 103n
payment to, 74, 75
prayers of, xliv
relief paid to, 45, 45n, 105
stock of wax (money), distributed to, 105
portable breviary, xxxviii
pound, *see* measurement, unit of
prayers for the dead, xliv
pulpit, cleat for, 108
ladder for, 69, 69n
Purgatory, lxvii

relic, arm, gilted timber, 124, 127
box full of, 125
enclosed in silver, 125
piece of Christ's cross, set in a cross, xxxvi, 125
purses containing, 125
relief, *see* tax
rent (farm), 43, 44, 54*, 57, 58*, 65, 75, 77, 78*, 86, 107, 127
for church house, 49, 61*
for common land ('comon plott'), 102, 115
for town house, 107*, 115*, 115n
reward to bellfounder, 79
road, common way, 121*
king's high way, 120
see also Places Index *sub* Mildenhall: roads
Romescot, *see* taxes
rood, xxv, 73, 135
canopy over rood, making of, 48
painting of, xxv
soldering of (or, sewing), 47, 47n
coat ('kote'; covering) for, 124
dormant (beam), painting of, 135
removing of, 135
framing for, 135
iron bar for, 135
making, painting & setting up, 135
making cross for, 135
rood-beam, statue of the Virgin on, 48n
rood-loft, xxv, xxxiv, xxxvii, 53
candlesticks on, scouring of, 95
carving of, 47, 47n
chest (hutch) on, 102, 102n
cleaning, 53, 60
cloth for, 53 (*see also* cloths: veil)
setting up of, 108
door, lock for, 52, 52n
entrance, xxv, plate 5
line for, 85
lock for, mending of, 96
mending of, 52
painted alabaster panels for, xxv
painting of, xxv, 46*, 46n, 47, 47n
removal of, lxvii, 110, 110n
setting up, 135
solar over, painting of, 44, 44n, 45
staging (scaffolding) for, xxv, 46, 46n, 47
sweeping, 66

timber for, 135
wooden spars ('strakys') for, 64
rood-screen, xxv, xxxiv
painting of, 47n
ropes, *see* bells; fixings and fittings
royal arms (on bell), liv
royalty, king, visit of (passing through), 46, 57, 57n
queen, visit of (passing through), 62, 62n, 70, 70n

saints, *see* altar; church: chapel; feasts and festivals; gild (religious); images; pictures
sand, *see* materials
sangred, *see* church services
'sayvype', 118
school, lxvii
school house, xliii, lxvii, 80n, 135
cleaning, 96, 104
daubing of, 107
door, irons (ironwork) for, 108
making of, 88
mending lock of, 80
making ground sill for, 84
mending, 96
nails for, 108
plastering with clay, 85, 85n
'wynd' making of, 87
sedilia, xxv
sentence book (form of excommunication), 62
sepulchre, *see* Easter sepulchre
sewing equipment, pins, 71
stays, 71
shears, making of, 68
sexton, xlii, xliii–xliv, 74*, 75, 133
keeping the clock, 74*, 75
wages of, xliii, 75n
shriving (shrift) pew, mending of, 69, 88, 96
shriving stools, making of, 55
sick, copper cross carried to, in the hour of death, 126
sluice, making of, 105, 105n
solder, *see* materials
spouts, stirrups for, 65
squint, xxv
staging (scaffolding), xxv, 46, 46n, 47
stalls ('stoles'), making of, by carpenter, 110
mending of, 124
statue of Virgin Mary on rood-beam, 48, 48n
status, abbot, lix
archdeacon, xxxi, lix, 48, 63n
bishop, 136
clerks of the register, 74
commissioner, 102n, 119
communicants, 118, 118n, 119*
dame (lady), liv, lxii, 7, 32, 33
dean, 46, 48, 68, 118
Dom., 45
elder, 155 (will 28), 173 (will 48), 175 (will 50)
esquire, 7n, 121

Father (older man), 135
fen reeve, 119
gentleman, li, 99, 112
Goodman, 134
Goodwife, 117
husbandman, lx
inhabitants, 114, 120, 136
lord mayor of London, xxix*, lxiii
Master (Mr), 45, 48, 50*, 54, 61*, 66*, 71, 74, 75, 86*, 93, 96, 102*, 107, 116, 119, 122*, 124, 128
member of Salters' Company, lii, 49
men who served the king, 105
Mistress, 67, 117
monk, liii
Mother (older woman), 50, 65, 97, 99, 103*, 115*
parishioners, 45, 76*, 77*, 79*, 83
  the parish, 110
servant, 27
sir (lord), 29n
sir (non-graduate priest), 43*, 43n, 49, 50, 53, 62, 67, 92, 109, 125, 128, 133*, 155 (will 29)
visitor, 102
visitor's scribes, xxxvii
widow (relict), 17, 28, 38, 67, 151 (will 22), 157 (will 33), 172 (will 47), 178 (will 53)
woman (day's work of), 117
yeoman, lx, 173 (will 48)
younger, lxix, 83, 110, 114, 123, 141
see also clergy; parish officers; occupation
stone cross, 121
stool (or stall), before St Christopher, 102, 102n
  choir master's, mending of, 87
subsidy, see taxes
suit of court, 68, 68n
supplication, 101
surety, see pledge

tabernacle, xxv*
  mending of, 95
taxes, 37
  Peter's Pence (Romescot), 47, 47n, 48, 52*, 55*, 58, 59, 61, 62, 64*, 66, 68, 71, 72, 75
  relief, 116, 124
  subsidy, 114
teaching, xlix
  see also school
textiles, buckram, xxxv, 70
  blue, 98, 99
  canvas, xxxv, 69, 69n, 98, 128
  chamlet, green, 111
  cloth, 57, 60, 71, 96, 100*, 104
    fine, 124, 127
    finest weave, xxxvi
    of gold, xxxv, 111, 125
    of twilly, lxiii, 16
    white, starched, 111
  corse, green, 125
  damask, 128

blue, 125, 128
  with 'peckockes of golde inbrodered', 111
  green, 128
  'popynggay grene', xxxv, 125, 129
  red, xxxv, 125
  white, xxxv, 111
    powdered, 124
  diaper, xxxvi*, 106*, 111*, 124*, 126*, 127*
    fine, 111, 126*
    silk, white, 111
  dornix, 111
  embroidered, xxxiv
  fustian, white, 111, 129
  hair cloth, xxxvi, 69, 69n, 72, 72n
  lace, 99*
    crewel, xxxv, 99
    silk, gold, xxxv, 98, 99
    silk, silver, xxxv, 98, 99
  lawn, 135
  leather, liii, 45, 87
    'horse heyd (hide)', 54
    red, 81, 82
    white, 69, 70, 70n, 74, 74n, 96
    white hide, liv
  linen, xxxiv, xxxv, 62, 97, 108, 111, 127
    lining of, 111
    white, fine, 115n
    white, with bars of blue, 111
  orphrey, xxxv
  ostrich feathers, 125
  painted or stained, xxxvi
  plaincloth, 106*, 111*, 124, 126*, 127
    linen, 111
  ribbon silk, xxxv, 70, 72
  ribbon, 70
    red silk diaper, 111
  russet, 125
  satin of Bruges, 128, 128n
    white, 128
  say, 72
    red, 125
  silk, xxxiv, xxxv, 36, 48, 64, 70, 124*, 126, 127*
    embroidered with gold, 124, 127
    red, xxxvii, 124, 125*, 126, 127
    red with white, 126
    white, 129
  thread, blue, 98
    of various colours, xxxv, 98
    silk, 70
  tapestry, 129
  'tapr'' (for girdles), 98
  velvet, black, 128
    blue, xxxv, 111, 125, 128
    motley, 111, 125
    red, xxxv, 125
    with ostrich feathers, 125
  'ynkyll' (linen tape), 91
thatching, 70, 104, 104n
  binds (binding threads), 45, 104
  rye straw, 45

sways, 45, 104
    thatch, 8, 8n, 45, 70, 84, 104*, 104n
thieves, damage by, 87, 87n
thurifer, 52n
timber, *see* materials
tools and equipment, besoms, 104
    cradle (for work on the tower), 56
        mending of, 57
    irons, 93*
    ladder, 58, 91, 97
        for clock, 109
    lantern, 52
        horning of, 82
            new, 72, 82
    mattock, 118
        mending of, 47, 118
    pan,116
    saw, 109
        filing of, 109
    scaffolding (staging), 46, 46n
    shears, making of, 68
    shovel, 52
        shoeing of, 80
    tackle ('taklyng'), 89*
town house, rent for, 107*, 107n, 115*, 115n
    thatch for, 110*
    thatching of, 110
    yard, gravel for, 93
travel, riding, 89, 95

Valor Ecclesiasticus, l, li, 74n
vessels, pan, 100, 103
    brass, 102
    pot, 90, 100
    brass, 102
    pewter, 124, 127
vestment (unspecified), xxxi, xxxiv–vi, xxxvi,
    lxviii, 103n
    black, xxxvi
    damask, red, 128
    fustian, red, with white drips, 129
    mending of, 59, 64, 68, 70, 75
    red, 128
    satin of Bruges, red, 128
    say, red, 125
    silk, red, 125*
    suit of, xxxv, 124*, 125*, 127*, 128*
    velvet, blue, 128
    white, 125
        for the low altars, 125
    (occasion specified), for double feasts, 125
    for Good Friday, 125
    for Jesus Mass, 125
    for Lent, 125
    for Sundays, 125
    for work days, 125
    (wearer specified), for deacon, 124, 125
    for priest, 124, 125
    for subdeacon, 124, 125
    alb, xxxv, 70, 111, 115*, 115n, 124*, 125,
    128*

cloth for, 70, 71, 96
    mending of, 61, 69, 75, 92, 92n, 96*, 97*
    new, 63
amice, 111
    mending of, 92, 92n
cassock, 59
chasuble, xxxv, 124*
coat, 128
cope, xxxv, 111*, 124*, 125*, 128
    best, 98, 98n
    black, for Requiem Mass, 125
    cloth of gold, 125
    damask, blue, 125, 128
        red, 125
    for Sundays, 125
    gold and silver lace for, 98
    green, 125
    old, 125
    laces to mend, 72
    making new cope, 98, 98n
    mending of, 48, 59, 62, 64, 70, 97
    powdered with garters, 125
    red, with lilies, 125
    russet, old, 125
    satin, white Bruges, 128
    velvet, blue, 125
        black, 128
        red, 125
    with garters, 111
dalmatic, xxxv
girdle, xxxv, 56, 60, 62, 63, 70, 125
    green corse, harnessed with silver, 125
    'tapr" for, 98
    'ynkyll', 91
maniple, xxxv
purse, xxxiv, 86
    containing relics, 125
    gold (cloth), 125
    motley green, 125
    set with pearls, 125
rochets, 47
    for the choir, 128
stole, xxxii, 87n
surplice, xxxiv, xxxv, 52, 52n, 62, 64, 69, 86,
    128
    cloth for, 96
    for priest, 58, 108n
        making of, 108
        mending of, 96
    mending (making) of, 61, 63, 68, 71, 72,
        82, 87, 95, 97, 104, 115, 118, 123
    washing of, 48, 95, 118*, 119
tunicle, xxxv, 124*, 128*
visitation, 48, 48n, 63, 63n
    bishop's, 80, 80n, 136
    chantry commissioners', 104, 104n
    commissioners', 102, 102n
    dean's, 118
    expenses of, 74, 74n, 104
washing (church cloths, linen, napery), 52*, 53,
    53n, 55*, 55n, 57*, 58, 59, 60, 61, 62*,

63*, 63n, 64, 66*, 68*, 69*, 70*, 71, 72*, 73, 74*, 75*, 79, 80, 81*, 82, 83*, 87, 88*, 91, 92, 93, 95, 96*, 97*, 98, 99, 104, 108, 109, 110*
  and mending, 116, 124
wax, *see* candles; materials
whitewashing, 103, 103n
wine, *see* bread and wine
woman, day's work of, 117
wood, *see* materials
work days, vestments, for 125
working year, builder's, liii
workmen's wages (costs, payment for labour, workmanship), 36, 45, 52, 56*, 58, 59, 60, 61, 64, 70, 71*, 73n, 74*, 75*, 80*, 81*, 82*, 83*, 84, 87*, 88*, 89*, 90*, 91*, 92*, 93*, 95, 98*, 99, 102, 103, 105, 107, 108*, 109*, 110*, 112*, 116*, 117*, 118*, 119*, 123*, 128, 133, 136
writ of distraint, 89*
writing, accounts, payment for, 97, 97n

books for the town (parish), 109
  copying out bishop's inventory, 118
  in books, 81, 81n
  inventory of church goods, 108, 109
  materials, paper, 101, 108, 109, 119
    for the clerk, 72
  parchment, 36, 71, 82*
  vellum, 82
  of will, 63

yard, *see* measurement, unit of